LOVERS AND KILLERS

Marlene Olive was a pretty teenaged girl who wrote sensitive poems when she wasn't tripping on drugs, or acting out her bizarre occult and sexual fantasies. Chuck Riley was a virginal, overweight newsboy turned drug dealer who became Marlene's lover and virtual slave. In the California youth culture of the 1970s, the chemistry between them was perfect—for murder. . . .

BAD BLOOD

A Family Murder in Marin County

"The most deftly-written, engrossing reconstruction of grisly 'true crime' since Capote."
—*Village Voice*

"Shocking, explosive, unforgettable, *Bad Blood* will haunt you." —*South Bend Tribune*

"It is difficult to imagine a much better book . . . this is non-fiction writing at its best."
—*Los Angeles Herald Examiner*

Gripping Reading from SIGNET

BAD BLOOD

A Family Murder in Marin County

RICHARD M. LEVINE

A SIGNET BOOK

NEW AMERICAN LIBRARY

TIMES MIRROR

This is an authorized reprint of a hardcover edition published in the United
States by Random House, Inc., New York. The hardcover edition was
published simultaneously in Canada by Random House of Canada Limited,
Toronto. Portions of this work originally appeared in somewhat different
form in *Playboy* magazine.

Grateful acknowledgment is made to the following:

Avon Books for permission to reprint an excerpt from
The Satanic Bible by Anton Szandor LaVey.
Reprinted by permission of the publisher.

Steinberg Music Co. for permission to reprint lyrics from
"Bad Blood" by Neil Sedaka and Phil Cody. Copyright © 1974, 1975
Kiddio Music Co. & Top Pop Music Co.
International copyright secured. All rights reserved.

First Signet Printing, November, 1983

1 2 3 4 5 6 7 8 9

In memory of Kenny Levine

Preface

This is a story of parents and their children that takes place in Marin County, California. Not the familiar Marin County of encounter sessions and hot tubs in eucalyptus groves, but one that exists farther up the freeway, where tract houses surrounded by high fences come in four standard colors, and the streets are as deserted at three o'clock in the afternoon as they are at three in the morning. Terra Linda, eighteen miles north of the Golden Gate Bridge, is such a suburban development, populated largely by people who left their pasts in distant places to take part in California's golden dream, and, in time, by their curiously listless children, who shared neither those pasts nor that dream. It is the story, in particular, of one suburban family whose dream turned to nightmare and ended in death.

The murder of Jim and Naomi Olive by their teen-aged daughter and her boyfriend on the first summer day of 1975 struck at the heart of Terra Linda, a residential community riven by generational strife. According to the editor of the local paper, "The morning after the case broke parents took a hard look at their children across the breakfast table and couldn't help wondering about the outcome of their next family quarrel." These parents were "middle Americans" with a vengeance—middle-aged, middle-class and, in the case of the majority of men who commuted to corporate jobs in San Francisco, middle-management. They were hard-working, success-oriented believers in the American way, in upward mobility and rising expectations, but by the mid-seventies they had lost faith, many of them, in all that they held most dear—their community, their marriages and, especially, their children.

The community had been developed two decades earlier according to the suburban values of the time, its low-slung glass-and-plywood houses with central atriums designed to bring the outdoors inside and provide a touch of modernism at knockdown prices. Its population, which would eventually grow to 10,000, was so racially and economically homogeneous that even the most expensive homes were simply tract houses with extra features. To assure maximum privacy, all the houses were surrounded by six-foot-high fences on every side but the front, while the town itself was bounded north and south by Marin's bosomy hills and on the east by Route 101, the only connection to the county seat of San Rafael. Terra Linda's hub was a huge shopping center that fed the consumer passions of those first young residents, many of whom had become entranced by the area's natural beauty when they were stationed at nearby military bases and had decided then that it would be a fine place to raise a family when the time came. When it did, they vowed to give their children "the best that money can buy," in the reassuring cliché of the day—a good public school system to educate them, liberal churches to mold their values, an extensive parks-and-recreation department to amuse them, and if things went wrong, as they inevitably did, a model juvenile hall to detain them. Then the men—and increasingly their wives as well—devoted themselves to their careers to pay for it all, assured that their kids were in the best professional hands.

Throughout the sixties and early seventies, property values escalated so rapidly that when these families were ready to move from a "starter" house to a larger or more luxurious place in the approved manner, they found that they could not afford to. Since younger couples could no longer buy into the community, a transient population of renters moved into single-family homes that had been converted to multi-unit dwellings. Educational and municipal services declined, along with the will and the tax base needed to maintain them. (One primary school had already been closed and more would need to be as the baby boom went bust.) In the 1970 census the area lost population and thus much needed state and federal funds. Like middle-class Americans elsewhere, Terra Lindans sensed that they were losing ground, and a new and very unsuburban term—"downward mobility"—was coined to describe the slippage.

By the mid-seventies the urban discomforts that Terra Linda residents had fled had arrived in the suburbs in full force, from the pollution of a nearby "industrial park" to a growing crime problem. In the San Rafael area that includes Terra Linda the rate of "serious" crime was increasing by 20 percent annually. Most of it was property crime committed by neighborhood kids, often to finance drug habits but sometimes to no discernible end at all. Teen-age vandalism became so serious that a combined police and sheriff's unit was created to patrol favorite targets, while both the high school and the shopping center hired armed guards. In 1975, when a seventy-year-old widower was terrorized at knifepoint by a gang of local toughs, the first of a series of town meetings was called to discuss all aspects of juvenile lawlessness.

For most of Terra Linda's adult inhabitants keeping up with the Joneses was hard enough; keeping up with their own children was impossible. Unlike the more liberal-minded residents of Marin's posh southern suburbs, some of whom reportedly smoked dope with their kids, Terra Lindans didn't even try. And since their sons and daughters were growing up on the thin edge of California's youth culture, the generation gap became an unbridgeable chasm, probably as wide in Terra Linda as anywhere in the country.

I had talked with some of those children that spring to research a magazine article about how high school kids had changed since the early sixties, the era portrayed in the film *American Graffiti,* which had been shot in the area and in which many of those kids had served as extras. They were the younger brothers and sisters of the kids who didn't go off to college in the movie, and I wondered how they were doing, a dozen years and a social revolution later. I found them as disillusioned as their parents, with the same uneasy feeling that they had arrived too late for their generation's main event, in their case not the suburbanization of America but the social ferment of the late sixties, so much of which had originated in nearby Berkeley and San Francisco. They had inherited that era's props and preoccupations—its music, drugs, casual sex and fascination with the occult—but not the time-bound urgency that had provided their older brothers and sisters with some sense of direction, or at least of energy. It had all gone suddenly stagnant, with the drug of choice changing from myth-generating psychedelics to mind-lulling "barbs," the sex oddly routinized and the music second-rate and hand-me-down. Even the occult had lost its mystery.

They were a generation going nowhere, and boredom surrounded them like the heavy fogs that seep over the coastal hills. Somehow these kids had become jaded without becoming experienced, and so their only way of rebelling against their parents' striving was to do nothing. But even "hanging out" was difficult in Terra Linda, for there was no place to gather, no Main Street to cruise. On weekend evenings, groups of kids could be found in a section of the shopping-center parking lot exchanging drugs and information about parties in the area until the guards chased them away. One pizza parlor where the kids had once congregated had changed ownership recently, and the new proprietor, in an attempt to attract a family clientele, not only raised prices but, to add insult to inflation, replaced the jukebox with a live organist playing old standards. It worked. When "September Song" replaced "Satisfaction," the kids fled in droves.

The phenomenon of downward mobility affected the young in particular. Fewer Terra Linda High School graduates were going to college than in years past, and a growing number of kids were not even finishing high school—a particular irritant to their education-minded parents. An especially malicious feature of the local newspaper's "People" column were wry items about middle-class kids stuck on the lowest rungs of their fathers' professions—a school janitor whose father taught history, a drive-in carhop whose parents owned the town's best French restaurant, a chimney sweep who serviced some of the same houses his building-contractor father had constructed.

Perhaps because their rebellion had grown more lethal for being so severely circumscribed, these kids expressed a degree of hostility toward their parents that seemed to go well beyond normal adolescent anger. Domestic conflict had grown so severe in many households that one widespread arrangement for dealing with it was for teen-agers to live with the families of friends, with their own parents paying room and board. Or sometimes, when adults placed children in Terra Linda's "model" juvenile hall on grounds that they were "beyond parental control," with the state picking up the tab. A lot of those kids graduated from "status" offenses that only juveniles can commit to criminal activities such as house burglary, and their parents were often their first victims. The war between the generations was not an empty phrase in Terra Linda.

I had been researching my high school story for several weeks when Marlene Olive and her boyfriend Chuck Riley were arrested for murder. It did not come as a complete surprise to some of my young informants. Several of Marlene's friends and even acquaintances at Terra Linda High School told me that they had known about her desire to kill her parents, and even about the specifics of various schemes she had devised for doing so, but had not taken her seriously. "We all *say* we're going to get rid of our parents," one of them explained, "but no one ever *does* anything about it."

I don't mean to suggest that family killings were epidemic in Terra Linda (although that same summer, rumblings from the other side of the generational fault were heard when a mother in neighboring San Rafael murdered her two teen-aged children), but merely that the death of the Olives reverberated ominously in many households, for it struck the discordant note I had been hearing elsewhere too loudly to be ignored. The story was prominently featured in the local media for a few days and then, as usual, dropped as soon as the lurid details of the crime and its aftermath were exhausted. Since it was clear that the real story lay behind the tabloid headlines, I decided to try to find out not just what happened inside that pleasant ranch house on a tree-shaded, floral-named suburban street but, as far as possible, why it happened, and what it said about the surrounding community, the warring worlds of the kids and their parents. In time, in too much time, the original magazine article metamorphosed into this book.

I don't know if all happy families are alike (although I suspect not), but Tolstoy was surely right when he said that each unhappy family is unhappy in its own way. Certainly the Olives of Terra Linda were. Still, there was something quintessentially American about them, despite—or perhaps because of—the fact that they had lived much of their lives abroad: Jim Olive, "a bound-for-glory salesman who never got there," in the words of an old friend; Naomi Olive, an alcoholic housewife in a domestic cocoon; and Marlene, who had to teach herself to be an American teen-ager and went about her lessons with a convert's misguided enthusiasm. Like many of their neighbors, they formed a lethal configuration, a nuclear family set for explosion. The difference was that in the Olives' case the ultimate family nightmare actually occurred.

As I began to learn about the Olives' lives—and those of Chuck Riley and his family—I was drawn to the available detail of the story and could only hope that such specificity would imply a larger picture, in the way that a faithful rendering of the giant's toes would indicate his stature. I had a lot of help. The Olives themselves were dead, of course, but friends and relatives in California and South America were able to describe their family life over the years. Like his daughter, Jim Olive was a diligent letter writer and record keeper, and Colonel Philip Royce, his friend and business partner, afforded me access to his files. Eventually police, school and juvenile authorities were persuaded to open up sealed records and talk about their contact with the Olives as family problems culminated in an act that nearly everyone had anticipated and no one could do much to prevent. Finally, before I was allowed to meet Marlene, her guardian, Carolynn Shaalman, provided me with notebooks of her poems, and this running account of an adolescent's inner turmoil seemed to me to constitute an extraordinary document, a rhymed and metered diary of a murder in the making. Marlene was clearly an intelligent, complex young woman whose consciousness of her situation was increasingly undermined by fantasies that threatened to live a life of their own.

In Chuck Riley's case the richness of personal detail was even greater and certainly more unexpected, coming as it did not just from conscious recall but from a much less conventional journalistic technique—hypnosis. As indicated by his submissive relationship to Marlene ("akin to slavery," one psychiatrist would testify), Chuck was extremely hypnotizable, a fact that his lawyer would put to dramatic use during his trial. In and outside the courtroom, experts disagreed about the ability of even the most hypnotizable subject to lie in a deep trance when his very life is at stake, as Chuck Riley's was, but no authority has suggested that such information would be inaccurate when the subject has little or no reason to misrepresent the facts. When I asked a psychologist to rehypnotize Chuck in weekly sessions after his trial, I was, for the most part, interested in details of his past that he could not otherwise recall but would have no reason to fabricate. I tried to verify the information whenever possible, and if that wasn't possible, I omitted facts that seemed too clearly exculpatory. Hypnosis is a controversial, and no doubt fallible, technique that journalists have hitherto ignored as an investigative tool, even though it is probably less fallible than our usual method of reconstructing the past, a subject's conscious recall. It is certainly more effective. Here was a way to get beyond the grim facts of a family murder by following the thoughts and feelings of one participant as well as his conversations with the other. Although they were only used to supplement personal interviews and documentary evidence, Chuck Riley's hypnotic recollections provide a glimpse into one person's psyche that novelists may imagine but nonfiction writers must normally do without.

It was not until his trial ended, six months after the murder, that I was able to talk to Chuck. By then I had come to know his parents, Oscar and Joanne Riley, well-meaning, plain-speaking people blinking in the glare of sudden media attention. For them Chuck was still the kid he had once been before, as Oscar put it, "he got into the pot scene and Marlene put her spell on him." By then, too, I had met many of Marlene and Chuck's friends, who taught me most of what I learned about the ordinary teenage world that had become the crucible for such an extraordinary event. Some of them take their part in the narrative under their real names; others requested anonymity. To all of them I'm extremely grateful.

But most of the story came directly from Chuck and Marlene themselves, in hundreds of hours of interviews conducted over a period of several years. While at first they may have talked to me so frankly simply because an adult was not just listening to them but taking notes, in time a trust and friendship developed. The interviews are long over, but I have stayed in close touch with both of them, and what they have become since the crime—Chuck in jail and Marlene on the streets—may be the most important part of the story. Neither will entirely escape that airless bedroom at 353 Hibiscus Way where the bodies of the Olives once lay. But as I hope the following pages attest, both have tried in their own manner to understand an event that at first seemed impossible and became, in reconstruction, almost inevitable, not so much a question of whether as when.

One

After it was done Chuck walked past Marlene into the Olives' living room, his yellow sport shirt splattered with blood. He slumped down on the new cloth-covered couch and stared into the fireplace. Either the stereo, tuned perpetually to the progressive rock of radio station KTIM, was barely audible or the shots had temporarily deafened him. He was still high from the drugs he had taken that morning and now he felt dizzy and sick to his stomach as well. As always when he felt "out of it," he closed his eyes and pictured himself driving fast and expertly along the winding hillside roads that led to the ocean from his home, then out along Highway 1 between the granite cliffs and the swirling water far below. Behind the wheel of a car was the only place Chuck felt completely in control. He hardly took notice when Marlene came over, curled up next to him and began to run her hand through his silky chestnut hair—his best feature, she thought—and nuzzle his neck. "It's going to be all right now, Chuck," she said soothingly. "Everything will be okay. They can't interfere anymore."

She got up to bring him a can of Coors from the refrigerator and searched through her pocketbook for a couple of Valium tablets. He swallowed the tranquilizers absent-mindedly and guzzled down the rest of the beer. Marlene was now sitting on the carpet in front of him with her head on his lap, stilling the nervous bounce of his knee and saying all the things he had dreamed she would say since they first met nine months before—that she loved him and there would be no other guys for her from now on, that no one would ever take her away from him again

1

and they could even get married if he still wanted to. Then she left the room.

Marlene had been away a few minutes before Chuck began to feel uneasy again and went to look for her. He found her in her bedroom, toying with some cream-colored plastic beads on the bed. There were seven of them. They were round and flat, each with a different black letter repeated on both sides and a hole punched through the middle for a missing string. She had taken them out of a tiny plastic box and was trying to form a word with them: E-R-T-I-D-G-J . . .

Abruptly, Marlene scrambled the letters and started over again: J-E-T-I-G-R-D . . .

"What're those?" Chuck asked.

"My baby bracelet from the hospital I was born in," Marlene answered. "My daddy said it had my real mother's name on it and when I turned twenty-one I could find out what it was."

Although Marlene had talked often, almost obsessively, about the fact that she had been adopted at birth by the Olives, this was the first Chuck had heard about a hospital ID bracelet. When he attempted to add another letter at the end of the row, Marlene quickly mixed up the order again, swiping the beads in her fist as if they were jacks on a sidewalk. With her back half turned to him, she began rearranging them. Chuck wasn't sure whether the slight tremble to her shoulders and the sharp bursts of air through her nostrils meant she was laughing or sobbing.

R-I-D-G-E-T-J . . .

Marlene tried several more combinations before she gave up, banging her fist down on the bed and scattering the beads, only to search them out one by one and carefully place them back in the plastic container. "Now I'll never find out who I am," she said. But to Chuck, watching this curious performance, it seemed as if she didn't really want a name to emerge.

Afterward Marlene began unbuttoning his outer shirt and lifting the black tank top underneath. Chuck's body, just coming down from the acid high, responded to her prompting almost automatically. Never much for sexual preliminaries, she moved on top of him quickly. And when they were finished she lay beside him, whispering welcome endearments into his ear. After a time Chuck reached for a cigarette, and Marlene searched for the turquoise kimono-style robe that her mother had given her not long before.

It wasn't easy to find amid the clutter of her room—glittery, sequined clothing and pairs of six-inch-high platform shoes strewn over the floor along with boxes of her "personal papers," mostly letters from friends she had left behind when she moved to California, rough sketches of the latest fashions inspired by the women's magazines she collected, and page after page of hurriedly scribbled poems that would eventually be recopied into her loose-leaf "poetry books." A self-confessed pack rat, Marlene never threw anything away—or even *put* it away, her mother had constantly complained. On the headboard and wall behind her bed and on the night table beside it were several peacock feathers in a glass vase, a bowl filled with marijuana seeds, a half-dozen bottles of prescription drugs, posters with soft-focus scenes and romantic inscriptions—and the only reminder that Marlene had spent nearly all but the last two of her sixteen years in Ecuador—some wooden llamas hand-carved by Indian craftsmen from the Andes. The room, as Naomi Olive had never tired of suggesting, was a "disaster area," with barely enough cleared space to walk around on tiptoe. It was a typical ongoing dispute between a teen-age daughter and her mother, one of an endless series of blowups between the two of them which had finally reached, as the evidence in the bedroom opposite Marlene's grotesquely demonstrated, a most untypical resolution.

When Marlene found the robe on the floor, the mischievous black-coated Rascal, her favorite cat (the other was a tiger-striped tabby named Mishu), was using it as a pillow. "My God, the cats!" she said in sudden panic. "I don't want the cats to get in there, Chuck. Move him inside." Across the narrow hallway Chuck, dressed in his undershorts, grabbed hold of Marlene's father under the arms and dragged him farther into the small bedroom so that his legs no longer blocked the doorway. Jim Olive was, even in death, a pleasant-looking, compulsively neat man who appeared to be a decade younger than his fifty-nine years. He wore his favorite weekend outfit, dark slacks and a belted khaki-colored safari jacket with deep front pockets. His thick auburn hair, with only the slightest trace of gray at the temples, was combed straight back, and the faint grimace around his mouth might have come from biting into a wedge of lemon rather than from four bullets fired point-blank into his chest.

"Get his wallet and keys and everything else out of his pockets," Marlene ordered. Chuck took some change and a key

ring from one of Jim Olive's front pants pockets, Rolaids and
chewing gum from the other. The outside pockets of the safari
jacket yielded a small date book, which he handed to Marlene;
she glanced at it just long enough to notice that the only appointment that her father had scheduled for the following week was a
routine dental checkup on Tuesday afternoon, three days away.
Still searching for a wallet, Chuck turned the body over on its
stomach, a maneuver that required some effort, for Jim Olive,
although only five feet six inches tall, was a thick-set man.
Chuck patted down the back pockets. Nothing. "He sometimes
keeps it in his inside jacket pocket," Marlene said. Chuck rolled
Mr. Olive over on his side and unbuttoned his jacket. Four
coin-sized spots of blood, one on the left shoulder and the others
grouped together above the heart in what Chuck, an expert
marksman, would later call "a tight pattern," had seeped through
the dead man's orange Bahama shirt. He unclipped a plastic
penholder from the breast pocket of the shirt and noticed with a
twinge that it advertised ABC Brakes, a client of Jim Olive's
small-business consultancy firm to which the older man had once
recommended Chuck for a job. Finally he reached deep inside
the jacket pocket and found the wallet. After riffling through it,
Marlene tossed its contents—a Social Security card and a driver's
license, several gas credit cards and a BankAmericard—onto the
small pile of her father's belongings. "The rings, too," she said.
Chuck removed a gold wedding band from Jim Olive's left hand
and a jade school ring (Penn State, class of '37) from the index
finger of his right hand.

In the meantime Marlene had found her mother's black patent-
leather purse on the desk between the bed and the windows and
dumped it out on the faded green shag rug that carpeted the
whole house, even the bathrooms. Naomi Olive, who had rarely
gone out by herself in recent months, had relied on her husband
for her immediate cash needs, but Marlene picked out some store
credit cards and a plastic-coated ID card the State of California
issues to nondrivers for check-cashing purposes. Moving quickly,
she went down the hallway to the master bedroom, which her
father had occupied alone (as if to apologize for insisting on
separate sleeping quarters, Naomi Olive had kept most of her
clothes and jewelry there). She found her parents' joint checkbook lying on top of the double dresser, and returning down the
hall, threw it on the growing pile of their belongings. Next she
unhooked a small gold watch from her mother's wrist and turned

her attention to the plain gold wedding band and the diamond engagement ring lodged together on her left hand, which hung limply from the bed. Marlene had to struggle to remove the rings, for Naomi Olive had grown thick-limbed and arthritic since the time, thirty-one years earlier, when the rings had first been placed on her finger two weeks apart. With a wrench that almost sent her sprawling backward, Marlene finally pulled them off. "They never should have been married," she muttered to herself. "And now they're not."

A bloodstained claw hammer with a red wooden handle lay on the carpet near the head of the bed. Marlene took it out to the kitchen sink, rinsed it off and left it there among the unwashed breakfast dishes. She came back with some dishtowels, sponges and two spray bottles of Rex all-purpose detergent. "Help me get the bedroom cleaned up," she said.

There were bloodstains all over the mustard-colored walls, especially the one behind Naomi Olive's bed, and spots of blood on most of the furniture. Without talking much, Chuck carried the furniture and accessories into the living room, where Marlene wiped them clean. First he brought in the objects that stood on the mahogany night table beside the bed—a cloth-shaded lamp, a clock radio, an empty teacup, a plate holding a section of an apple, an ashtray overflowing with Naomi Olive's cigarette stubs, and some copies of her favorite magazine, the *Ladies' Home Journal*—as well as the night table itself. (Before handing the night table over to Marlene, Chuck noticed a piece of flesh clinging to its side and flicked it away.) Then they emptied the bookcase of several hand-carved wood figurines from Ecuador, assorted glass and china bric-à-brac, and a round fish tank containing several guppies (one of many fish tanks of all shapes and sizes scattered throughout the house). Next they maneuvered the bookcase itself into the living room. Marlene removed the oil painting above the bookcase—a crude semiabstract woodsy landscape that had been purchased in Ecuador. Although it had been hanging a good eight feet away from Naomi Olive, the painting, too, was spattered with droplets of blood.

All this time both Chuck and Marlene were trying to avoid looking directly at the center of the carnage. Naomi Olive was lying on her back with her head twisted toward the door. She was partially covered with a light blanket. Her metal-frame glasses lay broken and askew on her face. Blood soaked the roots of her graying hair and ran down her cheeks in rivulets onto the pillow and sheets, eventually to collect in a small pool beside the bed. Her forehead had been struck repeatedly above the left eye with a hammer, leaving massive contusions surrounding a gaping hole in her skull the size of a golf ball.

Chuck pulled the bed out from the wall. The wall itself looked as though someone had flicked a paintbrush at it. The thick elongated tracks of blood immediately above the head of the bed became smaller and more widely spaced higher up, with a few red specks reaching to the ceiling. An oil painting of Marlene as a child that hung directly above the bed was similarly spotted with blood.

The portrait, perhaps Jim Olive's proudest possession, had been presented to him on the occasion of the Olives' twenty-fifth wedding anniversary by colleagues at the Gulf Oil Company in Ecuador, over which, at the time, he presided. It was painted by a local artist from a photograph of Marlene that had lain, until its mysterious disappearance one day, under the glass top of Jim Olive's desk—a picture of an extraordinarily pretty and carefree young girl with light-brown hair combed into bangs, widely spaced bright-green eyes, a freckled nose, a suggestion of dimples, and an even row of sparkling teeth. The painting itself duplicated every detail of the photograph, down to Marlene's buttoned-on Mary Jane collar and green-and-red-print dress, except, oddly enough, for her eyes, which were colored brown rather than green and made too large, so that the final effect of the portrait was reminiscent of those saucer-eyed children sold by the yard in schlock art galleries. Chuck wiped some blood off the gilt frame and brought it out to Marlene in the living room.

The contrast between the ten-year-old girl in the painting and the young woman who studied it with a look of great annoyance was striking. At sixteen Marlene was large-boned and slightly overweight. She was still very pretty but adolescence had coarsened her features, drugs had dulled the gleam in her eyes, and the prevailing teen-age fashion, in the form of the thick-soled platform shoes she favored, gave her movements a lurching quality. She wore jeans and a white T-shirt that promoted the recent "North American Tour" of one of her favorite rock groups, Yes. The unbridled hostility Marlene felt for her mother burst forth again as she was wiping the streaks of blood off the portrait. "Curse that bitch!" she said aloud. "Getting her blood all over my picture."

With the painting removed, Chuck proceeded to scrub the

bedroom wall with the spray cleaner and rags. It was hard work. Even though he applied all the elbow grease he could muster, the wall remained streaked with pinkish stains. The shag carpet was even more hopeless. Marlene soaked up the puddle of blood beside the bed with a rag, wrung it out in the bathroom sink and repeated the process. She finally unscrewed the bottle cap of the detergent and poured the liquid over the spot, leaving it to soak in. Then she took Chuck's yellow shirt, the blood-soaked pillow from under her mother's head as well as the rags they had been using to clean up the room and attempted to burn them in the living-room fireplace. When she couldn't get the fire started, she called for Chuck. He crumpled up some magazine pages, shoved them under the rest of the debris and lit the pile.

By now Chuck was getting restless. Try as he might, there was no way he could push the killings from his mind with the evidence right under his nose. Unwelcome images kept flashing into his consciousness. He wanted desperately to forget what had just happened, to be around other people. When he had left his best friend Michael Howard's house to walk over to the Olives' he said he would be back soon with Marlene. The two friends had planned to drive to the beach with their girl friends. That was nearly two hours ago. "Let's walk over to Mike and Nancy's and see what's happening," he finally told Marlene. "We can finish this later."

"I've got to feed the cats first," Marlene said.

While she opened a can of cat food and emptied it into a plastic dish on the kitchen floor, Chuck cleaned his gun, a single-action .22-caliber Ruger pistol that he had bought several months before from "a friend of a friend" for $30, assuming, without asking too many questions, that at that bargain price it was "hot." He had fired it thousands of times during target practice sessions at China Camp, a desolate stretch of marshland and woods bordering San Francisco Bay, and was so good a shot that he could routinely burst beer bottles set on an oil drum fifty feet away. As with his driving, shooting was "something I could do better than the others," and he took considerable pride in his marksmanship. Always meticulous about caring for his guns, he would clean them thoroughly as soon as he was through firing them. Today was no exception. He took some 3-in-One oil from a kitchen utility drawer and worked it with a cloth through the gun's barrel and six cylinders. He carefully polished the black metal exterior of the weapon, reloaded it and dumped the rest of the bullets into a plastic Baggie when he couldn't rearrange them neatly in the box they came in.

Before leaving the house, Marlene stuffed her parents' checkbook and credit cards into her purse and gave the cash from her father's wallet to Chuck, who generally took care of money matters. The two of them then pulled the light summer blanket over her mother's head. "That's the last time I'll have to look at her," Marlene announced with what Chuck would later call a "mocking grin."

The contrast between the scene inside the house and the unruffled normality outside could not have been more extreme. If some latter-day Norman Rockwell were looking to paint the bright side of American suburban life, he could do worse, at first glance at least, than choose Terra Linda. This being the first day of summer and a warm Saturday afternoon, many of the Olives' neighbors were out mowing their subdivided plots or trimming the azalea bushes that lined their driveways or washing their cars, more often than not station wagons like the green Chevrolet Vega with simulated wood paneling that sat in the driveway of the Olive residence at 353 Hibiscus Way. If any neighbors had heard unusual noises coming from that house in the early-afternoon hours or looked up from outdoor tasks a couple of hours later to see a hand-holding teen-age couple walking down the block, they did not remember it afterward. Privacy is a much cherished value among Terra Linda residents, the search for it being the reason most of them had moved there from crowded urban centers in the first place. It is, moreover, a value made almost mandatory by the houses they had moved to—houses virtually barren of front windows and surrounded by six-foot-high wooden fences on the remaining sides.

Chuck and Marlene strolled down Hibiscus, crossed center-divided Las Gallinas Avenue and cut through a pathway that led to Orange Blossom Lane, where Mike Howard lived. It was on this pathway that the teen-agers had often met secretly during the three months since Jim Olive forbade them to see each other, a restriction that had recently received the added authority of a court order.

Since no one answered the bell at his friend's house, Chuck correctly assumed that Mike and Nancy, having grown tired of waiting for him to return, had gone to the beach by themselves.

He searched his pockets for a piece of paper, scribbled a hurried message for his friend to call him at home on the inside of a matchbook and stuck it in the brass door knocker. Then he and Marlene cut through some backyards and crossed Manuel T. Freitas Parkway, Terra Linda's main thoroughfare, to the parking lot of Northgate Mall. As they were crossing the road Roger Kyle, a dapper, smooth-talking clothing-store salesman whom Chuck had recently come to admire for his social grace and appeal to women, saw them and honked his car horn, but they were too preoccupied at the moment to notice. Earlier that day Chuck had paid Kyle a visit to temporarily retrieve the object he had given his new friend as security on a small loan—his .22-caliber pistol. Driving past on the way to his sister's birthday party, Kyle wondered if Chuck had managed to sell the gun, as he had promised he would in order to repay the debt.

Northgate was Terra Linda's commercial hub, if such an enormous shopping center (actually three distinct shopping centers) could be said to be the "hub" of such a relatively small town. With two major department stores and dozens of smaller shops of every variety, surrounded by fifty acres of parking space, it seemed more appropriate to say that Terra Linda was Northgate's periphery, so completely did the commercial center, which drew customers from all over northern and central Marin, dominate the residential area.

Chuck and Marlene continued walking across the vast parking lot to T-Burger, a favorite luncheon place, where Chuck bought a pack of cigarettes from a machine and dialed Mike Howard's house on a pay phone just to make sure he and Nancy hadn't been asleep or "screwing around" when he had rung the bell a few minutes earlier. His need for the distraction of other people seemed to grow by the minute; nervously, he rang the number a second time when there was no answer. Then they headed across the mall toward the Rileys' house, stopping off on the way at Goodvi's, a clothing store where Chuck's younger brother worked. Kerry, who had recently become weekend assistant manager at the store, was showing a new salesgirl the ropes when Chuck and Marlene walked in, and he introduced her to them.

Only a year apart in age, Chuck and Kerry had shared many of the same interests as well as the same bedroom all their lives, although they were, in both looks and disposition, opposite types. Thin and sharp-featured, Kerry resembled his father, while Chuck had inherited both his ample girth and his easygoing manner from his mother. There was nothing unusual about Chuck and Marlene stopping by the store to shoot the breeze and try on the latest in flared hip-hugging Levi's and crazy-patterned sport shirts. But today Chuck seemed jumpy, "white as a sheet and bug-eyed," according to Kerry, who thought his brother was "flying" on drugs. "Hey, bro, what's happening?" Kerry asked in his usual jive-talking manner. "You look higher than a kite in a breeze." But Chuck cut their normal bantering short to ask if Kerry could give them a ride home. After Kerry explained that he had just come back from a break and wasn't due off for another two hours, Chuck said, "Well, catch ya later," and led Marlene through the store to the rear entrance. "Is she always so quiet?" the new salesgirl asked about Marlene, who had not said a word the whole time she was in the store.

Chuck and Marlene walked the remaining half mile from the mall to his house—past the Guide Dogs for the Blind training center, where Chuck had often played as a kid; past Rev. Walter Werronen's split-level Faith Lutheran Church, which his parents occasionally attended; past Hartzell elementary school, which he had attended; across the railroad tracks to the Rileys' modest three-bedroom house in Rafael Meadows. Technically a part of the city of San Rafael, Rafael Meadows was definitely "on the other side of the tracks" from upper-middle-class Terra Linda, even if the trains, a freight-carrying branch of the Southern Pacific, hardly ran anymore. The houses there were also tracts, but smaller and less expensive than Terra Linda's, while the residents more often than not held blue-collar jobs in the area instead of commuting to more lucrative work in San Francisco. Although the Meadows was often described as "run-down" (or "lived-in," depending on whom you were talking to), it had a neighborly, back-fence feeling that Terra Linda conspicuously lacked—a lifestyle perfectly suited to Oscar and Joanne Riley.

Oscar Riley got home from his job later than usual on Saturdays, the day he stayed at work to fill out the weekly sales report for the baked products that he delivered by truck to most of Marin County for the Dolly Madison Company. Otherwise there might have been more of a stir when Chuck and Marlene walked in, for Oscar Riley and his son were currently not on the best of terms. Only the night before, Oscar had, as he put it, "read the riot act" to his son for continuing to see Marlene despite the court order and for repeatedly breaking the midnight curfew they had agreed on. Furious about his father's interference in what he considered his "private affairs," Chuck had told him in no uncertain terms that Marlene was "the only thing that matters to me," and stomped out of the house, slamming the door behind him.

Joanne Riley, a nurse's aide at Ross General Hospital, was more conciliatory that her husband by nature. She had known all along that Chuck and Marlene were still spending a lot of time together, a fact that she did not view as harshly as her husband did. It was easier for her to understand how much the steady companionship of an attractive girl meant to Chuck, a "late bloomer" who, although he had recently turned twenty, had never had a girl friend before Marlene. For years she had been after him to lose the excess poundage that hindered him socially, but it was only in the past eight or nine months, since he became hopelessly infatuated with Marlene Olive, that he had felt motivated to slim down.

So when Marlene and Chuck walked into the house, Joanne Riley did more than hold her peace; she invited them to stay for dinner. But Chuck, who had felt "uncomfortable" around his parents ever since he first became involved with drugs at fifteen, said that they would probably "do something with Mike and Nancy," who had called just before he got home.

When Chuck returned the call, Mike Howard readily accepted his standard excuse that "something came up with Marlene" and agreed to drive over to pick them up. (Chuck's car, an unregistered, much ticketed 1966 Buick Skylark with a plywood board in place of a hood, had been "grounded" by Oscar Riley.) Quickly changing clothes and grabbing a lid of marijuana and some cocaine from the drug stash he kept in a footlocker under his bed, Chuck was off and running again, leaving even his normally forbearing mother slightly miffed at the way he neglected his family and just about everything else for Marlene. Joanne Riley couldn't help but think of her husband's angry words when Chuck came home at two o'clock in the morning. In another of those tense hallway confrontations that had become all to familiar around the Riley household, Oscar Riley told his son, "One of these days you're gonna get burned bad and I won't be there to bail you out."

Now, a few minutes later, Mike Howard was waiting outside in his girl friend Nancy Dillon's car, a bruised and battered old Mercury. With Mike's mother and younger sister visiting relatives in England and his father living away from home, he and Nancy, the girl he met the same day that Chuck had met Marlene, had the house to themselves. Mike was a rangy, wispy-bearded twenty-year-old with a peculiar tick in his throat, a kind of low-pitched croak that acted up whenever he became excited, as he was now. "Where the hell *onk* have you *onk onk* been?" he asked Chuck. "We waited nearly an hour."

"Sorry, man," Chuck said. "I guess I lost track of time."

Mike and Chuck had been close friends since shortly after the Howards had moved from San Francisco to Terra Linda in 1971, although some tension had developed between them in recent months. His friend's failure to show up for the trip to the beach was, in Mike's view, "a typical Chuck move." These days he was always late for appointments—or forgot them completely. And he had begun cutting corners in other ways. He owed people money, Mike included, and didn't bother to repay the debts during the times when he was flush. He had even started to cheat in his drug dealings, giving customers a sample "taste" of high-quality pot or cocaine and selling them inferior dope later on. For someone who had started dealing more to make friends than money, who had often given away more drugs than he sold, Chuck's behavior seemed pointless. It was all done, his friends assumed, to support his most expensive habit—Marlene. He had gone "completely bonkers" over her, Mike thought, receiving "only grief" in return.

Partly as a peace offering, when Chuck got back to Mike's house he carefully removed the Howardses' mahogany-framed living-room mirror from the wall, carried it to the kitchen table and brought out a gram of cocaine that was packaged—his special "trademark"—in a tiny clear plastic coin purse with a zippered top. "I brought some dynamite snow and this primo Oaxacan," Chuck said, tossing a cellophane bag of marijuana onto the mirror along with the cocaine. Nancy chopped up the coke into a fine powder with a kitchen knife and made eight parallel lines out of it while Chuck rolled some joints and started one around the table. Then he rolled a dollar bill into a tight cylinder and they all snorted the coke, one line to one nostril. Marlene was sitting on Chuck's lap; protectively, he held her long hair back when she leaned over the mirror.

He was feeling expansive now, getting a buzz off the coke but an even bigger one from Marlene's changed attitude toward him. She generally kept her distance from him in public, rarely returning his sometimes clumsy attempts at affection or allowing others to see her as his "old lady." Now she was sitting on his lap, whispering into his ear. Even Mike and Nancy noticed the difference in Marlene's behavior—and Chuck *knew* they noticed it. Maybe he had finally won her over, Mike thought, although it was hard to believe. Chuck started another joint around. "Rub my feet, would you?" he asked Marlene. "These new boots pinch." Mike and Nancy watched in amazement as Marlene pulled off Chuck's cowboy boots and massaged his stockinged feet. "Kiss it," Chuck said after a time. Chuck always blows it by coming on too strong, Mike thought, but Marlene bent over and kissed his friend's outstretched foot.

The conversation turned to the Yes concert coming up the following week at the Cow Palace. Mike and Nancy had bought tickets as soon as the concert was announced in the papers. By now the show had long since been sold out and Mike knew that Chuck hadn't gotten tickets. "You guys going to Yes next week?" he teased. "We're goin'," Chuck said. "One way or another, we're goin'."

Everyone had a beer except Marlene, who didn't drink much. Another joint was passed around. Mike got down on his knees and blew smoke into his dog's nostrils. Merlin, an old black Labrador, shook his head but refused to budge. A few minutes later he wobbled away on rubber legs and bumped into an easy chair. Getting Merlin stoned was an old joke, but everyone laughed.

A Jimi Hendrix album was playing on the stereo in Mike's music room off the kitchen. Hendrix was Marlene's favorite musician (her *very* favorite song was his version of "All Along the Watchtower") and his music always turned her on sexually. She pulled Chuck down the hall into the bathroom and they made love against the cold tiles. They came back into the living room still rearranging their clothes.

"I'm getting hungry," Nancy said.

Chuck whispered something in Marlene's ear and she nodded. "We'll treat you guys to dinner out," he said.

Before the group left the house Marlene said that she had to tell her parents where she was going. "You think you can get permission?" Mike asked skeptically, knowing that Marlene had recently been restricted from going out nights after a particularly violent fight with her mother. "Sure," Marlene reassured him. "My parents are being pretty cool these days."

She dialed her number on the kitchen phone and cheerfully said, "Hi, Daddy, is it okay if I go out for dinner with Mike and Nancy?" There was a brief pause before Marlene said, "Thanks a lot. I'll be back by seven. Bye."

In the car Chuck suggested the Travelers Inn, a restaurant his parents frequented just off the freeway on Third Street in downtown San Rafael. On the way there he passed around another joint so they would all get "the munchies." The Travelers Inn was an odd conjunction, a rowdy Irish bar that served Chinese food in an adjoining room, both of them more run-down than atmospheric. In the late afternoon the restaurant was empty except for the occasional drinker getting a head start on Saturday night who stumbled in accidentally from the bar. They ordered four Number Three dinners—"the monosodium glutamate special," Mike Howard joked.

Marlene grew more withdrawn during the meal, hardly eating or talking at all. Chuck was more cheerful but clearly restless. At one point he got up and wandered around the bar area. In the men's room he put a dime in a vending machine that sold different brands of cologne and pushed the "Brut" plunger. By now he was fairly well "spaced." The events at the Olive house were a nagging thought in the back of his mind which, every so often, would surface in a rush from the depths of his consciousness like an out-of-breath diver. Staring out of the restaurant's lettered plate-glass windows, he remembered everything for an instant before he shook off the recollection with a toss of his head so violent that Mike asked his friend if something was wrong.

On the way back to Terra Linda, Chuck and Marlene, after some whispered exchanges in the back seat, asked Mike and Nancy if they wanted "to get a room and party at the Villa Rafael." Mike had heard from Chuck that he and Marlene often rented rooms in local motels to spend time together unharrassed by their parents. Occasionally, Chuck had hinted, they were joined by another couple or even a single male whom Marlene had chosen and Chuck had procured. Indeed, some months ago Chuck had casually asked Mike if he would ever like to help him "turn Marlene on," but the offer was vague and nothing came of it. This more specific invitation made Mike apprehensive, but before he was pressed for an answer there were more furtive exchanges in the back seat and Chuck said, "Forget it. Let's just go back to your place.'' Marlene had reminded him that they had ''some work to do'' later that night.

Back at Mike's house more joints were passed around while everyone pondered the usual Saturday-night conundrum of what to do and where to go. Marlene had picked up a mimeographed handout advertising a rock concert that night (''Start the summer off right''), but it was across the bay in Hayward. Mike knew about a party in the area, but Chuck said he was too tired. He looked at the movie listings in the San Rafael *Independent-Journal* and saw that one of the features at the 101 Drive-In was entitled *Death Race 2000*. Anything about cars fascinated him and he lobbied for the movie in spite of Mike's assurance that it would be there all week, while the party wouldn't. Since no one was willing to compromise, Chuck and Marlene decided to go off to the movie by themselves, although they took down the address of the party in case they could rejoin their friends later in the evening.

It was dusk as Chuck and Marlene walked toward Hibiscus Way; house lights were being turned on, sprinklers off. Neighborhood kids, hurrying to reach home before dark, pedaled their bicycles standing up past Chuck and Marlene. The roar of souped-up engines being gunned down these straight suburban streets by their older brothers—one of the prevailing nighttime sounds in Terra Linda—could already be heard nearby. If only, Chuck thought, he could keep his mind off the two bodies in that airless room.

Inside the Olive house the telephone rang and rang. The caller was Colonel Philip Royce, a retired Army officer who was Jim Olive's closest friend and his associate in a General Business Services franchise for which they had recently rented office space in San Rafael. Although Royce had moved into the downtown office two weeks earlier, a delay in the installation of telephone lines had kept Jim Olive working out of his office at home, a spare room at the far end of the hall near the master bedroom. Royce knew that his partner was to have transferred business records and office equipment into the new quarters that morning, and he was anxious to find out how the move had gone. It was the first of many increasingly anxious attempts he would make to contact his partner before he finally called the San Rafael police six days later.

At Chuck's prompting Marlene ignored the telephone. They

both steered clear of Naomi Olive's bedroom (which had been Marlene's room the last time Chuck was allowed into the house). Marlene seemed nervous about Mishu pacing before the closed door and shooed him away. They had not discussed a plan for disposing of the bodies, although it was clear that nothing could be done until after dark. Chuck still felt strange inside the house, somehow fearful that Jim Olive would find him there and carry out his angry threats to shoot him on sight if he did. In the house he had to fight even more desperately to block out the violence of the afternoon, but the dreaded images would reappear, as he later told a psychologist, "like a slide show in my mind." Although an hour remained before the eight o'clock show, Chuck and Marlene left the house quickly. Marlene grabbed her rabbit fur coat, and Chuck, for no clear reason, picked up his pistol from the coffee table in front of the couch and stuck it in the Vega's glove compartment. As an afterthought he reached into the utility refrigerator the Olives kept in the garage and removed a six-pack of beer.

The teen-agers spent the next half-hour aimlessly driving around Terra Linda, through the streets near Hibiscus, most of them also named after flowers, to the somewhat posher section of Marinwood, whose street names ended in "stone," and out the Lucas Valley Road past the point where the developments ended and the dairy farms began, then back across the freeway to the desolate marsh fill where the 101 Drive-In was located. Chuck felt "mellowed out" by the drive, again completely forgetful of recent events. "It sure is nice of your dad to let us have the car," he said to Marlene, intending no cruel irony.

If Chuck's purpose in wanting to attend a movie that evening was, as he later stated, "to be around people," the crowded drive-in fitted the bill admirably. But if it was also to keep his mind off of the recurring flashes that had plagued him all day, he could not have picked a worse movie. For soon after the opening credits it was abundantly clear to Chuck that *Death Race 2000*, a low-budget Roger Corman production, was hardly the simple "racing flick" he had bargained for.

Set in the year 2000, the film depicted the annual road race from New York to "New Los Angeles" that had by then replaced baseball as the national sport. Five male-and-female racing teams competed against one another by running down pedestrians along the route, scoring from 10 points for "women in all age categories" to 100 points for the old men who were wheeled onto the road during Euthanasia Day at the geriatrics hospital. A bloodthirsty television commentator greeted each score with enthusiastic cries of "Beautiful kill! Neat kill!" By the time the movie was fifteen minutes old it had gone through every conceivable variety of death and destruction on the highway.

Chuck could not keep his mind in check; images from the afternoon pressed on his consciousness with increasing persistence. The awful gurgling of Naomi Olive choking on her own blood. Jim Olive screaming "Oh my God, Naomi . . . Oh my God!" and turning around to catch sight of Chuck. "I'm going to get you, you bastard." The glint of a kitchen knife. The four quick shots that sent the older man spinning to the floor.

By the middle of the movie it was impossible for Chuck and Marlene to continue to avoid the problem at hand. Marlene first broached the subject of what they were going to do with her parents' bodies. They discussed the possibility of making it look as if the Olives had been killed during a robbery, a cover-up that had been dramatized on a recent *Kojak* episode the two had seen. But Chuck realized that they had already gone too far in cleaning up Mrs. Olive's bedroom to make the plan work. "What about pushing their car over a cliff near Stinson Beach?" he suggested, taking his cue from a scene in the movie they were now scarcely watching. But Marlene didn't want to give up the Vega, and besides, she had recently lost a favorite piece of jewelry, a turquoise-studded silver ring, and she thought that maybe it was somewhere in the car. On the screen a multiple collision set off a racing car's gas tank and consumed the driver in a blazing furnace of heat.

"Do you keep any gasoline at home?" Marlene suddenly asked. Chuck said there were only a couple of empty gas cans lying around the side yard for "emergency use."

"We're going to get rid of everything once and for all."

"Where?" Chuck asked.

"I'll tell you later. Just go get the gas cans when this is over."

Chuck had trouble following the rest of the movie, which now included a terrorist plot to kill the President interspersed with all the twisted automobile wreckage. Somehow the hero, a racing-car driver named Frankenstein, ended up throwing in his lot with the terrorists and becoming President himself. He told the TV announcer in a post-race interview that his first act in office would be to abolish the whole competition. The announcer protested vehemently. "Sure it's violent," he argued, "but that's the way we love it. It's the American way of life." Then the announcer ended the movie with a little homily that made Chuck shudder: "Murder was invented even before man began to think. Now, of course, man has become known as the thinking animal."

The lights were already out at the Riley house when Chuck pulled up a few doors away. "It's me, Rascal," he called out in a loud whisper just to make sure that the family dog, a notoriously bad watchdog in any case, wouldn't set off a racket at an unfamiliar noise. Carrying a flashlight that Marlene had found in the Vega's glove compartment, he snuck around to the overhang along the side of the house and took a battered red two-and-a-half-gallon gas can with a piece of cloth jammed into the spout. Then he drove to the all-night Shell station just off the downtown San Rafael freeway exit and put a gallon of premium (Chuck always bought premium even when he was near-broke) in the gas can, paying for it, as a sign said he must at that hour of the night, with exact change.

On the drive back to Terra Linda, Marlene said, "When we get to my house we're going to wrap the bodies up and load them in the car."

"Where are we taking them?" Chuck asked again.

"A special place," Marlene answered this time. "Out by China Camp."

"Right then and there," Chuck would later tell the police, "I knew it was gonna be involving her witchcraft."

Turning onto Hibiscus, Chuck drove past the Olives' driveway and backed the car up as close as possible to the door that led from the garage directly into the dining L and living room. The move required some precision, since the garage, which had never housed the family car, was crowded with unpacked belongings from Ecuador and old furniture that had recently been replaced.

"Take your clothes off so we don't get bloodstains on them," Marlene, beginning to unbutton hers, instructed Chuck. Chuck obediently stripped naked, leaving his clothes in a pile in the hallway, and opened the door to Naomi Olive's bedroom. He was not more than a half step inside when the smell of dried blood and flesh that was already beginning to rot hit him like a physical blow, an odor made all the stronger by the heat trapped within the small, closed room for ten hours. Slamming the door shut, he gasped for breath to keep himself from vomiting. "Christ, it stinks in there," he said. "We better do something about that." Since Naomi Olive was somewhat prissy about offending odors, there was more than an ample supply of room freshener in the house. Marlene quickly fetched two spray cans of Lysol from the hall closet and handed one to Chuck. They both held their breath and emptied the entire contents of the two cans into the room. When Chuck entered the room through the pine-scented mist the offending smell was still evident, but it was bearable now.

The whole day had seemed like an ambulatory nightmare to Chuck, a "bad trip," and there was a part of his mind that kept telling him that he would wake up momentarily, that when he entered the bedroom it would be empty. But there was no mistaking Jim Olive's outstretched body, half turned on its side with one arm held awkwardly overhead in exactly the position it had settled in after Chuck's search. At least Chuck could be thankful that he had had the foresight to pull the blanket over Naomi Olive's face earlier. He desperately wanted to avoid having to look at that battered skull ever again. And to make absolutely certain he wouldn't be forced to, the first thing Chuck did in the room was to slip a pillowcase over the blanketed head while Marlene lifted the body a few inches off the bed.

Driving to the Olive house, they had agreed to wrap the bodies in sheets and blankets secured with cord, so Marlene had gathered up the extra bedding from the overstocked linen closet in the hallway (Naomi Olive's supply of towels and bedding would have met the needs of a fair-sized hotel) and brought in a spool of laundry line and some twine she found in a kitchen drawer. They tried to lift the body enough to put a blanket underneath it but found the dead weight too much for them. The alternative was to tie the body up in the original bedding, which was now stiff with congealed blood, then to roll it off the bed with a leaden thump onto a blanket spread out on the floor and secure this second layer of wrapping around the first, switching to the roll of twine when the laundry line ran out. Next they repeated the process with Jim Olive, but had more difficulty because his outstretched left arm had already stiffened with rigor mortis and refused to be budged.

Afterward Chuck struggled unsuccessfully to lift Jim Olive to a standing position, the problem being not only his stocky 155-pound frame but the fact that the mummylike figure had no balancing point. Even with Marlene's help he found the body too heavy and unwieldy to carry. Marlene ran off to get a heavy handmade quilt out of the linen closet (it was, in fact, a treasured wedding present from Naomi's foster mother) and they rolled the body onto it and dragged it through the living room and out the door to the garage, where the Vega waited, its hatchback open and its back seat turned down. Gingerly they leaned the body against the car while they protected the carpeting with a canvas tarp that had served happier, leaf-gathering duties in the past. Chuck pushed the body in head-first as far as he could and then went around to the front seat to pull it up farther. Then they went back for Naomi Olive and maneuvered her beside her husband the same way.

Before they drove off, Marlene gathered up some towels that had been used in the cleanup and stuffed them into the washing machine in the garage. The uncovered, bloodstained mattress met her eye. "Let's put it on top of the bodies in case we get stopped by a cop," she said. "We can always say that we're just moving some furniture." In fact, Marlene had already decided to use the spare furniture in the garage to turn Naomi Olive's bedroom into a "family" room—in effect, to make it seem that the bedroom itself, along with its occupant, had never existed.

By now it was nearly midnight. At the stop sign on the far side of the freeway overpass Chuck suddenly caught sight of a patrol car sitting on the gravel road shoulder. The cop was eating a sandwich and did not seem to notice them, but Chuck, who considered the surprise encounter "a bad omen," held his breath until the Vega moved on. He slowed down to the exact speed limit, an interminably crawling 25 mph, and kept the speedometer needle fixed on that figure, not a mile faster or slower, for the rest of the trip.

The road now bordered the artificial lake in back of the Civic Center, where Chuck and his friends often gathered to get high, and curved past the county jail. At the other end of the complex the big red light, the only spot of vivid color in the midnight landscape, seemed to take forever to change, and in his impatience the thought occurred to Chuck that it might be broken. Finally he could turn east on North San Pedro Road, and he continued another three miles past all the developments to the water.

The place they were headed for, China Camp, had a curious local history. It was founded a century ago by Chinese laborers who had been lured to this country by the dollar-a-day wages paid to workers on the Southern Pacific Railroad. When the line had been completed they sent for their families, and since most of them had been fishermen in China, established a thriving settlement at the edge of the bay that resembled, with its ramshackle wooden huts built on stilts over the mudflats, the villages they had left behind. They fished off their junks for tiny bay shrimp and oysters until, shortly after the turn of the century, the water became too polluted to support the catch, and, slowly, the Chinese drifted away to other parts of the Bay Area. By the 1950s the village, which once had a population of 10,000, consisted of a few dozen abandoned shacks, which were burned to the ground during the filming of a scene in a John Wayne movie.

Since that time the whole area, only nominally patrolled by the county sheriff's office, had taken on the aspect of a local badlands in the midst of Marin County's well-groomed affluence. Dirt bikers came to blaze their own trails across the deep-pitted surface of the land. Teen-agers lost their virginity—or refused to—in the wooded hillside a few hundred yards off San Pedro Road. Marksmen tested their skill against beer bottles set on tree stumps. It was even widely rumored that on full-moon nights a satanic cult gathered in the woods—a truly forlorn landscape of gnarled and leafless scrub-oak trees surrounded by sparse underbrush—to perform their most secret rites. Few people claimed to have actually caught them in the act. Only Marlene had hinted broadly that she was a member of the cult, and Chuck, for one, had become convinced that his girl friend was a witch or "something damned close to it" (she certainly had strange powers over him). It was a conviction that would be strengthened when he realized, weeks later, that that very day, June 21, was the summer solstice, traditionally an active night for sorcerers of all persuasions.

Chuck had been going to China Camp with his friends for years to ride motorbikes, practice target shooting or just plain "party." They generally drove through the woods along a dirt fire road to a clearing known as the firepit, actually a concrete cistern, a circular structure three feet high and twenty-one feet across that had once stored rainwater for a now abandoned dairy farm. In recent years the firepit had occasionally been used by hunters to barbecue a hapless deer they had shot (most of the wildlife native to the area had long since been scared away); more often, townspeople used it as a convenient, if illegal, place to burn refuse. Chuck and his friends would set up targets on the ledge of the cistern or on a nearby abandoned wreck and try to outshoot one another. With his steady eye and continuous practice Chuck usually won. In the six months since he bought the used Ruger he had fired it many thousands of times in China Camp.

Now Chuck turned onto the dirt fire road and headed for the woods a few hundred yards away. He could see that the spring rains, aided by the weekend motorcyclists, had left deep ruts in the road, and he made a quick decision to drive through the tall grass that bordered it. But the dew-laden grass made the wheels spin, so he moved back onto the road, thinking that if he proceeded carefully and cut across the ruts at an angle, he could avoid getting stuck. The strategy seemed to work until, just as he was nearing the broad incline that led into the woods, he felt a sharp jolt that he knew instantly "spelled big trouble."

Chuck had done enough four-wheeling in worse terrain not to panic right away. He tried rocking the car by shifting rapidly between low gear and reverse. At first the car would move forward a few inches before the wheels lost traction, but after a while they just spun in place, digging themselves deeper into the rut. He got out to examine the situation. It was even worse than he'd expected. The back wheels were stuck in such a deep rut that the chassis was actually touching the ground, leaving the wheels free-spinning on air. Chuck asked Marlene to sit on the trunk for added weight on the rear wheels, and when that didn't work he told her to drive while he pushed, again to no avail. Even with the sticks and stones Chuck placed under the wheels for traction, they refused to hold. Now Chuck was growing panicky; sweat poured down his face and burned his eyes. Dirt flying out from behind the spinning wheels caked every part of his body that wasn't clothed. During breathers he looked back at North San Pedro Road nervously. So far, two cars had passed them without the drivers noticing anything amiss. At the approach of the first car Chuck turned off the headlights, removed his gun from the glove compartment and stuck it in his belt "just in case."

He asked Marlene to help him unload the car to reduce its weight and also to make the jack under the spare tire accessible. Grunting from the strain, they hid the bodies behind a clump of tall grass. "Scout around here," Chuck said. "Find some branches and rocks." For once he was giving the orders. He jacked the car up and stuck as much of the debris as possible under the rear wheels before setting them down. The wheels still spun wildly, sending out two streams of pulverized debris behind them.

"Motherfucker, *mother*fucker," Chuck cursed. He was beside himself, sure that at any moment a patrol car would drive by and find them stuck in a ditch with two bodies half hidden in the grass not ten yards away. He took out a flashlight and looked under the car. One of the back wheels was not even touching the ground. He found some two-by-fours and used them to jack the car up even higher, then worked the mattress under the right rear wheel, which had dug itself deepest into the ditch. "Floor it," he yelled to Marlene and grunted as he pushed from behind. Maddeningly, the car inched forward, then settled back, the free-spinning back wheel sending tufts of mattress stuffing all over the area. Chuck thought about putting the bodies back inside and "torching" the car right then and there, but decided to make one last attempt to free it.

Since the mattress gave him the height he needed under the wheel but not the traction, he jacked the car up once again and replaced it with the Vega's spare tire. Then he revved up the motor and, in a frustrated rage, threw the clutch into gear. The car shot forward with a violent metal-clanging lurch and Chuck sped over the remaining ruts until he reached the edge of the woods. He ran back to Marlene and the two of them dragged the bodies to the car, leaving the tattered mattress by the roadside. Chuck ran back again to pour some gasoline over the mattress but thought he'd better light it on the way out.

Before driving on, Chuck walked into the forest a few paces checking the ground with a flashlight. The dirt fire road that ran up the wooded hillside seemed passable, but both Marlene and Chuck felt a quiet dread replace the panic of the past hour. The full moon, seeming to balance on the treetops like a Christmas decoration, highlighted wrecked cars, a heap of abandoned tires, a picnic table in a small clearing. Marlene kept an anxious vigil as Chuck drove a couple of hundred yards into the forest, turned a sharp left across a dry creek bed and pulled up near a large log that lay a few feet out from the firepit. Chuck turned the car around to face the road and left the headlights on.

They carried out Naomi Olive's stiff, blanket-swathed body first but had trouble lifting it over the concrete rim of the firepit. Instead they dragged it up against the log and placed Jim Olive's body head to head beside his wife's. Chuck poured gasoline on the prone figures and directed Marlene to help him find some wood. There was no lack of fallen branches around the firepit, and by the time they finished scouting the immediate vicinity—

Marlene walking in front of the headlights, Chuck taking a flashlight in the opposite direction—the stack of wood on top of the bodies reached waist-high. They tossed Naomi's bloodied bedding on the pile and Chuck emptied out the gas can. He remembered an arsonist's trick he had seen in some movie which would give them a few minutes to escape before the fire blazed up. Putting the unlit end of the cigarette he was smoking inside a pack of matches, he closed the cover over it and tossed it on top of the woodpile. "Come on, let's move," he yelled and drove out of the forest at top speed, skimming over the ruts. When he got close to North San Pedro Road he ran back and set the mattress aflame.

Once on the main road, Chuck and Marlene strained to catch a glimpse of the burning woodpile through the forest cover but could see neither flames nor smoke. Just when Chuck, worried that his trick hadn't worked, made a U-turn and doubled back he saw a column of smoke rising above the trees and obscuring the moon. He sighed audibly and continued on to San Rafael. He felt relieved but still scared. If only Marlene would reassure him that everything was going to turn out all right, but she had been in one of her "out of reach" moods for hours. He traveled through downtown San Rafael to an all-night Jack-In-The-Box and gulped down four large orange juices to Marlene's one. "You been fire-fightin'?" the guy behind the counter asked. Chuck smiled weakly. The clock on the wall of the drive-in read 2:35.

Chuck was too keyed up to head back to Terra Linda right away, so instead he announced that he needed to "do some driving" and turned south on Route 101 toward the Golden Gate Bridge fifteen miles away. He wanted to "break loose" on the deserted freeway, putting the car through the kind of 360-degree spins and hairpin turns that always won him the admiration of his peers and a measure of self-confidence. Instead he kept the speedometer needle glued to the speed limit. He took the last possible turnoff before the bridge, continuing out to Fort Cronkhite on the Marin headlands, an abandoned Army base where once big artillery guns guarded San Francisco from enemy attack. Chuck meant to go to a hilltip vantage point that offered a view of both the bay and the ocean to "relax and get high and look over everything," but the early-morning summertime fog was already drifting in and he missed his turn. A military police car followed them warily all the way back to the freeway.

Marlene suggested that Chuck had better get out to China Camp at daylight to make certain the bodies had burned. Chuck also wanted to be up early in order to return home before his parents awakened. It was bad enough that his father probably knew he had stayed out past his curfew. If Oscar Riley realized that he had been out all night, he'd "blow his stack." Inside the house Marlene steered Chuck to the master bedroom and, suddenly amorous, insisted on having sex. It had been a longstanding "fantasy" of hers to make love on her father's bed, but Chuck was clearly not up to the moment. Exhausted from the evening's strain, he lasted only a few perfunctory minutes before dozing off. It was after four.

At six o'clock the alarm on the clock radio sounded. Marlene, who had scarcely slept at all, was already dressed. "You better get out there before the bikers," she said. Chuck reached into his coat pocket to get his plastic purse of cocaine, holding a pinch under each nostril for his usual "wake-up snort." He dressed quickly and drove behind Long's drugstore in Northgate Mall, where he knew there would be stacks of pine flats used to carry shipping crates—wood that would come in handy if the bodies had not burned completely to ashes. He piled several of them into the back of the Vega, then stopped at a nearby Phillips 66 station to put another gallon of gasoline in the red storage can. "I see you're getting an early start on the lawnmowing," the cheerful attendant commented.

China Camp was still deserted when Chuck arrived, and it was easy in the early-morning light to avoid the bigger ruts. The fire was still smoking a little from a few live embers, while the underside of the large log was glowing brightly. Next to the log Naomi Olive's body was almost completely incinerated except for several of the larger bones, part of the rib cage and the skull, which was charred black but complete, recognizable not only by the bone structure but by the large hole on the left side of the forehead. Chuck could not shake off the feeling that the skull was looking directly at him.

Jim Olive was another matter entirely. His legs had disappeared without a trace, but his torso and head, although very badly burned, were still intact. Parts of his clothing were still visible and his left arm was stuck in the air exactly as it had been when Chuck and Marlene had bundled him in the blankets.

Chuck tried to concentrate the fire this time. Using a stick, he pried Jim Olive's torso up against the log on top of his wife's scattered bones. Then he dumped the wood he had brought with him over the remains, scavenged the area farther afield for more branches, poured out the gasoline and lit the whole pile. With a great whoosh the fire blazed up as high as the lower branches of the surrounding trees.

On the way back Chuck stopped at a 7-Eleven store on North San Pedro Road and bought a large bottle of Seven-Up and a box of chocolate doughnuts, which he proceeded to devour as he drove. When he got back to the Olives' house, Marlene's hair was still wet from a shower. She had already moved some of the furniture and knickknacks that had been scattered around the living room back into her mother's bedroom and was down on her knees working out the large stain in the carpet with soap and water.

He told her what he had found at China Camp and what he had done about it. But Marlene had something else on her mind, asking Chuck a question she would pose in various forms several times in the coming days: "Did my daddy see you? Before you shot him, did he see who you were?" Chuck hesitated before replying. Certainly Mr. Olive had seen someone, had called out, "I'm going to kill you, you bastard." But Chuck had lost a lot of weight since Jim Olive last laid eyes on him three months earlier, and his hair had been trimmed from shoulder length to a much shorter cut. He told Marlene he wasn't sure her father had recognized him, although in fact he thought Mr. Olive probably had.

Now it was after seven and Chuck was anxious to get home before his parents awoke. Since Marlene didn't want to stay in the house alone, they drove the Vega to the parking lot of a church near the Rileys' house. Chuck told Marlene to wait a half-hour or so before walking over. When he got home he was relieved to find that his folks were still asleep. He took a long revivifying shower and changed clothes. By the time he walked out to the living room his mother was busy preparing breakfast.

"Morning, sleepyhead," she said. "Are you hungry? Bring the paper in for Riley and I'll fix some pancakes."

Opening the front door to retrieve the Sunday *Independent-Journal*, Chuck saw Marlene walk around the corner and was annoyed that she hadn't waited longer. He took the paper into his parents' bedroom with what his father, who had not forgiven him for their bitter encounter two nights before, recognized as his son's "hangdog look."

"You're up with the cows for a change," Oscar Riley said. "At least you must've stayed out of trouble last night."

Two

In sharp contrast to the early-morning commuter bustle of weekdays, Terra Linda wakes up reluctantly Sunday mornings, much of it with a nasty hangover. On summer weekends drinking habits change from the secret afternoon tippling of bored housewives and "happy hour" libations of commuting husbands to the open pours of backyard barbecues. So not many people were up and about in Terra Linda around the time Chuck and Marlene were sitting down to breakfast with the Rileys.

One quick-stepping exception to the general somnolence was Vince Turrini, a lanky, clean-cut twenty-two-year-old who lived, with his new wife, just two blocks from the Rileys. Unlike most of his peers, Turrini had followed through on his boyhood ambition to be a fireman by actually becoming one. This morning he had arrived at the Santa Venetia station, which is located on North San Pedro Road just three miles from China Camp, promptly at eight o'clock. It was two days after the official beginning of the county's summer "fire season," when the slightest spark, fueled by the combination of strong ocean breezes and parched foliage, could set whole hillsides ablaze within minutes. The Santa Venetia area serviced by Turrini's station was particularly susceptible to summer brush fires, since many of the houses were surrounded by undeveloped grassland. For that reason the small station had just been allotted a new four-wheel-drive "squad," a specially outfitted red-and-white Dodge pickup truck designed for normally inaccessible terrain.

The Sunday before, when Turrini had taken the squad out to the flattrack area of China Camp for a test run, he encountered a dirt biker whose motorcycle had broken down and loaned him some tools. Shortly before ten o'clock exactly a week later the same man walked into the station. "There's something burning out there at the firepit," the man said. "From the looks of it some fool roasted a deer *outside* the rim."

The news came as no surprise to Turrini. Somebody was always doing something stupid out at the firepit. In only a year on the force he had already put out several small grass fires in the vicinity, not to mention a 1962 Oldsmobile, which a couple of teen-agers had stolen, run aground and ignited.

Turrini and a summer helper, eighteen-year-old Craig Carroll, scrambled into their pickup truck and sped out toward China Camp with sirens roaring. When they arrived at the firepit they could see a thick funnel of smoke but no flames. The fire had already burned down to embers. "Squad Sixty-four to Woodacre," Turrini radioed back to headquarters. "Ten-ninety-seven, smoldering fire, code four, fifteen minutes for mop-up"—which meant that he had arrived at the scene of a smoldering fire and could put it out in short order without additional help.

Turrini and Carroll pulled the high-pressure hose from its reel and wet down the coals, raked the ashes around and wet them down again. Since they couldn't turn over the still-smoldering log by hand, they wrapped a chain around it and towed it a few feet away from the rim of the cistern so that Turrini could reach the underside with a hose. To make sure no sparks remained to spread the fire up the hillside with the aid of a sudden wind, the two young men shoveled the ashes into the debris-filled cistern. It was then that Turrini first noticed several small bone fragments, the largest of which he would later describe to police as "triangle-shaped, maybe two-and-a-half inches long and curved, like a piece of a volleyball." He also noticed black streaks on the ground underneath the ashes, which he knew meant that gasoline had been used to start the fire.

In the report that Turrini filled out upon his return to the station he listed the smoldering object at the firepit as a "carcass (probably deer)," more because of the motorcyclist's remark than from any evidence he had viewed first-hand. And yet, in retrospect, the odd thing about the whole incident was that all week long, while this explanation for the small fire went otherwise unquestioned, Turrini's colleagues in the Marin County fire department teased the rookie fireman about the report, suggesting that it probably wasn't a deer that had been burned at the firepit, after all. It was probably a human being.

Another early-rising Terra Linda resident that Sunday morning was Colonel Philip Royce. Royce had already jogged his daily two-and-a-half-mile course wearing, as was his custom, a pair of well-worn combat boots. By eight o'clock the lean and stiff-spined West Point graduate (class of '39) was seated in his pew at the Church of the Nativity, a relentless modern wood-and-stone structure that not merely pointed the way heavenward for its parishioners but looked as if it might momentarily take off from its hilltop perch and transport them there.

The eight o'clock mass at the Episcopal church was a "said service," more traditional and, lacking any choral accompaniment, shorter than the better-attended ten o'clock mass. According to Rev. David Barnette, the parishioners who attended the earlier service were a "special breed," men who had neither the time nor the inclination for the more relaxed ten o'clock version and the convivial socializing, accompanied by coffee and doughnuts, that followed it. In short, they were busy men for whom Sunday, far from being the traditional day of rest, was simply another workday that happened to begin with church. Phil Royce, who enjoyed being addressed as "Colonel" even though he had retired from active service fourteen years earlier, generally met Jim Olive at the early service.

Throughout the short mass and Rev. Barnette's sermon on "the human condition," Royce kept glancing back at the entrance to see if his friend had walked in. He was still anxious to find out how Jim Olive's move into their new offices had gone the day before and to discuss some business matters that had come up during an important all-day meeting the two had attended in Sacramento on Friday. After the service Royce shook hands with the modish-looking prelate, who wore his graying hair shoulder-length and sported several large turquoise rings on his fingers. "I wonder what happened to Jim," Royce said. "It's not like him to oversleep."

It was, in fact, Rev. Barnette who had introduced the two men the previous summer following such an early-morning service. At the time Royce, who had completed an M.B.A. degree after an earlier business venture went bankrupt, was talking to another parishioner outside the church, explaining his plan to start a small-business counseling service in San Rafael. Jim Olive listened for a few minutes and then said, "I have just the ticket for you. We should talk." He went on to explain that he had purchased the central Marin County franchise of a national small-business consulting firm, General Business Services. He wanted to expand his operation by purchasing the Northern California regional directorship but needed someone to "put out the home fires" in his local area. Would Royce be interested in forming some sort of partnership? The two men met several more times, and by October, Phil Royce had quit his insurance job in San Francisco and bought into Jim Olive's franchise. They had worked out of their homes until a few weeks before, when they rented an office in nearby San Rafael.

In the meantime the partnership had flourished. Jim Olive was an excellent salesman and brought in a steady stream of new clients, while Royce had developed the technical business training that his partner, who had spent most of his life in one marketing venture or another, admittedly lacked. More important, the two men, less than a year apart in age, became fast friends, finding that in terms of both personality and life experience they had a great deal in common. Like Royce, Jim Olive had been attracted to the military life and maintained his commission in the active reserves until 1971, when he retired with the rank of lieutenant colonel. And both exhibited the same square-shooting rectitude and unflappable politeness that might be considered virtues especially prized in the military. The two men also faced the world with a certain easygoing affability that masked deep-seated tensions and flash tempers held, at no small cost to their blood pressure, firmly in check. Moreover, both had experienced major career disruptions relatively late in their lives, Royce when he left the military and Jim Olive, more recently, when he was forced out of his job as an oil-company executive in Ecuador, where he had spent thirteen years, and returned to the United States to start his own business. They were, in short, both survivors, men who had become, by dint of much unwanted practice, good at starting over again.

There were even some small but uncanny coincidences in their backgrounds. Phil Royce had spent his first three years in the military as an infantryman based in Panama and had taken a keen interest ever since in Central American affairs. Jim Olive had grown up in Panama as the son of a pioneering American newspaper publisher and had spent some of those same years stationed only a few miles, albeit on opposite oceans, from his future friend.

Perhaps the oddest coincidence of all was that their Central American experiences had led both men to identify closely with a bizarre and little-known figure in American history. In the 1850s an adventurer named William Walker—by all reports a short, quiet and unimposing man, a lawyer and sometime journalist—had outfitted a ragtag brigade of freebooters in San Francisco, set sail for Central America, and after some bloody skirmishes with the local authorities, established himself as president of the independent republic of Nicaragua. Before he was executed by the Honduran government three years later for leading an expeditionary force into its territory, Walker left behind a romantic legacy that would become, in an age less squeamish about American adventurism, the stuff of a dozen pulp novels— the legend of a Walter Mitty who actually lived out his most swashbuckling dreams.

Of course, the choice of a hero is never accidental or even so fortuitous a matter as geographical proximity. Jim Olive and Phil Royce, two level-headed, family-oriented, Rotarian-joining businessmen, shared a thwarted romantic side. "I could have made general if I'd stuck it out," Phil Royce would often say somewhat wistfully, in the next breath disparaging "McNamara and the other accountants" who ran the "lovers' war" in Vietnam. And Jim Olive wrote to a friend in Ecuador two weeks before he died: "Here I am doing bookkeeping and tax accounts. Not that I'm unhappy. This is a great place. But it's not exactly the world of high finance." So that the final resemblance between the two men was that they had failed to live up to the large ambitions they had set for themselves and were a little surprised and disappointed at where they had ended up. In some sense both men, one literally and the other metaphorically, jogged along well-tended suburban streets in combat boots.

Perhaps even more curious than the fact that Phil Royce and Jim Olive had the same little-known nineteenth-century filibuster for a hero was that they never discussed the matter. It was only after Jim Olive died and Phil Royce became the executor of his estate that the matter came to light. One day several weeks later, as Royce was going through his friend's personal papers in the Olives' drafty, padlocked house, he discovered a whole shelf of books about William Walker, most of which he himself had read. And, nearby, a metal file cabinet held hundreds of neatly typed 5 x 8 file cards crammed with information on Walker's life. For Jim Olive, whose secret and largely unfulfilled lifetime ambition was to become a published author, had spent two decades collecting this information with the intention of one day sitting down to write the kind of full-scale, judicious biography of Walker that had never been attempted.

In the coming weeks and months Phil Royce learned a great deal more about Jim Olive's life, through personal records and correspondence as well as visits with friends and relatives, much of which seemed to trace, in the light of what had occurred, the footsteps of disaster. He realized how hard his friend had tried to hold the disintegrating pieces of his private life together "with a smile on his face and all ten fingers in the dike." And for the first time he wondered whether the deep emotional reserve that made it so difficult for even such good friends to discuss their personal problems might not have contributed to the final tragedy.

As Phil Royce found out from old letters and journals in the file cabinet, Jim Olive's Scotch-Irish ancestors had settled near the small town of Cuba in western New York State around the middle of the nineteenth century. Cuba was a quiet agricultural community surrounded by gently rolling farmland, a center for the production of fine aged Cheddar cheese. By the time he died, Jim Olive's grandfather, who had started out as a day laborer, owned one of the largest dairy farms in the area, and the Olive family was among the small town's social elite.

Jim's father, Chester, was saved from leading a life of small-town respectability by an adventurous boyhood friend who, in 1925, was about to start an English-language newspaper in Panama and needed a level-headed business manager. Chet Olive and his wife, Elsie, took their children—Jim and Eunice, aged nine and thirteen—out of public school and boarded a Grace liner for Panama. But when they arrived there was precious little business at the fledgling paper to manage. For several years Chet Olive had to sell off such personal belongings as his wife's engagement ring to meet printing costs, then delivered stacks of papers in his Model T to outlying towns up and down the Panamanian coast. Meanwhile Elsie went door to door collecting accounts from the leisured ladies of the Canal Zone, and young Jim sold papers on the streets of Panama City. It was the first of many sales jobs for him. In what was perhaps the key document of his life, the detailed job résumé (headed "James F. Olive,

Marketeer'' and accompanied by a different but always out-of-date photograph) that he kept adding to and sending out far and wide each time he met with a career reversal, Jim Olive was to write: ''My experence in foreign sales began at the age of nine, hawking the new tabloid in company with a screeching horde of unwashed urchins. They taught me colloquial Spanish, the elements of street fighting, and the value of persistence in salesmanship.''

Within a few years the *Panama American* became bilingual (adding a Spanish section to its back pages) and began to prosper, along with the Olive family. Jim Olive grew up a ''thoroughly Latinized American,'' as he liked to put it in later years, a bright, personable youth with carrot-colored hair that would turn auburn with age, and a facility for dreaming up hopelessly impractical get-rich-quick schemes. If his short stature was a social disadvantage, he made up for it by being an excellent dancer and an engaging storyteller. But like his less convivial father he was nevertheless a very private person, reluctant to express his inner feelings. If the conversation turned too personal, one would likely find him staring off into space, lost in thoughts of his future fame and fortune.

At Pennsylvania State College he enrolled in a science program, switching to business administration two years later, after he and a friend were responsible for an accidental explosion in the chemistry lab. In his freshman year he joined the Triangle Club, an engineering fraternity, although from the beginning he seemed to stand apart from the rest of his sober-minded fraternity brothers in those Depression years. George Koth, a childhood friend and neighbor, was a senior engineering student when Jim Olive entered college. ''Jim always looked and acted younger than his age,'' Koth recalls. ''He had a terrific imagination and would always be dreaming up great exploits for himself—barnstorming the country in a biplane or striking it rich in the Andes—things the rest of us might have dreamed about but never said aloud.''

After graduating from college in 1937, Jim worked briefly for a literary agency in New York. (''Here I learned,'' the future salesman wrote in his résumé, ''the value of personal contacts.'') Shortly thereafter he returned to Panama and tried his hand at developing a tract of land his father had recently received in the sale of the *Panama American*. The land, which Jim named Seacliff Acres, was lovely beachfront property, but unfortunately it was on a remote stretch of the Panamanian coast near Costa Rica. No lots were ever sold.

In 1941 Jim Olive was called to active military duty, and because he was bilingual, assigned to Army intelligence work as a mail censor, first in Panama and then in the Burma theater. While others lived the adventures he dreamed of, Jim searched their correspondence home for breaches of security, rising to the rank of major for his diligence. It was during this period that he received a letter from his mother that included a picture of herself together with a beautiful young lady named Naomi Wagner, the foster child of Anna DeKay, one of Mrs. Olive's best friends from Cuba, New York. It is more than possible that the photo represented some subtle matchmaking on Elsie Olive's part, for Jim had not long before asked his mother to buy a diamond engagement ring for him so that he could offer it in absentia to an English-woman living in Panama—a proposed union that Mrs. Olive did not wholeheartedly bless. In any case, the young woman standing beside her in the photograph did not go unnoticed by her son, who wrote his sister that he had just seen "a picture of the DeKay girl, who is a honey."

She was indeed. At nineteen, Naomi Wagner had an almost doll-like beauty, with a trim figure, long chestnut hair that fell in ringlets, sparkling green eyes and a wide, dimpled smile. On home leave in the summer of 1944, Major James F. Olive, duly smitten, met, wooed and won Naomi Wagner, all in the space of a month. There is a wedding picture that shows the two of them standing arm in arm against a bank of gladiolas in Mrs. DeKay's living room, Jim in his dress uniform and Naomi in a long velvet gown with an enormous orchid pinned to it, marginally taller than her husband and, a week short of her twentieth birthday, nearly ten years younger. Both bride and bridegroom are beaming broadly.

For Naomi, marrying into the locally prominent Olive family must have promised the security and respectability that had escaped her during an emotionally disruptive childhood. Her father, Robert Wagner, was a handsome, amiable man who worked as a hired hand on several farms around Cuba and also in a gristmill owned by Anna DeKay's husband. Very little is known about her mother beyond the barest facts of her short life. She came from a local farm family and is remembered as being exceptionally beautiful. At the age of twenty-six, when Naomi was two, she seems to have fallen ill, possibly of tuberculosis, and entered Willard State Hospital on Lake Seneca, where she was confined until her death six years later. It was widely believed at the time that Teresa Wagner was mentally ill and that the official diagnosis was either the cover story used to explain their mother's sudden disappearance to Naomi and her younger brother, David, or that she had indeed suffered from both physical and mental ailments. Whatever the truth, the cruel legacy of this experience for Naomi Olive was that she lived all of her adult life fearful that she might have inherited her mother's mental illness.

Naomi was only allowed to visit her mother twice during her years of confinement, and her brother just once—facts that tend to confirm the suspicion of mental illness. While their mother was still alive the children were moved between both sets of grandparents. A year after Robert Wagner remarried a much younger woman, Naomi was "adopted out" to the well-to-do DeKays while her brother remained at home. The decision—while not uncommon in hard-pressed rural areas during those Depression years—must have left its scars, for the young girl saw very little of her father and brother after she left home. Neither was invited to her wedding.

The DeKays appear to have provided a loving home for Naomi, guiding her through high school (where her grades were excellent), taking her with them on annual winter vacations to Florida and encouraging her, after graduation, to enroll in a secretarial course at a nearby junior college. By the time she married Jim Olive, Naomi Wagner's traumatic years seemed far behind her, and from all outward appearances she was a bright, popular, very pretty young woman whose general contentment with life was marred only by occasional depressive moods and girlish temper tantrums it was assumed she would outgrow.

A month after the wedding Jim was unexpectedly assigned to intelligence work in the Philippines for the duration of the war. Soon after his discharge he and Naomi moved down to Panama, where the real estate market was now booming and some of the family-owned land could be sold at a tidy profit. "This taught me the importance of timing in sales," he would note in his résumé.

Panama disagreed with Naomi Olive from the start: the relentless tropical heat and six-month-long rainy season, the fly-infested native market where she was expected to shop for strange foods, the dirt and squalor she encountered once she stepped out of the

Balboa district, where they lived, and most of all the unfamiliar language. What was worse, her husband was a jovial fellow who seemed to know everyone in the republic, Panamanians and Americans alike, so that the Olives were quickly swept into a frenetic social whirl and expected to respond in kind. Naomi began to dread these gatherings, where the talk always got around to local politics, about which she knew little and cared not at all.

Jim Olive soon got the first in a long string of jobs in the oil industry—Central American advertising manager for Standard Oil of New Jersey. The work frequently took him away from home to carry Esso's latest promotional material to outlying service stations, a situation that did not further endear Naomi to her new lifestyle. When Jim was appointed Esso's division manager in El Salvador four years later, Naomi was elated. The promotion meant a step up in their standard of living, which would now include a handsome company-owned house in the capital city of San Salvador replete with domestic help, including a gardener, a cook and a maid. More important, Naomi was far away from Jim's forbidding mother and all those other relatives and friends in Panama who were, she felt, always "judging" her every move.

But the job also meant more obligatory business entertaining of a kind that terrified Naomi. The result was that she retreated further behind the whitewashed walls of her house, throwing herself into a frenzy of domestic activity, which sometimes took odd turns. It was during this time that she first developed a compulsion to buy bathroom towels, a collection that eventually grew into the hundreds, with matched sets of every conceivable color and size. Convinced that the maids were stealing from her, she would also make elaborate lists of all dirty linen before giving it to them to launder, checking off the articles one by one when they were returned.

A month-long trip by car through the American West in the summer of 1951 seems to have been a happy time for the Olives, as do several shorter trips that Jim and Naomi took to neighboring Nicaragua so that he could pursue his research into the life and times of William Walker. But once back in El Salvador, Naomi would step up her agitation to return to the States permanently, and the following year Jim agreed. His mother had recently died, leaving him with a substantial inheritance. With it he bought a small eight-unit apartment building in St. Petersburg,

Florida, which Naomi helped him manage, and threw himself
into a round of chamber of commerce activities and get-rich-
schemes of his own. The most peculiar of these ventures—all
notoriously unsuccessful—involved exporting to South America
some of the pedigreed Brahma bulls raised for breeding purposes
in central Florida.

Jim had little luck with his writing career as well, which he
now had the spare time to pursue in earnest. Having amassed
mounds of information on Walker, he was determined to turn it
into a historical novel on the grand scale. First he tried to
structure his tale around a series of dispatches on the campaign
sent by a fictional correspondent to his newspaper, the New
Orleans *Weekly Chronicle*. But after several episodes the device
became patently artificial, so he switched to a loosely related
series of sketches about Walker and his men which he hoped to
place in adventure magazines. Although the whole rather seedy
Walker affair was absurdly romanticized in the sketches (Walker
himself was at one point described as that "steel-eyed leader of
mystic power, the Gray-Eyed man of Toltec legend") and the
dialogue could take on a certain archness at times (one of the
soldiers refers to a brass cannon as "a right smart little persuader"),
several of the New York agents to whom Jim Olive offered his
literary efforts praised his fluid writing style ("especially as you
are a relative newcomer to the field," one of them added somewhat deflatingly). However, all but one, Scott Meredith, found a
variety of excuses for their inability to represent him.

At the time Scott Meredith, who would go on to become one
of the most high-powered literary agents in New York, offered a
service to neophyte writers whereby he would "analyze and
critique" manuscripts sent to him at a charge of $5 for those
under 9,000 words and $10 for those over that length. Through-
out the summer of 1955 Jim Olive sent the agent sketch after
sketch, and a lengthy correspondence ensued. Meredith also
praised Jim's "fine lucidity of style" and wrote that he had "the
basic equipment to achieve success in the field." But the major
problem with the sketches was so often the same that Meredith
would explain his reason for returning one of them, "Gold Coast
Adventure," by saying, "You've guessed it: plotting flaws."
Jim was so weighed down with his knowledge of the Walker
campaign that in his fictional portrayal of it, the agent explained
gently, "the background has sometimes eclipsed the foreground."

But instead of improving his writing technique Jim Olive, true to his training, would come up with new strategies for marketing his work. At one point he wrote Meredith: "I am a civilian again now, having completed my annual two-week stint, so you no longer have to refer to me as 'Colonel.' However, the title might prove attractive to a publisher, considering the subject matter of my story, and I have included it in my by-line." And toward the end of the correspondence, after Jim read a book review of another historical novel about William Walker, he thought perhaps the time was ripe to give his agent a harder sell. It was, after all, the centenary of Walker's Nicaraguan campaign, and Jim was sure a new book on the subject "could mean plenty to the Nicaraguan Tourist Commission . . . if a well-directed campaign of publicity were put on, built around the 6,000 ghosts of Walker's army of adventurers." The letter concluded with an all-stops-out sales pitch to the agent that perfectly captures Jim Olive's go-getting style:

> I hate to miss a good bet. When a parade comes along it seems that everyone jumps on the bandwagon. I don't mind standing on the curb, but I don't want to miss the spectacle completely. . . .
> This thing has dynamite in it. If it's sales ideas you need, I got 'em. If it's maps or authentification you need, I got 'em. I've got a library of books written by Walker and his men. I've got microfilms of Nicaraguan newspapers of the period. I've got topographic maps, personality files, unit histories. Nobody's got what I've got. I've even been to Nicaragua!
> Let's get on this thing, Mr. Meredith. There's a big parade a'coming.

The correspondence breaks off abruptly late in 1955 (to resume briefly ten years later), when the Olives were preparing to move to Norfolk, Virginia, where Jim had purchased a franchise to sell Phillips Petroleum products. None of his Florida ventures had brought him much of an income, and Naomi, whose early upbringing gave her a perpetual wolf-at-the-door outlook on life, was growing increasingly insecure about it. She had also begun drinking more than was good for her, perhaps partly as a response to a medical test that weighed heavily on her. After years of trying, Naomi was told that she would probably never be able to have a child.

Jim had chosen Norfolk for his dealership because it was, as he wrote in his résumé, "a fast-growing community of high potential." What he did not say was that Norfolk would soon be serviced by fifteen major oil companies, most of which distributed their products directly to service stations rather than through jobbers. In such a glutted market Jim worked harder than he ever had in his life just to keep his head above water. He had become a disciplined, determined man, a compulsive list-maker and time-scheduler who worked twelve-hour days, weekends included, and had few, if any, outside interests except for an occasional round of golf. With what Russell Sommer, a socially prominent Norfolk lawyer who befriended the Olives, called his "fireball personality," he had many acquaintances but few close friends and no one in whom he confided. "He held himself aloof from his emotions," Sommer recalls.

Lacking Jim's extroverted ways and professional interests, Naomi was even more isolated socially. She resisted the efforts of some acquaintances to draw her into the gilded social life of Norfolk's leading country club, the Princess Anne. She was also becoming less attractive physically, thick-waisted and prematurely gray. The drinking, which had begun as a social necessity in San Salvador and had become a private need in St. Petersburg, grew worse in Norfolk. The couple began to bicker constantly, often about Jim's futile attempt to keep watch over the liquor in the house or refusal to replenish it. More than once Naomi locked Jim out of the house overnight.

Until then it seemed a conventional marriage with all of the conventional fifties problems of people who had cut themselves off from their roots and grown apart. And the Olives chose the conventional solution. After fifteen years of marriage they decided to raise a child—in their case, necessarily, an adopted one. "It wasn't really Jim's idea," recalls Ann Ellis, a family friend in those years. "Naomi wanted a child desperately. She needed something of her own." At the time the Virginia adoption laws were much more informal than they are today. Jim Olive simply mentioned his and Naomi's desire to adopt a new-born infant to John Courtenay, Russell Sommer's law partner and a friend as well. Courtenay spoke to Dr. Harley Ferris, a country-club sailing mate who was also the Olives' family physician. As it happened, Dr. Ferris had another patient, a prominent Norfolk society woman whose teen-age daughter had become pregnant in those pre-pill days after a brief affair with a Scandinavian sailor on shore leave. Arrangements were made through the county welfare department for the Olives to take the baby home from the hospital the day after Dr. Ferris had delivered her on January 15, 1959. The natural mother never even saw her infant daughter. Formal consent papers were signed by both parties ten days later (Marlene's natural mother signing her name in a florid, mature script that belied her nineteen years) and, as agreed, Jim Olive wrote out a check to cover the hospital costs. Standard procedure would have dictated that the hospital identification bracelet for an adopted child read simply "N.I."—No Information. It is not known how it came about that Jim and Naomi carried home with them an unstrung baby bracelet containing the scrambled letters of the natural mother's name along with their healthy eight-pound baby girl.

The Olives made no attempt to conceal the fact that Marlene was adopted, although they told friends and neighbors in Norfolk that her natural parents had both been killed in an automobile accident shortly after her birth—a fabrication eerily similar to one that Marlene would put forward to the San Rafael police sixteen years later when they were investigating the Olives' sudden disappearance.

After the required three home visits by a county welfare inspector, a final order "in the matter of an unnamed girl child" was filed in the Norfolk circuit court in the spring, together with an amended birth certificate naming the baby Marlene Louise Olive.

From the first wrist-tested bottle feeding, Jim was a doting father. But friends noticed immediately that Naomi had extended her compulsive housekeeping to include her daughter, as if an excessive concern for Marlene's welfare could substitute for genuine intimacy. Indeed, for the first six months of Marlene's life Naomi never came near her daughter without wearing a gauze mask, and she insisted that everyone else, Jim included, do so as well. She also repeatedly sterilized every object that might come within Marlene's grasp. "She was very clinical in her approach to motherhood," according to Russell Sommer, a frequent houseguest at the time. "I don't remember her being overly loving in a spontaneous way. It was not a question of lying in bed and bouncing Marlene around on her tummy." After fifteen years of unemployment, Naomi had finally found a full-time job. "She would never go out," Ann Ellis recalls, "not even to the movies or a dinner party. 'Nomi,' I'd tell her, 'you'll smother the child to death.' ''

Certainly there must have been more relaxed family moments, at least for the camera. Jim Olive took some home movies of the first year and a half of Marlene's life, domestic scenes that are remarkable only if one knows what lay ahead. There are glimpses of a gurgling Marlene seated in her highchair being spoon-fed by Naomi and playfully tossing around a black-and-white stuffed panda. There are shots of Marlene in a playpen pretending to hide from her parents by putting her hands over her eyes. There is footage of a Christmas dinner and of Marlene opening up presents under a lit tree. There is a scene of Marlene blowing out a single candle on her first birthday cake, and another of her wearing a crinoline and a white baby bonnet at her christening. Later, there are backyard scenes of Marlene taking her first tottering steps, looking like a diminutive astronaut in her hooded baby jumpsuit.

The real dislocation in the Olives' family life came not with the adoption of Marlene but the following summer, when the gas and oil distribution company Jim Olive had formed went bankrupt. Jim lost all of his life savings, but he hardly seems to have flinched from the blow. Naomi was another matter, however. Everyone who knew her in Norfolk agrees that whatever problems Naomi had exhibited up until then, she became completely unhinged by Jim's financial setback. During conversations she began to ramble on endlessly about the most trivial matters. In a nervous tic that stayed with her thereafter, her eyebrows would jump up and down as she talked, like two runners constantly assuming their mark. At times her behavior became more bizarre. Ann Ellis remembers one occasion, shortly after Jim's business failed, when his sister was visiting Norfolk and she and the Olives came over to her house for dinner, bringing Marlene with them. "My daughter was there too, so I told Naomi, 'Don't worry. Evie can baby-sit for Marlene.' But she was overprotective in the extreme and never would leave the child, even to come to the dinner table in the next room. Naomi stayed in the bedroom while the rest of us sat down to eat. When it became clear that Naomi could not be coaxed out of the bedroom, I fixed a plate of food and Jim took it in to her. Well, the next thing I knew the bedroom door opened and Naomi hurled the plate of food at Jim and stomped around yelling, 'You threw away a hundred and fifty thousand dollars. How could you do that? You've thrown it all away.' Jim and my husband had to pack her home and I spent the rest of the evening scraping food off the walls. The next time I met Naomi she was perfectly sweet and never once mentioned the incident.''

Not long after his business folded, Jim received an attractive offer from the Tennessee Gas Transmission Company (Tenneco) to become its marketing manager in Ecuador. He left in advance of his family to make the necessary living arrangements and liked what he found. Located on the Pacific, between Colombia and Peru, Ecuador is a small country that manages to contain mountains, jungle and a fertile coastal strip in close proximity. Its culture, like its population, is the forced issue of the once mighty Incas and their Spanish conquerors. Politically, the country has long exhibited an almost orderly procession of elected civilian governments overturned by military coups (so orderly, in fact, that the last group of colonels who plotted to overthrow the elected leader, President José María Velasco Ibarra, waited a few days before carrying out their plan so that his daughter could be married in the presidential palace). Economically, Ecuador was then in a long slump caused by the blight-induced failure of its cocoa crop (hitherto the country's leading export), a recession from which it did not fully recover until the discovery of large oil reserves in the mid-sixties. It is not untypical of the general state of the Ecuadorian economy that the country's most famous export has become universally, albeit mistakenly, known as the Panama hat.

Quito, the beautiful neocolonial capital city of Ecuador, lies in the grassy sleeve formed by two volcanic mountain ranges in the Andean highlands. Guayaquil, the country's busy commercial center, is located on the coast. The two rival cities, each with its own climate, dialect and traditions, are so totally different that Ecuadorians say they might as well be distinct countries. It was a pity that Naomi Olive had to follow her husband to the second of those two countries.

Guayaquil's steamy climate alone could unhinge a much lesser paranoid than Naomi Olive. In the rainy season the mosquitoes that once made Guayaquil the yellow-fever capital of the world still swarm into the city from the surrounding swamps, particularly in the early evening when the wind dies down and the lights go on. And during one two-week period in the rainy season the mosquitoes are accompanied by fat crickets called *grillos*, clouds

of clattering insects so thick that a pedestrian must literally wade
through them and then pick them off his clothing when he
reaches shelter, which is generally as soon as humanly possible.
The most characteristic sound in Guayaquil during the rainy
season is the soft pop that *grillos* make when they are run over
by automobile tires.

Except for the orange-flowering acacia trees and the *malecón*—
the broad promenade that runs beside the swift-flowing, chocolate-
colored Guayas River—Guayaquil is not an especially lovely
city. But it does have the pulsing energy of a major port, for
nearly everything that enters or leaves Ecuador does so through
Guayaquil. The city was once a pirate's haven and today it is
ruled by their successors, robust, rough-edged men who have
made their fortunes in bananas or coffee or shipping. Particularly
at night and along the fetid waterfront streets, the city exudes an
almost palpable sense of foreboding, an overripeness verging on
corruption. Like most foreigners and wealthy natives, Jim Olive
protected his family as best he could by renting a house surrounded by a high concrete wall in the plush Barrio del Centenario,
a long way from the waterfront.

Jim Olive felt at home in Guayaquil from the moment he
arrived. With his fluency in Spanish and familiarity with Latin
American ways, he was well liked by Ecuadorians of all classes.
He would introduce himself as Jaimie O-li-ve, dividing his last
name the way it would be pronounced in Spanish, and many of
his Ecuadorian acquaintances did not even realize that he was a
norteamericano. In sharp contrast to most of the city's foreign
colony, much of Jim Olive's social life was spent in the living
rooms of Ecuadorian friends, where he loved nothing better than
joining a group singing traditional Ecuadorian folk songs or dancing the spirited, handkerchief-waving *cachullapi* or the more
stately *pasillo*.

As Tenneco's sales and distribution manager in Ecuador, Jim
assembled a staff of young and ambitious "nationals" whose
loyalty to him he returned by paying them well and advancing
their interests with the home company. (Thanks to the start he
gave them, several rose to high positions in the Ecuadorian
business community.) He worked harder than any of them,
arriving in his office at precisely eight o'clock, returning home at
noon for the traditional two-hour siesta, and going back to work
until six-thirty, when he would meet friends for a drink at one of
the city's social clubs. He also traveled widely throughout the

country setting up distribution centers and service stations and sometimes just garnering favorable publicity for his company. A frequent item in the local paper, *El Universo,* would be a photograph of Jaime Olive seated in a native canoe and wearing a Panama hat and a huge grin, heading downriver to present some tribal chieftain in the interior with a Tenneco shield and his first barrel of oil (never mind that the sign would be a rusted hulk six months later or that there was no machinery to lubricate).

If Ecuador provided Jim Olive with a full and varied life on an economic scale that he could never have afforded at home, his wife's existence gradually became a nightmare. At first Naomi took Spanish lessons, ventured warily into the local markets as well as to Guayaquil's version of a supermarket, and spent afternoons around the country-club pool or at the nearby beach resort of Playas or attending the weekly meetings of the Damas Británicas y Norteamericanas. There is a blown-up photograph from the time showing the Olives and another couple playfully posing for the camera at the annual Halloween ball put on by the American consulate in Guayaquil. All four are wearing war paint and mock fierce looks on their faces, fringed buckskin outfits and long braided wigs held in place by beaded headbands—although the intended effect is somewhat marred by the white vinyl handbag Naomi is holding on her arm. But her old insecurities and paranoid fears soon got the better of her and she began to go out less and less. The maids took care of the shopping, and Jim went to parties alone, always careful to parry any questions about Naomi's absence by saying she was "feeling under the weather" or simply wasn't "up to par." After a while people stopped asking.

The less contact Naomi had with the outside world, the more fearful she became of its encroachments. Merchants were forever short-changing her. The American wives at the country club were always conducting "whispering campaigns" against her, and some were more actively trying to steal away her husband. But she could not be safe even inside her own home. She suspected that the maids were stealing the silverware and that the drinking water, despite her insistence that it be boiled twice, remained contaminated. She spent more and more time alone in an upstairs sewing room, where she made her own clothes while sipping the Scotch she had hidden in the sewing-machine cabinet. And when she drank she would release her bottled-up rage in temper tantrums, during which she hurled glasses or ashtrays

against the wall and ranted on about Jim's infidelity or the
hostility of other American wives or the amount of time he spent
away from home on "so-called business trips." On the rare
occasions when she invited friends over, she was sometimes
unable or unwilling to receive them by the time they arrived.

By then Marlene was a button-cute, energetic five-year-old
with pale skin, close-cropped blond hair combed into bangs, and
two missing front teeth. In one of those accidents of propinquity
that sometimes befall adopted children, she looked remarkably
like Naomi as a young girl. It was, of course, much less remarkable that she seemed to resemble her mother emotionally. For
Marlene was also a painfully shy and quiet child, subject to
frequent bouts of moodiness. She learned to curtsy prettily for
adults, but as soon as it was permissible she would seek refuge
behind her mother's skirts. Naomi, for her part, remained an
overprotective and fearful mother, reluctant to let Marlene go
outside alone or, at times, outside at all. "Naomi kept Marlene
under her wing," recalls Marissa Moss, a family friend at the
time, "and when she withdrew, the little girl did, too. She
seemed to use the child as a crutch, a companion to talk to when
she lost contact with others, almost like a pet. You never saw
Marlene out screaming and running about with friends like kids
should. There was great love and concern from Naomi, but it
was often misguided."

Jim's relationship with his young daughter was much less
complicated. He doted on her, talked about her constantly to
friends and, like many men who become fathers at a relatively
late age, spoiled her terribly. He never came back from a business trip to the States without the latest Barbie doll or children's
game, until Marlene's room came to resemble, by Ecuadorian
standards at least, a fair-sized toy store. Neither did it help the
young girl's sense of responsibility that there was always a
dark-skinned Emelda or Andalina or María (Naomi had trouble
keeping maids) to pick up after her.

In the summer of 1964 the Olives stopped off to see Jim's
sister and her children in Panama on their way north. Eunice
Richard was alarmed at Naomi's drinking and "erratic" behavior and managed to persuade her sister-in-law—whose fear of all
forms of psychological therapy, and especially of mental hospitals,
dated back to her mother's illness and could not have been
assuaged by her suspicions of her own—to make an appointment
at an outpatient psychiatric clinic at Corozal Hospital in the

Canal Zone. On her first visit Naomi was interviewed by a psychiatric social worker. Under the heading "Factors leading to Admission" on the standard medical history form, the social worker wrote:

> Patient is isolated in Ecuador where she feels she cannot stay because of the difference of culture and the lack of family life and freedom that American women have in the country. She has been depressed for the past two years and then she started to drink heavily. She gave up drinking a month ago and then she became more depressed. She would not sleep or eat properly. She cries and was hopeless and frightened that something would happen to her or her husband.

During their two-week stay in Panama, Naomi and Jim together attended four group-therapy sessions under the guidance of Dr. Milton White, a staff psychologist. In a "progress report" after his last consultation with the Olives, Dr. White stated that he prescribed an antidepressant and tranquilizers for Naomi and recommended strongly that she continue therapy after she returned to Ecuador. His "final diagnosis" of his patient was: "Schizoid personality with paranoid features."

Naomi would never again be induced to seek psychological help. "You'd just love to see me locked up, wouldn't you?" she told Eunice before returning home. "That way you could have your little brother all to yourself." Indeed, the group-therapy sessions she had attended marked the beginning of an implacable grudge that Naomi held against her sister-in-law for the rest of her life. And thereafter, whenever Eunice or anyone else broke through Jim's extreme reticence about family matters to suggest some sort of professional help for Naomi, he quickly cut short the conversation by saying that it would cause a "revolution" at home. What Jim Olive jokingly referred to as his job of "preserving domestic tranquillity" was relatively easy in those days, since Marlene was still a child and there were long periods when Naomi seemed perfectly normal and Jim could glimpse the lovely, shy, adoring girl he had married twenty years earlier.

The summer after the group-therapy sessions, the Olives moved back to the United States for good, or so they thought at the time. The reason seems to have been less Naomi's hatred of

Ecuador (she had actually improved considerably during the year on Dr. White's tranquilizers and antidepressants) than the fact that Jim, having successfully overseen the sale of the Tenneco subsidiary to a local oil company, had worked himself out of a job. In his résumé he added: "I was also anxious for my small daughter to receive an American education and background." In gratitude for his service Jim expected Tenneco to reward him with a lucrative distributorship covering several Northeastern states, but after a period in the company's Denver office, he was offered only a routine marketing job in Albuquerque, New Mexico ("inadequate for my experience and background," according to the résumé), that brought with it a considerable cut in salary and responsibility. As a result, instead of taking heart at the family's return to the States, Naomi once again saw red ruin all about her.

Then, less than a year after the family had moved to New Mexico, Jim Olive was fired. This time Naomi was not the only one to be thrown into a tailspin, although Jim took the setback in considerably better spirits. "It took me a week," he wrote Eunice, "to teach Nomi not to use the word 'fired' around the house unless she was referring to the stove, or 'canned' unless she was talking about dinner. These words are the kind that bounce in and out of little kids' mouths, and besides they are bad for morale. My morale is OK for a guy who just got shot out of the saddle while crossing the Mojave Desert. I know everything will turn out alright but the suspense is killing me." He began the whole wearisome process of applying for work again, well aware that a forty-eight-year-old salesman was not the most sought-after prospect on the job market. As a stop-gap measure, he got a job representing the New York–based Alexander Hamilton Institute, a business correspondence school that offered, for $325, a "lifetime subscription" to materials designed to lift readers "from the crowded ranks of junior and middle-level executives," where Jim himself had long languished, "to the top 5% of management," where he fervently wished to be.

Whether under the institute's influence or not, at this point in his life Jim Olive arranged by far the biggest sale of his life. In 1966 a consortium of Texaco and Gulf discovered the rich reserves of oil deep in the jungles of Oriente province that would make tiny Ecuador an OPEC member and the second largest (after Mexico) petroleum-producing nation in Latin America. In the meantime Cautivo, the company that had bought Tenneco's interests in Ecuador, did not have the resources to use its large refinery anywhere near to capacity. Jim immediately saw that it would be in Gulf's interests to purchase Cautivo and refine some of the Oriente yield for an expanding Ecuadorian market. After several visits to Gulf headquarters in Coral Gables, Florida, he managed to convince the company to back his plan and appoint him general manager of a newly formed Petróleos Gulf del Ecuador. In that capacity his first official act was to have a dozen boxes of personal business cards printed in English and Spanish announcing his new position—cards which he continued to hand out long after he had been demoted.

In the beginning the only problem with the new job was that Naomi had no intention of following Jim back to Ecuador; the couple agreed that, for a time at least, she and Marlene would rent a house in Miami while Jim set himself up in Guayaquil and came back to visit as often as possible. Naomi seemed about the same as she had been for several years, that is, perfectly normal for days and even weeks at a time but subject to sudden and inexplicable fits of an angry paranoia—especially when she had been drinking too much—that were reminiscent of her childhood temper tantrums. One such alcohol-fueled tantrum that Marlene would never forget, or forgive, occurred when Eunice Richard sent her niece a stuffed doll and Naomi grabbed it away from her and tossed it in the garbage.

The family's frequent dislocations and Naomi's erratic behavior began to take their toll on Marlene, now a dimple-cheeked, freckle-faced eight-year-old. Any emotional strain she underwent was followed by attacks of asthmatic wheezing that were severe enough to require medication and the nightly use of a room humidifier. She developed hay fever and other allergic reactions and, more disturbingly, a persistent bed-wetting problem caused by a chronic bladder infection. A ten-day stay in Miami's Children's Hospital for a kidney dialysis (a procedure that would have to be repeated several times in the coming years) is Marlene's fondest childhood recollection of her mother. For once Naomi's overprotectiveness suited the occasion. She was at Marlene's bedside constantly, reading to her, teaching her to knit and helping her cut out paper dolls. (It was, especially, the mental image of the paper dolls she and her mother worked on together that would stay with Marlene in the more troublesome times to come.) But under normal circumstances such solicitousness toward Marlene could turn in a flash to a sullen withdrawal.

"There was no in between with Naomi," her friend Ann Ellis observes. "She either smothered Marlene or ignored her. It wasn't that she didn't love her. She loved her desperately. It was more that nobody had taught Naomi how to be a mother."

Partly because of Marlene's psychological symptoms, Jim was able to induce Naomi to join him in Guayaquil. He had taken a house near their old one that met Naomi's single condition, a bedroom of her own. Her insistence on sleeping apart might have been an act of domestic revenge for her unwarranted suspicions about Jim's infidelity (at least she told people in Guayaquil that she had stayed away so long because of her husband's "girl friends"). In addition, she had recently undergone a hysterectomy and was having what she would describe to even chance acquaintances as a "difficult menopause." As always Jim tried to put the best face on trying personal circumstances. "Naomi and Marlene arrived here about two months ago," he wrote his friend Russ Sommer in Norfolk, "and we are all set up again in great style. Things seem to be a little better for us this time than the last and Naomi seems to be enjoying herself."

In fact, there were happier times when Naomi was able to break out of her self-imposed isolation. On such social occasions she took great care to limit her drinking and gave every appearance of being a perfectly normal housewife with a somewhat annoying propensity to ramble on endlessly about petty domestic matters and an excessive pride in her husband's position in the world. As a couple Jim and Naomi almost always got along well in public, although people were often surprised to learn that Naomi, with her graying hair and whiskey-bloated face and figure, was nine years younger than her husband. In the fall of 1969 the Olives threw a day-long silver-anniversary party for themselves that is still fondly recalled by their friends in Ecuador. "They rented a beachfront hotel in Playas for the whole day," their friend Alicia Reed recalled years later. "Jim was so outgoing and courteous. The kids all played together on the sand and at night there was dancing under the stars and a lobster bake. It was one of those thoroughly pleasant days that stay with you always."

But in the long run Naomi never really adjusted to Guayaquil's rough-mannered, tropical ways any better than she had the first time. (From another letter Jim wrote to Russ Sommer: "Guayaquil is a mess this week. We have a 'wet' carnival here. And the fun consists of sloshing everybody with buckets of water followed by handfuls of flour. Naomi thought the whole thing was pretty barbaric.'') She stayed in her room much of the time, sometimes even asking the maid to bring meals upstairs. In addition to sewing and playing with her two cats, Naomi added a new interest: tropical fish. Ever since Marlene had brought home a goldfish she won at a Miami street fair, Naomi had begun collecting them, and she now owned several large tanks that housed a dozen different species. She would spend hours feeding them, changing their water or simply staring into the mysterious, fern-filled world they inhabited, so calm and effortless compared to her own.

With her mother closeted in her room much of the day and her father working long hours and traveling frequently, Marlene was spending most of her time with the two live-in maids, going shopping with them and even accompanying them to Catholic mass on Sunday. More important, they served as her confidantes and advisers when Naomi was unresponsive to her girlish concerns, and thus it was always a psychological blow to Marlene when the maids were fired, as they inevitably were, for some imagined offense. Moreover, she was now at an age when she could spend after-school hours and sometimes "overnights" at other friends' houses, and while she eagerly sought permission to do so, the visits created a new problem in her life. For the first time it became abundantly clear to Marlene that her mother wasn't like the other mothers she met—busy, outward-reaching women, generally much younger than Naomi, who ran their houses with a crisp efficiency and often held down jobs or did charity work as well. And what was even more hurtful, the contrast became equally apparent to her girl friends, who shied away from coming over to Marlene's after once seeing her pallid, distraught mother wandering around the house or being told by Naomi in a slurred voice that it was time to go home. On other occasions Naomi would just sit and stare at the young girls as they played, and that was even worse. But Marlene's real fear was that someday her mother would throw a drunken fit in a friend's presence.

One other crucial event in Marlene's life occurred when she was ten. She discovered on her own what her parents had never told her—that she was not their natural daughter. Playing in her father's study one day, she took to rummaging through the file cabinet he kept there for personal papers. As Jim Olive was a meticulous record keeper, the cabinet held neat rows of green file folders identified by typed headings on gummed labels: "Personal Correspondence"; "Tenneco"; "Real Estate"; "Nicaragua 1850s"; "Wm. Walker"; "Alexander Hamilton Institute" . . . But stuck in the back of the bottom drawer was a bulky brown folder that stretched out like an accordion. Marlene untied the string and found that it contained a number of official-looking documents: her parents' marriage certificate, her father's Penn State transcript, her own birth and baptismal certificates, and various expired passports and visas. But the document that immediately drew her attention, perhaps because there were a half-dozen copies of it or because of its air of importance, was a legal-sized typewritten paper embossed with an official seal reading: "Circuit Court—City of Norfolk—Virginia." It was headed: "In the matter of the Adoption of an Unnamed Girl Child under the age of Fourteen years."

Marlene tried to read the document, realizing that it had something to do with her and her parents but, being unfamiliar with the legal vocabulary, failing to grasp exactly what. That evening at dinner she asked her father what the word "adoption" meant, and when he wanted to know why she was interested, she showed him a copy of the document.

Jim and Naomi had always intended to tell Marlene that she was adopted when she seemed ready to understand the situation, which she never had. Caught unprepared, Jim tried to explain that parents who are not able to have babies of their own sometimes get them from other parents who cannot take proper care of their children. Marlene was just as much their child, he emphasized, as if her mother had given birth to her. But what made Marlene really special was that while most parents had to take their own child home from the hospital whether they wanted to or not, Jim and Naomi had chosen Marlene from all the babies there because they loved her so much. Not unexpectedly, the "approved" explanation of adoption was a tattered comforter to throw over a puzzled child. A thousand questions would come to her mind in time, but right then, without knowing precisely why, Marlene began to cry. "I was so confused because I didn't understand how that other woman was my mother and my mother was, too," Marlene recalled years later. "I was angry, so angry, because I thought that I had been bought. I began to wonder if they loved me or were just taking care of me and didn't love me or what was happening. Then I started thinking about who my real mother was, but I didn't say anything about it for a long time.''

Over the years it became a poisonous thought, this incessant dwelling on her "other mommy." But at the time the main effect of Marlene's discovery was simply to crystallize her growing resentment against Naomi. The two would have loud, bitter arguments whenever Marlene felt that Naomi was restricting her growing sense of freedom, arguments that would end with Marlene biting her own forearm or banging her head against a wall in frustration. The longest-lasting of the Olives' maids, a hefty, strong-willed Jamaican woman named Jenny, remembers a time when Marlene was playing around in Naomi's jewelry box and refused to stop after her mother told her to. Naomi picked up Jim's belt to frighten Marlene. Suddenly beside herself with rage, Marlene grabbed the belt away and started to strike out at her mother before Jenny could contain the young girl, kicking and screaming, in a bear hug.

The reverse side of Marlene's hostility toward her mother was her affection, bordering on adoration, for her father, a normal enough tendency for a young girl entering adolescence but one which, like so much else in the Olives' family life, eventually reached a worrisome extreme. For his part Jim continued to be a doting father, snapping photos of his daughter at every opportunity, driving her to the country club and waiting for her while she swam, taking a group of her friends to Saturday-afternoon matinées of American movies dubbed into Spanish, buying her presents at every opportunity. "There's no doubt that Jim spoiled Marlene partly to make up for Naomi," Alicia Reed says. "I remember a time when my daughter, who went to the Colegio Americano with Marlene, came home with an excellent report card. My husband, Francis, was so proud he took it into the office the next day and Jim's reaction was, 'What are you going to buy Caroline?' 'Nothing,' Francis said. 'She always gets good marks.' Jim shook his head in amazement. 'If Marlene ever came home with a report card like that,' he said, 'I'd have to give her a horse, at least.' '' (The only critical comment on Marlene's Colegio Americano report card in those years stated that "she tends to carry around a hundred-*sucre* note [about four dollars] while most of her classmates have just enough for lunch. It makes their eyes bulge.'')

On weekends Marlene would accompany Jim on his round of errands in town; if some pressing business came up at the office, she would play there until he took care of it. She took day-long trips with her father to the Gulf refinery at Cautivo, a hot and dusty camp which Naomi avoided at all cost, and, occasionally, weekend excursions to Quito, a spectacular two-hour flight over the Andes. Often Marlene, who was perfectly bilingual, spoke Spanish rather than English to her "papita," as she would affectionately call him, a habit she developed at least partially to exclude Naomi—who had never learned more than enough Spanish to be able to communicate with the maids—from the conversation. And when Marlene played "house" with her dolls, as she did until much later than most girls, a Barbie doll would take her part and a Ken doll would take Jim's. In Marlene's childhood games nobody ever played Naomi.

In 1970 the Olives moved from Guayaquil to Quito. By then oil drilling and exploration in Oriente province rather than marketing had become Gulf's main concern in Ecuador, and it made more sense for company executives to be in closer touch with the government bureaus that controlled those areas. Naomi was delighted to trade the steamy coast for the moderate temperatures and breath-taking scenery of the Ecuadorian highlands. It is hard to blame her, for Quito is one of the world's most pleasant cities, spread out in the folds of the Andean foothills like an enormous picnic blanket.

The Olives moved into a small villa with polished wood floors and wrought-iron balconies that Jim had rented in the posh residential quarter of El Batán, a hilltop near the Hotel Quito with a spectacular view of the city below, and beyond it to the west, of snow-capped, cloud-shrouded Mount Pichincha. Like most of Quito's better houses, this one was completely surrounded by a high stone fence and a spiked gate that opened electronically. Besides the physical isolation of Quito's better residential housing there was, of course, the larger cultural isolation of an American enclave in a foreign land. "Families who come to Quito from the States are thrown back on their own resources," says Holley Bell, the public information officer at the American embassy there. "The situation tends to intensify family life, for better or for worse."

The lucrative oil boom was drawing thousands of Americans to Ecuador, most of them skilled technicians who left their families in the capital while they themselves lived in makeshift camps in the Oriente for months at a time. Where the Texaco-

Gulf consortium had led the way, now a dozen international conglomerates were drilling for oil, and they had together financed an intricate 300-mile pipeline that brought the resources of the jungle over the Andean passes to the seaport of Esmerald. Clearly, oil was now too big a business to be left in the hands of a marketing man, and Jim Olive, while remaining head of Gulf's sales department in Ecuador, was quickly replaced as general manager by a more experienced executive. Even with his reduced responsibilities he was probably still out of his depth in the high-stakes game of corporate politics, as proved by the incident still recalled in Quito business circles as the "92 octane gas fiasco." Jim managed to convince his superiors in Coral Gables that Ecuador needed a high-octane gas. An enormous catalytic converter was imported piece by piece, along with new gas pumps and storage tanks, all of which rusted away at the refinery for months before the Ecuadorian government decided, for political reasons, not to grant Gulf the permit it needed to market the more expensive fuel.

Nor was Naomi much of a help in her husband's career. Wives of Gulf executives abroad were expected to do a certain amount of entertaining to bolster the company's image, but whenever Jim arranged a dinner at home for Ecuadorian officials or visiting VIPs from Coral Gables, it was always catered by the nearby Hotel Quito, and while the food was good and the hotel waitresses were gaily costumed in imitation Incan get-ups, the evenings lacked a certain domestic touch. Frequently Naomi stayed upstairs in her room, and when she did attend these and other company functions, there was often reason to wish she hadn't. Toward the end of the Olives' stay in Quito, Naomi appeared at a company Christmas party and drunkenly accused Jim's boss in Ecuador, Bernardo Díaz, of wanting to replace him. After that, company functions were stag affairs whenever possible.

Even when she was in her worst moods, Jim was a solicitous, if helpless, husband. To avoid friction at home he would sometimes eat lunch and take his siesta at his friends the Sosas' house, and neither the *capitán*—a dapper, mustachioed man who had served for twenty years in the Ecuadorian army—nor his high-born wife, Tamara, would question him about Naomi's whereabouts. Only once, after seeing Naomi belligerently drunk, had Captain Sosa taken his friend aside and suggested that it might be a good idea for Jim to send Naomi to an alcoholism clinic in the States. Jim shook his head sadly and said that Naomi was fine much of the time and that even when she drank and carried on he remembered the way she was when he married her, young and beautiful and helpful to him in his work, and he didn't feel that he could "abandon" her now. What worried him most, he added, was the thought that since both his wife and daughter had been adopted children, Marlene might in time develop some of Naomi's "difficulties."

In fact, Jim already had some cause for concern. When they came to Quito, Marlene had been enrolled in the sixth grade at the Colegio Americano, where her teacher was an energetic, no-nonsense young woman named Mary Lou Pasquel. That term Mrs. Pasquel became pregnant, and her students took a keen interest in the course of her expanding stomach. "One day," she recalls, "we were discussing motherhood, what it's like to be a mother and how your life changes. Marlene raised her hand and said, out of the blue, 'I hate my mother.' Just that matter-of-fact. Well, the other kids were shocked into silence and I guess Marlene felt she had to do some more explaining. So after a while she added, 'She's not my real mother. I'm adopted. That's why she doesn't love me.' "

One day after school Marlene wanted to know if Mrs. Pasquel could tell her how she could find out who her real mother was. She said that her father had promised to help her learn the woman's name when she was twenty-one, if she still wanted to know then. Because the adoption notice mentioned an "unnamed girl child under the age of fourteen," Marlene had somehow gotten it into her head that she would find out when she turned fourteen, in three years, and she was very upset about the delay. "I told her I didn't know how she could find out and it wasn't that important," Mrs. Pasquel remembers. "But I could see right away that it was very important to her." A short time later Marlene failed to hand in some assigned homework, and when Mrs. Pasquel asked her why, she said that her brother and sister had made so much noise the night before that she couldn't concentrate. Since Mrs. Pasquel knew that Marlene was an only child, she resolved to talk to Jim Olive about more than his daughter's school work at their next conference.

When Brigadier General Rodríguez Lara overthrew the government in the spring of 1972 with only a token show of force, a two-day period of martial law was declared, during which people were prohibited from congregating in the streets and staying outdoors after ten o'clock. Naomi locked herself inside for weeks, and when she finally ventured out, it was to stock up on canned foods by the case, enough food to allow her to stay inside for years if she chose to. For a long time afterward she was excessively worried about Marlene going out alone, even to her friend María Sosa's house a few blocks away. To mollify his wife, Jim agreed to drive Marlene everywhere she wanted to go.

As she got older Marlene increasingly began to chafe at these restrictions on her sense of independence. Once she took advantage of the fact that her father was in Guayaquil on a business trip to stay late at a friend's house. As it got to be dark Naomi began calling Jim's business associates in a panic, and by the time Marlene came home an hour later she was met by her mother and a half-dozen Gulf salesmen. On another occasion, when Marlene refused to obey her mother's order not to leave the house with a friend, Naomi called the militia, and the two were swiftly apprehended and escorted home by a detachment of mounted cavalry.

When Naomi was drinking, which was much of the time now, she would often forget that she had already given Marlene permission to do something, and an argument, frequently a violent one, would ensue. Nor was Marlene especially blameless in these altercations. As she grew older she became openly more abusive toward Naomi, routinely telling friends who came over after school or on weekends to "forget her, she's drunk." If nothing aroused her adopted mother's wrath quite so quickly as a volley of questions about her natural mother, Marlene took aim and fired away: What was her name? How old was she? Was she pretty? Did she have other children? Why didn't she want to keep her baby? In fact, Naomi almost certainly didn't know the answers, but the questions would send her into a tantrum, during which her normally pristine vocabulary would turn to foul invective and her face would bunch up at the center as if it were pulled by a drawstring. In her anger she would tell Marlene that the woman was a "gutter tramp" who didn't want any children. Once she added that by the time Marlene was adopted she and Jim no longer wanted a child either. The remark wasn't true, but it served to confirm the young girl's conviction that her mother didn't love her. "Even though you know someone's angry," Marlene would say later, "there are words you never forget."

After these arguments Marlene often packed a small suitcase and "ran away" to the Sosas, at which point the captain would promptly place a call to Jim at the office. If Marlene spent the night, Señora Sosa invariably found that the bedsheets were soaked with urine the next morning. But usually Jim picked Marlene up after work and tried to negotiate a temporary truce at home, scolding his wife and daughter for "fighting more than fishermen's wives." He could never bring himself to punish Marlene physically, however. On the few occasions when Naomi insisted that she be spanked for some misdeed, he would march his daughter into the library, close the door behind them and thwack a stuffed pillow while Marlene cried out in mock pain.

Jim was in an impossible situation. Both his wife and his daughter were very demanding of his attention and jealous when the other received it. Each would call him at work frequently with petty complaints about the other. Marlene, particularly, became very adept at manipulating her father by making him feel guilty about her mother's behavior. "*Papa, dame plata,*" she would say in an ingratiating, little-girl manner, and Jim was only too willing to hand her money for whatever she wanted if it would ease the tension in the house. "Let's not rock the boat," he would tell Marlene. "You know how sensitive your mother is."

Besides using her father as a buffer against her mother, Marlene developed a rich fantasy life as her surest escape from domestic discord. At times the fantasy was no more complicated than a game of bingo or "go fish" attended by imaginary companions. But more often it involved her extensive doll collection, which Marlene would take out from the cedar chest where it was stored. She invented elaborate family scenarios for her dolls, all of which included a happy brood of brothers and sisters as well as wise, adoring parents. She would stage long dinner-table conversations, speaking the dialogue aloud using different voices for different members of the family. In one of her favorite fantasies, Marlene went back to visit her natural mother in Norfolk. Imagining her to be wealthy and beautiful, Marlene always dressed her in Barbie's finest full-length red velvet gown and diamond jewelry. This particular scenario had several variants. Sometimes Marlene would simply watch her mother's activities throughout the day from across the street. If she approached the house, she pretended at first that she was a new neighbor or an Avon saleslady. There would be some introductory chitchat with the woman, then the revelation that Marlene was the daughter she had put up for adoption long ago, and a happy, tearful reunion. But if Marlene came into the house and there were other children present, she would either refuse to reveal her true identity or do so almost casually, adding quickly that she was very happy with her adoptive parents and her new life. It was an attempt to inflict punishment on the woman who had given Marlene away and kept her other children.

In the seventh grade Marlene began to turn some of her fantasy life into poetry; for a time the poetry and the doll games continued apace and then the newer activity subsumed the older. At first Naomi encouraged Marlene to write, perhaps because the anxiety-ridden, adolescent fantasies her daughter produced mirrored some of her own inner turmoil and her attempts to deal with it. The first poem Marlene ever wrote described a young girl who was shipwrecked on the high seas, and instead of drowning, lived a weightless, will-less underwater existence among strange flora and fauna. Isolated with her tropical fish and the plastic flowers she imported from the United States (although the city bloomed with a rich profusion of real ones), it could not have been difficult for Naomi to identify with the heroine. In any case, she delighted her daughter by praising the poem and asking for a copy of it.

Marlene often signed the poems with her favorite among the several pseudonyms she was constantly trying out, Maria Lucia Miranda—Maria Lucia because it resembled a Spanish version of Marlene Louise; Miranda, the name of a classmate, because of its mellifluous sound. Unconsciously, the pseudonym provided Marlene with a means to distance herself from her most intimate and threatening thoughts. And on a conscious level, she felt that it was perfectly plausible for her to adopt a new name, since she didn't know her original name anyway and wasn't who she thought she was. Moreover, she couldn't even be sure of her real age, for if the only birth certificate that existed for her had been "amended" to include her adopted name, what guarantee was there that her birth date had not been altered as well? Sometimes she felt considerably older than her thirteen years, and with her height and full-blown figure, she certainly looked older. At other times, sitting on the bedroom floor playing with dolls or kicking and screaming and sometimes even biting herself in a temper tantrum, she felt and acted younger.

Despite these various escape fantasies and identity subterfuges, Marlene's childhood years in Ecuador were not entirely unhappy ones. Indeed, after she moved back to the United States she would look upon them fondly as a simpler, more carefree time and dreamed of returning one day. Even the darkest cloud over her childhood—her generally bleak relationship with her mother—sometimes dispersed enough to allow light-hearted, affectionate memories through. There were recollections of Naomi teaching Marlene how to embroider and to bake fruit-filled Christmas cookies, others of the two of them shopping for Jim's birthday present, bathing and grooming the cats, or playing in the yard with the family dog, a boxer named Chatka. There were family gatherings around a stunted but gaily festooned Christmas tree that had to be imported in sections from less tropical climates and then wired together. There was the succession of homemade Halloween costumes Naomi skillfully fashioned for her daughter—a polka-dot clown's outfit one year, a gossamer-winged fairy godmother's another and a pillow-stuffed fat girl's still another. There was the time Naomi helped Marlene with a school assignment to draw the inside of a flower, when the young girl was amazed at her mother's accuracy at portraying the stamen and pistil and bent-down petals of a perfect blossom. There were the nights when Marlene's asthma attacks prevented her from sleeping and Naomi eased the congestion in her lungs with vapor rubs. There was a vividly recalled occasion when Marlene, at the age of twelve, had her first period and Naomi happened to come upstairs from some adult gathering. Finding her daughter sitting panic-stricken on the bathroom floor staring uncomprehendingly at the droplets of blood, she hugged her and reassured her that she was not coming apart on the inside.

In particular, there were two public events in Marlene's young life that her mother attended. One was a grade-school theatrical called *Sourdough Sally,* in which Marlene played the title role of an Alaskan girl in gold-rush days. Naomi didn't say much after the play but it was enough for Marlene that she had come. The other was Marlene's confirmation, which took place just after her eleventh birthday. She wore a blue taffeta dress with a gold cross around her neck and carried a tiny black missal in one white-gloved hand. She paired off with the other girls in her confirmation class to walk down the aisle and kneel briefly at the altar, and when she came back she glanced at her parents and thought she saw tears in her mother's eyes. Later, after a family dinner at the Conquistador Club, she asked Jim if that was true and he said yes indeed, Naomi had been crying all through the ceremony.

But these were still rare oases of communication surrounded by vast tracts of stony silence or heated argument. Jim continued to provide Marlene with most of the parental support she received. The two were inseparable. At home in the evenings they would often play Scrabble together in Spanish or sing Ecuadorian folk songs to Jim's halting guitar accompaniment. On weekends he often took her on day-long drives down the Chillos Valley outside Quito to visit the Indian markets at Gayamba, Cumbaya and Santa Domingo de Corales. During the week-long Fiesta de Quito in December, when the world's best toreadors gathered in the city, Jim and Marlene would get an *abono* of tickets and spend every afternoon at the bullfights. In the summer there would be long afternoons around the palm-bordered pool of the Quito Tennis and Golf Club, sometimes extending into dinner and dancing in the evening. Indeed, so close did Marlene's identification with her father become during this period that she often wore his favorite clothes around the house, especially when he was away on long business trips.

As Naomi became more reclusive and Marlene older, Jim began to take his daughter with him to social and business affairs where men would normally be accompanied by their wives. With mock formality he would introduce her as Señora Olive, but one of Jim's Gulf colleagues, seeing Marlene at these adult functions, nicknamed her *la mujercita*, the little mistress. Almost fourteen, Marlene had lost some of her childhood cuteness, but she was still an attractive young lady suffering from the typical complaints of her age. She was beginning to develop acne and had put on some weight, which she self-consciously hid underneath a loose-fitting poncho. "She's become a woman almost overnight," Jim told a friend, and as with many another adoring father, it wasn't entirely clear how he felt about the situation.

Around this time Marlene's friends changed from a group of Ecuadorian girls she had grown up with to American girls she had recently met at school. They were much more advanced socially than Ecuadorian girls from good families, who do not go out on dates until they are at least sixteen and even then are heavily chaperoned. In some ways this change in her circle of friends provided Marlene with a brief period of adjustment to life in the United States, but when the time came for the Olives to leave Ecuador it was still a transition that both she and Jim were extremely fearful of making.

*   *   *

Jim Olive lost his job at Gulf in January of 1973, a few months short of the time when he could have collected retirement benefits. He was given two months to look for new employment while still drawing a salary, but no other severance pay. It was agreed that the official reason for his leaving would be the new Ecuadorian government's intention to nationalize part of the oil industry. In fact, Jim Olive was fired because he lost out in a power struggle within Petróleos Gulf del Ecuador and because, being a middle-aged salesman caught in an economic squeeze, he was, quite simply, expendable.

It was time to update his résumé again and start the all too familiar letter-writing campaign. With the exception of an eighteen-month period in the middle, he had spent the last thirteen years in Ecuador, and his enthusiasm for the place was reflected in the working title of a book he had begun to write about it: *The Greatest Little Country in the World*. He desperately wanted to stay where he felt most comfortable, and for a few weeks it looked as though his friend Captain Sosa would be able to use his good offices with the new junta to get him a consulting position with CEPE, the state-owned petroleum concern. When that proved politically infeasible and several other local possibilities fell through, Jim decided to move back to the United States and go into business for himself. He tried to talk some of his Ecuadorian friends into investing in a horse-breeding ranch in Texas with him, but their overall lack of enthusiasm was no doubt influenced by the fact that several of them were still paying off the debt on the last sure-fire moneymaking scheme he had promoted, a brick-manufacturing plant that went bust when it failed to fulfill a large government contract. Then he saw a General Business Services advertisment in the *Wall Street Journal* that seemed perfect: "Become the businessman's businessman. America's leading business management and tax service offers franchises to qualified counselors." He wrote away for a prospectus and arranged to visit the company's headquarters in a Washington, D.C., suburb on a job-hunting trip.

There Jim had some difficulty choosing an area as he gazed at the map of the United States pricked by nearly a thousand red pins. He wanted one where the local economy was healthy, the climate similar to Ecuador's and—his greatest concern—where the public schools were good. His first choice, the San Diego area, was cluttered with pins, but farther north a part of Marin County was available. He made a few calls to friends in California (including George Koth, his old Penn State roommate, who now lived south of San Francisco) and was assured that Marin County, with an expanding population and a highly regarded school system, more than met his qualifications. A quick check in an atlas showed that the Bay Area, like San Diego, had a large Spanish-speaking population, a fact that promised to make Jim's bilingualism an added asset.

In late March, Jim called Naomi and Marlene from Washington and told them that they were moving to Marin County, and that it was "the third richest county in the country." Naomi was delighted at the news. For years she had blamed most of her troubles on either Ecuador or the Gulf Oil Corp., and now she was rid of both of her nemeses at once. Moreover, she thought that Jim's new job meant that he would spend more time at home. And a home of her own in a quiet suburb of a city whose language she could speak was all that Naomi wanted out of life. During the next few weeks she was more active and cheerful than she had been in anyone's memory.

Marlene, on the contrary, was completely disconsolate at the prospect of moving. She moped around the house for a week. Then she began crying a lot. Part of her reaction was simply fear of the unknown. She had spent twelve of her fourteen years in Ecuador, all of the last six. She spoke Spanish better than English and considered herself as much Latin as American— more. She saw the United States, to use one of her father's favorite phrases, as "the land of the great PX," the place where you stocked up on items that were hard to get in Ecuador. But an equal measure of her reaction had to do with the little she did know about the United States. It came from the advice columns and cautionary short stories in her favorite magazine, *Seventeen*, and from American movies and TV programs she had seen, as well as loose talk around school. And it could be summed up in one hair-curling word: drugs. Eve Ortega, a friend with whom Marlene had corresponded since the two were neighbors in Miami, had written that everyone in her tenth grade class *came* to school stoned. She had read about rock musicians like Jimi Hendrix and Janis Joplin O.D.'ing, and on a trip to Miami one summer, she herself had seen a high-flying hippie walk straight into a brick wall. She had also heard a close friend of her father's talk about what happened to his children, who had also been brought up in Ecuador, after they went off to college in the United States. Within two years his son had been kicked out of Louisiana State and was living in a radical commune, and his daughter was a member of a Los Angeles drug rehabilitation center. "I told my dad that I was going to get sucked into the drug scene and we were going to grow apart," Marlene remembers. "I told him that I didn't want to go and I cried and cried. He just said you'll make new friends soon and there's nothing we can do about it now."

But Jim was just as anxious about his daughter's adjustment to California as she was. "I hope Marlene can keep her feet on the ground," he said to Nancy Sotomajor, the headmistress of the Colegio Americano's international section, who did not try to discount his fears. "I told him that thirteen- and fourteen-year-old kids—particularly girls—often react very badly to being uprooted. They're terribly insecure and conformist at that age, neither fish nor fowl. They need so much peer acceptance. We'd had some bad experiences."

In short order the movers had crated up whatever the Olives were taking with them, and the rest of the furniture had been sold to a military attaché at the West German embassy. The attaché also led away Chatka, as Marlene, who had not been able to persuade her father to let her take the dog along, looked on tearfully. Mother and daughter did manage to convince Jim to allow them to take the two cats, the affectionate tiger-striped Mishu and Rascal, a mischievous black cat that Marlene had found in the Presbyterian churchyard just as the caretaker was about to throw him into a can of burning leaves and then presented to Naomi one Mother's day.

In the last week the Sosas threw a party for the Olives. Naomi appeared contented and carefree—"like a princess," according to Marlene, who had never seen her mother looking so beautiful. Everyone danced and sang and the band serenaded the Olives with spirited renditions of Ecuadorian folk music. The Sosas said that whenever Marlene wanted to come back to Ecuador she could stay with them, and Marlene made her father promise that in a year or two she would be allowed to return for the summer. And then suddenly it was time to head for the airport accompanied by a large contingent of Jim's friends, who loaded the Olives down with gifts and flowers and waved until their orange-colored Braniff 747 lifted off. "Buy me an *abono* for the next fiesta!" Jim yelled back as he walked onto the tarmac.

When the Olives landed in San Francisco they rented a car and made their way across the Golden Gate Bridge and up the freeway toward the Holiday Inn in Terra Linda, arriving around midnight to start their new life.

Three

In nearly every way Chuck Riley's upbringing made him a representative product of his environment. Like most of central Marin's adult population, his parents had come there in the fifties from distant parts of the country, lured by the temperate climate and economic opportunity of postwar California. And as was true of many of their neighbors, the original impetus for the move had been the military—not, in their case, a wartime leave or temporary stationing in San Francisco, but Joanne Riley's assignment, in 1954, to the military hospital at Hamilton Air Force Base, ten miles north of San Rafael.

Joanne had grown up in the coal-mining town of Pottsville, Pennsylvania. Her father, an easygoing, heavyset man whom her elder son would come to resemble in her mind, worked as a brakeman on the Lehigh Valley Railroad. After high school she decided to join the WAFs in order to benefit from the specialized nursing training and adventurous travel the Air Force recruitment posters promised. She ended up at a base in Lackland, Texas, learning to become a teletype operator, and there she met a young man whose restlessness and aspirations for self-betterment matched her own.

Oscar Riley had been born in the delta section of Arkansas near the Louisiana and Mississippi borders, the youngest son in a family of nine children. His father was also a railroad man, a section foreman on the Missouri-Pacific. Even though he was president of his class, Oscar dropped out of high school in the middle of his senior year when he and two friends were arrested in a drunk driving incident. It was the first time the "Riley name'' had been tarnished, and Oscar was ashamed to go home. He worked long hours at low wages as a nightclub bouncer for the man who had bailed him out of jail. He also labored in the cotton fields, weighing the pickers' bulging gunny sacks at the end of the day alongside another Pine Bluff resident more suited to the arduous task, Sonny Liston. Years later, when Liston had become heavyweight champion of the world and was preparing for a fight against Zora Folley, Oscar visited his training camp outside Denver, and the resulting picture of the two former field hands—the huge black man holding his trunklike arm around a short, frail-looking white man with slicked-back hair and thick glasses—is one of Oscar's favorite mementos.

In 1953 he joined the Air Force, intending to finish the credits he needed for a high school diploma (which he did the following year) and to get his flight wings (which he never got a chance to do once it was discovered that he was color-blind). He met and dated Joanne Hensley during his basic training at Lackland, although the flourishing romance was cut short when Oscar suddenly developed a severe case of pneumonia and was shipped to Fitzsimmons Hospital in Denver. She visited him regularly during the six months he was there, only a fraction of which was spent recovering from the lung infection. By then he had become a full-blown morphine addict due to a medical mixup. An Air Force doctor at Lackland had prescribed the painkiller on a short-term basis, and when he was transferred to Denver, Oscar continued to receive it three times daily until he was ''sitting up in bed before each meal waiting for my fix.'' He spent months in the hospital ''drying out, nothin' else you can call it,'' and the experience left him so wary of narcotics that ever since he has refused even the dentist's routine offer of Novocain.

The Rileys were married in June 1954, after Oscar was medically discharged from both the hospital and the Air Force, and they moved shortly thereafter to Marin County so that Joanne could report for duty at Hamilton. Less than a year later, after giving birth to Chuck at the base hospital, she retired to full-time homemaking. The Rileys had a second son, Kerry, two years later and a daughter, Michelle, in 1961. Oscar worked as a gas-station attendant while waiting to get into a barber school in San Francisco, an occupation he chose principally because all the men on his mother's side of the family in West Texas had been barbers. When no ''chair'' opened up he began attending the College of Marin, graduating from the junior college with a business major. Then he took what he thought would be a temporary job at the Lucky supermarket in downtown San Rafael; he stayed for seven years, eventually working his way up to head clerk. It had once been Oscar Riley's great ambition in life to capitalize on his junior college education by rising out of the ranks of blue-collar workers, perhaps by becoming an insurance or real estate agent. However, as the years passed and his family responsibilities grew, he resigned himself to his job delivering Dolly Madison baked goods around Marin.

Neither did Joanne Riley ever become the nurse she had aspired to be, but since she was of an easier disposition than her husband, the failure bothered her less. Once Chuck and Kerry started school she began working at several hospitals and convalescent homes as a nurse's aide. She is a large, sharp-featured woman who gives off an air of no-nonsense maternalism, and the work seems to suit her. For several years now she has worked the night shift at Ross General Hospital, beginning at eleven o'clock and getting off at seven in the morning, then sleeping until the early afternoon. A hand-lettered sign tacked to the Rileys' front door reads: "Do not disturb. Daytime sleeper. That means you." But a more accurate indication of Joanne Riley's gregarious ways is the framed print that hangs over the living-room mantelpiece—a portrait of an Indian chief in full headgear above the motto "O great spirit, grant that I may not criticize my neighbor until I have walked a mile in his moccasins."

For someone who would soon develop such a severe weight problem, Chuck Riley started off life a normal-sized child with brown hair that his mother kept closely shorn and large brown eyes that were always laughing. Oscar Riley's home movies show him perpetually clowning for the camera, decked out with toy six-shooters sticking out of ridiculously low-slung twin holsters. In one scene Chuck and Kerry are playing on a backyard seesaw (by then Joanne's hand can be glimpsed weighting down Kerry's side for balance). In another (Oscar's favorite), a six-year-old Chuck is seen, lunch box in hand and name tag fastened to his shirt, walking to his first day of school with a look of studied confidence on his face.

Chuck's accepting, happy disposition made him the darling of the Rileys' military friends. He loved to care for the parakeets and fantail doves he kept at home, and whenever one of Kerry's rabbits gave birth it was Chuck who would patiently feed the runt of the litter with an eyedropper. A favorite family story tells of the time Oscar won a duck from a place called Ducks Unlimited through a church raffle. Chuck, then four, stood in the kitchen watching his father and uncle scald and pluck the bird, then he took it out on the porch and tried to set it upright on its legs, saying, "Stand up, Mr. Duck. You'll probably feel better." "I cooked the duck," Joanne recalls, "but nobody could eat it."

Oscar would often take his sons to the Marin Rod and Gun Club (which Chuck always mispronounced "Rotten Gun Club") to fish for sea bass along a rickety pier that extends out into San Pablo Bay across from San Francisco. As proof of his son's basic gentleness Oscar often cites the fact that he always insisted on throwing undersized fish back into the water. At the same time, it was a cautionary convenience to have San Quentin so close by. Whenever Chuck or Kerry misbehaved, Oscar would march them out to the end of the pier and point to the looming presence of the maximum-security facility a few hundred yards away, with its windowless expanse of mustard-colored stucco and circular guard towers. "If you don't watch your step," he would warn them with mock severity, "that's where you'll end up."

Chuck began getting fat around the time he entered kindergarten, and by the age of ten he was a chubby-cheeked, barrel-shaped kid who weighed nearly 200 pounds and could rest his elbows on his stomach. Because he drank so much liquid Joanne thought he might be diabetic, but tests showed that he was overweight for a more obvious reason—he overate. It was through food that Joanne showed her love and also compensated for the love that Oscar was sometimes unable to express. Oscar could be rigid and authoritarian toward his elder son, and Chuck remembers feeling uncomfortable in his father's presence from an early age. When the tension between them would burst into open argument over one behavioral infraction or another, Joanne often tried to negotiate a peace at the large round kitchen table, the center of the Riley household. As he grew up, Chuck's waistline became an ever expanding and vicious circle. Whenever he became emotionally upset he ate more, and whenever a classmate called him "fatso" or "butterball" he became upset, however good-naturedly he learned to take the teasing on the surface.

In 1964 Oscar Riley got a "wild hair" to bring Joanne and the children back to Arkansas so as to be closer to his family and eliminate the annual cross-country treks to visit both sets of grandparents. He got a job selling a line of grocery products door to door. But he soon discovered that he could no longer take the countrified pace, the sweltering heat and frequent tornadoes of backwoods Southern life. Because Chuck's reading and spelling scores were below average, the Rileys agreed to have him repeat the third grade—a decision Chuck secretly resented. But if Chuck lacked interest in school, he was fascinated by his uncles' collection of hunting rifles, which he learned to shoot with unerring accuracy. From then on guns vied with every conceivable variety of wheeled transportation as the ruling passion of his adolescence.

The following year, soon after the Rileys moved back to California, Chuck began to earn spending money—as much as $60 a month—as a delivery boy for the San Rafael *Independent-Journal*, Marin's leading newspaper. He delivered the *I-J*, an afternoon paper, when school let out, making his rounds first on his bicycle and later on motorcycles. He kept the job until he was seventeen and is remembered by his boss as "one of the three or four top carriers I ever had and maybe the best salesman." His customers liked him because he would accommodatingly "porch" papers upon request, and his employer liked him because he would consistently sign up more "starts"—new subscriptions—than any other delivery boy, a feat he achieved largely by keeping a sharp eye peeled for moving vans in the neighborhood and then soliciting the new residents. His diligence won him the standard $1 bonus for each new subscription (he would regularly get twenty or thirty a month, several times the average) as well as numerous special pirzes in *I-J* contests, which ranged from pen-and-pencil sets to twice-yearly excursions to Disneyland, a trip Chuck made nearly a dozen times.

Once, in the spring of 1971, Chuck was featured as "Carrier of the Month" in the newsletter the paper publishes for its hundreds of delivery boys. The blown-up photograph that fills the front page shows a pleasant-faced, doubled-chinned fifteen-year-old with an untamable cowlick and a barrel-sized waist hauling a bundle of papers from an *I-J* truck. The inside profile talks about Chuck's salesmanship, his family, his plans for college ("a bit vague right now") and concludes by describing him as "a jolly, likeable person who really enjoys meeting people."

Over the years Chuck won a record number of "Carrier of the Month" awards, which took the form of bronze statuettes of an old-fashioned newsboy in a peaked cap and shoulder bag, with the recipient's name inscribed on its plastic base. When, less than three years after he had delivered his last newspaper, Chuck Riley was on trial for his life, the *I-J* gave the event daily front-page attention. And one day when Joanne Riley found the paper's coverage particularly sensationalized, as she often did, she took down the twenty-one gleaming trophies that had stood side by side for so long on a high shelf in Chuck's bedroom and boxed them away in a corner of the garage.

With his first *I-J* money Chuck went out and bought a BB gun, the beginning of a small arsenal of pellet guns he collected before turning to more lethal weapons. He roamed around the hills in front of his house looking for targets (''pretend Indians'') and developed such a sure hand and eye that he once peppered his name on the wall of a friend's garage with pellets. At thirteen, after a year of steady pleading, Oscar reluctantly agreed to let Chuck buy a .22-caliber rifle, but insisted that he first take a gun safety course given by the San Rafael police department. Chuck would take the rifle to an undeveloped stretch of marshland across the freeway, known as Jack Rabbit Hill, and shoot at small game or at soda bottles set on a tree stump. In time he would enjoy the added power and authority guns gave him, but at that point shooting was simply something that an affection-starved fat boy could do better than the other kids on the block.

At about this time Oscar Riley was also prevailed upon to let his son buy a Honda 90 with money he had saved from his paper route. When the lightweight minibike wouldn't take the punishment Chuck gave it he eventually traded it in for a more powerful 100 cc two-stroke Kawasaki Trailboss, which he immediately stripped down and souped up for dirt racing. Every day after school a group of neighborhood kids, all of them too young to ride on the streets, would race their bikes along the fire roads that scarred the lush Marin hillsides, using an abandoned trailer as a kind of clubhouse. And most evenings one of them would walk his bike over to the Rileys' garage and pull Chuck away from the dinner table to fix whatever had gone awry during the day. Chuck was only too glad to oblige. He had always shown a mechanical flair, taking apart (if not always putting together) every clock and watch in the house, and he used this ability to win friends.

By the time he was in the sixth grade Chuck Riley was no longer just chubby—he was enormous. He weighed well over 250 pounds, most of it centered in a 48-inch waist. At one point, when he was fifteen, he went over the 300-pound mark, although how much over was at first difficult to say because 299 was the last calibration on the Rileys' bathroom scale. (At his heaviest, a visit to the family doctor eventually showed, Chuck weighed 340 pounds.) According to Oscar, it was nothing for Chuck to finish his paper route by snacking on half a dozen candy bars at Danny's Market, then eat "like one of those Japanese wrestlers" at dinner two hours later and top that off with a half-gallon of ice cream during an evening of television watching. Nor did the fact that Oscar would often bring home discounted boxes of Dolly Madison cakes and pies from work help shield his son from temptation.

Like most fat boys, Chuck suffered constant humiliation with generally good cheer. Joanne Riley had to buy him extra large men's pants by the time he reached his early teens, then cut a foot or more off the legs—either that or shop at special "big boy" clothing stores. Chuck was forced to bring his own bathing trunks to gym class when all the other kids were issued theirs. Indeed, gym class presented a never-ending series of embarrassments, especially during junior lifesaving classes or when basketball teams were divided into "shirts" and "skins," and sometimes Chuck would simply refuse to participate.

Oscar and Joanne tried to bribe Chuck into slimming down with a standing offer of $1 for every pound he lost and $5 for each inch he took off his waistline. The Rileys' family doctor tried to put Chuck on a strict 1,000-calorie diet, and when he failed to stick to it, prescribed Dexedrine to help him along. Chuck did take off weight for a while, but then he began using the pills more for the increased energy and sense of self-confidence they provided. At first one of the heart-shaped tablets would keep him "wired" for the whole day and then he needed two or three. Soon he was swallowing a fistful at a time and often staying up for several days without any sleep. Besides the strain such a regimen placed on his body, he found himself running out for post-midnight snacks at San Rafael's all-night Jack-In-The-Box (where, rumor maliciously insisted, he had a charge account) and thus putting back the weight he had lost. It seemed a hopeless situation. Some of Chuck's friends had formed a rock band and he enjoyed serving as their unofficial manager (which mostly meant that he got to carry the drums and set up the acoustical equipment when they played at parties) and in general became interested in rock music. Two of his favorite songs were "He Ain't Heavy, He's My Brother," a sentimental pop ballad about boyhood friendship, and "No One Knows What the Fat Man Feels." Chuck knew.

"Fat Man" was, in fact, one of the nicknames the kids gave him, along with Large Charles (often abbreviated to "L.C.") and "Boulder." A friend transformed the latter into "Rocko" and the nickname stuck, partly because Chuck himself encouraged its use, for it could be taken to indicate a certain hardboiled toughness (exactly the derivation that the district attorney would later encourage the jury to accept) rather than soft-bellied bulk. In fact, all of Chuck's contemporaries agree with Oscar's assessment that his son "didn't have a mean bone in his body." Generally, he was eager to please and generous to a fault, a fat kid near-desperate to win the acceptance and approval that his thinner peers could afford to take for granted. He was, from the time his personality first coalesced, a follower perpetually searching for someone to lead him—or just like him.

As soon as he turned sixteen and could drive legally Chuck bought his first car, a beat-up 1964 Corvair for which he paid $25. He put in a racing transmission and took the car out to the mudflats bordering a stretch of the highway, where he practiced precision turns and stops and learned how to accelerate out of spins and keep the car balanced in two-wheel drifts. He read hot-rod and racing magazines by the armful. For a while Chuck did odd jobs for a young stock-car racer who owned an auto repair shop in San Rafael and billed himself as "the world's fastest hippie." Chuck himself had the kind of quick reflexes and peripheral vision it takes to be a race driver, and it became his greatest ambition to get his NASCAR license and compete professionally. His ultimate dream was to win the Indianapolis 500. But for the moment he had to content himself with the reputation of being the best "wheel man" in Terra Linda High, certainly the most daring.

After the Corvair literally took a turn for the worse when Chuck tried jumping it off a motorcycle ramp, he began saving up for a '64 Nova he coveted, keeping a picture of the car in his room along with a chart of the amount of money he had earned. Working at the repair shop, he made the Nova into one of the fastest hot rods in the area. Chuck used the freeway behind his house as his own private drag strip, and once clocked the Nova over a measured distance at 157 mph, although the car's speedometer had long since quit. Another time he drove from San Rafael to Vallejo, a distance of 30 miles, in twenty minutes flat, much to the consternation of the other kids along for the ride. More than the speed, what worried them was the fact that it was late in the afternoon and commuter traffic was building. Indeed, Chuck loved nothing more than to get himself into some tire-screeching, speed-blurred situation on the thin edge of gravity with a carful of girls squealing for him to slow down, and then to pull out of it fine. He always did, too. It was the only time he felt "totally in control of a situation."

When the engine burst apart on the freeway while Chuck was pushing the Nova to 85 mph in second gear, he coasted the car off the San Pedro ramp to within a half block of his house. He bought a white '69 Buick Skylark, his last car. It had been involved in a front-end collision and the hood lock didn't catch, so Chuck secured it with a bungee cord. One day the cord snapped and the hood flew over the roof and down the freeway. He replaced it with a flat V-shaped piece of plywood, in the center of which he stuck a feathered dart. It was a fine conversation piece, but it was not the best means of remaining inconspicuous from the California Highway Patrol.

All this time the speeding tickets and license-revocation warnings had been piling up and Oscar Riley was getting, as he put it, "a bit hot under the collar," especially when he learned that Chuck had never bothered to take out automobile insurance. The obligatory six o'clock dinners in the Riley household were tense and silent. Afterward Oscar, a soft-spoken man who tries to keep a tight rein on his Irish temper at the expense of his blood pressure, would have what he called "stern words" with his elder son, as often as not about Chuck's "loose-footed" driving.

There were other signs of the trouble to come. Beginning in the ninth grade, Chuck's school record deteriorated badly and the Rileys would often get phone calls from his guidance counselor warning that he was failing courses. The problem was not so much incompetence as indifference, for although Chuck was always careful not to be counted absent and thus risk an immediate call home, he spent considerably more of his time hanging around the school grounds than he did inside a classroom. And although he never got into serious trouble, some of Chuck's extracurricular activities were questionable, to say the least. The Rileys never found out about the gang of kids who were going around stealing lawnmowers to power their minibikes, but they did hear about the shoplifting. Chuck's usual technique was to grab a baseball glove or a car stereo as soon as he entered the store, then walk up to a salesman and in his most personable manner explain that he had just received the item as a birthday present and already owned one, so would it be possible to exchange it. The ruse generally worked—until the day he tried it once too often in the same store and the manager called Joanne to find out just how many birthdays her son celebrated in a single year.

But what really got Oscar "all lathered up" was the suspicion that Chuck might be stealing at home, reaching into the trouser pocket of Oscar's work uniform, where he kept company money from the day's collection overnight, and helping himself to small amounts that Oscar would have to make up at the end of the week to balance his accounts. As often as not the money would be spent treating other kids to movies or buying beer for the group or in some other way that Chuck, who always felt isolated from his peers by his age and weight, could curry their favor. "A lot of kids would only pay attention to Chuck because they felt sorry for him," a boyhood friend named Bill Owen recalls. "Or if they needed a ride somewhere or wanted to use the miniature pool table in the Rileys garage."

About this time Joanne called up the family doctor, to complain that Chuck was getting moody and uncommunicative and had begun "buying friends." The doctor, who recognized that Chuck's weight problem had "psychological overtones," thought that family therapy might be worth trying and set up an appointment for the Rileys at the Family Service Agency in San Rafael. After much arm twisting Chuck agreed to attend the scheduled session along with his parents and brother and sister. It proved to be a disaster. The Rileys sat around in an uneasy circle while the therapist pointed his finger at one member after another and asked, "Now, how do *you* feel about Chuck being so fat?" Needless to say, there was only one session and the tension at home was, if anything, exacerbated by the experience. It was to get much worse when Chuck became involved with drugs.

Like Marlene, Chuck was a late starter in what Oscar Riley calls "the pot scene." He was known as a prodigious beer drinker who could down a couple of six-packs and still "maintain." But he did not begin smoking marijuana until he was sixteen, long after all the kids he was hanging around with, including his younger brother, were regular users. Partly this was a result of Oscar Riley's Air Force–induced paranoia about any kind of drug, what Chuck later called his father's "Jack Webb scare" about kids jumping off buildings or painting themselves red and walking into traffic.

What started Chuck smoking pot was the realization that he was already a heavy user of speed in the form of the large Dexedrine tablets the kids called elephant pills. It was also, of course, an act of rebellion against his father. Following another after-dinner argument in which Oscar threatened "permanent grounding" of Chuck's car (a neighbor had complained to the Rileys about their son's hellbent driving around the otherwise peaceful residential area), Chuck accepted some friends' dare to share the joint they were passing around. He did not jump off a building or paint himself red, although he vowed afterward that while he might accept marijuana when it was offered to him, he would never buy it on his own. A few weeks later he had bought his first one-ounce "bag" and was soon smoking daily. Within a few months he had taken his first acid trip, snorted cocaine, even sampled the white-powdered animal tranquilizer the kids called angel dust. As Bill Owen said later, "Chuck didn't just smoke weed, he smoked *lots* of weed. That was just Chuck, always overamping. He overamped on cars, he overamped on drugs, and when Marlene showed up he overamped on her."

He also began dealing marijuana, at first only small quantities to make his personal "stash." Everybody did it. The idea was that if you could find someone's older brother who dealt in large quantities, or had a connection who did, you could buy a quarter pound at the wholesale rate of, say, $50, then break it into four one-ounce lids, sell three at $20 each and keep one for yourself, thus taking care of your own needs and making some spending money to boot. Of course this was market economics at the most basic level. Far better to increase your profit margin and your stash by dealing in greater quantities, which was exactly what Chuck was soon doing. Either alone or with friends, Chuck would raise the $200 it cost to buy a pound of average-quality Mexican grass or even enough for a "brick"—a compressed kilo of cannabis leaves, stems and seeds—then break it up into one-ounce portions that were stuffed into plastic Baggies. This latter procedure was accomplished, when both his parents were out of the house, on the newspaper-covered kitchen table with the aid of a small balance scale of the kind druggists use, which Chuck had purchased at a local head shop.

It was not the admittedly lucrative financial rewards that attracted Chuck so much as the lifestyle of even a small-time dealer. One of his friends had already become pretty heavily involved in dealing. The fellow was always busy running back and forth between suppliers and customers, making calls from phone booths, using code names, keeping elaborate financial records like any up-and-coming entrepreneur. From his newspaper-delivery experience Chuck knew he was a persuasive salesman with a good head for keeping accounts, and he figured he could do the job just as well as his friend. But what really impressed Chuck Riley about a dealer's lifestyle was the fact that his friend was always so much in demand: kids sought him out on the streets, called him constantly at home, beat a steady path to his door. "For the first time I had people coming to me," Chuck later recalled. "I had something they wanted. That was my main motivation for dealing—just to become someone important to all these people." There were times, in fact, when Chuck gave away a lot more grass than he sold.

He prided himself on providing "good service" and dealing mainly with "return customers," who were in plentiful supply in hip, affluent Marin, where not only teen-agers but young adults not too far removed from their own flower-child days regularly indulged. Soon Chuck was buying as much as ten pounds at a time in large plastic garbage bags and thus getting a better wholesale price than his competitors. He was now no longer dealing casually with the older brothers of friends but with a few steady suppliers, middle-management types in the pot trade who were willing to "front" him the merchandise until he could break it down (no longer just into lids but into pounds), sell it off and pay back the debt. He was beginning to develop the reputation for trustworthiness and fair prices that would eventually make him someone to be reckoned with among his peers.

When the marijuana supply tightened up in the mid-seventies as a result of a U.S.-Mexican drug-control agreement, Chuck was in a good competitive position. The inflationary spiral had finally caught up with marijuana, and ordinary Mexican grass sold for $30 or more a lid—when it seeped through the border at all. Now Chuck was dealing mainly in the higher-priced varieties that carried "brand" names along with their greater wallop—high-altitude Oaxacan or coffee-colored Colombian, Panama Red or Acapulco Gold or even, occasionally, the black loamy Vietnamese grass brought back by returning GIs—all of which could demand upwards of $50 an ounce. Some of the most powerful Hawaiian varieties such as Maui Wowee or Kona Gold were so highly priced they were bought by the individual joint at $1 each. By the time he turned eighteen, Chuck had become known as the leading marijuana dealer at Terra Linda High. His familiar white Skylark, with its trunkful of merchandise, had been transformed into a traveling pharmacopoeia, a kind of new-style Good Humor van. Chuck was making several hundred dollars in an active week, but he used most of it to keep himself and a rapidly expanding circle of friends supplied with drugs.

About all that Oscar noticed of this frantic activity was that Chuck was hitting him up for spending money less often and was suddenly out of the house most nights. Also, that there were an awful lot of kids calling up for Chuck whose voices he didn't recognize. Generally they would refuse to leave a message or even their names.

For Chuck the best thing about his new-found popularity was being accepted, if only in a limited way, by girls. Dope dealers had a certain romantic cachet among teen-agers, and Chuck's street-smart nickname, Rocko, redolent as it was of knife fights in back alleys, fit the image he was trying to evoke. Not that any of the girls were dating him, but neither were they exploding in ill-concealed giggling fits when he approached, which had often been the case in the past. "It had always been an accepted fact that Chuck would never get a girl friend," his friend Bob Miller explains. For the most part he didn't even try, wearing his hair unfashionably short and dressing in blue-and-white-striped workshirts worn outside of cavernous Can't Bust 'Em overalls (once Kerry and three of his friends squeezed into a pair and hopped around as if they were in a potato-sack race), even to parties where all the other guys were wearing hip-hugging bell-bottoms and floral-print shirts.

Once, in the sixth grade, Chuck had asked a dimple-cheeked classmate to go steady with him; the abrupt turndown he received caused him to keep a safe distance from girls for years afterward, except in his mind. He would get crushes on girls that lasted for months, and fantasize about entering a party with a pretty date on his arm and coolly pretending not to notice that the music had abruptly stopped and everyone had turned toward him in shocked disbelief. Alas, these crushes on his "fantasy girl friends" were not only always unrequited but generally unrevealed, save for the bunches of flowers or pieces of costume jewelry that Chuck would leave on their desks at school. Whenever he shed his anonymity he was usually hurt. During one "Daisy Day" at Terra Linda High, when all the girls had to relinquish the embroidered daisy they carried around with them to the first boy who could make them talk, Chuck managed to trick the cutest girl in his class out of her silence, only to have her ask for the cloth flower back later in the day so that she could award it to her boyfriend.

What made a bad situation even worse was the fact that Kerry had turned out to be an aggressive, smooth-talking charmer who attracted more than his share of female admirers. As did Russ Mead, a tall good-looking fellow who played the drums in his own band and lived with the Rileys for a year after his mother died and his father, much to his dismay, remarried his aunt. "It was enough to make your heart break," Oscar Riley says. "Chuck would be real popular during the week taking the kids to drive-in movies in his Corvair, but come weekends, Russ and Kerry would shower and spruce up and go off on dates all chirpy in Russ's Dodge Charger, which would sit idle all week because he'd rather have Chuck drive him around. I'd throw Chuck the keys to the Impala. 'Forget about those boys,' I'd say. 'Have a good time.' " But just as often Oscar noticed Chuck "pulling the shades down on reality" by taking his old Kawasaki out of the garage to go tearing around the hills, where no one would notice him alone on a Saturday night.

All this improved somewhat when Chuck had, in his own words, "something to offer besides myself." At least now girls were coming to him to buy his wares or hang around for the "freebies" he gave out. But Chuck never did manage to have a steady girl friend, partly because he just tried too hard. Any girl who seemed at all interested in him was the recipient of such a headlong rush that she would inevitably back off. As he got older Chuck's lack of sexual involvement caused him no little embarrassment among Marin's consenting teen-agers, and he resorted to embellishing the truth to save face. One evening he walked into a gathering of friends with his hair and clothes in disarray and announced that he had been approached by a young woman in a nearby park who was looking for a quick liaison and that afterward *she* had paid *him* $20 for the favor. Needless to say, the story was greeted with some skepticism.

But if Chuck's social standing improved after he began dealing marijuana, what did not improve, in fact grew worse, was his school work. In his junior year of high school his reading and writing skills were still at grade-school level and he had failed or received incompletes in a number of required courses. He kept reminding himself that he would be about to graduate, as were several of his best friends, had he not been left behind in the third grade. More calls were made to the Rileys by Chuck's guidance counselor, Peter Paolino, and finally a family conference was arranged. Paolino enumerated the possibilities: Chuck could quit outright, he could go to an ''alternative'' school for problem students or he could attend night classes to make up work. He chose night classes, but it was clear to everyone that he would never attend them. Oscar Riley, the high school dropout who had arduously worked his way through junior college at night, was furious. Even though he himself had never managed to capitalize on his own hard-won education, he angrily told his son: ''Now you'll be wearin' some dumb dog tag on your shirt when you're fifty.''

''I'll get by,'' Chuck said, shrugging his shoulders.

''Not in my house you won't,'' his father fired back. ''Not unless you get yourself a job pretty damn quick.''

He did, making home deliveries in the evening for Shakey's Pizza Parlor in Terra Linda along with his friend Mike Howard. The job was a real boon for Chuck, since by definition it was highly mobile and thus combined wonderfully well with his drug-dealing activities. At one point it even became the rage among high school kids to get stoned and order out some gut-wrenching combination such as Canadian bacon, anchovies and pineapple—a Hawaiian Delight. (For added effect marijuana might be sprinkled liberally on the pizza in place of oregano, a nice turn on the usual herbal exchange.) Chuck was more than willing to provide all the essential ingredients.

When rising gas prices forced Shakey's to retire its delivery vans, Chuck reverted full-time to the fine art of ''hanging out,'' something he did with considerable expertise. In Terra Linda, for want of drive-ins or even ordinary restaurants that welcomed teen-agers, hanging out generally took place in the Northgate shopping center or in private homes. On any Friday or Saturday evening you could drive by Northgate Drugs, which was a kind of unofficial youth activities clearing house, and find out what parties were going on within a twenty-mile radius. This generally meant that someone's parents had piled younger siblings and animals into the family station wagon and gone off to Lake Tahoe for the weekend or, in the summer months, on longer trips to visit relatives back East. During the day there were a number of alternatives. Homes where both parents worked (an untypical situation in Terra Linda) became temporary hangouts until one of the adults discovered a small mountain of marijuana seeds or beer empties and blew the whistle. For Chuck and his friends there was always the "cabin" in the hills above Santa Venetia—really a kind of open-sided lean-to with a mattress-strewn "porch" overlooking a lovely sunlight-speckled eucalyptus grove—that they had built out of scrap wood years before and biked to frequently. Then, for a number of months Chuck and several of his buddies had rented a garage off the freeway, filled it with stereo equipment and gathered there daily until the noise prompted the neighbors to alert the police. The current hangout was a three-room apartment that two of Chuck's friends rented on Third Street in San Rafael.

But no matter where the gathering place was, the activities that took place there were the same. Someone whose parents had just kicked him out was always crashing on the couch. Someone was always cleaning and dividing up a supply of marijuana. There was always rock music blasting out of a stereo, and occasionally, since many of Chuck's friends played instruments, live jam sessions. A variety of drugs were always being smoked, sniffed or swallowed along with cases of beer and half-gallons of Gallo Mountain Red, the preferred teen-age wine, sugar-laden and cheap. Chuck himself was doing so many drugs around this time—acid at least once a week, cocaine and marijuana on a daily basis—that he kept a kind of diary in which he listed what he had ingested or inhaled on a particular day and how high it had gotten him, one star to four like moving ratings. On one locally celebrated occasion he became so impatient with the relatively relaxed pace of pot smoking that he put a handful of it in an empty beer can, punctured holes in the bottom and attached it to the intake end of a vacuum cleaner, thereby inventing a kind of motorized hooka.

Needless to say, Oscar and Chuck were now on worse terms than ever. Oscar could not understand why Chuck made no effort to find another job or attend night school and was rankled that his son, at nineteen, was living at home without contributing to the family's maintenance. He tried to persuade him to attend an auto-mechanics school in Denver he had learned about and live with old friends of the Rileys' there. Afterward, Oscar argued unpersuasively, Chuck might open up a repair shop in Sheridan,

Arkansas, a small garageless town where one of his brothers lived.

Oscar had no idea of the extent of Chuck's drug use and attributed the withdrawn stare and overall "listlessness" his son often exhibited at the dinner table to "adjustment problems stemming from his weight." Once he had smelled a half-familiar sweetly pungent odor coming from the boys' bedroom ("I've been in enough Marin County coops to know what pot smells like") and mentioned his suspicion to Joanne. For her part Joanne was well aware that Kerry and Chuck smoked marijuana (she had, in fact, once found a full pound of it under Chuck's bed) but had decided against informing her husband. Exhibiting, as usual, more bark than bite, she had repeatedly threatened to turn them in to the police if she caught them selling pot, and she once made a conspicuous display of writing down the license plate of a particularly suspicious character who had walked in the front door unannounced "looking like he was from outer space." Thereafter Chuck's clients parked their cars on the side street and tapped on his bedroom window. Oscar could not understand why Chuck protested so much that summer when he put up screens on the windows. Although the Rileys had acquired enough teen-age lingo to appear, according to Joanne, "with it" (Joanne especially took to sprinkling her conversation with such expressions as "that's cool" and "good vibes"), they were remarkably naïve, for the time and place where they lived, about drugs. When she glimpsed Kerry snorting cocaine from a distance, Joanne simply asked him, "What on earth are you doing with a straw in your nose?" And Oscar regularly would uproot the feathery, thin-stemmed weeds that sprang up along the side of the house without having the slightest suspicion that they had grown from marijuana seeds Chuck carelessly tossed out of his bedroom window.

But if the Rileys were naïve about drugs, they were sufficiently aware of their children's lifestyle to wonder how Chuck could have considerably more spending money without a job than he had with one. The answer, of course, was that he *had* a job and that he was doing quite well at it. Along with his bread-and-butter trade in marijuana Chuck had begun dealing cocaine, a considerably more lucrative and less cumbersome activity. He could buy an ounce (about 28 grams) of high-grade cocaine for $1,200 and sell it for $80 a gram, realizing a neat 100 percent return on his investment. And it was amazing how much of the high-priced white powder Terra Linda kids could afford. One of his best customers, a junior at Terra Linda High, consumed several hundred dollars' worth weekly. And more than a quarter of Marin's high school population, even if they did not have access to that kind of money, were frequent users of the drug, according to the county's hard-pressed narcotics squad. Occasionally Chuck would sell cocaine to one or another of the wealthy young rock musicians who lived in Marin, generally at a popular San Rafael club called the Lion's Share. The fact that he knew such rock-'n'-roll heroes as Elvin Bishop and Steve Miller—and could gain admittance to the coveted backstage area at the Lion's Share while his friends were forced to remain out front—gave him no small amount of reflected glory in their eyes.

At the time, Chuck was getting his cocaine from a flashy high-living Marin County dealer he knew only as Paco. Although Chuck's age, Paco drove an Alfa Romeo and rented a fifteen-room, $800-a-month hilltop house in which he kept several live-in girl friends and two mean Doberman pinschers. He also kept an enormous inventory of marijuana on hand in large screwtop jars neatly labeled Panama Red, Colombia, Acapulco Gold, etc., like so many herbal teas in a healthfood store. He kept his cocaine in a family-size mayonnaise jar, and the first time Chuck was at the house the jar was nearly full of the shiny white crystals—over a pound of the stuff, worth $20,000 on the street.

Cocaine passes through many hands in its underground passage from South America to a small-time dealer like Chuck Riley, and each middleman not only boosts the price but generally cuts the product—with a variety of substances ranging from sugar to speed—in the bargain. Since Chuck was dealing more for the prestige and acceptance it gave him than for the money, he tried to provide his coke customers, as he did his marijuana customers, with the best deal possible. Paco sold him high-grade coke, which meant that it was 80–90 percent pure, and Chuck prided himself on not cutting it further, or cutting it only minimally, never below 75 percent. But it was his method of packaging the grams and half-grams he distributed that Chuck felt really added "a touch of class" to his operation. Where most street dealers would simply wrap their merchandise in tinfoil or inside an intricately folded packet of paper, Chuck used tiny zippered plastic change purses that he bought, a few at a time so as not to arouse suspicion, at local five-and-dime stores.

Despite all his emphasis on fair prices and good service, Chuck still made a healthy profit on every ounce of cocaine he bought from Paco. True, his risks were now considerably greater, since California was about to liberalize its marijuana laws and the Marin County narcotics agents were much more interested in the coke traffic, but then, so was his income. With his newly expanded line of goods Chuck could easily make $500 a week profit working fewer hours than before, and when the occasional windfall sale landed his way, considerably more.

His coke dealing also had an unexpected side benefit. Since he generally had an abundant supply on hand, he was using it more himself, starting with a "wake up" snort in the early morning to get his "energy level" up and continuing at increasingly frequent intervals throughout the day. Cocaine, like the Dexedrine his doctor continued to prescribe, is a central-nervous-system stimulant and an appetite depressant, and so Chuck began to take off some weight—about forty pounds—in the months before he met Marlene, although at five feet ten and 250 pounds he was far from being a department-store mannequin.

Chuck was also surrounded, for the first time in his life, with a group of good friends. They were all fairly representative middle-class kids who shared a lifestyle that centered around music, cars and drugs. They seemed to be rebelling against their parents' social and economic striving but in a curiously listless way. They were totally devoid of ambition of any sort—either for college or careers or even new experiences. They neither sought out the cultural variety of San Francisco nor the natural beauty of West Marin that lay just beyond the expensive developments where they grew up. Occasionally they would drop acid and head for the beach. As Mike Howard described a typical scene: "Someone would always let a handful of sand sift through his fingers and say, 'Just imagine how many grains of sand there are on this beach.' Everyone would think about the question for a while and say 'Amazing' or 'Far out' and then we'd go home." Their rebelliousness, such as it was, had none of the social vibrancy of the sixties antiwar protests or search for alternative lifestyles, and they all felt great regret at having missed the heady excitement of that era, when so much seemed to be happening so quickly, much of it in nearby Berkeley and San Francisco.

They seemed to be continually fighting a losing battle with boredom. Everything they did—including the drugs they routinely ingested—seemed old hat. In a sense, there was no way for them to rebel that had not been tried by their older brothers and sisters, and almost, in the permissive atmosphere of mellow Marin, nothing to rebel against. Even the very listlessness that most characterized their protest seemed a repetition of old James Dean movies. In many ways they were an anachronistic generation, a throwback to the era portrayed in *American Graffiti*, that late-flowering fifties movie that was set in 1962 and filmed in San Rafael ten years later. (A few of Chuck's friends lucky enough to own period cars were hired by the movie company for the cruising scenes.) In fact, a brief exchange of dialogue in the film that perfectly captured much of their daily activity became a kind of running joke with the group at the time. "Where ya goin'?" one character asks another. "Nowhere," his friend replies, to which the first responds, "Well, you mind if I come along?"

Two crucial changes in teen-age lifestyle since the fifties made the comparison inexact—the abundance of both hard drugs and casual sex. For Chuck Riley, who was approaching twenty without ever having had a girl friend, only one change had occurred.

Four

After moving to the Bay Area, Marlene and her parents stayed at the Terra Linda Holiday Inn while they looked for a house to rent. The logical place to begin was Terra Linda itself, respectably affluent without being as expensive as some of the posher communities closer to the city (*"un barrio muy tranquilo,"* Jim wrote to his former secretary in Quito, Pilar Saajaramillo). At the first real estate agency, a young woman named Sandy Targ told them about an "Eichler"—a glass-sided tract house named for the man who developed Terra Linda—that was available a few doors down from where she herself lived on Del Ganada Road.

Naomi was, as Jim wrote to an Ecuadorian friend, in "seventh heaven," although "she would have preferred for us to spend our last *sucre* to buy a house right away." In the past Naomi had always seemed more stable and energetic after a move, when her small world of household shopping was, briefly, more important to Jim than his business affairs—and this one was no exception. The family shopped for living-room furniture, kitchen appliances and a new car—a green Vega station wagon, Jim's choice, practical and efficient. It even seemed possible that Naomi would become more active socially. When Sandy Targ got married shortly after the Olives moved in, Jim and Naomi attended the church wedding and the reception at her house following the ceremony. It was their first chance to meet some of their neighbors. Jim mingled with his usual glad-handed affability, jotting down names and phone numbers of potential friends and customers. Nervously, Naomi followed behind him nursing a single drink the whole afternoon, as was generally her custom in social situations. She managed to let people know that she was not thrilled with the need to cook and clean house again now that the family was living in what she referred to as "reduced circumstances."

It was perfectly true that without the company perks and cheap domestic labor of overseas life, the Olives were undergoing a certain amount of economic, along with a great deal of cultural, shock. Jim worked harder than he ever had in his life, but as in the past, his long-delayed dream of a business of his own meant precious little business at all. He got up at six in the morning without an alarm, picked up mail at the small post office down the block when it opened at eight, and spent the rest of the day trying to convince owners of marginal businesses that they needed to increase their overhead further by hiring him as a consultant. After renting office equipment, he spent evenings working in the converted garage until late at night trying to live up to his daytime promises—not very successfully, according to some of his clients. He joined the Terra Linda Rotary Club and the Tip Club, a group of local businessmen who traded information at weekly luncheons. He took a business accounting course at a University of California extension school two evenings a week. It was tough going for a man of his age, but he joked about his "nonprofit status" and remained, in the best Alexander Hamilton Institute tradition, optimistic and forward-looking.

Six weeks after arriving, Jim wrote Pilar Saajaramillo about his working day: "I felt just as backward and uncomfortable as if I had never sold anything in my life. I had to force myself to walk into people's stores and offices and tell them my story. And I didn't sell anybody anything. I didn't know my line well enough. I had two outright rejections ('Leave me alone, I'm busy'), four bored *impaciencias*, and two people who were much interested in my ideas but I just didn't have the knowledge to put it across. Then I got one guy who was sure I was going to save his life! And I have a date with him tomorrow. If I can make one Christian every day, I'll get rich. That's the nicest thing about selling. When you finally get rich, pie in the sky!"

The fact that Jim quickly became "buried under an avalanche of work" meant that he had little time for Marlene during a period when she desperately needed him. All spring and summer she kept begging him to take her to the beach and he kept begging off with the pressure of work. As soon as he could "pay the rent" he would take her to all the beaches she wanted. "Inside of a year," he wrote an Ecuadorian friend, "we'll all be sitting pretty—maybe I'll replace those golf clubs I sold in Quito."

It was a lot of deferred gratification to ask of a fourteen-year-old girl who had come to rely on her father's constant availability in a slower-paced world—particularly one who was going through the agonies of adjusting to a strange and frightening environment. When Marlene left Ecuador she was a shy and introverted girl, pretty but plump, who had never been to an unchaperoned party, much less smoked marijuana, and the distant rumors she had heard about drugs and sex being easily available to American teen-agers fed her anxieties. She was more at home with Latins than with Americans, in Spanish than in English (which she spoke with a slight accent and an occasional misuse of vocabulary). Her clothes (loose-fitting) and her taste in music (bubblegum) were all wrong for the cliquish, status-conscious teen-age world she was about to enter. A full year after the Olives arrived, Jim wrote to Pilar in an untypically downbeat mood: "We are completely rootless and have left all our friends behind. Sure we are making many new acquaintances here, but it is still too early to feel completely at home. Marlene still suffers from pangs of homesickness and nostalgia. Good reason. In Quito she was a privileged character. Here she is just another brat in blue jeans. But at least we are finally getting a smile out of her now and then."

Marin County, California, was a rude shock for Marlene. In the beginning she cried every day, slept a lot, and on weekends she watched TV from morning to night, getting up from the living-room couch only to go to the bathroom or get a soft drink out of the refrigerator. Jim tried to convince her to use the Terra Linda community center a few blocks away to meet friends, and gave her frequent small presents to coax her out of her lethargy—both to no avail. The few times she went outside, the streets seemed deserted. After one such tentative exploration she described her new neighbors in a poem as: "Graveyard people peeking out/Through half-drawn blinds . . ./Who live among straight lines."

Jim registered Marlene in the eighth grade at Vallecito Junior High School even though the term was nearly over. On Monday morning he drove her to school, accompanying her as far as her hall locker. After he left, Marlene couldn't find her way to class, and embarrassed to ask, sat outside on a schoolyard bench writing furiously in her notebook in order to look occupied. She was wearing a pleated skirt and a round-collared blouse with a sweater wrapped around her waist to further hide her chubbiness, and she felt horribly conspicuous amid the unisex school uniform of tight jeans and T-shirts. When she finally got to class she had no idea what was going on and felt that the kids were making fun of her for looking straight and talking funny and even for her name (when her English teacher read the roll a boy in the back of the room stage-whispered "Olive Oyl" to a flurry of half-suppressed titters). After the final bell she ran home.

For the next few days she wandered from class to class in a daze, "memorizing the floor tiles" so she wouldn't have to look around. Always shy and easily made to blush, she now found it impossible to look people straight in the eye for fear "they would see how scared I was," or to speak out in class beyond answering roll call. Before the end of the week she reported to the nurse during second period—her dreaded English class—with a stomach ache and was sent home. The next day she skipped her physical education class, embarrassed to dress in the skimpy gym uniform. The stomach ache and queasiness became a persistent low-level complaint, like "tiny mice nibbling on my insides." When the discomfort subsided it left a "cold, hollow feeling" behind.

The kids in school seemed unapproachable. She knew what was happening when a group of them would stand in a tight circle passing around a makeshift cigarette. But she could not at first understand why some of them—the hard-core "pillheads," it turned out—teetered through the corridors on rubber legs and sat through classes with eyes that looked like one-way mirrors. She longed for the weekend to arrive, but when it did, she stayed alone in her room. The Saturday-morning horror movies on TV, *Creature Features,* became a regular ritual, cathartic because they channeled an otherwise free-floating anxiety. She kept her room dark, and when she wasn't watching TV she lay for hours on her bed staring out the window at a small, thin juniper tree precariously planted in the side yard. The tree was so fragile that it had been braced to the ground with wire, and Marlene came to identify its leafless, lonely existence with her own. She began calling radio station KFRC to request her favorite pop songs and struck up a telephone friendship with one of the women who took requests, telling her how much she missed South America and longed to return. One song that was always on her list that first summer was Diana Ross's "Love Child," a narrative about a woman born out of wedlock who refuses to risk a repetition of the experience.

There were more active but equally solitary pursuits. Marlene quickly unpacked her beloved Barbie dolls (there were a dozen of them) so that she could make her daydreams palpable on the bedroom floor. No longer did they represent imaginary siblings. She chose the blondest, most dimple-cheeked among them to represent herself, and the others became girl friends who loyally helped her resolve her most perplexing problems, such as how to choose among the crush of boys who competed for her attention.

But her favorite activity—and most persistent escape—was writing. To improve her command of English, which others never saw as especially inadequate, she bought a paperback called *Power Words* that listed key words and phrases from different disciplines, and she began memorizing several of them at a time. She wrote long letters (some twenty or thirty pages) to friends in Ecuador or former schoolmates who had moved back to the States ahead of her. Some she sent. Others, clearly more therapeutic than communicative in intent, she simply stored away in her desk or dresser drawers. The unhappier she grew in Terra Linda, the more idealized became her memories of life in South America.

She also began writing reams of poetry, at first scattered efforts jotted down on scraps of paper and later more disciplined poems that she reworked in different versions and copied into her "poetry books"—loose-leaf-bound sheaves replete with jacket designs and tables of contents. Some of them were rhymed and metered, others in free verse. All of them, even the ones she reworked, were written quickly, often so quickly that they bordered on automatic writing. They contain a great deal of the self-indulgent, romantic posturing one might expect from a teenage girl—more poeticizing·than poetry. But there are many striking fragments that deal with real experiences, or at least fantasies that seemed real to Marlene. Loneliness was the prevailing—almost exclusive—theme of these early poems:·

> I sit in a cold, dark room
> listening intently
> for something that's not here.

It's just another empty space,
another empty day,
another empty moment.

There's nothing to do
but listen to my thoughts
and they are as empty as I feel.

I am lonely
but no one can help me
for I am lost within myself
in an empty space, trying to get out.

But there is no way out.

Because Marlene had been sleeping so much and complaining about stomach aches virtually from the moment the Olives arrived in Terra Linda, Jim decided to take her for a medical checkup in late May. The man who had been recommended to him as a family physician, Dr. Sheldon Tapley, was something of an eccentric in dress and manner—a sandy-haired, full-bearded general practitioner who spoke through clenched teeth and was much given to wild sport shirts, such as the pattern of red, white and blue stars he wore the first day he examined Marlene. Dr. Tapley took down a brief medical history of Marlene's past asthmatic and urinary conditions from Jim and listened to her talk about her problems at school. ("Not very happy," he scribbled in her medical record. "All make big joke out of conversations with me.") After Dr. Tapley gave her an upper GI it was immediately apparent to him that Marlene had developed a raging duodenal ulcer. He put her on a diet of baby foods and Maalox and wrote out prescriptions for a sleeping pill and sedative.

After that, Jim tried to spend more time with Marlene. He let her accompany him to the post office when it opened, and on weekends and holidays sometimes took her on his rounds visiting clients or the part-time bookkeeper he had hired to help him keep their accounts straight, Mrs. Winnie Stockstill. Father and daughter shopped for food together at Scotty's Market, searched out garage sales looking for household odds and ends, and frequently, when Naomi had locked herself in her room with a "headache," went out to dinner together. At home Jim taught Marlene to use his rented office machines and would pay her, in addition to her

$10 weekly allowance, ten cents each for addressing envelopes and making out bills. In the evenings Jim would watch television with Marlene before returning to his office to finish GBS paperwork or study his accounting textbooks until midnight. On Sundays, Marlene occasionally accompanied Jim to the early service at the Episcopal church he had joined in Terra Linda, and, briefly, she joined the youth group Rev. Barnette had organized. Even Naomi volunteered to help out at a summer camp for poor children that the church sponsored, putting in a busy day cooking and cleaning. Afterward Rev. Barnette's wife, Lulabelle, thinking she had found a "good, cheerful worker," called on Naomi repeatedly but could never again coax her out of the house.

One Sunday not long after the Olives moved to Terra Linda they visited Jim's boyhood friend George Koth, who had retired a decade earlier to Atherton, an affluent suburb south of San Francisco. Although the two couples had exchanged annual Christmas notes over the years, they had not actually seen each other since 1945, when George Koth was the production manager of the Acme Electric Co. in Cuba, New York. George's wife, Diana, a matronly woman who gave piano lessons, had preserved a mental picture of the shy and beautiful Naomi Wagner as fresh as yesterday's snapshot—"curly blond hair to her shoulders, blue eyes and a lovely, lovely figure. She never said a word, so I got accustomed just to looking at her." When Naomi Olive walked in the door three decades later, Mrs. Koth had to catch her breath from the shock. Naomi's skin was the pasty gray of newsprint, her hair a coarse steely brown thatch, her puffy, alcohol-bloated body clothed in a frumpy dress. Moreover, the woman who had never said a word now rambled on incessantly, much of her conversation only semicoherent, and all of it, according to the culture-conscious Mrs. Koth, who had fought hard to keep her head above the dishwater all these years, trivial beyond endurance. "It was like she had just gotten out of solitary confinement," Diana Koth recalls. "After what I learned later about her life I realized that's just what had happened."

When Naomi turned from her daily activities to more intimate subjects, they seemed equally trivialized—what she called her "female problems" and a long disjointed account about adopting Marlene. The latter, according to Mrs. Koth, came "out of the blue" and ended with "this nice doctor in Norfolk calling Naomi up one day and saying, 'I found just the one!' " But despite Naomi's insistence on telling the story, the Koths were both struck by the fact that mother and daughter scarcely exchanged a glance all day, whereas Jim and Marlene seemed to have an easy, affectionate rapport and several times made private jokes to each other in Spanish. Jim seemed equally solicitous of Naomi, putting her back on the mental track when she lost her thought or gently saying, when she wandered too far afield, "I don't think George and Diana want to hear about that, dear." Naomi, for her part, always referred to Jim, with obvious pride of possession, as "my Jimmy." Having tired of Naomi's company long before the group went out for a late Sunday lunch, Mrs. Koth made sure that she sat next to Jim at the restaurant.

He seemed hardly to have changed over the years. Mrs. Koth thought he was still "extremely likable, always smiling, the life of the party." At one point during lunch he offered to show her some Latin dance steps right then and there—an offer she politely refused. Back at her house after lunch Mrs. Koth asked Marlene into the playroom, hoping to "draw her out" and escape Naomi at the same time. "The thing she kept coming back to," Mrs. Koth recalls, "was how deeply in love she was with a Spanish musician. She said they were engaged and her parents wanted to keep them apart." In truth, Marlene was simply overdramatizing, as was her wont, the puppy love she felt for a guitar-playing Ecuadorian boy she had become friendly with shortly before moving to California.

The afternoon was a rare family outing for the Olives. Even the extra time that Jim tried to spend with Marlene skirted the edges of his sixteen-hour workdays and was further diminished in her eyes by comparison with the lavish attention he had been able to devote to her in South America. She felt abandoned by him, left with half a father just when she needed a father and a half. In a poem she titled "My Reasons for Leaving" (although she went nowhere, at least not then), she wrote:

> no one stops
> to step into my life
> and those in it have long ago
> fallen asleep.
> I have been empty for so long.

Although she wanted desperately to make friends at school, she remembers being so frightened of her classmates that she "jumped when someone said 'Hi!' to me." But toward the end of the school year she was befriended by a cute, diminutive, blond-haired girl in her ceramics class named Patti Metzger, who lived nearby. They stayed overnight at each other's homes, playing records in their rooms and talking about boys. At fourteen, Patti, like most of her contemporaries, was beginning to smoke marijuana, but whenever she offered some to her new friend, Marlene begged off, unconvincingly claiming that she was "allergic" to it. The girls often went to movies together that summer, including one called *Butterflies Are Free,* a maudlin story about the love between a fledgling actress and a self-sufficient blind boy. Thereafter butterflies of all stripes became a passion for Marlene. The more restricted she felt at home, the more butterflies she added to her collection—butterfly bracelets on her wrist, butterfly appliqués on her jeans, butterfly posters on her bedroom walls, and even, eventually, a butterfly tattoo on her thigh.

Marlene also grew fond of Patti's mother, a no-nonsense registered nurse with short-cropped hair and a trim figure. With her effortless juggling of domestic and career interests and her ability to be both friend and parent to her four children, Helen Metzger represented a painful contrast to Naomi in Marlene's eyes. (As with other friends' mothers she admired, Marlene started calling Mrs. Metzger "Mom" soon after they met, much to the older woman's surprise.) It was through the Metzgers that Marlene, to her father's dismay, became involved in Eastern religion.

Helen Metzger's own introduction to such unfamiliar ways had come about several years earlier, after her eldest son, who was ten at the time, was killed by a drunk driver as he and Patti were walking along a quiet street near their house. In her bereavement Mrs. Metzger found some consolation in Eastern religion, with its more pronounced emphasis on the eternal round of life and death than her Methodist heritage provided. For some time she and Patti had been involved in an organization called Nichorin Shoshu, a Japanese Buddhist sect whose followers believed that personal contentment lay in the rhythmic repetition of a simple chant: *"Nam-nyoto-renge-kyo"* ("Worship the doctrine of the good law"). The small San Rafael chapter of the sect held nightly meetings at the homes of adherents—often the Metzgers'.

As members were encouraged to bring new recruits to the meetings, Patti and her mother began to take Marlene. She was instantly attracted to the sect, as much for its exotic ritual (in

South America she had much preferred to attend Catholic mass with her Indian maids than her father's stripped-down Episcopalian service) as for the companionship it provided her. She bought a *gohanzan*, a Buddhist mandala upon which the devotee is instructed to fix his gaze while chanting, and housed it in her bedroom in a kind of altar, a black boxlike affair that resembles a children's puppet theater. Lighting candles and burning incense before the *gohanzan*, she would sit cross-legged and chant softly, "*Nam-nyoto-renge-kyo, nam-nyoto-renge kyo, nam-nyoto-renge-kyo* . . ." One night Jim passed by Marlene's room on his way to bed, heard the strange sounds and smelled the incense. He opened the door, peeped in, flipped on the lights, stared incredulously at the black box and said, "What the hell is *that*?"

Since just such skeptical parents were the very purpose of "home visitations" by long-time devotees, a few nights later a couple of young, clean-cut Buddhists appeared in the Olives' living room to explain Marlene's strange nightly doings as unalarmingly as possible. "We stress being a winner in life," one of them reassured Jim. "The philosophy is based on practical benefit and not faith. If you need a new house, a new car, a new job—chant for it. Then when you get the proof that the chant works, you'll have faith." Jim Olive, blind to the obvious parallels between Nichorin Shoshu's "positive thinking" philosophy and the Alexander Hamilton Institute's, remained skeptical. Although Marlene's enthusiasm for the Buddhist sect soon languished, until the end of his life whenever she got herself into trouble Jim Olive wondered aloud if "those crazy Buddhists" were involved.

At her father's prompting Marlene took a course in batik during summer vacation. It was a pleasant, all-girl class conducted on the patio of San Rafael High School by a goateed, pipe-smoking art teacher named Jerry Fitch, who for many years had also taught painting classes at San Quentin. With her fluent Spanish, Marlene helped out by translating for two summer exchange students from Mexico in the class. Initially Fitch was impressed with Marlene's "depth of experience," for it seemed, in the easygoing atmosphere of the art class, that whatever turn the conversation took, Marlene could contribute some personal anecdote, usually concerning her father. "If someone mentioned motorcycles, her dad was a champion racer," the instructor recalled. "If it was a foreign country, he'd been there. If it was jewelry, he was a master silversmith."

During her first summer in Terra Linda, Marlene also found that most elemental status symbol among teen-age girls—a boyfriend. It came about through the mediation of a neighbor of the Olives' on Del Ganada Road, Marian Robeson, who as the wife of a retired Air Force officer shared with them the experience of settling down in the United States after living abroad for many years. Marlene found in Mrs. Robeson a sympathetic listener to her problems of adjustment. Once a week Marlene would come over in the afternoon to clean house or occasionally just to do favors for the older woman. "She was just crazy about her daddy," Mrs. Robeson recalls, "and Jim about her. If she was still here when it got dark, he'd walk over to get her even though we're only a block away and the neighborhood's as safe as can be. I'd see them walking home with their arms around each other."

One day Marlene came over to ask Mrs. Robeson if she wanted her car washed. A short time later Mark Fowler, the neighborhood kid who normally performed the chore, roared up on his motorcycle to find out why someone else was washing the car, and the two teen-agers struck up a conversation that led to a date.

They saw each other for the rest of the summer. When Marlene wanted to leave the house after her ten o'clock curfew, she simply unfastened the screen on her bedroom window and crawled out to meet Mark at his house a few blocks away for long soul-searching talks or drives in his yellow Dodge pickup. But at other times of the day the young man, a courteous, clean-cut, hard-working fellow, was always welcome around the house. Long after he and Marlene broke up, Fowler did yard work and odd jobs for Jim Olive, and also served him as an unpaid consultant on teen-age mores when Marlene began getting into trouble.

In the fall the Olives bought the house at 353 Hibiscus, with Jim using his real estate experience to draw up the escrow himself in order to save money. As it was, Naomi had to give up her dream of a four-bedroom Eichler with an atrium for a more modest one-story tract house of similar design. The floor plan was L-shaped, with the shorter leg consisting of a combined living room–dining room with a sloping "cathedral" ceiling, a kitchen that was only partially enclosed, and a two-car garage. The longer leg was a narrow hallway that connected four small bedrooms and two bathrooms. Jim took the master bedroom at the end of the corridor and converted the adjacent bedroom into his office. Marlene and Naomi occupied the two facing bedrooms near the living room, although Naomi spent much of her time during the day in the master bedroom, where she kept her clothes and cosmetics. The rear wall of the L was almost entirely glass from floor to ceiling, but all that could be seen through it was the concrete patio area, a narrow fringe of grass and the six-foot-high wood fence that enclosed the house on all but the street side and isolated it from neighboring houses. The isolation was made more complete by the fact that the only window that looked out on the street was the smallest one in the house, located above the kitchen sink.

Even Naomi's attempts to brighten up the house with glass bowls of plastic fruit and, everywhere, vases containing red and white plastic flowers of indeterminate species had the opposite effect. But the most curious "decorative" touches were the paintings on the living- and dining-room walls, which seemed to indicate, as a psychiatrist who walked through the house after the crime would later testify in court, that "someone very disturbed lived there." The oddest one, placed near the front door, was a painting that made the viewer appreciate hidden nuances in the phrase "still life." It was a realistic, technically accomplished scene with traces of dislocation and decay apparent everywhere—in the pewter teapot with its lid ajar, in the dried-up twigs and leaves scattered around it on a burnished table, in the bunches of shriveled grapes discolored to a bluish-gray.

For a time Naomi continued to accompany Jim on social calls. One hot summer day they visited the clothing boutique that Alene Shilder, the wife of a GBS client, had recently opened in Petaluma. Wearing white gloves and her hair in a tight bun, Naomi seemed to the owner, a plain-talking, friendly young woman, too "prim and proper" for the casual circumstances and the wilting weather. "But that was what I'd have expected from Jim's wife," Alene Shidler recalls. "No matter how hot the weather, he was always wearing a suit and tie and had his fingernails perfectly manicured and every hair in place like he had just slipped out of a shower and gotten dressed. 'Jesus H. Christ, Jim,' I'd tease him, 'why don't you get a little daring and unbutton your collar!' "

But what did seem odd to Alene Shilder was the way Naomi relied on Jim for the smallest decision, even seeking out his approval before accepting a cup of coffee. "Naomi stood by the counter the whole time she was here holding her pocketbook in front of her with both hands while Jim went through the dresses and asked her if she liked this or that. Finally Naomi explained that she didn't like to try on clothes in stores because she was used to having them sent to her house for approval. At that point I said to myself, 'Lady, this place ain't Yves St. Laurent's salon and you sure ain't Jackie Kennedy.' "

Then, not long after the Olives bought their place on Hibiscus Way, a young couple from San Francisco, the Edemadfars, moved in next door and threw an open house for their friends in the city. Because she was used to the easier camaraderie of her old Haight-Ashbury neighborhood, Shirley Edemadfar was particularly struck by the fact that she hadn't so much as caught sight of a single neighbor in the two weeks since her arrival ("The Olives' bedroom was twenty feet from mine, but with these high fences and recessed doorways it might as well have been twenty miles"), and she invited them to the party. Jim and Naomi seemed to mingle well with the other guests and enjoy themselves. Naomi nursed a single Scotch the whole afternoon and her only conversational eccentricity was an obsessive concern with the mortgage payments she and Jim had recently incurred. What Shirley Edemadfar could not have known at the time was that the first agreeable social exchange with her new neighbor would be, with the exception of rare sightings at the Northgate Safeway, also her last—nor that the loud, invective-strewn arguments between mother and daughter would soon become her only daily confirmation of the fact that she did indeed have neighbors on Hibiscus Way.

As the months went by, Naomi's contact with the outside world became, as it had in Ecuador, increasingly sporadic, and for long periods of time could only be said to have existed at all because she answered the telephone in Jim's office when he was out on his rounds. And then one day she stopped answering it, with the usual complaint that he was neglecting his "family responsibilities" for business, and the usual justification that she was not, as she had been briefly when she helped him run the apartment complex in St. Petersburg twenty years earlier, his secretary anymore. Jim bought a telephone answering machine, and accompanied by Marlene, took over the bulk of the family shopping, while Naomi turned the house into a plywood fortress. Just as she had in Ecuador, she crammed the hallway closet and a storage recess in the garage with every conceivable variety of canned food—canned fruits, vegetables, soups, spaghetti, mushroom gravy—in quantities more suited to a thriving neighborhood market than to a private home, with only her rationale changing from the threat of political revolution to the threat of an earthquake and power failures. And what storage space was left over—the bedroom and hallway closets, a cedar chest in the dining area and a stack of cartons in the garage—was packed with the pastel-colored towel sets she still purchased by the dozen to cushion her isolation, like a mother bird whose nesting instinct has gone awry.

Alone in her room, Naomi read her women's magazines and chain-smoked Benson & Hedges, often while soaking her legs in a tub of hot water to relieve the drawing pains she had complained of ever since her hysterectomy. Other physical complaints, both imaginary and real, often kept her in bed, and even when she admitted to being well she napped every afternoon for two hours, lying on her back with the black cat, Rascal, resting on her stomach. To fill the empty hours Naomi watched police shows on television, her favorite being the endlessly reassuring *Barnaby Jones,* with its avuncular detective-hero who weekly overcame the world's evil through his wits alone.

It is a common phenomenon for habitual viewers of such shows to refashion the world in their image—seeing it only as a menacing place where the ordinary citizen is a helpless prey to criminals lurking in every shadow—and Naomi, whose natural suspicion this was in any case, certainly posed no exception. In South America she thought the wives of Jim's colleagues were out to do her in, but in Terra Linda, where she knew no one, her enemies became both more remote and more real, until eventually paranoid fantasies were her bedside companions.

What Jim and Marlene referred to as Naomi's "voices" had been going on for years, but the situation seemed to grow much worse in Terra Linda. Naomi would sometimes hold entire conversations with four or five participants besides herself, ghosts from her past that still haunted her, such as her brother and her father, or Jim's mother and sister, who had always "looked down" on her and had "stolen" the inheritance from under her nose. She would play all the roles in different voices, staccato bursts of angry invective that would suddenly burst into open speech, as if she could contain the early parts of the conversations in her mind until they reached a certain emotional pitch.

Then from behind her locked bedroom door would issue an angry argument between Naomi and, to all appearances, several previously unannounced visitors:

"How could you do this to me?"

"What do you mean?"

"You know perfectly well what I mean. Pry into my private affairs."

"Calm down, Naomi."

"She's only trying to help."

"The hell she is. I know her real motive."

"What?"

"Ruin my marriage."

If one of Marlene's friends, sitting in the living room or her bedroom across the hall, happened to overhear Naomi's "voices," Marlene would hasten to explain, quite matter-of-factly, "Oh, that's just my mom talking to herself. She's nuts."

Naomi's fears spurred her drinking, and her drinking, of course, exaggerated her fears. She was rarely falling-down drunk, but she often kept herself in a mild alcoholic daze by alternating sips of Scotch and her favorite Coors beer. Dressed in a housecoat, with her graying hair half trapped in a net, she would put one of her favorite Henry Mancini tapes on the stereo and swirl around the living room, reliving the days when she was the belle of the Friday-night dance at the lakeside, lantern-lit pavilion in Cuba, New York. Or she would wander distractedly from room to room all day indulging in her one true passion—the care and feeding of her beloved "fitzes."

Naomi had brought some of her fish tanks with her from Ecuador and purchased others at the Pet Arcade in Northgate Mall, until eventually there were nearly a dozen complete tropical aquariums spread throughout the house, ranging in size from ten gallons up to fifty. The largest tank contained hundreds of tiny guppies of every conceivable hue and stripe, with tails that were round or shaped into swords and lyres and opalescent, shimmering veils. Naomi lavished hours of attention on her fish each day, dropping just the right amount of tiny brine shrimp into their tanks through an eyedropper, isolating the sick and newborn in small bowls that she kept in the kitchen for special treatment, and laboriously changing their water. But most of the time she simply sat in front of an aquarium and stared at her fish for hours, learning to distinguish the sexes of different varieties, studying their feeding and breeding habits, the way the catfish sucked algae off the sides of the aquarium or the angelfish transferred their eggs from one leafy hiding place to another almost daily. She had favorites among the fish and would babble aloud to them, much to Marlene's embarrassment when she had a friend over: ''C'mere little fitze . . . tha'at's right . . . aren't ya looking *cute* today . . . yes you are . . . you are you are . . . you're my little baby . . . don't you let that big bad thing bother you . . .''

It was an orderly, self-contained world compared to the ragged one she inhabited, the fish sliding easefully among the plants and the rocks, nothing to disturb or frighten them. So peaceful. Every Wednesday—the day the Pet Arcade received its shipment of fresh brine shrimp—she made a trip to Northgate Mall to replenish and augment that world, her one planned venture of the week.

Naomi's mental illness and Jim's preoccupation with work made them both less attentive than they might have been to troubling changes in Marlene's behavior. The first indication that Jim could not ignore occurred shortly after Marlene began ninth grade in the fall, when she and a girl friend were arrested for shoplifting at the Payless drugstore in Northgate Mall. It was a routine event at the aptly named store, which had become such a frequent target of teen-age theft—especially girls stealing cosmetics—that it had been forced to hire a full-time plain-clothes security officer and make it store policy to call the police rather than parents if the value of the stolen goods exceeded a few dollars. That afternoon Marlene and her friend Sara Glenn were lingering around the cosmetics counter long enough to arouse the suspicion of secury officer Thomas Rodd, who watched them put several items in plastic shopping bags from a nearby boutique and set aside others to pay for. For Rodd, a veteran security guard, it was a standard MO; the ''vehicle'' to transport merchandise, the furtive looks around, the dodge of paying for some items. (''A real professional,'' he says, ''doesn't so much care if he's seen as that he gets away quickly.'') Rodd directed the two girls to his office, where five other teen-agers were at that moment waiting for the police to arrive on that sticky-fingered Saturday afternoon.

To instill a proper fear of the law into the two ''female juveniles,'' as the police report of the incident identified them, they were placed in separate windowless holding tanks until their parents could be called. When Jim arrived at the station house he and Marlene had their first joint encounter with juvenile officer Scott Nelson, a short, tousled-haired, gap-toothed cop who, although thirty-one, appeared younger than some of the kids he arrested. It was an image the boyish-looking lieutenant deliberately cultivated in order to "relate" better to his constituency. Instead of a police uniform he sported bold-patterned print shirts, bell-bottom slacks, platform shoes and enough turquoise-and-silver rings and bracelets to assure the most frightened runaway of being in sympathetic hands. For the fact was that Nelson's job as half of the San Rafael police department's two-man juvenile bureau was to keep the town's 14,000 potential "youth offenders" *out* of the overcrowded juvenile court system if at all possible. Officially he was not called a policeman or even a juvenile officer but a "diversion officer," and as such he had at his disposal a wide variety of community-oriented programs to help convince a wayward teen-ager of his wrongdoing, along with the counseling skills he had acquired in night-school psychology courses at the College of Marin. But with all these skills and community organizations at his command, the one element that Nelson knew mattered most in helping straighten out a confused teen-ager was the one he immediately spotted in Jim Olive—"a parent who really cares about what happens to his kid." It made his job not so much easier as barely possible.

Since he was well into his "Christmas rush," Nelson did not devote a great deal of time to Marlene Olive, a first offender charged with petty theft. He wrote out a juvenile citation, but true to the origins of the system, it was directed at Jim as the responsible party and not at Marlene, charging him to appear before Nelson at a "diversion hearing" a few weeks later.

According to Marlene, after a brief reprimand on the drive home Jim's reaction to the incident was to "let the whole thing slide." Naomi was another matter completely. Before Marlene even got out of the car her mother was on the slate walkway in her housedress screaming rhetorical questions at her for the whole neighborhood to hear: "Why do you do things like this? Don't you know you can get arrested? Don't your father and mother take good enough care of you so you don't have to steal?" The aftermath of the incident followed a pattern that would be repeated many times. Marlene was restricted to the house for the rest of the weekend and forbidden ever again to see her friend Sara, who was taken by the Olives to be the instigating party. Jim did his best to pacify Naomi, and after his initial outburst, Marlene as well. A month later, when Jim and Marlene reported to San Rafael headquarters for their scheduled diversion hearing, Scott Nelson stamped the juvenile citation "Reprimanded and dismissed."

The other disturbing change in Marlene's behavior, even before she entered ninth grade at Terra Linda High School that fall, was her extreme moodiness. She was either hypertense and irritable or tired and listless all the time, with seemingly no middle ground. She still slept a great deal, occasionally even dozing off in class, as her school guidance counselor, Bettina Pearce, reported to Jim over the phone, asking him if he knew what the trouble might be. Jim told her he thought it was just "nerves," the initial cultural shock of the move followed by the difficulty of finding friends and adjusting to such a radically different environment. In fact, the more immediate cause of Marlene's rapid mood shifts was the sizable dispensary of medication that Dr. Tapley had prescribed for his patient's asthma, ulcer and allergies—or, rather, Marlene's at first unwitting and then all too deliberate abuse of that medication.

It was the "downers" that Marlene came to favor. She loved the way they "washed over your head like a wave," smoothing away all the jagged edges of her life. Then nothing bothered her much—not Naomi, not English class, not the teasing she felt subjected to by other students. Over the course of a few months she became, without even knowing the term, a "downer freak." The outward effects, which she learned to control pretty well in front of her parents, were a heavy-lidded look, a certain slurring of her speech, and awkward motor movements. By the time she learned from other kids in school that prescription medication was as good a way to turn on as any other, she didn't really have to be told, although it was nice to know that it was acceptable as well as effective.

In fact, pills had certain advantages over other kinds of drugs, being perfectly legal if prescribed, and hard to prove illegal if not. They were bought and traded on the front lawn of Terra Linda High—dubbed "Space City"—with open abandon. They went by different, more descriptive names on the street than in drugstores—reds, yellow-jackets, ludes, perks, green amps, black beauties, blue heavens, orange footballs, speckled birds—but they produced the same effects. Or rather, side effects, since their value often had little relation to their retail cost and even less to their original function. For example, one Quaālude, a strong sedative and purported aphrodisiac, was worth several Libriums, a sedative without such a sought-after bonus.

In relatively small quantities the kids got their pills from permissive doctors or from the medicine chests of their oversedated parents; in larger quantities from other kids who worked in local pharmacies or from forged prescriptions or from their friendly neighborhood marijuana dealer, such as Chuck Riley, who would occasionally sell pills that he bought along with more basic staples from his connection, who got them, at however many stages removed, from illicit drug factories at home and abroad. Under-the-counter drugs were almost as good a business in Terra Linda as over-the-counter drugs.

In time Marlene would buy pills at school, but for the most part she continued to rely on Dr. Tapley's largesse. Except for the Dexedrine he prescribed for weight reduction and the sleeping pills that counteracted the stimulant's effects, all the other drugs could be renewed simply by calling in the prescription number to Northgate Drugs and charging them to the Olives' account, which sometimes, even on the discount "family plan," amounted to as much as $100 a month. Marlene would have as many as a dozen different prescriptions going at the same time—uppers and downers both—and she learned to tune her body like a twelve-string guitar. Eventually she became much less discriminating, simply throwing a bunch of pills into one container and swallowing a handful at a time. "Rock-'n'-roll stew," the kids called it.

Partly because of her drug use, Marlene's grades in high school were slipping and she was in danger of failing two subjects, algebra and English. Even in Spanish class, where she received extra credit as a teaching assistant by correcting tests and homework, she was only doing B work. Thus, in January, when Eunice's daughter got married in Riverside, California, with Jim as the best man, Naomi not only refused to attend the wedding herself but used Marlene's poor grades as an excuse for not allowing her to go either.

The mined silence that had prevailed between mother and daughter since the shoplifting incident suddenly detonated into a bitter argument, with Marlene, resorting to a favorite trick, screaming out that her "real mother" would have let her go, and Naomi, rising to the bait as she always did, yelling back that "your *real* mother was probably a whore." Later that afternoon

Naomi, by then well into her cups, paraded around the living-room stark naked, wiggling her hips obscenely, and as Marlene would later put it, "holding her snatch," in a grotesque imitation of the unknown woman who gave birth to her daughter.

By then Marlene had been in Terra Linda nearly a year and she felt more isolated than ever. Patti Metzger had moved to a different section of San Rafael, and Sara Glenn, whom Marlene was not supposed to see but did, moved to Illinois shortly after the shoplifting incident. One day Marlene divided a piece of paper in half and listed all her friends in Ecuador down one column and all her friends in the United States in the other. The result was a full page of names compared to a half dozen, most of whom were American friends from South America whose families had returned home. Marlene bought some pretty statio-nery and wrote what she called "friendship notes" to everyone on the list, but she received only a few replies.

For the most part Marlene relied for her day-to-day companion-ship on Jim, who was busier than ever. The datebook she kept from those days, with its daily telegraphed comments on her activities, really concerns Jim's life almost as much as her own, with such typical notations as "Daddy home—me too"; "Dad in San Jose"; "Dad *still* in San Jose"; "Today Dad took me to see *The Poseidon Adventure* . . ." Marlene spent some of her free time at a place called La Familia, a center for Marin's Spanish-speaking population. At Jim's urging she joined a school theatri-cal production, serving as a member of the stage crew. "Marlene is being a 15-year-old successfully," Jim wrote Eunice with his usual buoyancy. "Tonight she is out working behind the scenes at a high school production of *The Mikado*. (We will go see it tomorrow.) Big doings. More independent every day." But the truth was that Marlene had become a very frightened and isolated fifteen-year-old who spent much of her time on the living-room couch watching television or describing her feelings of loneliness and rejection in her poetry: "A broken sound/Cries out in pain./People hear/But they don't listen."

It was under such circumstances that Marlene began to associ-ate with a group of girls that Jim considered, as he repeatedly told friends and associates, "beneath her." He meant it largely in class terms. As Marlene began to get into trouble, Jim and Naomi became convinced that she had been rejected by the cliquish, status-conscious, upper-middle-class Terra Linda kids who would have been her natural companions under ordinary circumstances, and in desperation fell in with a group of "juvenile delinquents" who were leading her astray.

Of course, Jim's explanation of the changes in Marlene's behavior too easily excused his "baby" daughter. In fact, the group of girls who befriended Marlene a year or so after she had arrived in Terra Linda were not really juvenile delinquents, unless a fair proportion of the community's teen-age population so qualifies. In the broad social divisions at Terra Linda High the crowd they belonged to thought of itself as the "hippies" as opposed to the "greasers" (also known as "punks" or "gearheads") and the "straights" (including "jocks" and "worms"), a tripartite division which meant, according to one male member of Marlene's group, "that we smoked dope but didn't beat up on people."

For Naomi and Jim, who had both come from conventional small-town religious backgrounds and then lived their adult years in predominantly Catholic countries, divorce carried a much weightier opprobrium than it did for their neighbors, whose divorce rate was well over 50 percent and climbing rapidly. And so while it was true that many of Marlene's new girl friends came from broken homes, the fact was not as meaningful as the Olives thought. More significant, according to the Olives' own values, was that several of them lived with working mothers in the least fashionable areas of San Rafael, such as Santa Venetia, a flat stretch of tacky developments and cheap apartments behind the Civic Center. (When Terra Linda flushes, the standard local joke goes, Santa Venetia becomes flooded.) These girls tended to be held on a much freer rein than Marlene's other friends, and if they were not "looser" themselves, they could at least afford to give that appearance. Arlene Geary, Nancy and Sharon Dillon's mother, "worried when the girls didn't call home by midnight," whereas Jim still insisted that Marlene *be* home at ten o'clock on weekends and several times called the police in near-panic when she wasn't. (Nor did it help to allay his fears about the company his daughter kept when Marlene announced one night at the dinner table that Arlene Geary's current husband, Frank, had a long criminal record, which included a stretch in San Quentin for armed robbery.) Linda Fraser's divorced mother let her smoke pot openly at home (indeed often joined her) and did not especially object, as Jim Olive most certainly would have, to the fact that Linda, who was two years older than Marlene, dated guys from Marin City, the county's only black enclave. But there were others in Marlene's new circle of friends, such as Teri Kellogg and Leslie Slote, who came from Terra Linda homes as conventional in every respect as the Olives'. And, most often, it was precisely in those homes where the mutual resentments between parents and children grew into open warfare, where the normal generation gap widened into an unbridgeable chasm.

When Linda Fraser met Marlene in girls' glee club and asked her to join some of her friends on the front lawn during lunch period to "smoke a doobie," as was their usual practice, Marlene at first demurred. "She was so shy that she talked in whispers and wouldn't look you in the eyes," Linda remembers. "I thought that was the reason." But the real reason for Marlene's hesitation became clear when she finally accepted the invitation days later and joined a group of girls standing in a tight circle passing around a joint. When the joint got to Marlene she seemed flustered and handed it on quickly, mumbling her standard lame excuse about being "allergic" to marijuana. Linda, a slight girl with a cherubic face that belied her free-swinging ways, had never known anyone to turn down free pot.

But it was not long before Marlene loosened up enough to become accepted by the group, although for weeks she kept refusing the marijuana the girls usually smoked during breaks with the same excuse. Partly to avoid being thought too square by her friends, she began inventing an exciting past for herself—not so much making it up out of whole cloth as reweaving it into bolder patterns, often well past the point of recognizability. She told people that she was adopted and that her "real" name was Maria Lucia Miranda—the name she had taken for herself in Ecuador because of its mellifluous succession of syllables and Latin sound. Sometimes she would "Americanize" the pseudonym to Marlene Miranda and sign her poems or even school assignments with it. But her name was not the only part of her identity that Marlene seemed unsure of. The fact that as a young girl she had seen the "amended" birth certificate the Olives had routinely received during the adoption process caused her to speculate constantly about her "real" age. What if she had not been adopted at birth and her age as well as her name had been "amended"? What if the Olives had been able to have a child soon after their marriage instead of waiting fifteen years to adopt one? Then their daughter would be twice as old as Marlene was. Such thoughts led her to tell her friends, who were generally a year or two older than she was in any case, that she had three birth certificates, each with a different birth date on it.

Other stories exaggerated or invented incidental facts about her life in Ecuador. Her parents owned a "ranch" which she would inherit someday, Marlene claimed, passing around a photograph that showed her and Jim riding horses in the open countryside around Quito. She had been "engaged" in Ecuador, she told some of the girls, flashing a pearl ring of Naomi's that she sometimes wore. Another boyfriend had been murdered just after taking Marlene home from a date and stuffed down a drainpipe—an allusion to the older brother of a schoolmate who had indeed been killed in some Quito drug dispute and left beside a drainpipe near the Russian embassy. And always the same wildly exaggerated tale of her reluctance to leave Ecuador, which had her parents telling her that the family was only flying to Chile on vacation and then putting enough sleeping pills in her coffee so that the plane had landed in San Francisco before she awakened. In that story the genuine emotional turbulence that Marlene experienced in the first months after her arrival became a nervous breakdown so complete that her mother had to put her in a mental hospital—an almost dreamlike deflection of Marlene's long-standing hope that Jim would one day institutionalize Naomi.

As time passed and Marlene's crash course in Marin County teen-age life proceeded, her fantasies about her past life became more and more extreme. She had played in a rock band in Quito. She and her father had snorted "Peruvian flake" together. She had once acted in a French pornographic movie. (It even had a title: *To Die of Love*.) Her Indian maids had initiated her into various rites of native witchcraft. And—taking off from a favorite tirade of Naomi's that at first infuriated and then began to intrigue Marlene—her real mother was a whore. The stories were so exaggerated that they produced in their audience an effect directly contrary to the one Marlene had intended. Instead of finding her unacceptably "straight," her new friends began to think of her as a little too "weird."

Of course, it wasn't only her past that Marlene was busily revising. She had a lot of catching up to do in the present, too, in order to feel comfortable in her changed circumstances. "It felt good to have a bunch of friends," Marlene recalls, "but I was afraid I might blow it at any minute." The result was that she designed a speeded-up acculturation program for herself that allowed her, as she put it in one of her poems, "to crash the party/going 90 in a five-mile zone." (The next line reads: "It started getting scary when I tried to be alone.") First and foremost, her musical taste, formed in Ecuador, was hopelessly outmoded, no small matter in a teen-age world where rock 'n' roll was the common ground of social intercourse, its universal soundtrack. Marlene was still stuck in the "bubblegum" music of Donny Osmond and David Cassidy—idols of prepubescence her friends had long since outgrown. Moreover, they were not even listening to the few rock bands Marlene was familiar with—the "classical" sixties groups like the Beatles and the Rolling Stones.

By the early seventies the rock-music scene had splintered into several opposing directions, and the one Marlene's friends favored was an ear-splitting, pile-driving sound that a pop-music critic had dubbed Heavy Metal. It was the bad boy of the rock world, a mutant monster of its none too tame predecessors, not merely loud but deafening, not merely sexually suggestive but blatantly sadomasochistic, almost atavistic in its disregard of aesthetic niceties in favor of a primal scream. Heavy Metal groups achieved their characteristic sound through club-footed percussion, thick-thudding basses and brutal guitar riffs that were deliberately distorted and amplified through towering stacks of speakers—producing, in short, a sheer cliff of sound that threatened to destroy the audience at its feet by toppling over momentarily. Words—when they could be separated out of the amplified pandemonium—tended to be the usual anthems to teen-age angst that rock music has always provided. At home Marlene studied the records and tapes of these groups as if they were hieroglyphs to be decoded, which in a way they were. She copied whole songs into her notebooks and began the practice of heading her letters and poems with scraps of lyrics from them. They were the secret passwords into her new world.

Marlene's favorite rock star, however, was a somewhat maverick choice in her group. David Bowie was the self-styled "King of Glitter Rock," a brand of music whose heavily made-up, bizarrely costumed practitioners added multiple identities to the manifold confusions of Heavy Metal. Bowie could try on and discard different personae as if they were so many suits of clothing (in his case, sequined jumpsuits). Mainly he was Ziggie Stardust, a rock messiah who looked like a souped-up harlequin, with an ashen-white face, eyes heavy with mascara, and orange-colored hair that stood up on end as if he were plugged into his electric guitar. But at other times Bowie could also be a surrealistic spaceman, a leather-studded lowrider, a world-weary aesthete with sucked-in cheeks and flowing blond hair. Bisexual and literally multifaceted, Bowie never had to suffer the tyranny of commitment growing up implied. He could keep on trying.

For a while, at least, Marlene kept the distinction between reality and fantasy reasonably clear in her mind. She dreamed about becoming a rock groupie and made frequent trips with her girl friends to Prune Music Co. in Mill Valley, a store that sold musical instruments and was rumored to be patronized by many of the celebrated rock stars living in Marin. But a poem she wrote about meeting and seducing David Bowie was called, realistically enough, "In a Million Years." Like many other teen-agers she also fantasized about becoming a rock star herself. In the privacy of her bedroom she would take out Jim's old guitar and accompany her records with appropriate hip swivels and silent mouthings. (She sent some lyrics she had written to a vanity press and received a form letter back congratulating her on taking her "first step into the exciting world of music.") And yet in another poem, entitled "Living a Dream," she wrote self-deflatingly:

> I want to be a rock and roll star
> and dance around and scream;
> but I look at what we really are
> and realize it's only a dream.

At the end of the poem Marlene repeated the line "I want to be only me" down to the bottom of the page, each successive repetition becoming smaller and smaller until the line was reduced to an ink speck on ruled paper. Here was Alice disappearing down the rabbit hole. In the very act of affirming her identity, Marlene unconsciously negated it. "I want to be only me" becomes a hollow, half-hearted incantation. She also, of course, desperately didn't want to be herself, and her rock fantasies provided a glamorous, high-energy alternative to the void she felt in her own personality.

Marlene's very favorite song on her favorite Bowie album ("The Rise and Fall of Ziggy Stardust and the Spiders from Mars") was called "Lady Stardust." The song presents a clever metaphor for androgyny, one that changed sexes in mid-lyrics and linked performer and audience, rock star and groupie, into one hermaphroditic whole. Marlene had no trouble identifying with the solitary youth who seemed such a misfit until his triumph on the stage. The conceit struck such a responsive chord in her that she adopted the name Lady Stardust, as she had once adopted Maria Lucia Miranda, as her new alias, signing it to poems and letters and even writing it in silver spangles on her favorite jeans belt.

Under the influence of Bowie's music, Marlene's whole manner of dressing changed radically, as she began to transform herself into what she called a "glitter chick." Some of the change was simply a matter of dressing like the natives did—she could not be expected to go around in the brown-and-white saddle shoes and cutely embroidered, round-collared blouses she had brought up with her from Ecuador and wore on that first mortifying day in school. But Naomi fought even minor changes, refusing for months to let Marlene buy a pair of denims and consenting, finally, not to the tight blue jeans her daughter craved (Naomi said "the dye would come out in the wash"—the whole point!) but to a pair of *white* jeans that didn't look like jeans at all. With Jim's connivance Marlene finally got her blue jeans and halter tops and three-inch-high platform shoes, although each time they brought home a purchase, Naomi's standard response would be: "That's so *gaudy*. Why do you need to show off like that?"

But even Jim balked at the more extreme fashions that Marlene began to buy—or sometimes shoplift—at Marin's trendy boutiques: the satiny blouses and the rhinestone belts and the six-inch-high glitter-encrusted platforms the girls called "watchtowers" after the popular Jimi Hendrix version of "All Along the Watchtower." Despite her normal shyness, when it came to dressing she began not only to imitate but to outdo the most far-out "look" of some of her friends, particularly Teri Kellogg, whose special "trademarks" were the two or three rings she wore on every finger but her thumbs and the fifteen or twenty bracelets that practically immobilized one of her arms like an Egyptian mummy's.

But it was Marlene's make-up that really bothered Jim, who had always been so quick to compliment his daughter on her good looks. She took to wearing enough mascara to make her look like a football player on a rainy Sunday afternoon. She often mixed alternating bands of several eye-shadow shades. She wore a "shiny" foundation and a "sparkling" cheek blush and she bought long false nails that she painted every color of the rainbow and some—such as the black nail polish with specks of silver sparkle she especially favored—that were never seen in rainbows. To fit into her slinky new image, Marlene convinced Jim to buy her a $300 course at the Gloria Marshall weight-reducing salon in Northgate Mall, where she quickly lost the twenty pounds she had put on since moving to Terra Linda.

"You're so pretty," Jim would gently chide his daughter, "I don't know why you wear all that make-up." But Marlene didn't feel very pretty. "I was lonely and frustrated and insecure as Marlene Olive," she says. "But when I was Lady Stardust I didn't think about that other person. It put me in a different world—all sparkles and happiness. It made me feel good."

It made Naomi feel terrible. The battles about Marlene's make-up and dress taxed all of Jim's efforts to negotiate some sort of domestic truce between his wife and daughter. Often Naomi would insist that Marlene remove most of her make-up before she could leave the house. And once, Marlene recalls, when she appeared in the living room in her full Lady Stardust regalia for a rock concert in San Francisco, Naomi "had a cow." Marlene was wearing a low-cut black dress with irides-cent red, green and blue threads running through it, and her long fake nails looked like a color-TV test pattern. She had silver glitter in her hair and on her eyelashes, and a rhinestone teardrop stuck with nail adhesive an inch from the corner of one eye. The uproar that ensued after Naomi told Marlene she could not go out of the house until she "looked decent" was more than normally abusive, with both mother and daughter cursing each other and Marlene finally spitting at Naomi in a fit of rage before storming off to the concert. As Marlene recognized in a poem she wrote shortly after the incident, what little understanding and self-restraint had existed between the two of them was fast vanishing and the future battle lines were being drawn:

> I don't know what your world's about
> I can only live in mine
> It's funny about that imaginary line
> That's no longer imaginary
> It's scarlet
> Don't call me a harlot.

By the time school ended and summer vacation began, the arguments had become more frequent and bitter than ever—a continuous domestic conflagration that flared up at unexpected moments like the dry-season wild fires that ravaged the surrounding hillsides. In addition to Marlene's appearance, the fights would often concern her new friends, in particular the hours she began to spend talking to them on the telephone (which she would answer on the first ring no matter where she was in the house for fear that either her mother would get there first or the caller would hang up). At other times fights would break out when Naomi felt that Marlene was deliberately doing some trivial household task improperly—cutting the celery straight instead of on a bias, setting the knife on the wrong side of the fork—or, more often, not doing some assigned task at all, such as washing the dinner dishes or straightening up her room. But whatever the original point of contention, arguments that started out on the common ground of all such parent-child tension quickly reached extraordinary heights of antagonism.

"I'm going out," Marlene would yell at Naomi.

"Not until you straighten up that mess in your room," Naomi would yell back from her bedroom across the hall.

"I don't wanna do it now. I'll do it when I come back."

"I don't wanna hear any more 'I don't wanna's.' You can't leave until your room is clean."

"Heil Hitler!"

"None of your smartass remarks, you hear me? I'll tell your father you've been saying that again and then you'll see if you can go out."

"Screw you! See if I care."

"Don't your curse at your mother, you no-good swine."

"Who you callin' a swine, crazy lady? You're the one who lays around like a pig drinking all day."

At some point Naomi would usually lunge for Marlene, who, being by far the quicker of the two, would run into the bathroom they shared, lock the doors (one leading to Marlene's room, the other to the hallway) and wait for Jim to come home. The bathroom was carpeted with the same green shag rug that covered the rest of the house and had a wall heater near the floor, which made it comfortable even on cold days. It became Marlene's favorite hiding place. Separated by locked doors, mother and daughter would give full vent to their resentment and anger, both growing progressively hysterical until Naomi began screaming at the top of her voice and banging on the door while Marlene, seated on the floor next to the heater, bit her arm until she drew blood or hit her head against the tile wall in a tantrum. Just picturing Naomi's face in anger—her mouth and eyebrows seeming to move up and down in lockstep—made Marlene furious.

"Besides, you're not even my mother," she would yell out, and the battle would rage again.

"Thank God for that. She's probably some gutter tramp who couldn't take care of you . . ."

"Even if she is, I'd like to find her. She'd be better than you."

"Some two-bit whore who—"

"Don't you go callin' my mom a whore, bitch! Crazy lady! *Puta chingada!*"

Naomi must have known that Marlene's natural mother wasn't a whore, but she also knew that the word would always get a quick and furious reaction out of the girl. Afterward, with nowhere left to go, the argument generally sputtered to an end. By the time Jim came home Marlene and Naomi would both be suffering from battle fatigue, the one curled up in front of the bathroom heater, the other lying on her bed. He would make his usual remark about the two of them acting like "fishermen's wives" and would listen to each one's self-justifying complaints, but he would do nothing to resolve the long-range problem, thankful for the brief respite. Except in the most temporary sense, his conciliation efforts were unsuccessful, for Jim Olive represented the problem far more than he did the solution.

Marlene and Naomi viewed each other more as rivals for his affections than mother and daughter. When Naomi angrily accused Marlene, as she often did, of wanting to "split up the family" or "take my home away from me," it was clear that her perpetual fear of losing her husband had now focused almost entirely on her daughter. At a time when Marlene was coming into full womanhood, Naomi looked older than her fifty years, and she took every opportunity to remind her daughter, and anyone else who would listen, that she had once been a very beautiful woman, showing youthful pictures of herself to prove the point.

In a sense Naomi's fears about her daughter were not entirely unjustified. Marlene and Jim had always enjoyed a rapport that went beyond the typical father-daughter relationship precisely to the extent that Naomi had long since abdicated her social role. This continued to be true even during the time that Marlene and Jim were fast losing their special closeness. Many of Jim's Terra

Linda acquaintances had never met Naomi, whereas Marlene was a familiar figure even at social functions, such as Rotary dances and Tip Club "mystery trips," that were normally reserved for husbands and wives.

"Here's my *other* girl friend," Jim would say with a wink by way of introducing Marlene, even though he was always careful to explain that Naomi couldn't come because she didn't feel well. Although there is no evidence that the sentiment was reciprocated, Marlene clearly fantasized her father as a lover. She pointedly told friends that her parents never slept together. She continued to hop into Jim's king-sized bed in the master bedroom at the slightest unfamiliar late-night noise, just as she had always done as a child. Marlene, rather than Naomi, helped Jim buy his clothes, encouraging him to wear more youthful-looking fashions and to switch from horn-rimmed to metal-frame glasses. She even wrote unmistakably romantic verse about herself and Jim, such as these lines of self-description from a poem entitled "Daddy's Sweetheart": "Long brown hair could entice any man/And her green eyes could light the night./Daddy couldn't have chosen any better."

Despite all of Marlene's protestations about her "pure" love for Jim, as time went on her feelings became much more ambivalent than she was willing to admit to herself. She was angry at him for spending so little time with her and for his weakness in dealing with a deteriorating domestic situation. As she began to get herself into more serious trouble, Jim was always the one who doled out the fitful punishments she received—the restrictions and curfews that he could never quite make stick. Although Marlene was generally careful not to use abusive language in Jim's presence, he once slapped her for referring to Naomi as "your old lady." She thought of her parents together as "matching robots," with Naomi playing her "crazy lady role" and Jim playing the "white knight protector." And it was true that Jim tended to side with Naomi in family disputes, if only to pacify her. As he had done since Marlene was a child, he continued to tell her that the two of them had to "take care" of Naomi, to make sure she didn't get "overexcited." His loyalty to Naomi—even, in his own way, his love for her—further angered Marlene. In regard to his wife he was, Marlene wrote in a poem, "living in a land that was," a place she felt excluded from.

If Marlene's love for her father was a mixed emotion, the same could be said of her hatred for her mother. She would tell her friends how much she detested Naomi, but to the few adults she confided in, such as her high school Spanish teacher Edurado Montoya and Helen Metzger, she said that her mother didn't love her. There were also rare moments of affection between mother and daughter, no less genuine for the fact that they often revolved around Jim. On one such occasion Jim had driven to Sacramento for a meeting of GBS area directors, and when a bad thunderstorm broke out before he had returned, Marlene and Naomi, concerned about his safety and frightened themselves, huddled in the master bedroom to comfort each other.

During her second summer in Terra Linda, Marlene began to smoke marijuana with her friends, having become tired of repeating the lame excuse about being allergic to it and feeling, as Chuck Riley had earlier, that so long as she was getting high on prescription drugs anyway, she might as well not buck the social pressure to try pot. When none of the dope-crazed scenarios she had played out for so long in her imagination occurred—indeed the first few times *nothing* occurred—Marlene became a regular user, although marijuana never replaced the free-floating, softly cushioned feeling she got on downers, a feeling, she wrote, that resembled "gliding down some childhood river on an innertube."

Marlene's major preoccupation during the summer was a lanky, baby-faced schoolmate with shoulder-length blond ringlets. Like Marlene, Larry Pederson wrote soul-searching verse, preferred the downers he swallowed in mind-blurring quantities to other drugs (although as his nickname, "Weed," implied, he rarely passed anything by) and fought constantly with his businessman father and "semialcoholic" mother. (Instead of running away, Larry would camp out in the hills above the Pedersons' expensive Eichler for weeks at a stretch, sneaking home to shower every few days when his parents were out.) Marlene got Linda Fraser to introduce Larry to her after she had already developed a crush on him from a distance. He found her "shy and withdrawn" and "desperately clinging," someone who could only speak her mind through indirection, a habit she had no doubt learned from Naomi. "The first day we met," Pederson recalls, "Marlene said, 'Can I tell you a secret? I know a girl who loves a guy and he doesn't even know it.' It blew me away."

Larry and Marlene went out all summer and the relationship was heavily sexual from the start, with Marlene playing a passive, although far from unwilling, role. Telling her parents that she was sleeping at Linda Fraser's house, she would often stay over at Larry's on summer weekends when his parents went to their Lake Tahoe cottage. On weekdays they would make love at the Frasers' apartment or even, on one ill-fated occasion, in Marlene's bedroom. On that occasion Naomi woke up from her afternoon nap to the sound of labored breathing and bedframe creaking across the narrow hallway and yelled out, "Marlene, what's going on in there?" In the midst of the ensuing fracas Larry Pederson hid in the bathroom and eventually snuck out of the house undetected. "Tramp!" he heard Naomi scream at Marlene. "Guttersnipe! Little whore!" Marlene was shouting back invectives of her own, but by the time she slammed the front door and left the house a half-hour later to rejoin Larry, she was sobbing convulsively.

Besides sex, Marlene's other new interest that summer was the occult, into whose more arcane reaches she was initiated by Larry Pederson. Of course, in a teen-age subculture where one's sign was often better known than one's name, everybody believed in astrology, UFOs and extrasensory perception, or their Eastern analogues, the *I Ching*, tarot cards and the mysteries of the pyramids. Even the merits of such harder-to-swallow occult phenomena as black magic, witchcraft and demonology were generally accepted. To most of the kids in Marlene's new circle of friends, the laws of the occult were as axiomatic as the laws of geometry—and far more widely known. Each of them could have reeled off a dozen rock songs with demonological allusions, the Rolling Stones' "Sympathy for the Devil" being only the most famous. And they all knew that some of their rock heroes— such as Jimmy Page, the lead guitarist for Led Zeppelin, who had bought Aleister Crowley's house in London—dabbled in black magic outside of the recording studio.

After Marlene read the popular paperback *Psychic Discoveries Behind the Iron Curtain*, she and Larry Pederson tried ESP and dream-telepathy experiments together, both without notable success. But during one astral-projection experiment that called for Marlene to relax on her bed before leaving her "physical body," she did notice a "tingling sensation" in her arms and legs, and when she got up she found an empty beer bottle on the floor—an unfamiliar brand that she was sure had not been there before.

One day Larry Pederson told her that he was a warlock and could perform magical spells and rituals. He lent her a paperback called *The Book of Ceremonial Magic*, which she pored over excitedly. "I figured if Larry could do it, so could I," Marlene later recalled. "It was powerful and different, something I could be recognized for." Next she bought all the books she could find on black magic, witchcraft and fortunetelling, the beginning of a small library of books on the occult that she eventually collected—and the police eventually confiscated.

But Marlene's first essays into the world of the occult were no more successful than her experiments in psychic research. For one thing, she found that she didn't have most of the specialized equipment many of the ceremonies mentioned in her books required—the witch's regalia of censers, pentacles, wands, white-handled knives and lengths of knotted rope. And even when she finally collected them, the results were disappointing. In the patchy grass of the Olives' backyard she drew a circle outside a pentagon with Jim's old officer's sword and placed a Bible in the center of it—a sure-fire method of putting a curse on the hapless person who picked up the book, according to one of her occult sources. But as far as Marlene could tell, Naomi did not go out back for the next few days or even so much as peer through the drawn living-room curtains. Following instructions from another book, Marlene would close her eyes, focus her concentration and begin to doodle on her sketch pad in an attempt to produce "automatic writing," but the results were always gibberish. Nor were her attempts to summon forth spirits with the aid of the ouija board she had purchased at Brentano's in Northgate Mall any more successful, no matter how carefully she followed the incantations that came in an accompanying instruction booklet.

There were, however, a few more hopeful signs. One of Marlene's occult books indicated that the way to recognize a "true witch" was by a special "mark" on her breast—and sure enough, she had a mark of a kind, a tiny blood spot on her right breast. A witch, it was also suggested, had a particularly penetrating glance that riveted people's attention, and Marlene had indeed noticed since coming to Marin County that people seemed to "look her straight in the eyes and listen attentively, like they were expecting some kind of message to come out" (it was not until much later that she realized that such intense eye contact, in the very capital of consciousness raising, may have had a cultural rather than a supernatural explanation). She also thought back on the number of times she had predicted the outcome of events or been able to read people's faces correctly—that kind of psychological insight, the books agreed, was another sure sign of a witch.

But as a novice witch Marlene could not manage to hold the attention of Larry Pederson, who drifted away at the end of the summer because "she wanted to cling and I didn't want to be clung to." She was back to spending many of the long hot days alone in her room, as she had the summer before. Of course, the bedroom, which had become the launching pad of her fantasy life, looked different now. There were peacock feathers sticking out of old wine bottles and altar candles on the night tables and trendy posters on the walls, including an outsized calendar that featured a full-color illustration of a different variety of marijuana plant each month. Along with the Bowie tapes, the occult books and the sequined clothes, these were the props of her new world. To make room for them she packed up her Barbie-doll collection and other childhood souvenirs she had long since outgrown. As she wrote to herself, "The stories are all read/Winnie the Pooh is dead/And the teddy bear no longer/Sleeps in your bed."

Marlene still spent a great deal of time writing poetry, which she now collected in a loose-leaf binder that she titled *Paper Gods*. (On the front cover was a collage of teen-age idols and villains that included newspaper pictures of Richard Nixon, Ted Kennedy, Nelson Rockefeller, national guardsmen, the Beatles, Elvis Presley, and Yoko Ono, as well as the wrapping from a package of Zig Zag cigarette papers and a drawing of a bejeweled Hindu deity.) The poems themselves expressed her old theme of loneliness, and in a series that she entitled "Freedom Poems," added a new and increasingly more urgent theme, the near-desperate need to shake off any external constraints on her actions:

> Don't want no ties, no strings to bind me
> Can't handle being in a cage with bars all around
> Won't tolerate living without being free
> Won't bother with money, 'cause I'll get where I'm bound
> No hours to be in at night
> No lessons to be learned
> I'll believe what I feel is right
> To make my own decisions is a privilege I've earned.

It was the universal plea of adolescence, the cry of half the rock-'n'-roll songs ever written. Like so much else in the American teen culture that she had come to late and adopted with a convert's fervor, Marlene took the message and its implications literally. She had none of the distancing perspective on her adopted culture of the native-bred, the ability to distinguish metaphor from literal statement, wish from fulfillment.

One other event that touched the Olives' lives in a curious way occurred before their second summer in the United States was over. In late August the wife of the assistant principal of Terra Linda High, Edward Gilbright, was stabbed to death just inside the front gate of her Eichler. The Gilbright murder made everybody in the neighborhood extremely apprehensive—the more so as the weeks went by and the killer was not apprehended—but no one quite so much as Naomi Olive. It was the realization of all her paranoid, TV-influenced fantasies, *The Streets of San Francisco* come to the streets of Terra Linda. She insisted that Jim install new locks on the garage door and always double-bolted the front door when she was inside the house alone. And just in case some Houdini of a cat burglar managed to work his way inside when she was taking her afternoon nap, Naomi set up a barricade behind the door made up of wastebaskets, buckets, chairs, brooms and vacuum cleaners, all of which had to be laboriously removed piece by piece when the occasional visitor had convinced her of his legitimacy. But when genuine trouble came to 353 Hibiscus Way, it did not come from the outside.

Five

Chuck Riley remembers the bright fall day that he met Marlene Olive "like it was my birthday." He and Mike Howard had been over at their friend Steve Donnelly's house cleaning and bagging some marijuana. The house had become a frequent meeting place for Chuck and his friends, partly because it was only two blocks from Terra Linda High School (Chuck could carry the amount of dope he expected to be able to sell in his pockets, and if necessary, return for more) and also because Donnelly's parents, who both worked, were away all day. But the real attraction of Donnelly's house was Donnelly himself. A tall, rangy twenty-one-year-old, Donnelly had recently returned from a three-year tour of duty with the Special Forces in Vietnam, and he went around Terra Linda dressed in combat boots and a flak jacket, as if he were still there. When he talked about fights he was not talking about schoolyard brawls but about firefights on jungle hilltops.

That day, as was his custom, Chuck went over to the high school around "brunch period"—the midmorning break when everyone would be outside—to see friends and "take care of business." Although to an outsider's eye the 2,000-member student body of Terra Linda High School appeared as relentlessly white and middle-class as the surrounding community, it was, in fact, as caste-ridden and turf-conscious as any inner-city gang. The "jocks" hung out in the central courtyard of the sprawling two-story brick building, the "greasers" in the parking lot and the "heads" on the front lawn, no doubt so they could monitor the movements of patrol cars along the streets. Chuck gravitated toward the front lawn, where a group of kids was standing around one of the frail, wire-braced trees that had such trouble taking root, although the marijuana seeds that had surreptitiously been planted around them flowered luxuriantly. The focus of the group's attention seemed even frailer than the tree that supported her—a girl sitting cross-legged on the ground, her downcast face hidden from the onlookers by the curtain of her long hair. Several boys were dancing around the tree trying to catch her attention with arm-waving gestures and taunting remarks.

"You're an orange and I'm gonna peel you."

"You're a kite and you'll never come down."

"Watch me cut your string."

"Hey, Marlene, you're a rabbit. I bet I can make you disappear."

Between stifled sobs Marlene was pleading, "Please stop it! Just leave me alone!"

Chuck soon found out that the girl was on her first acid trip and it was quite clearly turning into a bad one, in no way helped by the callous initiation ritual she was forced to undergo. Whether it was the fetal position she had assumed on the grass, the demure lace-bordered blouse she was wearing that day or simply the fact that it was her first acid trip, Chuck was struck by "a kind of innocence" in Marlene Olive. He got the others to back away and then, kneeling beside her, reassured her that everything would turn out all right, that he would stay with her. He handed her a marijuana joint to "level her out," but she refused it, as she did his attempts to find out her name or strike up a conversation. A few minutes later Sharon Dillon came up and led Marlene inside to the bathroom.

It was also a day that Marlene Olive would never forget, although for entirely different reasons. As Marlene recalls the experience, all of the girls she had become friendly with over the summer were out on the lawn and "everyone was getting loaded." That morning both of the Dillon girls had taken acid, and when Sharon handed the tiny tab of tinted gelatin to Marlene, she quickly swallowed it with a gulp of Coca-Cola. What she did not realize immediately was that Sharon and Nancy had each taken one section of the "four-way windowpane" and given the rest—a double dose—to Marlene.

At first the LSD had a pleasant effect, making the scene around her glow with an inner radiance, as if the love poster on her bedroom wall had suddenly sprung to life. Even inanimate objects felt alive and sentient and, somehow, seemed to sway to her will. She laughed uncontrollably from the sheer joy of the vision. (Later she wrote in it: "Picking up a twig/she could count each pore/which she never noticed before.") All too soon, however, the scene became "crystallized," broken into a million jagged pieces like a radiant reflection in a shattered mirror. She hid her face in her hands, peeping out occasionally to see if she could bring the pieces together again in her mind. But it was impossible. When Chuck Riley knelt beside her she could not understand what he was saying nor even keep his face, peering at her from inches away, in focus. Soon afterward she would write a poem describing the experience that begins:

> It started out one day in October
> The weather was nice, I guess, I wasn't sober.
> Sitting on the grass
> Thinking about the past
> Never knowing who was by my side.

For Marlene the rest of the day was a blur of half-comprehended activity, time itself dissolving in an acid bath. She and the Dillions took a bus to a medical clinic in nearby Corte Madera, where Sharon was scheduled to have an abortion. The short time Marlene spent in the doctor's office was a "nightmare" for her. The door to the waiting room seemed to "breathe open and shut by itself." A baby screamed on the floor and Marlene, who felt uncomfortable with children under the best of circumstances, yelled for it to stop, finally rushing out of the office ahead of her friends. Late in the day the three girls made their way back to the Dillions' house, arriving in time to catch the final bullet-ridden, blood-splattered scene of *Bonnie and Clyde* on television.

Later that night Sharon gave Marlene some well-meant advice. She should try to lose some of her shyness and "stop staring at the ground all the time"; she should go out with more boys, have more fun and, in general, "loosen up." Although the advice seemed unremarkable at the time, in retrospect Marlene came to feel that her personality changed radically from that day on, that she "became more like Sharon"—that, indeed, her friend had "reprogrammed" her during the acid trip. And what is certainly true is that throughout the school year Marlene became increasingly immersed in a sexually permissive, drug-oriented teen-age subculture for which neither she nor her parents were the least bit prepared.

Even her initial attempt to heed Sharon's advice ended badly. Late that same night she called up Andy Orrick, the boy she was going out with at the time, and asked him to come over. After the two of them made love on Sharon's bed, Marlene was suddenly, unaccountably, overwhelmed by a wave of anger, and she began swinging wildly at Orrick, striking him repeatedly with her fists until he managed to contain her forcibly. Clearly, it would take some time before she felt entirely comfortable in her new world.

Throughout the day Chuck Riley had been walking around "on cloud nine," thinking that Marlene was "the most beautiful girl in the world." Chuck had an "instant crush on her—I guess you could call it love at first sight." He tried to find out all he could about her from friends at school, but aside from her name, only learned that she had spent most of her life abroad and was considered shy and a little "weird." The next day, a Thursday, he went back to the schoolyard at the same hour to seek her out. It was the first time Chuck had ever actually asked a girl for a date (although he had been out many times with his friends and *their* girls), and he was in a fine sweat about the matter, having rehearsed his lines to himself all morning.

He found Marlene sitting in a circle of friends on the front lawn and offered them some grass—his usual "calling card." After joking about her condition the day before, Chuck asked her if she would go to the drive-in with him the next night. Marlene hesitated. She liked the fact that Chuck seemed popular, and now that a goatee and mustache masked his baby face, he looked older than his age and certainly older than her classmates, most of whom she found embarrassingly "silly." On the other hand, even though Chuck had begun to diet seriously during the summer, he still weighed over 250 pounds, a fact that the loose-fitting "kung fu" jacket he wore failed to hide. Marlene said that she would like to go to the movies Friday night but she had invited Nancy Dillon to sleep over at her house. Maybe some other night. But Chuck, who was not about to be spurned so easily after he had worked himself up to such a fever pitch, quickly offered to find Nancy a date, too. When Marlene reluctantly agreed, Chuck arranged to pick her up after dinner the next night and went bounding off toward home to see if his friend Bill

Owen, who lived down the block, was willing to do him a big favor—two, in fact, for he needed Bill not only to take out Nancy Dillon but to provide transportation, his own car having recently had another of its well-deserved mechanical breakdowns.

After he had recovered from the shock that his friend had actually gotten a date, Bill Owen agreed to double with him the following night, especially when Chuck said he would pay for the whole evening. At the appointed hour the two of them pulled up to 353 Hibiscus in Owen's Dodge van, and Chuck, who had spent hours selecting his clothes and brushing down his cowlick, rang the bell. He heard Marlene yell for her mother to answer it while she finished dressing. After introductions, Naomi Olive led Chuck to the dining-room table and continued clearing away the dinner dishes. Since it was "just about the only time I'd met parents because I was taking out their daughter," Chuck responded nervously to her probing questions about his age, employment and interest in Marlene. A few minutes later Jim Olive came out of his office down the hall to meet Chuck and continue the interrogation. Where were they going? How were they getting there? Did Chuck happen to know the phone number at the 101 Drive-In in case they needed to reach Marlene? (No, he said, but if the Olives called the box office they'd make an announcement over the car speakers.) What time could he have Marlene back? (Anytime Mr. Olive wanted, Chuck suggested politely, realizing that "you have to be careful about these things if you want to stay in good with parents.") Jim Olive told Chuck to try to have Marlene back by eleven o'clock at the latest. Chuck nodded, although the curfew seemed a little stringent for a Friday night. But then, the Olives, who appeared to be a good ten years older than his own and his friends' parents, seemed more anxious about their daughter's whereabouts than most Terra Linda parents would be.

Chuck searched his mind for a general topic of discussion. Two weeks earlier, in an attempt to placate his father (who not only insisted that his son look for a job but often wondered aloud how he could possibly have so much spending money without one), Chuck had found part-time work as a door-to-door vacuum-cleaner salesman. Now, catching sight of a well-used vacuum cleaner in the corner of the dining alcove, he decided to "hit the Olives with a sales pitch before they could throw any more questions at me."

"I see you have a pretty old machine over there," Chuck said.

"Are you in the market for a new one by any chance? I'm a Kirby salesman and I could let you have one of those at a discount."

"Actually," Mr. Olive began, "we're quite satisfied—"

"Do you know about Kirby . . ." Chuck raced on. He had recited the company's sales pitch dozens of times since taking the job, usually in great haste and sometimes with his foot literally in the door, but all he had to show for it was about $100, his commission on two orders. "Perhaps you'd like to see their new line. Kirby has the most powerful motor of any vacuum cleaner on the market for greater suction. And it has the exclusive patented vibrating 'Beaterbar' that shakes the grit and dirt out of the matting of the carpet. Dirt in the matting cuts the life of the carpet in half, you know . . ."

Just then Marlene and Nancy appeared in the living room and Chuck breathed more easily. "I like your father," he said to Marlene on the way to the car. "He seems like a real nice guy." Chuck also had the feeling that Jim Olive's first impression of him was a good one—and he was right. "Seems like a fine young man for a change," Jim had said afterward, according to a report that Naomi gave her daughter the next day. "A real go-getter."

In San Rafael the two couples stopped at a liquor store known to be fairly relaxed about checking IDs for proof of age, and Chuck went in to buy a bottle of tequila and some orange juice. Marlene turned down the tequila when it was offered to her at the drive-in, as she did Chuck's clumsy attempts to put his arm around her, but she accepted the joints he kept rolling and passing around the van all evening. By the time the double feature was over, Marlene recalls, she had "moved over to the edge of the back seat as Chuck kept inching toward me." The teen-agers drove to the all-night Jack-In-The-Box, and Nancy Dillon accompanied Chuck inside to place an order. According to Bill Owen, a strapping, handsome fellow who has never lacked for girl friends, Marlene "came on to me pretty strong" while Chuck was out of the van. "I can't stand Chuck," he remembers Marlene telling him. "He makes me sick."

Alone in the car, Bill and Marlene arranged to meet the following afternoon. The next day he picked her up, drove to the Civic Center lake, and after an hour of desultory conversation during which Marlene talked about her interest in "white magic," took her home. A few days later Marlene mentioned the incident to Chuck, discounting her own role in initiating it. Chuck told his friend that it didn't bother him because Marlene had sworn that Bill didn't mean anything to her. "It blew me away," Bill Owen recalled later. "He was already talking like her fiancé and I knew she didn't even like him."

Indeed, Chuck was hopelessly infatuated with Marlene from the start. Just how infatuated was apparent to Mike Howard the following week when he saw his friend, who normally never left home without a guaranteed ride in both directions, cheerfully pedaling his bicycle to Marlene's house in the rain. It was even more apparent to Marlene after Chuck left a note for her that read, in its entirety: "I'm happy happy happy happy. In love love love love. Do with me what you will."

Chuck began to drop by the high school whenever he thought Marlene would be out on the lawn. Often he would bring her flowers, a public demonstration of affection that embarrassed Marlene no end. With his car operating again, he offered Marlene rides after school, plied her with free dope and gave her the first of a series of more expensive gifts he would buy her in the coming months, a pair of silver earrings. It was all to little avail. In public Marlene avoided Chuck as much as she could, embarrassed by the way "he'd just stand around looking lovesick at me." But she did encourage him, as she encouraged everyone, to call her up at home. She felt popular and accepted when the phone rang often, deeply depressed when it didn't. Since Chuck sensed that the one side of him that clearly appealed to Marlene's imagination was his drug dealing, he began to spin grandiose, and largely apocryphal, tales about his South American cocaine connections, his rock-'n'-roll clients and the big-money deals, involving what he described as "mountains of snow," that were just about to "come down." He told her that he used the nickname Rocko to guarantee his anonymity in dealing drugs and showed her the small mahogany-handled .22-caliber pistol he kept in the glove compartment "in case anyone starts pushing me around."

To make himself more desirable in Marlene's eyes, Chuck embarked on an intensive self-improvement campaign. He bought a Spanish-language primer and began memorizing words and phrases that he would toss out in the course of his telephone conversations with Marlene to impress her. He studied up on glitter-rock music, particularly David Bowie's albums, and bought a few popular paperbacks on witchcraft and the occult. Knowing that Marlene wrote poetry, he began addressing poems to her. As might be expected from someone whose worst subject in an aborted high school career was English, most of them were doggerel, but a few were amazingly good—the ones he copied out of an old poetry anthology Oscar owned or from the liner notes of rock records. For the sake of added authenticity Chuck would change all the women's names to Marlene and insert references to people and events she would recognize.

He also began to be aware of fashions in men's clothes and bought some dress slacks and bold-patterned sport shirts to replace his usual uniform of workshirts and ballooning overalls. But Chuck's chief self-improvement program was weight reduction. Marlene provided him with the motivation to diet successfully for the first time in his life, and over the next several months he managed to lose more than sixty pounds, reducing his waistline from 44 inches to 36. He quit smoking, gave up beer and sometimes, with the help of prescription diet pills and frequent inhalations of cocaine, would go all day without eating. Just about every other week Chuck would make a ceremony of putting a new notch on his belt an inch from the last, and several times during this period he had to buy—or steal—a whole new wardrobe. When his weight finally stabilized at around 200 pounds, Chuck was lighter than he had been in many years. He was still somewhat pudgy, but for the first time since his early childhood he could no longer be described as a fat boy.

However, at first everything Chuck did backfired. Until he slimmed down, his more stylish, tighter-fitting clothes only served to make him look heavier. His Spanish seemed laughably rudimentary to Marlene, who also discovered that Chuck had cribbed some of his poetry to her. Soon after they met she heard a song on the radio by the Jefferson Starship, "Caroline," that was virtually identical to a poem Chuck had slipped in the Olives' mailbox, "Marlene."

When Chuck asked Marlene to be his "old lady" two weeks after they met, she refused politely, saying that she didn't want to be tied down and wasn't "together enough" for a steady boyfriend. Occasionally Marlene would allow Chuck to take her to a rock concert at Winterland or the Cow Palace in San Francisco, but she never failed to insist that one of her girl friends come along. Chuck was always careful to meet her parents' eleven o'clock weekend curfews, even though this meant leaving the shows early and racing back to Terra Linda. The result was that of all of Marlene's new friends, Chuck quickly became Jim Olive's favorite. He was unfailingly polite, dressed well and seemed responsible. When Chuck expressed an interest in GBS, Jim took him into his study and showed him a wall map with his own region colored red and the two adjacent regions that he hoped to acquire soon shaded lightly. From his contact with local employers, Jim was constantly hearing about job possibilities, and he often passed the information on to Chuck. Once he went out of his way to recommend Chuck highly to a client who had a mobile brake-repair service, but the potential job fell through when the man asked to see Chuck's driver's license, which was in its usual state of suspension because of traffic violations.

But for the most part Chuck only got to see Marlene in the company of the group of students who began meeting regularly on the Terra Linda High School front lawn that fall to smoke his dope and trade pills. They were probably the first generation of Terra Linda students who not only attended high school but actually graduated from it dead stoned. It became a kind of game among them to regulate their body chemistry according to their class schedule—taking downers for the popular "Bach to Rock" music class and Jerry Fitch's art class, in which Marlene and several of her girl friends were enrolled, or getting "beaned out" on uppers for the more physically demanding courses such as gym and modern dancing. Soon the group began cutting classes and shifted their activities to Steve Donnelly's house, where some sort of party was always in progress. Until she fell in with the group, Marlene had been fairly diligent about school work, and her grades had been decent, but she, too, began skipping classes with the others. She signed absence excuses with her father's signature, which she had learned to imitate with a check forger's precision by filling up page after page in her school notebook with dry runs.

Most of the group were at least a year or two older than Marlene, which was one reason why she made up that odd story about not knowing her real age. (Chuck, for one, thought Marlene was seventeen until her sixteenth birthday in January.) They were also much more advanced sexually. That fall would be remembered by the group as, in Steve Donnelly's words, "the days of the great feast." Couples would bump into one another on their way in and out of the master bedroom. There were also experiments in group sex that began one day during a collective acid trip, when Donnelly announced that Wesson oil rubbed on the skin glows iridescent in black light. A quick shopping expedition was undertaken, after which those present stripped off their clothes and began pouring bottles of cooking oil over each other. When word got out, "Wesson oil parties" became a regularly scheduled event, although neither Chuck nor Marlene, who were both still overweight and extremely self-conscious about displaying their bodies, participated in them. Chuck was still a virgin at nineteen, and Marlene, although she had slept with a few boys, was relatively selective in her choice of mates compared to her girl friends' permissive ways. But just as in other areas of teen-age manners and mores, Marlene quickly went from relative sexual inexperience to overindulgence, so that in a short time she would develop a reputation not so much for being overly permissive as for being kinky. As a line in a poem she wrote about that time put it: "The light said red but I saw green."

What was true about sex was even more true about drugs—her "chemicals of mirth." She tried LSD several times after her first acid trip and began smoking pot regularly and snorting cocaine whenever someone, usually Chuck, provided it. (She described her reaction in a felicitous couplet: "I sniffed it pleasingly./Angels were teasing me.") She continued to abuse the sedatives Dr. Tapley had prescribed for her various nervous complaints, especially when, after arguments with Naomi, she had trouble catching her breath, a remnant of her childhood asthma attacks. She wrote about the "plush, warm world" she lived in on pills, her "velvet-lined box." Naomi's repeated assertion that people who used drugs were "savages" only made them more attractive to Marlene. But for a long while she was able to hide the extent of her drug habit from her parents. Every time Marlene came home stoned—which would soon be pretty nearly every time she came home—she would pause on the front steps before unlocking the door and repeat to herself "One . . . two . . . three . . . *straight*" until she felt in control. And there were occasions when she did not come home because she could not. After one such experience she wrote:

> I'm coming down, I'm coming down
> Hope to see you on the ground
> 'Cause I'm coming down
> Touched the sky
> Got too high
> Time to die

> Don't ask why
> Just don't cry
> I'm coming down, I'm coming down.

That afternoon she had swallowed acid, a variety of downers and several cans of beer. Then, wobbly-legged and glassy-eyed, she had asked a young man she had just met at Donnelly's house to drive her home. There Naomi immediately began yelling at her, not for her state of intoxication, which Marlene managed to hide, but for bringing "strange men" into the house. Jim came out of his office to see what the ruckus was all about and met Travis Wheeler, who was indeed, as Jim would write to a South American friend, "the most shining example to date of the sterling breed of friends Marlene has made since we moved here."

At twenty, Travis Wheeler, a wiry, good-looking fellow with a wispy mustache, curly blond hair and blue eyes, had already been in and out of a half-dozen Youth Authority institutions since the age of eight, when he stole a speedboat and smashed it against a jetty on the San Rafael canal. He found the Marin County juvenile hall to be "summer camp," with outings to local attractions and plenty of social workers to dote on him. Two weeks later he was returned as a runaway, and since then he had been back frequently, his most recent incarceration—for possession of two kilos of marijuana—having ended just a few days earlier. What earned him his nickname of "Houdini" was that he had escaped from "juvy" and, most recently, county jail, almost as many times as he had been committed there. He was generally caught a short time later under circumstances that were reminiscent of Keystone Kops capers, such as the time he had swallowed a chewing-gum foil and convinced the doctor at the Marin County jail, after x-rays were taken, that he had in fact swallowed his razor blade. When he arrived at the hospital in a sheriff's car he made his break, but he was easily overtaken after a hundred-yard chase when he tripped over a lawn sprinkler.

Flamboyant and reckless, Wheeler appeared more rogue than criminal, and he was a popular figure in the teen-age world Marlene had entered. Even his Youth Authority number, 007, added to his image, as did the 1963 silver-toned Cadillac he drove, which was lined inside with fun fur and had large stereo speakers in the back window. Marlene was fascinated by the tattoos on his arms and chest—among them images of Father

Time, a naked woman, a phoenix and the legend "Born to be Wild." Clearly, Chuck Riley provided little competition for Travis Wheeler.

Marlene spent much of the next several weeks with Wheeler, who initiated her further into a lifestyle of petty crime. As had happened many times before, Wheeler had been kicked out of the house by his mother and her third husband (his real father was serving time in Florida for armed robbery) and was living out of his car. He seemed to have a scam for everything. When he needed gas he simply pulled off the side of the road, put on one of several discarded license plates he kept in his trunk and used a stolen credit card. He "shopped" for groceries with a "booster bag" pinned to the inside of his jacket and cashed bum checks at local stores with fake ID cards.

With Wheeler, Marlene was the pursuer instead of the pursued. She bought him clothes and supplied him with some of the dope Chuck regularly gave her. She told him self-aggrandizing lies that she knew would intrigue him, saying, for example, that the Ecuadorian dope traffic was controlled by a friend of her father's, and if Travis went down there, he could buy large quantities of cocaine at rock-bottom prices to smuggle back. But it was in the realm of the occult that Marlene's imagination really began to work overtime in her pursuit of Wheeler, especially after she discovered that he had the word "Satan" tattooed on his arm in large block letters. Wheeler told her that he was "a member of the Satanic religion" and that, according to a popular paperback on the occult he had read, the turquoise phoenix on a ring that Chuck had given her was a traditional sign of the devil. Using the mystique of her South American background again, Marlene, in turn, told Wheeler that her maids had taken her to "black masses" as a child, and she concocted a fanciful tale about having recently attended a candlelit séance during which a naked woman in a trance began "bleeding from her pores" and thrashing about as if possessed.

While a table-raising session that Wheeler had organized ended disappointingly, Marlene's belief in her own occult powers was strengthened by her success in reading people's fortunes with the aid of tarot cards. Prodded by Wheeler's belief that one of his other girl friends could "predict things," she bought several books on the tarot with instructions for laying out the cards and interpreting the mysterious images, and when she tried out her technique the results were truly astonishing. She told one friend,

Jeff Flagg, that he would lose his job as a postal clerk, and two weeks later he was indeed laid off. The same evening she told Don Messner things about himself, such as his tendency to "live like a hermit," that everyone present found eerily accurate, especially considering the fact that Marlene had never met Don before. But the tarot reading that actually frightened Marlene—and made her think she might indeed be a witch—occurred the night she told Andy Orrick not to drive home along the Lucas Valley Road. Andy had laughed at her warning, although he took another route home for safe measure. The next morning a front-page picture in the *I-J* showed the twisted wreckage of a car that had careened off the tortuous road into a telephone pole.

When Marlene laid out her own tarot cards, the one that seemed to come up most often was the High Priestess—a robed figure seated between two fluted columns that symbolizes spiritual enlightenment. She began to carry the card in her pocketbook and to tell friends that she was the High Priestess or sometimes the High Priestess of the Satanic Church.

This latter notion was inspired by a book on witchcraft that Travis Wheeler had given her, *The Satanic Bible*, a mass-market paperback that featured the bald-headed, goateed picture of its author, Anton Szandor LaVey, on its back cover. The book was especially popular among Bay Area teen-agers, in part because LaVey, a former circus animal trainer and carny barker turned cult leader, lived in San Francisco, where he had founded the Church of Satan and built it into an organization of several thousand dues-paying initiates. The book was both a philosophical tract on the virtues of hedonism and a how-to guide to Satan worship. Marlene read *The Satanic Bible*, several times as part of what she called her "research" into witchcraft, and it became her favorite occult text. One passage that especially stuck in her mind concerned the proper object of ritual sacrifice, for it seemed to Marlene that her mother fit the description perfectly:

> The question arises, "Who, then, would be considered a fit and proper human sacrifice, and how is one qualified to pass judgment on such a person?" The answer is brutally simple. Anyone who has unjustly wronged you—one who has "gone out of his way" to hurt you, to deliberately cause trouble and hardship for you. When a person, by his reprehensible behavior, practically cries out to be destroyed, it is truly your

moral obligation to indulge them their wish. . . . The "ideal sacrifice" may be emotionally insecure, but nonetheless can, in the machinations of his insecurity, cause severe damage to *your* tranquillity or sound reputation.

Marlene also learned from *The Satanic Bible* that the seasonal solstices and equinoxes were witchcraft "holidays" and that both "vary a day or two from year to year, depending on the lunar cycle at the time, but usually fall on the 21st or 22nd of the month"—in the case of the summer solstice, on the 21st or 22nd of June.

Witchcraft had entered Marlene's rich fantasy life, becoming, as she put it, "my greatest escape." She knew it was a make-believe world and yet it sometimes seemed "realer than my real world. Sometimes I was convinced I *was* a witch." She wrote a sequence of poems called "Devil's Disciple," one of which begins:

> I'm evil, I'm so evil
> I'm darkness in disguise.
> I know just what to do to steal
> The color from your eyes.

She told her friends that she had become initiated into the Church of Satan and attended its black masses, or sometimes that she belonged to a coven of witches in Marin County that met at China Camp on full-moon nights. She decorated her room with witches' regalia such as candles, incense burners and the five-pointed sign of the pentagram. Attaching a mystical significance to the color black ("Black is the night/Mysterious delight . . ."), she began to dress entirely in dark clothing, bought black satin sheets for her bed and sensed a special kinship with Rascal, the Olives' frisky black cat. She also began to feel that she had an uncanny power in her green eyes—which she thought were her best feature, anyway—to command people to do her bidding by menacingly staring them down. (This notion was reinforced by *The Satanic Bible*. "Learning to effectively utilize the command to LOOK is an integral part of a witch's or warlock's training," the book instructed an initiate. "To manipulate a person, you must first be able to attract and hold his attention.") As she put it in another poem, she would become a "Soul shaker/Mind breaker/Maker of evil delights."

Besides witchcraft Marlene's other "great escape" continued to be rock music. When she tired of calling herself Lady Stardust she began calling herself Freebird, after a popular Lynyrd Skynyrd song that described the feelings of a free-spirited soul who refuses, as Marlene felt she must refuse, to be caged in. In her poetry she often fantasized about what it would be like to be a groupie to famous rock stars:

> She wore a silver dress
> All eyes upon her breasts
> And stepped into the fire
> Of everyone's desire.

At first it seemed relatively harmless, what she called in another one of her poems "my game of self-pretend." Around this time she began telling friends that her father was going to give her a Dodge Charger for her birthday, a month away. The car would be silver and she would call it "Highway Star," after the popular Deep Purple song. Occasionally she would say that it wasn't her father who was going to give it to her but her Uncle Bob, a wealthy, powerful protector who became increasingly important in Marlene's fantasy life as her love for her father grew more ambivalent. Only her protector's name held a semblance of reality. She was once picked up hitchhiking home from the East Bay by an older man driving a black Cadillac, and when she asked him his name he said, "Just call me Uncle Bob." But she never saw him again.

One day Marlene drew up a list of twenty possible aliases in her poetry book ("They call me different names/Now every one applies/Let me start you off, alphabetized") that began with Acid Queen and ended with a childhood nickname, Wizzy. In a letter she later sent to Chuck she wrote: "I have so many dreams but am afraid everything I wish will crumble like pie crust. I'm counting on you to help me find my place. It's your choice, not only mine." What followed was another wide-ranging list, this one of "careers" and "fields of interest":

Music
Foreign Affairs
Fashion (design/store owning)
Photography
Modeling/Acting

Dealer
Cocktail waitress
Mechanic (fast cars/custom paint jobs)
Pro racer
Stewardess
Groupie
Poet/Writer
Massage lady
Hooker

As she wrote in a poem called "Illusive Woman," she was fast becoming "So many different people/it sometimes/seems unreal."

The last-named career choice assumed a tighter grip on her imagination as the year went on. It was first suggested by Naomi, who frequently told Marlene that she looked "like a cheap whore" during arguments about her manner of dress and kept repeating that her natural mother had been a prostitute. "I couldn't understand why my real mom would give me up unless maybe she was a hooker and was forced to," Marlene later reflected. "So maybe I'd become one, too." The possibility became more real after Marlene met a friend of Linda Fraser's named Jim Pickett, a sharp-dressing, fast-talking pimp who lived in Marin City and worked out of the sleazier motels bordering Route 101, sometimes employing local high school girls in his "stable," according to information developed by the San Rafael police. Marlene refused Pickett's repeated suggestions that she would make a "fine fancy lady," but she was, in a curious way, flattered by his attention and more than willing to entertain the offer in her mind, if not in reality. But as time went on, the line between her imagination and reality, between the proposition and its acceptance, was as thin as the ice Marlene knew she was treading—and getting thinner all the time. A poem she wrote then began: "The ice is thin/You're taking a chance./You mustn't give in to everything/That enchants you."

Still, there was always a line in her mind and in those of most of her friends. "I was trying to come across weirder than I really was to impress people," Marlene explains. It did impress people, but the results were not always what she intended. On Halloween Eve, sitting outside her house in Andy Orrick's car, she had suddenly begun to stare at him in the manner recommended by *The Satanic Bible* and to chant, in an odd, trancelike voice, "We want you. We need you. We want you. We need you . . ." After that, Orrick decided that Marlene had "totally weirded out" and never went out with her again.

Other friends began to feel the same way. Teri Kellogg wore a medallion imprinted with signs of the zodiac that Marlene claimed had been cursed by a sorcerer centuries ago. The way to get rid of the curse, according to one of Marlene's occult books, was to place the medallion on a satin cloth surrounded by four candles, sprinkle blood from a sacrificed animal on it, recite a certain chant and bury it. At first Teri thought her friend "had gone a little loose upstairs," but after she broke up with her boyfriend and got kicked out of her parents' house in the space of a week, Marlene's crazy notion about the cursed medallion stuck in her mind, and eventually she did bury it, although she couldn't bring herself to perform the complete ceremony.

Other members of Marlene's group, such as Leslie Slote and Kim Ferguson, both firm believers in the occult, were also, by turns, skeptical and frightened of her preoccupation with witchcraft. Even such a self-described modern-day "Satanist" as Travis Wheeler, who would testify at Chuck's trial that Marlene was an "apprentice witch," added that he believed "about one-eighth" of what she told him. "She was insecure and always trying to convince people that she was something she wasn't. I never really took her that seriously."

Only Chuck Riley did. During the weeks that Marlene was going out with Travis Wheeler, she ignored Chuck more than ever. He continued to send her gifts of flowers, dope and jewelry. Occasionally he took her to rock concerts in the company of other friends, but after an angry confrontation with Marlene at Donnelly's house one afternoon, he decided to "stay out of the picture until things blew over." Chuck had taken Wheeler aside and tried to persuade him that he loved Marlene and considered her his "old lady." When Marlene heard about the conversation she screamed at Chuck in front of their friends to "stop acting like you own me." The rest of the day Chuck sat gloomily in the middle of Donnelly's living room rolling dozens of marijuana joints and tossing them up in the air for friends to grab. The next day he nearly killed himself.

That afternoon Donnelly and a couple of other friends had asked him if he wanted to go four-wheeling with them, which involved taking a jeep to nearby Nicassio Lake along with a bottle of whiskey, and "spinning doughnuts" in the mudflats. Earlier Chuck had filled a plastic Baggie with several kinds of pills, mainly sedatives, and now he was swallowing them a few at a time with the whiskey as if they were so many M&Ms (which was, in fact, the street name for a downer in great favor with Terra Linda teen-agers). It was a long night, since the jeep got stuck in the mud and had to be towed out. On the way back to town the group stopped at a bar. After several more drinks Chuck became sick and vomited, which may have saved his life. By the time they got into town and met up with Mike Howard and the Dillons at Donnelly's house, he was nearly comatose except for his incoherent mumbling about Marlene. Mike knew he couldn't take Chuck back home in that condition, so they drove around for hours, at one point stopping off at Marin General Hospital, where an orderly pronounced Chuck out of serious danger. Around three in the morning Mike dropped Chuck off at Northgate Mall at his request. From there he walked over to Marlene's house and sat on her front lawn until dawn writing his heart out to her—telling her "my life is nothing without you," begging her to "be mine for a while" and allow him to be her "servant." When he looked at the pages in the first light of day they were, except for scattered phrases, completely illegible.

The events of that night led Chuck to take what he called Marlene's "witch talk" more seriously, since it became clear to him that, whether or not Marlene possessed the occult powers over others that she claimed, she held a very real power over him. "I thought that if there was such a thing as a universal force," he later recalled, "maybe it could be funneled through certain people who could use it for good or evil, and maybe Marlene was one of them. I began to believe—without *really* believing it—that maybe Marlene was a witch." Certainly Marlene did nothing to discourage that belief. When she wanted her way about something she would stare at him with what friends called her "do-it-or-else look" and say, with all the menace she could muster, "Chu-uck."

One day, as she had done with Andy Orrick, Marlene decided to nudge Chuck more concretely along the path of conviction. On that occasion Marlene was sitting on the living-room couch before the fireplace working on a painting of a bird flying into a blood-red sunset, when she suddenly went into what Chuck took to be a "trance." She stiffened and stared unblinkingly into the middle distance, seemingly insensible to Chuck as he called out her name and waved his hand in front of her eyes. She had read all she could find in her books about automatic writing, a subject that especially interested her because of the way she often dashed off early versions of her poems, filling page after page without much reflection. She had made frequent attempts to experience the phenomenon without any success. Now she simply faked it, picking up a pad of paper and hastily improvising a series of made-up "letters" on a handy napkin. Then she began mumbling some sounds that Chuck couldn't understand. After ten or fifteen minutes Marlene suddenly appeared to snap out of her trance, whereupon she simply resumed the conversation with Chuck where she had left off as if nothing had happened.

"Boy, you were really out of it," Chuck said.

"What are you talking about?"

"You must have been in a trance. You were mumbling something and writing on this napkin."

Marlene looked at the napkin. "I don't remember a thing," she said. "I wrote that? That's the witches' alphabet."

Then, Chuck later recalled, "she just kinda smiled."

It seems clear that Marlene's first thoughts about killing her parents were a similar kind of playacting, what psychologists call "projected fantasy." Certainly they were taken that way by most of her friends. The first time she mentioned killing her parents in public, as Chuck recalled the occasion under hypnosis, was during a gripe session at Steve Donnelly's house: "We were all bitching about things we didn't like—school, being hassled by the police, our parents laying down all these rules. Marlene began talking about how much she hated her parents. She said, 'I wish they were dead. I wish someone would kill them.' 'I know what you mean,' I said. 'My parents are a real drag too.' "

As Christmas vacation approached, Marlene began to talk about killing her parents more and more frequently. At first none of her friends made much of a distinction between these remarks and what Chuck would later call "normal teen-age talk about wishing your folks would drop dead." "Sure, Marlene kept saying she wished her parents were dead," Nancy Dillon would later recall. "But no one took her seriously. We all sometimes wish our parents were dead."

Nor was anyone especially alarmed when Marlene first began speculating aloud about how she would kill her parents. Around that time she mentioned to Patti Metzger that it would be so easy to poison the soup she was sometimes called upon to heat up for Naomi at lunchtime. "I could lace it with fifty tabs of acid and watch her space to death," Marlene said. Patti took the remarks, as she took her friend's stories about her involvement with witchcraft and various rock stars, as "Marlene talk." On another occasion, after having an argument with Naomi while waiting for Travis Wheeler to pick her up, she slammed the front door and said to him, "I hate those sons of bitches. Do you know anyone who'd get rid of them for me?" Not long before, while rummaging through her father's papers for a copy of her birth certificate, Marlene had seen the will Jim kept in his office filing cabinet, which named her the sole heir to his estate in the event that he and Naomi died together, and she told Wheeler then that she would inherit "a bunch of money" and could afford to pay the killer handsomely. "I thought she was just blowin' off steam," Wheeler later said. "I used to get mad at my mom, too."

There were several reasons why the tension in the Olive household escalated around the time of the Christmas holidays, not the least of which revolved around the family telephone. The fact that Marlene had always spent an inordinate amount of time on the phone had long been a sore point with her parents. The problem was further aggravated by Marlene's habit of making frequent long-distance calls to friends from South America who had moved back to distant parts of the States, and even to Eve Ortega, her childhood friend in Miami. The result was that the Olives' home telephone bill was generally much higher than Jim's office bill, and in the preceding few months, as Marlene acquired a whole new set of friends to call, the bills had skyrocketed. By September, Jim had told Marlene to limit her local calls and pay for her long-distance calls out of her allowance. But the October and November bills were higher than ever, the latter coming to nearly $100. At that point Jim put a lock on the family phone, which meant that Marlene could receive calls but not make them. To do that she had to ask Jim's permission to use his office phone and limit her conversations to ten minutes, often in his presence. The situation infuriated Marlene, who had come to rely on telephone calls as confirmation of her new-found popularity. It also caused several big rows with Jim, the worst coming after he learned from Naomi that Marlene was circumventing his restrictions by using his office phone when he was out on his rounds, and from the December bill that she had been telling friends to call her on the home phone and reverse the charges.

There were other arguments about Marlene's growing problems at school. In some courses, especially English, she was doing quite well. (Marlene had become fascinated by Dostoevsky's novels and had written a well-received paper on the Russian writer that would unsettle her teacher when she reread it after the crime. It focused on the theme of parricide, which was for Dostoevsky, Marlene wrote, "the highest symptom of social decay, a disruption of human ties that contradicts the obligation of universal forgiveness and the promise of resurrection.") But she was also in danger of failing several courses that interested her less. When the head of the Spanish department, Eduardo Montoya, told her that she could no longer be a teacher's aide because of her poor overall academic performance, she broke down in tears. She had enjoyed the authority the position gave her and had also formed a friendship with Montoya, confiding to him stories about her mother's drinking and their terrible fights, more than once calling him at home after one of them to seek immediate advice and comfort. Now Montoya took her to Bettina Pearce, to whom she had also related the family's problems. The school guidance counselor decided that Marlene's scholastic slide had gone far enough, and so she telephoned Jim and asked him to come in with his daughter the following morning.

As always, Jim appeared both concerned and contrite about Marlene's behavior—the very model of a devoted parent. He talked about the culture shock of moving to the States, Marlene's initial isolation and the influence of a new set of friends—"fast kids," he called them. He seemed to have a grasp of some of the causes behind Marlene's recent truancy, and thus Mrs. Pearce took heart when he promised that he would talk the matter over with his daughter at home and take steps to resolve it. But she felt less sanguine when she brought up Naomi's drinking and her relationship with Marlene, for Jim visibly stiffened and quickly changed the subject. And what the elderly guidance counselor could not know was that once outside her office Jim angrily warned Marlene never again to "wash our dirty linen in public."

Besides Eduardo Montoya, the teacher who knew Marlene best was Jerry Fitch, her instructor in the batik class she took the previous summer. Now she was back again in his art class, together with Nancy Dillon. He found her greatly changed. Aside from her behavior, what had also changed for the worse was Marlene's penchant for telling elaborate tales of exotic adventures, many of them still revolving around her father. But now her fantasies were "more intense and dangerously out of control." And mixed in with Marlene's hero worship, Fitch would overhear derisive remarks about both her parents that showed "a very high level of anger and even hatred."

What Fitch calls "the bubble of Marlene's fantasies" burst for him the day she wore an exotic-looking bracelet to school that consisted of two strands of pewter-covered brass connected by a helix-shaped center band, all of it stamped with odd hieroglyphic markings. Fitch knew that even though the bracelet looked like expensive silver, it was, in fact, a common piece of Egyptian costume jewelry that many American women who travel to the Middle East bring home, as had his own wife. He started to compliment Marlene on the bracelet when she launched into an elaborate tale about how, with her father's help, she had fashioned it out of silver and added "mystical" Incan symbols herself. Since he didn't want to embarrass her in front of the other girls, Fitch simply listened in growing amazement as Marlene spun the story. Soon afterward Marlene began calling Fitch at home to ask if he wanted to buy the bracelet, and if not, where she could sell it. The reason she needed the money so urgently kept changing from one call to the next, but it always involved helping a friend over some emergency—a smashed car, an abortion—without the friend's parents finding out. At that point Fitch decided that Marlene's stories went beyond "simple lying" to "a situation that needed professional attention."

All of these problems—Marlene's deteriorating school work, her telephone calls, her "fast" friends—added a new and unaccustomed dynamic to the Olives' family life. No longer was the tension solely between Naomi and Marlene, with Jim playing his usual mediating role. To be sure, mother and daughter fought as bitterly as ever. More than once, in fact, their quarrels had gone beyond shouting matches to physical abuse. One routine argument, witnessed by Nancy Dillon, escalated to such a pitch of fury that Naomi hurled a hot iron she was using at Marlene across the room. It glanced off her wrist, leaving a red welt and eventually a scar that became a vivid symbol of Marlene's hatred of her mother.

But now Jim and Marlene began to argue frequently as well. She still tended to see her father's disciplinary actions as his way of "kissing my mom's toes" and felt jealous that he paid so much attention to her. Their arguments were over quickly, flash floods of emotions compared to the season-long storms between Naomi and Marlene, and her feelings about Jim remained ambiguous to the end. She continued to address adoring poetry to him ("O gentle moon, how I love to/bathe in your light./My love would grow just to gaze at your sight . . .") and clearly wanted to replace her mother completely in his affections and, if possible, in actual fact. Several times she raised—and Jim angrily rejected—the possibility of committing Naomi to a mental institution as the only hope for family accord. "It's either me or her," Marlene yelled on one such occasion. "Take your pick."

"I'll do no such thing, young lady," Jim replied. "She's your mother and you'll learn to get along with her."

But Jim was still Marlene's only protector, if an increasingly inconstant one. She continued to have a recurrent nightmare in which her father held up the brick walls of a crumbling school auditorium until she and her classmates could escape, before allowing them to collapse around him.

Then on Christmas day the walls of their own house almost tumbled down, or so it seemed to Naomi with more justification than usual. It all began auspiciously enough. Early that morning the family gathered around a small synthetic Christmas tree to unwrap presents. Marlene received a clock radio, bedroom slippers and a cosmetic set. She gave her father a leather briefcase and her mother a brass teapot that she had bought at Jim's urging. Afterward Jim and Naomi went out to buy a few last-minute items for the Christmas dinner they were preparing, Naomi having made it clear the night before that she had no intention of cooking. She was annoyed that Jim, in an attempt to heal recent family wounds, had encouraged Marlene to invite several friends over for turkey and trimmings. Marlene had asked Nancy and Sharon Dillon as well as Chuck, with whom she had become more friendly after breaking up with Travis Wheeler. ("Hiya, stranger," she had recently greeted him over the phone. "Where you been keeping yourself?")

Chuck was in particularly good favor with the Olives. A few days earlier he had sent Marlene and her mother a dozen roses each for Christmas and then came to the house to present a very surprised Jim Olive with a bottle of his favorite Scotch. The latter gift was "kind of a bribe, too," according to Chuck, since he wanted Jim's permission to take Marlene to a New Year's Eve concert in San Francisco. The strategy worked. "For some reason I trust you more than Marlene's other friends," Jim told Chuck. "You're the only one who ever has her back here when you say you will."

Marlene had also invited Ron Maddox, a young man she had met through Chuck and was instantly drawn to. Maddox was cast from the same mold as Wheeler, although he lacked Travis' raffish charm. Raised by his divorced mother in nearby Concord, he had been in trouble with the juvenile authorities early and continuously, becoming a ward of the court at the age of nine. Now he was living with an aunt in Terra Linda and paying expenses by burglarizing houses in Marin's wealthier neighborhoods. When Chuck felt that he needed a show of "muscle" on some of the larger coke deals he had graduated to, he hired Ron, who was adept at karate and the use of guns. Maddox set his fee at $100 if all went well, and double that if he ever had to "drop the hammer." When Marlene invited him to her house, Maddox told her that he had never been to a Christmas dinner. As it turned out, he arrived late and brought half the San Rafael police force with him.

What had happened was that Maddox had been driving to the Olives' house with a friend named Warren Creasy, who had recently run away from the Marin County juvenile hall, when the transmission on his borrowed car got stuck between gears. Maddox managed to pull into a nearby driveway to examine it. The owners of the house were on vacation, but a neighbor, fearing burglars, called the police. One of the policemen in the squad car that came around recognized Creasy, who immediately took off across the lawn. The officer fired a warning shot over the young man's head and then radioed for help. The shot, resounding eerily in the otherwise night-still neighborhood, brought everyone in the Olive house outdoors except Naomi, who had gone off to her room after dinner to watch one of her favorite TV police shows, *Cannon*. While Maddox ducked behind the car, Creasy, who knew Marlene and had in fact been over to visit her earlier that afternoon, headed for the Olive house, dashed through the front door shouting "Hide me, hide me!" and ran into a closet in her room.

Naomi looked up from the TV set to see a real police car sitting in the middle of her front lawn, its siren screaming and its red light rotating in the dark. Other police cars were pulling up alongside the curb. Several cops entered through the front door; others went around the back. Creasy was caught trying to climb out a window, wrestled to the floor, and after putting up quite a struggle for a reed-thin fifteen-year-old, handcuffed and dragged out of the house. When a grease-stained Ron Maddox walked in a few minutes later, he was greeted excitedly by Marlene and her other guests. Jim's welcome was considerably more restrained. He was somewhat relieved when Marlene and Ron falsely told the police that they knew Creasy but assumed that he had been released from juvenile hall rather than escaped. Naomi, however, was transfixed with horror and well beyond any reassurance. "It's just like on television," she kept muttering. After the incident she added two more locks to the front door, making an even half-dozen.

Of course, the excitement that day made Ron Maddox all the more appealing to Marlene. After the police left and her parents were out of earshot, she plied him with fervid questions about the incident. "I was out of the picture just when I thought I was back in," Chuck recalls. A few days later he walked into a friend's house looking for Ron Maddox and found him in bed with Marlene.

Chuck left to do some dealing, saying he'd return soon. On the way back he stopped off at Danny's Market to buy a six-pack of beer and recognized two plain-clothes detectives outside the store. He decided to put on an act to impress Marlene. Taking his gun out of the glove compartment, he knocked impatiently on his friend's front door with the butt end. Once inside, he locked the door, moved quickly to a window and peered through a crack in the curtains at the street as if he were being pursued. He opened the revolver, spun the cylinders to make sure it was fully loaded, cocked it and put it down on a table along with his cocaine supply. "Some cops have been hasslin' me," he announced dramatically. "They're not gettin' me or the drugs without a fight." After keeping up the charade for half an hour, he said, "I guess I lost 'em on the way over." Then he hung around the rest of the day looking downcast when he wasn't staring accusingly at Marlene. But late in the afternoon when Naomi called to tell Marlene to come home, Chuck readily agreed to drive her there.

For the next several weeks Marlene spent most of her time with Ron Maddox. Chuck was often around, always willing to do her bidding. He told Maddox that he loved Marlene and would "always be there for her." She, in turn, used her new-found sexuality to keep both Chuck and Ron in a continual state of jealousy by snuggling up to one of them in the other's presence (although she slept with Maddox and still refused Chuck's clumsy advances). Just as she had done to Chuck, she tried to make Ron think that she had occult powers by predicting his future, and once by going into a "trance" that he couldn't shake her out of for fifteen minutes. After she saw *The Exorcist* on television Marlene practiced the look of satanic possession that Linda Blair used in the film whenever one of her "premonitions" was coming over her, gritting her teeth and rolling the pupils of her eyes off to the side or making them disappear altogether.

Around New Year's Marlene became consumed with plans to run away from home, announcing her intention to anyone who would listen. She explained to Raul Fernandez, the director of the Spanish-speaking social club La Familia, that she planned to make enough money on a drug deal to buy a car and then head for Florida with Ron Maddox. Linda Fraser's mother tried to talk Marlene out of it. "With your baby face, I told her, they'll pick you up at the first red light."

Practically any older woman who befriended Marlene became a substitute mother figure. "I feel closer to you than I do to my real mom," she told Gloria Fraser. "I can tell you anything and it wouldn't shock you." A part of her longed to be a dutiful daughter. "Once when Jim picked her up here," Mrs. Fraser recalls, "she said, 'See, I even washed the dishes without being asked.' " But another part of her was growing angrier than ever at both her parents. One night, after a bad fight with Naomi, Marlene called up Jim's business associate Kathy Kane and, crying hysterically, said, "My mother hates me because I'm from Ecuador. She hates everything Latin."

Until now Marlene's talk about killing her mother had been vague enough to be taken lightly by her friends. With Ron Maddox she formulated elaborate and quite specific murder plans. At first they involved hiring someone Maddox claimed to know who would do the job for a fee. "I was thinking about what you said," Marlene wrote Maddox. "About that man who would take care of my mom. I think we should talk it over together, you and I. I'd be worried about what would happen after she died but whatever did wouldn't keep me away from you."

Soon Marlene drew Maddox into her plan directly. He had told her that he sometimes borrowed a friend's rifle—a .30-06 with a telescopic sight—to go deer hunting in the mountains. "She had mentioned wanting to kill her mom before, but I never thought anything would come of it. One day she called me up and said, 'I've got to get rid of her or I'm gonna kill myself.' She had it all worked out.'' In the plan Maddox was supposed to break into a recently vacated house across the street from the Olives. After Jim left early in the morning Marlene would get Naomi to pick up the paper at the foot of the driveway, where Maddox would have a clear shot at her. Maddox took Marlene seriously enough to actually borrow the rifle. ''She had little ways of getting to you. She'd put you on the spot. She'd say, 'Were you serious when you said you'd help me or was that just talk?' Or else she'd come on with an 'I guess I'll have to find someone else' type thing.''

Days would go by when Marlene didn't bring up her murder plans, but every time she raised them, according to Maddox, ''she was a little more up to her eyeballs with everything. She had to plan to poison her mother one night when her dad worked late and she had to cook dinner for the two of them. She said she'd leave an empty bottle of pills by the bed to make it look like suicide. She talked about hitting her mother over the head and making it look like she was drunk and fell in the driveway. She had a lot of crazy ideas. How many ways can you kill a person?''

Eventually Marlene came up with a bizarre plan that involved killing Jim in order to drive Naomi ''over the edge.'' It was worked out in considerable detail. ''She'd ask her dad to drive her to a friend's house on the other side of China Camp,'' Ron Maddox explained. ''She'd make up the friend's name and tell her mother. When the car was going through China Camp she'd pretend that she was sick or just lose something out the window. Any distraction to stop the car and have him get out of it. I'd be up on a hill and when he got out of the car I'd hit him. Then we'd stuff him back in and drive into the woods and bury him. Everyone knew how crazy her mother was, or at least they would after she told them her husband was driving Marlene over to a friend nobody'd ever heard of. People would think the old man just up and left. And with him gone Marlene figured there was ninty-nine out of a hundred percent chance her mom would really go overboard and have to be put away. Then she'd be home free.''

Once again Maddox took the plan seriously enough to go out to China Camp, pick a likely spot on a rise above the dirt road and fire off some practice shots. But after thinking it over, he decided not to carry out the plan. "Her father, that was what my mind snagged on," he said later. "I knew him. He was a reasonable man. Why do I want to do this? I could get a good twenty years if not life for some screwy dream of hers."

After rejecting the plan, Maddox told Marlene he didn't want to talk about the subject anymore, and eventually "the whole idea just sorta faded out." But even if he had not backed out, it is far from clear that Marlene would actually have carried out any of her proposals. When the police finally searched her room they found letters to Maddox describing this and other detailed plans to kill her parents in a cardboard box under her bed, along with her poems and fashion drawings. Most of the schemes involved killing Naomi alone, but a few included Jim. They were all written in a hasty, angular scrawl instead of her usual practiced penmanship, as if to relieve a surge of anger, and, of course, they had never been mailed.

Since Maddox's change of heart made it more difficult for Marlene to even entertain the thought of killing Naomi, she finally carried out her alternative plan for freeing herself from an increasingly intolerable domestic situation. On January 15, her sixteenth birthday, Marlene ran away from home.

She had cut school that day and spent the morning with a group of friends at Steve Donnelly's house. Chuck gave her a necklace consisting of a tiny silver coke spoon on a chain, and she invited him over to her house for the birthday dinner the family was planning. (Ever since the Christmas Day incident Jim had become increasingly hostile to Ron Maddox, who thus joined a growing list of friends either he or Naomi refused to allow in the house.) In the afternoon Marlene went shopping at Northgate Mall. She paid for the merchandise with a Sears credit card she had stolen from Naomi's pocketbook that morning, showing the clerk a note she had forged in her mother's handwriting giving "my daughter Marlene" permission to use it. After three o'clock, when school would be out, she went home. Since it was her birthday, Naomi's angry outburst caught her by surprise.

The school attendance office had called again to say that Marlene had been absent without excuses all week. In addition, Naomi had discovered that her credit card was missing, and her suspicion that Marlene had taken it seemed confirmed as soon as she walked in the door carrying shopping bags. Marlene's quick denial did not stop Naomi from launching into the all too familiar litany of complaints about Marlene's school work, her "no-good friends," the way she was "whoring around" and "dressing like a tramp." Marlene fought back for a while and then stormed into her room, slamming the door behind her. When Chuck came over for dinner she signaled to him to wait for her down the block. Then she filled a suitcase with clothes and her poetry books and told Naomi she was "returning some of Sharon's things." Before Jim came home from work Naomi found the abrupt note Marlene had left on her bed: "I'm taking off with Ron Maddox. Please don't look for me." Later Marlene wrote a poem about her decision to run away that ends:

> My words are hollow and echo in this house
> Filled with the crumpled paper thoughts
> Of my parents . . .
> Now their thoughts pile up
> In the rooms and halls
> And deaden the echo.

Six

Marlene had no intention of going very far. She told Chuck to drop her clothes off at Arlene Geary's, trusting that Sharon and Nancy Dillon's mother would allow her to stay there for a time, as she had any number of other "runaway" Terra Linda kids. At that very moment, in fact, the small house in Santa Venetia looked more like a juvenile crisis center than a family dwelling. Nancy Dillon, who had recently left her father's house in nearby San Anselmo, was staying with her mother, as was Sharon and a younger sister. Ron Maddox, whose mother threatened to turn him in to juvenile authorities if he ever came back to Concord, had been staying there for several days, and Teri Kellogg had been at the Gearys' since November. That was when her parents kicked her out of their comfortable house in Marinwood for being a "bad influence" on her younger sister and agreed to send Arlene a biweekly check to cover her upkeep. So it was a good bet that the easygoing Mrs. Geary would allow Marlene to stay at her house, although the older woman did insist that she telephone her parents that evening to let them know she was safe.

By the time Marlene called two hours later, Jim and Naomi were panic-stricken. A quick check of her room had verified that she had taken many of her belongings; it also turned up a cigar box full of marijuana seeds that Marlene had collected, intending, she later claimed, to string them into a necklace, as well as a note that said "Buy acid/cocaine." While Naomi railed against all the forces she was sure were corrupting her daughter, she was also genuinely concerned about Marlene's safety and even contrite about her role in starting the fight. With Naomi's help, Jim immediately launched into a frenzied search for Marlene that would continue unabated until the police found her five days later.

Characteristically, he kept a detailed record of his activities, which began with the notation "6:30 P.M. Arrived home. Marlene missing 15 minutes." He called Chuck, who misled him by saying that Marlene might have gone to a party at Ed Tucker's house down the block from the Olives' but responded to Jim's request for a list of her friends and their telephone numbers. In his datebook Jim noted: "Chuck cooperative. Doesn't know whereabouts."

Next Jim drove to the Gearys' house, where he suspected Marlene might have gone. At first Mrs. Geary feigned ignorance of Marlene's whereabouts, but Jim spotted her suitcase in the living room and insisted on taking it back. "You may think you're doing her a favor by covering up for her," he said, making an effort to control his anger, "but you're not." He drove to Ed Tucker's house. "Kids party going on," he noted when he got back. "No knowledge of Marlene."

Just then she called. "Said she was with friends in Novato," he continued writing after a terse conversation. "Would be home tomorrow. Would not reveal location. Crying. Seemed to be hazy, disconnected." By this point Jim was as angry as he was concerned, and he told Marlene that she'd "better be home in 24 hours or I'll call the police."

No wonder Marlene was hazy and disconnected when she called home. Chuck had gone over to a friend's house with Marlene and Sharon to break up five pounds of prime Jamaican grass and make some sales. Since then the small group of teen-agers had liberally sampled his merchandise, dropped some acid that Ron Maddox had brought with him, and with the adults in the household away on vacation, gotten into a collection of fine wines that was stored in the cellar. Chuck was very upset at the thought that Marlene might run away with Ron Maddox. Influenced by his state of mind and the occult books he had been reading, he experienced a frightening LSD-induced hallucination during which he saw himself standing in a pool of fire conversing with a robed figure he took to be Satan, who told him that Marlene had the power to destroy life with her mind.

Marlene spent the night at the Gearys'. Around noon the next day she called home again. "I'm sorry I took the credit card," she told her father. "I'll pay for the things I bought."

"I'm not concerned with that now," Jim said. "I want you to come home. Your mother feels very badly."

"I'm not coming. I need to lead my own life without any interference from her."

"Come home and we'll work things out."

"You can't get her to change. She's always drunk and on my case."

Afterward Marlene reported to Arlene Geary: "My dad said to come home and things would be better. He's said that so many times and it never is. He can't do anything."

Since it was clear that the first place the police would look for Marlene was the Gearys' house, Marlene and Ron Maddox moved in with a neighbor named Maurice, a good-looking young man who made his living largely as a gigolo to wealthy older women. He and Ron Maddox struck up a quick friendship. At night the two would go off together to burglarize houses in Tiburon and Sausalito, fencing the fur coats, stereos and color television sets they stole, while giving most of the jewelry to Maurice's girl friend and Marlene.

For all her brave words about independence, the five days Marlene spent away from home were a miserable time for her. Like any other sixteen-year-old she felt more frightened by her sudden freedom from parental control than liberated by it. Most of the time she stayed in bed with severe stomach pains, half hoping that Jim would find her. He and Naomi spent every waking moment trying. Once and sometimes twice a day Jim telephoned or personally visited everyone on a three-page list of people who might possibly have heard from Marlene. Even Naomi made calls, including a long tearful conversation with Kim Ferguson in which, according to Marlene's friend, "she asked me what I thought they could do to get Marlene back on the track. I told her to ease up a little—kids are different up here from where Marlene grew up."

After Marlene had been away for three days Jim informed the San Rafael police about the situation, although there was not much they could do to find her beyond keeping a close watch on the Geary house. Two days later, when a girl in a rabbit-skin jacket was spotting walking into the house, the police contacted Jim and waited for him to arrive before making their entrance, as he had requested them to do. It turned out that the girl who had aroused the police's suspicion was Teri Kellogg, wearing a coat identical to Marlene's; Marlene was in the bedroom sick with cramps and a fever. Ron Maddox tried to block Jim's way by demanding a search warrant, but by then, Marlene admits, she "wanted home." Jim was so relieved to see her that he put aside his anger for the moment and bent over the bed to hug her, although he did not, as Marlene would later recall, burst into tears. Because she was ill, Jim was able to convince the two policemen who accompanied him to release Marlene in his custody immediately rather than take her to the juvenile hall, which would have been the normal procedure.

Jim and Marlene didn't talk on the way home, but when they arrived, Naomi couldn't contain herself. She repeatedly threatened to prosecute Arlene Geary for harboring a runaway. "Let's just drop it here," Jim intervened. "Let's start all over." But he was equally intemperate on one subject—Ron Maddox. "You are never to see that little bastard again, young lady. If I ever catch him around this house, I'll make sure he regrets it." In the end Naomi and Marlene promised Jim to try to get along better, and they all agreed to keep an appointment for family counseling with juvenile officer Scott Nelson, although Naomi was only convinced to go when Jim told her that her presence was required by law. Belatedly, Marlene received her birthday presents— hot curlers, a blow dryer and a set of plastic bracelets.

Because of his interest in psychology, Scott Nelson conducted preliminary family counseling sessions during which he probed the relationship between parents and teen-agers to determine whether more professional help was called for. It was a service frequently used by families who attached a special opprobrium to psychological counseling but did not mind sitting down together with a friendly cop. The day after Marlene returned, Jim called Nelson to set up an appointment. Over the telephone he pointed to Marlene's relationship with Naomi as the reason why she ran away. But he seemed even more concerned about what he referred to as her "drug habit."

When the Olives arrived for their late-afternoon appointment, the first thing the psychologically oriented juvenile officer did was make a mental note of how they arranged the folding chairs that he deliberately kept stacked against a wall. If the parents sat together and separated themselves from their son or daughter, he knew he was in for a difficult, generally unproductive session. If they all sat together, particularly with the child in the middle, as the Olives did, his hopes rose.

The second thing Nelson did was take out his "parents'

education kit'' and display it on his desk top. Nelson hoped that by examining his collection of easily obtainable drug paraphernalia—everything from tiny roach clips to enormous, tentacular water pipes—parents would lose some of the fear and ignorance about the whole subject that made them less than rational in dealing with it. ''Look,'' he said, pointing out the cigarette he was holding, ''when I was a kid we played with candy cigarettes and now I have a pack-a-day habit I can't break.'' He handed Jim a metal box of what seemed like scented confectioner's sugar. The label read: ''Lemon Snow Dust. Pure White Sniffing Powder. A Cokesnuff Product.'' He handed Naomi a syringelike dispenser of sourballs. ''Eight-year-old kids can buy this stuff in any head shop in town,'' he said for emphasis.

There was a poster of the wall behind Nelson that depicted the parts of a marijuana plant in blown-up detail. ''We know about those, don't we, young lady?'' Jim said, pointing to the seeds. It was his first reference to the box of seeds he had found in her bedroom, and Marlene, caught unaware, blushed. ''I was only going to soak them in water and string them on a necklace,'' she said unconvincingly. Nelson relieved the tension by pointing out a Doonesbury cartoon next to the poster that showed two beer-bellied cops searching for marijuana seeds in a kid's car. (''Hey look,'' one says, ''there's three.'' ''Three?'' his partner exclaims. ''Why he must be a dealer. Geez, that's 30 years, ain't it?'') It was one of Nelson's principles as a counselor never to let himself be identified with either parent or child and to keep both sides in a conflict slightly off balance. Now he handed Marlene the piece of paper on which she had written ''Buy acid/cocaine'' and asked her what it meant. ''There was nothing I could say,'' Marlene later recalled. ''I just sat there like a dummy.''

It was almost a relief when Nelson changed topics, launching into his favorite therapeutic technique, ''reverse role playing.'' The idea was to get parents and teen-agers to appreciate each other's point of view by switching identities, but the problem was that few of them, and certainly not Marlene and Naomi, had enough distance on their relationship to make the necessary imaginative leap. Nelson asked Marlene to introduce herself as Naomi. According to Nelson, ''Most kids are very guarded in this situation. They don't want to pay for it later. But Marlene seemed to enjoy sticking it to her mother.'' He recalled that Marlene, playing Naomi, began by saying, ''I used to be beautiful but now my face is wrinkled and the veins in my legs show," and went on to talk about spending her days drinking, feeding the fish and, of course, "bossing my daughter around." Curiously, Naomi, playing Marlene, also started out with a physical compliment that immediately became a complaint: "I could be very beautiful if I didn't wear make-up and cheap clothes."

With introductions made, Nelson asked Marlene and Naomi to take each other's parts in a typical fight. They more or less replayed the argument that followed Marlene's return home from the Gearys' and, again, Nelson was surprised by the degree of anger and invective each displayed. "You know all the sassy remarks," he said afterward, "but how well do you understand each other's real thoughts and feelings?" At the end of the session Nelson recommended that the family undergo psychological counseling and wrote down the names of a few agencies that provided the service. But he suspected that the Olives would not follow his advice and, indeed, they never did. On the way home Naomi swore that she'd never allow herself to be "dragged through that cesspool again."

Whatever determination the Olives made to resolve their differences faded within a few days of Marlene's return home. She continued secretly to see Ron Maddox in the face of Jim's angry warning, while telling her parents that he had moved away from the Bay area. (She even had him address an envelope to her, mailed it to her friend in Florida with instructions to send it back, and then made sure her parents saw the envelope with its Miami postmark.) But she chafed at Jim's interference, which could not, as other restrictions could, be blamed on Naomi's influence over him. One afternoon in late January, Ron Maddox drove over to see Marlene, as usual sending a friend to get her out of the house. Naomi spied him from the kitchen window and yelled out to Jim, who had come to blame much of Marlene's actions on the young man's influence. In a cold rage he took his old unloaded army pistol from a locked desk drawer and strode out the door. He ordered Marlene inside before directing his attention to Maddox. "If I ever see you near this house again," he said, holding the pistol by his side but taking steady aim with his words, "it will be the last time."

It never went beyond a verbal confrontation because Maddox did, in fact, move away from the Bay Area a few weeks later. With the police on his trail after the string of house burglaries, he had gone back to live with his mother in Concord but then had been caught stealing a car battery. Having been in and out of juvenile halls for so many years, Maddox was now faced with doing, as he put it, "good time or hard time." The juvenile court judge allowed him to volunteer for a Job Corps program in Oregon. On several occasions Chuck agreed to drive Marlene to the East Bay so that she could visit Maddox and deliver a series of love poems to him.

On the way back from their last trip Marlene told Chuck, according to his subsequent recollections under hypnosis, that "there was something different about me, a kind of glow that she had never seen before. It was just that I was happy Ron was in juvenile hall and maybe now I finally had her to myself. There was no one left." While Chuck was driving, Marlene began unbuttoning his shirt and playfully pulling the hair on his "Italian" chest. "Then Marlene lay down with her head on my lap and began just rubbing her hand up and down my leg. Then she began to feel me. She unbuckled my pants and played with me. It was the first time we did anything related to sex."

With his much vaunted driving skills meeting their most severe challenge ever, Chuck managed to reach the lake behind the Civic Center. A nearly full moon reflected off the still water. He went on reminiscing under hypnosis: "I unbuttoned her blouse and unsnapped her bra and bent over to kiss her breasts. Then I unsnapped and unzipped her pants. They were skintight and it was pretty hard to do. She said, 'Here, let me help you.' Then I just didn't know what to do next. I mean I knew how to but I didn't know if I should have sex with her or if this was just a game she was playing with me or what. We talked for a few minutes and I saw that it was getting late and I said I ought to be taking her home." When they arrived at the Olives' house and Chuck tried to kiss Marlene good night she turned away abruptly, which puzzled him. Nonetheless, months later, when one of the psychologists who hypnotized Chuck before his trial asked him what the happiest day of his life was, he answered, "It was the night by the lake coming back from Concord. I think that was the happiest day."

Chuck finally slept with Marlene the next day. Marlene was over at his house to see Joanne Riley off to the hospital, where she was scheduled to undergo a hysterectomy. Marlene enjoyed the same close, confidential relationship with her that she did with the mothers of many of her friends, and she had agreed to do some cooking and cleaning around the house in Mrs. Riley's absence. After Joanne left the house, the teen-agers went to listen to records in Chuck's room, where Marlene, according to the detailed account of the rest of the day that Chuck would eventually relate under hypnosis, took the lead in seducing him:

"She started to undress and I just sat there and stared at her. She unbuttoned my shirt and told me to get in bed with her. I said all right. I was enthralled. I never thought it would happen. And so we had sex for a short time and I climaxed really fast and then I almost blacked out when I got out, I just couldn't believe it. Then a few minutes later we had sex again for about 45 minutes to an hour. Afterwards she said that she wants sex in her own time and in her own way. That she would come to me, I wasn't to try to take her.

"Later I took her home and had dinner over at her house. After dinner Mr. Olive went into his office and Mrs. Olive went into her room and we sat watching TV and kind of had our arms around each other. She was very jumpy about that and whenever she heard someone coming she told me I was to take my arm off her. At night I had to leave the house by ten, and about 15 minutes before then Mr. Olive would come into the living room, kind of like checking up, and tell me it was time. That night I looked at Marlene and told her that I had always loved her and that I would be a part of her life, even if I have to be second. And then she slid up and laid me back on the couch and was just completely teasing me, running her hands up and down my legs and wrapping her thighs around my waist and pressing her whole body, squeezing it against mine as tight as she could. And she was just saying, 'Ah, oh, baby,' all hot and bothered. And she laughed. I just put my arms around her and held her. Then I went to kiss her again and she did the same thing she had done the night before. She turned away."

After that first time Marlene and Chuck made love nearly every day. When Joanne Riley was well again and working the day shift, Chuck would pick Marlene up at school in the morning and drive back home. At other times they would have sex at some friend's house or in the isolated shack that Chuck had helped build as a boyhood retreat or, simply, in the ample back seat of his Buick. Often Chuck rented rooms at the Villa Rafael motel in the afternoon. He would drive Marlene home in time for her ten o'clock curfew, pick her up at school the next morning and return to the motel room until checkout time. He would always keep the room key as a memento, a fact that the police discovered after the murders when they searched his room and found the collection in a shoe box.

Chuck was the first boy Marlene had gone out with who was less experienced sexually than she was, and from the beginning sex with him became a means of control and, sometimes, of humiliation. She delighted in arousing him while he was driving and helpless to return her advances, several times doing so in the presence of girl friends. But primarily Chuck (who had told her that he was a virgin when he started to sleep with her) provided Marlene with a blank canvas on which to create sexual fantasies. Although they soon became as lurid and death-obsessed as other areas of her imagination, at first they seemed innocent enough. (One of Marlene's poems from those days began with the invitation to "Let me show you Paris/In a satin-sheeted bed.") She encouraged Chuck to dress all in black and sometimes to rip off her clothes and otherwise treat her roughly. Once she showed him a photograph in *Penthouse* of a nude woman she claimed to be her. More often Marlene would clip out nude pictorial displays from men's magazines, imagining that she was the model in the photographs and making up sexually suggestive quotations about herself, which she would then paste over the real ones. "Making love underwater to the delight of a school of trailing dolphins," she captioned a provocative sailing layout. " 'I can unleash my body out at sea,' says Marlene, 'especially when I'm with a sensitive, commanding lover.' " And beside another photograph she wrote: "There's something about the raw power and brooding moods of the sea, the constant pulsing of waves disguising deep hidden fury, that makes sex in the silent waters so intense."

More inconvenient for Chuck was Marlene's insistence on what he called "telephone sex." In general, the telephone became a kind of umbilical cord connecting Chuck to Marlene, a way for her to keep him in tow and exact a certain revenge on her parents for limiting her outgoing calls. Having ignored Chuck for months, she now wanted him to check in with her frequently throughout the day to tell her what he was doing. Before Chuck dropped her off at night she would often ask him to call her an hour later, when she knew her parents would be asleep. She would pick up the receiver at the first sound and the two would often talk through the night. One time Chuck called Marlene at midnight, as she had instructed him to do, and was still on the phone when Oscar got up for work at six o'clock, an expensive "talk-a-thon" that he was quick to criticize.

Although it was far less comfortable, thereafter Chuck generally called from a public telephone outside a nearby 7-Eleven store, using rolls of dimes he kept in his glove compartment for just that purpose and wrapping himself in a sleeping bag to ward off the cold. During these hours-long early-morning conversations Marlene enjoyed a captive audience for her fantasies about her future as a rock star, actress or high-class call girl. She would also give full vent to her hatred of Naomi, recounting their latest argument in minute, if often misleading, detail. She talked about her plans to find her "real" mother and speculated about the woman's identity. And at some point in the conversation she would bring up the game of "telephone sex," asking Chuck to pretend that he was making love to her and give a graphically explicit account of his actions while she masturbated.

It was during one of these telephone conversations that Marlene first elicited Chuck's help in killing her mother. If she and Chuck could come up with enough money by pulling off a big coke deal, she mused, maybe she could hire someone to do the job.

"It's either me or that bitch," Marlene said, after relating her latest argument with Naomi. "Either I'm gonna do her in or myself. You *must* know someone who'd do it to help us out."

"Maybe I do," Chuck said casually. "Let me think about it."

"Think now," Marlene suddenly challenged him. "What about one of your connections?"

"Well," Chuck said, wriggling on the hook, "if anyone can do it, or at least knows someone who would, it's Fred Griffin. He's a really big-time dealer with a lot of underworld contacts in the city."

"Talk to him," Marlene urged.

Actually Fred, the elder brother of Chuck's friend Gary Griffin, was a supermarket clerk living in San Francisco who had, several years back, provided the boys with some marijuana when they first started dealing. "It wasn't exactly that I picked a name out of the air," Chuck said later. "He was a real person, so if she checked up on me she couldn't say I was lying. Plus, she couldn't find him by herself very easily since he lived somewhere in the city and even I didn't know where. I figured that after she blew off some steam about her mom the matter would drop."

It did, at least for a time. In March, Marlene entered a new school and, for two weeks, a new family as well. Despite her repeated promises to improve her school work, her grades and attendance continued to slide. She failed one course and received incompletes in two others. At a final meeting with Bettina Pearce, Jim pleaded that she not be sent to Madrone, a "continuation" school for problem students, fearing that "she would be associating there with an even worse element than she already is." Impressed with Jim's concern, the guidance counselor agreed to allow Marlene to begin the spring term at Pacific Crest, an experimental public school housed in a church in downtown San Rafael. Naomi tried to turn an embarrassing situation to its best advantage. "We've finally got Marlene into a good private school," she told several people. "You can't imagine how much they cost these days."

An outgrowth of late-sixties permissiveness, Pacific Crest had originally been designed to provide a more flexible, "creative" environment than regular high school for students who, for a variety of reasons, thrived best in such an atmosphere. The school had few obligatory courses (even state-mandated requirements such as physical education could be fulfilled by riding a bicycle to school or hiking on weekends), refused to list failures on report cards and allowed students to hold down jobs by attending adult-education courses at night. Students even had played a role in choosing the school's two teachers, Joan James and Gunard Solberg, both young, committed and interested in the arts, the former an accomplished photographer and the latter a published novelist. But as a reaction set in against educational liberalism and the community's share of state funds dwindled along with its school-age population, Pacific Crest had recently been forced to take an increasing number of "referrals" from the area's regular high schools, students who were there not by choice but, like Marlene, because they were doing poorly elsewhere.

In his first meeting with Jim and Marlene, Gunard Solberg was struck by what an "incongruous pair" they made. "Here was this superstraight businessman of a kind you don't see anymore, at least in California—conservative suit and tie, gold-rim glasses, squeaky-clean. And his daughter—wearing a sexy leather skirt, lots of blue eye shadow and huge rings on every finger—looked like a Sunset Strip hooker." But Solberg was encouraged by Jim's pronouncement that Marlene was "a good student and just needed to be in a stimulating environment." And he also thought it an encouraging sign that Marlene, hoping to make up the credits she had lost the past term, signed up for an unusually heavy schedule, including such no-nonsense courses as sociology, marine biology and creative writing. At the end of the meeting Jim handed Solberg his business card and said, "Please call me if there's any problem."

Solberg taught the creative-writing course on Wednesday evenings at his house, encouraging students to read their work aloud and discuss it. The first week Marlene was too shy to read, but the sheaf of poems she handed in further buoyed her teacher's optimism about her abilities. They also provided an insight into Marlene's personality that gave him cause for concern as he became more familiar with the Olive family's problems. Solberg later recalled his initial reaction: "I thought the poems were the best student work that I had ever seen—technically polished, thematically interesting. Most kids write pretty slapdash free-verse poems. Hers had a more formal elegance, maybe because of her Latin background. Most of them were very self-absorbed, often about love but with a lot of violence thrown in for its shock value. Here was an adolescent ego crying out for people to notice that she was alive and special."

Unfortunately, Marlene's scholastic diligence at Pacific Crest faded quickly. She dropped several courses and simply failed to attend others, so that by the end of the school year she would only receive credit—an A—in her creative-writing class. In an attempt to promote responsibility the school required its students to furnish excuses if they intended to be absent or late. In the course of a week Marlene would give Joan James or Gunard Solberg a bewildering variety of excuses—doctors appointments, job interviews and, in time, court appearances and meetings with her lawyer—and leave before class began to meet Chuck in the parking lot. When Jim found out that Marlene was still cutting classes, a nasty row ensued. He had already insisted on dropping her off at school every morning; from then on he took to making unannounced stops there during his daily rounds to check up on her. Since no other parent had ever done that before, it is hard to say whether Marlene was more embarrassed when Jim caught her cutting school than she was on the rare occasions when he found her in class.

It was about this time that Marlene hit upon the idea of finding a foster home to live in, an arrangement, she had learned, that the juvenile authorities sometimes made in cases of extreme friction between parents and children. She made an appointment with Scott Nelson to explore that possibility. Although by now the juvenile officer was well aware of the family's problems, he was amazed at the level of hostility that Marlene expressed toward Naomi. "Marlene told me that the mother hated her and was on her case for every little thing, sometimes getting physically abusive when she was drunk," he recalls. "She showed me a cut on her arm that she said she got when Mrs. Olive pushed her through a plate-glass window. She said that her mother slept in the spare room opposite her bedroom because her father couldn't stand sleeping next to a drunk and that she kept Marlene up at night talking to herself. She even made a point of saying the parents never had sex. She kept calling her mother 'that bitch.' The only complaint she seemed to have about her father was that he kowtowed to the mother to keep things peaceful."

Nelson told Marlene that finding a foster home involved a court procedure and was probably not possible in her case, but he was sufficiently impressed by her litany of complaints to suggest that she might find a family who would agree to take her in until she and her mother could come to some sort of terms. In the next few weeks this notion became an obsession with Marlene. She asked Jim's business associate Kathy Kane and several of her friends' mothers if she could stay with them. She told Helen Metzger that her relations with her mother were "getting out of control" and she had to leave home. "I didn't know whether to believe her stories," the petite blond nurse would testify in juvenile court, "because she always overdramatized and took things to the limit. She told me that Naomi had thrown a knife at her and had beaten her until she bled. That's why she had ulcers."

Joanne Riley finally found a family that was willing to care for Marlene in return for some light baby-sitting chores. One of her colleagues at the nursing home had relatives in nearby Novato, the Hermandezes, who both worked during the day and needed someone to be home when their two young granddaughters returned from school in the afternoon. It could not have been a better choice, for the couple, Mexican-Americans fluent in Spanish and English, proved to be devout middle-aged people who loved and understood children, having raised five of their own before taking on the responsibility of bringing up two more.

All that remained was for Marlene to convince Naomi and Jim to give their consent to the scheme. In fact, that evening Jim was quickly persuaded by her argument that it would be a temporary situation to relieve the pressure at home. "It's a lot better if you know where I am than if I run away again," Marlene said, driving home her point with a not so veiled threat. Jim agreed to call the Hernandezes, and after a pleasant conversation in which he discovered that he knew Luis Hernandez, the owner of a small auto repair shop, he told Marlene that she could live there "as an experiment."

Everything went smoothly for the first week or so. Then problems developed in a rush. Marlene became less than conscientious about being at the Hernandezes' house when the two girls arrived home from school. Late one afternoon when Marlene was entertaining several friends in the living room, Mrs. Hernandez thought she smelled marijuana, a fact that Marlene later ruefully confirmed. On another occasion, when Mrs. Hernandez, removing Marlene's pocketbook from the dining-room table, asked why it was so heavy, Marlene showed her the kitchen knife she carried around "for protection." Even more ominous was the fact that each morning Marlene appeared at breakfast dressed in a new expensive-looking article of clothing, and when Mrs. Hernandez asked her how she could afford them, she said that her father was "feeling guilty" about her absence and giving her the money.

When she called Jim to discuss Marlene's behavior, Mrs. Hernandez learned that the girl had lied about her father's generosity. And that wasn't all—he had not seen his daughter since he drove her to Novato two weeks before, despite the fact that Marlene told the Hernandezes that she had spent the past Saturday night at home so that she could go to church with her father on Sunday morning. Confronted with her lies, Marlene cried and asked for another chance. But the following Friday, after Marlene had been with the family three weeks, she and Chuck left for a concert in San Francisco, promising to be home by one o'clock. Marlene did not get back until the next morning, and at that point a weary Mrs. Hernandez, who had waited up all night for her charge, told her that she would have to return to her parents. "Marlene, you need a mother and father," she added consolingly. "You don't need two strange people." When Jim came to pick Marlene up a short time later he apologized profusely for his daughter's behavior, and with tears in his eyes, told Mrs. Hernandez that the family would "have to try harder."

Even with the best of wills, it may have been too late, for Marlene and Chuck were already embarked on a whirlwind shoplifting spree that would end three weeks later when they were arrested and charged with grand larceny. By then they had amassed more than $6,000 worth of stolen merchandize of every description—dozens of blouses, pants, dresses, shoes, purses, articles of jewelry, and bottles of perfume and bath oil from Marin's best department stores and trendiest boutiques.

The ill-fated adventure began when Marlene decided that she "wanted some action, something challenging." One day she and a girl friend stole some clothing at the Emporium department store in Northgate Mall. When she told Chuck about the theft he tried to talk her out of repeating it, motivated not so much by moral conviction as by a fear of losing her. "I knew that if she got into trouble and her parents came down hard on her, she'd just run away again," Chuck explained later. When she insisted on returning to the scene of her crime the next day, Chuck decided to go along "to act as a lookout," as he later put it under hypnosis. "So we drove to the Emporium in my car. Marlene stole some gloves and she saw a scarf she wanted and stole that. We went to the make-up department and she palmed a compact and put her arm around my waist and the next thing I knew it was in my back pocket and I was helping her. She had a way of sticking her hands in my pocket like a girl friend would and putting rings in there, too. She liked to put me on the spot."

At first Marlene took nearly all the initiative in their shoplifting. She would hide large items inside a tear in the lining of Chuck's leather jacket or in a cloth "booster bag" that she pinned to the inside of her own rabbit-skin coat, a trick she had learned from Travis Wheeler. Even in the beginning, Chuck admitted, Marlene could always get him to participate actively to "win her appreciation" or just by saying that if he didn't steal something, then she would. Several times she refused his offer to buy her what she wanted.

When their presence in the neighborhood shops became too risky they moved farther afield to shopping centers closer to San Francisco—in San Anselmo, Corte Madera, Tiburon and Sausalito. They became an expert team, one of them distracting the sales clerk while the other shoplifted. Mounds of stolen merchandise piled up in the trunk and back seat of Chuck's car. After every heft Marlene would carefully remove and save the price tags and enter the value of the items in a notebook. Only occasionally would Chuck take something for himself.

As time went on, Marlene kept upping the ante. She began to see Chuck and herself as a modern-day Bonnie and Clyde, an identification made more complete by the fact that Bonnie wrote poetry. She wrote a "Bonnie and Clyde" series of poems and told Chuck that they should pattern themselves on the outlaw couple and "do what we like and take what we want."

In a jewelry store in San Anselmo, Chuck stole a $750 topaz ring that he gave Marlene as an "engagement present," although any plans that they had discussed to get married were set in the vague future—"after I'm eighteen," Marlene repeatedly explained. In a Mill Valley jewelry store they were almost caught stealing another ring by a sharp-eyed clerk, but Marlene, who had stuck it in Chuck's pants pocket, managed to talk her way out of trouble. Since she was determined to steal a diamond, the two of them cased a number of stores before realizing that the security was too heavy for their normal distractive tactics to work. Nor is there any indication that Marlene actually meant to carry out an elaborate plan she devised—involving masks, a decoy car and a change of clothing—to rob a local Wells Fargo bank.

One day at a boutique in San Rafael, Marlene handed Chuck two glittery evening gowns and walked out. Almost unconsciously, he followed her—and nobody stopped him. After that their modus operandi became much simpler. Marlene would tell Chuck what she wanted and he would carry it out by the armful, without making much of an attempt at concealment. Experienced security officers claim that such a shoplifting technique is actually rather sophisticated, since it is more difficult to spot at an early stage than a furtive approach, and so perhaps it is not surprising that Chuck and Marlene got away with it as long as they did.

Other members of their group knew that Chuck and Marlene were shoplifting (in fact, Marlene gave her girl friends much of the stolen merchandise) and warned them to stop before they got caught. Chuck's old friends, in particular, saw his latest activity as one of a series of worrisome changes in his recent behavior, as a result, they all assumed, of Marlene's influence over him. There was no question that having a steady girl friend boosted Chuck's morale and confidence. Nor that he looked far better than he ever had now that he had lost so much weight, styled his hair neatly, and under Marlene's careful tutelage, exchanged his old baggy overalls for designer jeans, hand-tooled boots, leather vests and silk scarfs.

But his total absorption with Marlene made him careless of his old friends. He was uncharacteristically aloof and short-tempered, borrowed money that he forgot to pay back, and put together elaborate drug deals with silent partners who became more vocal when the expected return on their investment failed to materialize. For the first time Chuck began to "step on" the cocaine he was dealing (cutting it with speed to increase his profit margin) and to give customers a "taste" of high-grade marijuana and then sell them inferior weed. And for someone who had always been so circumspect in his drug dealings, he was becoming surprisingly sloppy, leaving the floor of his car strewn with marijuana seeds and roaches, and keeping a razor blade and mirror for chopping up cocaine on the dashboard.

To some extent even Chuck recognized what was happening to him. "Every time I heard that Marshall Tucker line 'Can't you see what that woman's doing to me,' I'd get a nervous twinge." Marlene was Chuck's "most expensive habit" and he increased his drug dealing "to support her in style." ("I don't want you to stop dealing," Marlene had recently written him in one of her "farewell" letters. "I want to be able to hear you're going higher in the business. I want to hear you went to Kezar Stadium and sold dope to Pink Floyd and Lynyrd Skynyrd and had a good time.") He stepped up another rung on the local drug hierarchy by dealing directly with Paco's supplier. Chuck could buy larger quantities at cheaper prices, but if the potential profits were larger, so were the attendant risks. The largest drug deal Chuck was ever involved in—the sale of an "eighth" (of a kilogram) of cocaine, then worth $5,000, to members of a popular rock band— fell through after Chuck flew to Los Angeles with the merchandise because the buyers rightly suspected that it was not the same as the sample they had originally tasted.

His friends noticed other danger signals. Ever since the time when Chuck was employed briefly by the San Francisco Opera Company two years earlier, he had begged his friend Bill Owen, who worked full time for the company as a truck driver and prop man, to find him a similar job. In March, Chuck got a chance to join the opera company on a month-long tour through the Southwest. He was initially overjoyed at the opportunity to travel and, not incidentally, to get Oscar off his back for not having a regular job. He joined the touring company for several warm-up performances around the Bay Area and enjoyed driving the big rigs, setting up the scenery and helping with the sound effects backstage during performances. But when Bill came by to pick his friend up on the morning that the company was scheduled to leave for Tuscon, Chuck was still in bed. "I have to quit," he explained. "Marlene said if I leave now, that'll be the end of our relationship."

Like Chuck, Marlene linked their relationship to a favorite pop song—the Electric Light Orchestra's "Evil Woman." She noticed that she could get Chuck to do practically anything for her by simply staring him down, and her power over him worried her. ("Chuck's always thinking of me," Marlene wrote in her diary. "His friends notice and in a way despise me for it. I have heard people say that I have him so tied to my pinky that he has no other life.") But on the few occasions when he defied her will, she could show a quick and nasty temper. Once Mike Howard and the Dillon girls were astonished to see Marlene suddenly become angry and bite Chuck through the sleeve of his leather jacket hard enough to draw blood from his arm. Later Chuck admitted to Mike that Marlene had bitten him before in anger. Then he took off his shirt to show his friend something that Mike found even more astonishing. One day after he and Marlene had made love in the cabin, Chuck explained, Marlene had insisted on carving her initials into his shoulder with the kitchen knife she carried in her purse. And by then the three neatly executed, inch-high letters, MLO, had turned from raw welts into permanent scars. At that point Mike told Chuck that he was "too hung up" on Marlene. "She's using you and you let her," he added.

"Yeah, well, she's not using me," Chuck said. "And even if she were, you're right, I'd let her. I don't care."

The result of Chuck's growing estrangement from his parents and friends over Marlene was that he spent almost all his time with her. Their relationship had become intensely sexual, with Marlene's fantasies becoming increasingly sadomasochistic. A poem she wrote at that time, entitled "Gonna Crush Him Under My Feet," commanded her unnamed lover to "Crawl across the room/beg for more/let me hear you beg for more." She searched her collection of men's magazines for the kind of display-window S&M scenes the editors seemed to favor and gathered together the most common props. She and Chuck would bring a sack of

whips, ropes, knives, guns and other paraphernalia to the cabin
in the eucalyptus grove. Marlene always insisted that Chuck
dress for the occasion as what she called "the master of the
whores"—shirtless, wearing only black leather pants and a suede
ski mask he had borrowed from a friend at Marlene's encourage-
ment. (She had promptly dubbed it the "executioner's hood.")
Then, using all the articles they had brought with them, they
would act out Marlene's rape fantasies. On one such afternoon,
as Chuck related under hypnosis, "We took the gun and some
knives and lengths of rope up to the cabin. I held the gun on
her—it wasn't loaded but I told her it was—and tied her wrists
up against the banister on the side of the cabin, and when I
stepped back she kicked me backwards. So I sat down on her
legs and tied them up. I took the knife and cut all of her clothes
off—her shirt button by button, then her bra and panties. Then I
held the knife at her throat and fucked her. Afterwards I cut her
loose and she jumped up and grabbed the knife and started to
come at me. But one of her legs was still tied and she tripped
and I grabbed her and knocked the knife out of her hand and
pushed her back on the floor. She kicked at me and called me a
bastard and a punk and said who did I think I was and spit in my
face."

On several occasions Marlene would masturbate with a hunting knife that Chuck kept in the car. Afraid that she would "tear
her insides to shreds," he taped the blade. Then she began using
the barrel of the .22-caliber pistol Chuck kept in the glove
compartment of his car.

"The first time I was in my bedroom and had just cleaned the
gun and left it on my desk," Chuck's hypnotic account continues.
"I went out to the living room and when I came back I saw that
she had taken the gun and put it inside her and was gently riding
back and forth along the barrel. I said, 'Marlene, don't do that.'
She just looked at me and smiled. And she cocked the hammer
back on the gun. I had left the gun loaded and I didn't know if
she had emptied it. I was frightened that she would shoot herself
with it. I finally convinced her to give me the gun back and it
was still loaded. I put the hammer back down.

"After a while I started using the gun to masturbate her. 'Tell
me it's loaded,' she would say. 'Pull back the hammer.' She
would become really turned on. I didn't like it at first. I had
always thought masturbation was totally obscene, the worst thing
you could do to yourself. But I'd given up trying to stop her. She

had already told me about using long-necked bottles and the butt end of a hammer and other things. When I used the gun Marlene would become very aroused. Her whole body would quiver, so I felt that what I thought wasn't as important as the pleasure it was giving her.''

Not all of Marlene's erotic fantasies were carried out, including one, which derived from a magazine photo spread, to build a wooden medieval stock into which her head and hands would be locked while Chuck, wearing his executioner's hood, whipped her with a cat-o'-nine-tails they had improvised out of rope. Another unrealized fantasy involved Marlene's frequently expressed desire "to become a high-class hooker with an elite clientele" and have Chuck pimp for her. She did, however, pressure him to solicit other men for her, and once, in an evening of unintended comedy, pushed this fantasy to the edge of realization.

She had already told him about making love to three men in a French pornographic movie. ("Her fantasies were so vivid and strong," Chuck would later recall, "she could say just about anything and it would sound true") and expressed interest in repeating the experience, which Chuck had managed to resist. One night at the Villa Rafael she reviewed a list of likely sexual partners among their friends and insisted that Chuck bring Steve Donnelly back to the motel. After his protests were rejected Chuck finally drove around aimlessly for a time and came back to report that he couldn't find Donnelly. Marlene suggested several more candidates and each time Chuck would leave the motel, drive around for a half-hour or so and come back with the same story. Finally she told him to "just pick someone off the street." At that point Chuck felt that he had "run out of excuses" and drove over to his friend Doug Nolan's house. "I said, 'Let's go for a ride,' " Chuck recalled, "but I never told him where or why. I knew that he was going with a girl he was really faithful to and it hurt me too much to admit that Marlene wanted someone else."

Doug walked into the motel room and saw Marlene lying in a flimsy black negligee on the black satin sheets she had brought with her. "We smoked some bush," he remembers. "Chuck had some Making Love body lotion and we gave her a rubdown. Chuck took his clothes off and said I should. They started going at it and I said, 'Sorry, I've got an old lady and I'm really happy.' I watched the boob tube in the corner for a while and then Chuck drove me home. I could tell he was real uncomfortable about the whole scene and we never talked about it again.''

When Chuck and Marlene finally engaged in group sex, the third party was a female. Marlene had always encouraged Chuck to express his sexual fantasies as insistently as she indulged her own. But Chuck's fantasies were generally much more prosaic, involving making love in a variety of sexual positions and outdoor locations. One afternoon at the Gearys', Marlene suggested that she and Sharon give Chuck a ''body rub.'' The massage quickly turned sexual. After Marlene and Chuck made love, she said that ''it wouldn't be fair to leave Sharon out,'' and walked out of the bedroom. The experiment was repeated on several other occasions, always at Marlene's prompting.

Marlene also initiated erotic photography sessions in which Chuck and Sharon participated. She claimed that her fictitious ''Uncle Bob'' had a connection with *Penthouse* magazine and had encouraged her to send in some nude shots for possible publication. One session was held in Sharon's bedroom, with Chuck using Jim's Olympus camera to take the pictures and Marlene, surrounded by fur pillows as props, pouting and posing in perfect imitation of the models in the men's magazines she collected. Another nude picture-taking session was held outdoors near Nicassio Lake. One of those photographs, taken by Sharon, showed Marlene spread across the plywood hood of Chuck's Buick in tongue-lolling ecstasy while Chuck performed cunnilingus on her. (The district attorney later introduced it into evidence at Chuck's trial to illustrate the ''perverse teen-age culture'' out of which, he claimed, the murder germinated.) Marlene told Chuck and other friends that the pictures had been enthusiastically received by *Penthouse* and would soon appear in print. In fact, after the crime the police found the film in the same cardboard box under Marlene's bed that contained her letters, poems and other papers. Like so many of Marlene's fantasies, it remained undeveloped.

If sex was one way that Marlene, in her words, ''got some power over Chuck,'' witchcraft was the other. She continued to read all the books on occult phenomena she could find in bookstores and libraries. She thought about joining Anton LaVey's Church of Satan, but ''never had the nerve to attend'' one of the black masses over which he presided in his San Francisco headquarters. Intrigued as she was by the possibility that she might have ''psychic powers,'' she still recognized that her interest in witchcraft "was something I did because I didn't want to be a carbon copy of everyone. I wanted to be different."

Chuck felt none of Marlene's ambivalence about her occult powers. "Did you really believe that she was a witch?" one of the psychiatrists later asked him under hypnosis. "When I first heard it," he answered, "I was just playing along, but after a while I became more and more convinced of it."

Marlene continued to play on Chuck's credulity. Under hypnosis he would later describe a sacrificial ceremony that Marlene said she had assisted at in Ecuador. "She told me it involved a young virgin who they laid on top of a marble slab that had the sign of the pentacle in the middle. A black cloth was draped over the slab, and the virgin, who had been put in a trance with some herbal drink, was dressed in a white gown. After saying some chants, which she wouldn't tell me what they were, Marlene untied the gown and cut the sign of the pentacle on the virgin's belly with a knife exactly over the pentacle on the slab. Then the priest cut her wrist and collected her blood in a goblet that was passed around for everyone to drink." The account is an almost verbatim recital of a medieval satanic ritual sacrifice that Marlene had read about in one of her occult reference books.

Marlene also told Chuck that she belonged to a coven of witches in Marin but was sworn to secrecy about its activities. Every so often she would abruptly break off a late-night phone call by announcing that she had a "meeting" to attend. Pressed for more information, she once told him that the coven met on full-moon nights on "sacred ground" in China Camp. She even showed him a poem she wrote entitled "Invitation to My Coven":

> Drink from the silver goblet
> Blood that pours through the veins.
> Focus your anger on evil,
> Notice the knife in your hand.
> The sweet aroma in the air
> Makes it easier to follow your dare.

In fact, China Camp had once been sacred ground, not to Marin County witches but to the Miwok Indians, whose burial mounds, containing corpses covered with clam and mussel shells, had been thoroughly plundered years earlier. Chuck and his friends agreed that the place was still "spooked," which was one reason why they continued to frighten themselves at night by driving through the wooded areas that were thinly populated by gnarled and fire-damaged scrub-oak trees.

This was exactly what Chuck and Marlene, along with Mike Howard and Leslie Slote, decided to do one night in mid-March when they had all gotten high on grass. Chuck drove them deep into the China Camp woods and was amusing himself and terrifying the others by maneuvering his car off the fire roads and in and out of the stunted trees at faster and faster speeds, crunching the undergrowth beneath the wheels. A slight breeze stirred the pale leaves, and when Chuck stopped the car the power lines that stretched from hilltop to hilltop added a forlorn electric hum to the eerie atmosphere. When someone noted that it was a full-moon night, the group grew very quiet.

"I'm scared," Marlene said. "This isn't a good place to be tonight."

"Did you see the dead body we ran over?" Chuck teased her.

"It feels like there are ghosts flying around," Mike Howard chimed in.

"Chuck," Marlene pleaded, "let's get out of here. Please! Now!"

All of a sudden Marlene let out a blood-curdling scream and then began crying hysterically. She grabbed Leslie and said, "This isn't funny. Every minute I'm in here tonight means a year off my life." Chuck started the car up and drove out of China Camp as quickly as he could. "At that moment total terror ran through us all," he remembers.

Just after they got back on the road, according to Leslie Slote, the others were still "freaked out" but Marlene "just started smiling, like she was a different personality completely. 'Did you see them, Mike?' Marlene said. 'Did you really see ghosts?' He goes, 'Yeah, sure,' trying to be brave. 'Well, maybe I'll take you to a meeting,' Marlene said. I'm going, wow, maybe all that stuff she was laying out about being a witch and the High Priestess and belonging to the Satanic Church—maybe it's all true."

Soon after the China Camp incident Marlene gave Chuck a necklace of wooden beads and told him that each one of them represented a past life that he had led. In most of these lives, she went on to explain, the two of them had some connection, including one time in seventeenth-century Salem when Marlene had been accused of being a witch and Chuck was the only person in the town to defend her. "As long as we have some karma to work out," Marlene concluded, "you'll always come back to me."

Then Marlene gave Chuck the helix-shaped Egyptian bracelet that had been the object of such imaginative invention in Jerry Fitch's art class that fall. "At first she gave me the bracelet because I really admired it," Chuck said under hypnosis. "Later she said she never was going to tell me this but the bracelet gave her the ability to communicate with me without words and over distances. The bracelet was magical and it had an incantation that she had put on it." Afterward, whenever Chuck felt a "tingling" or "pinching" sensation on his wrist he would call Marlene, and more often than not she said she had been trying to get in touch with him. "I know it sounds off the wall," he would later claim, "but I really felt that she could communicate with me through that bracelet."

Marlene continued to experiment with tarot and other fortune-telling cards, sometimes coming up with readings that her friends thought were astonishingly accurate. Toward the end of March she laid out Chuck's tarot and told him that there "was some kind of trouble coming which will make things hard for us. You will go to the Tower."

Chuck and Marlene were arrested on March 26 at the Emporium department store in Northgate Mall. The day had been fairly typical of the life they had been leading for the past few weeks. Chuck had picked Marlene up at Pacific Crest in the morning and driven her to a Planned Parenthood clinic in San Rafael for a pregnancy test—a frequent necessity because of Marlene's irregular periods and her refusal to use birth-control pills, which she thought made her fat. They spent the rest of the morning shoplifting and then went back to the clinic for the results.

There Marlene met a girl named Sue Evers, who had also come for a pregnancy test. Although only twelve, she had spent time in juvenile hall on several occasions, had smoked marijuana for years, knew all about the San Rafael prostitution scene and said she had once been raped. Marlene remarked on the fact that Sue resembled her somewhat, and when she learned that the girl was born in Virginia and had also been adopted, she conceived the notion that Sue might be one of the long-lost sisters she had always dreamed about, a real-life version of the Barbie dolls that she had not played with in years but still kept tucked away in the back of her closet. She told Sue about their shoflifting exploits and invited her along to "pick out a present for yourself."

"We went back to the Emporium," Chuck's account under hypnosis continues. "Marlene and this girl that she thought was her sister started looking through bathing suits. I stole some for them. Then I came back in the store and decided that I'd go and get myself something for the first time, as long as I was stealing all this stuff. I walked over to the men's department and saw four shirts that I liked and put them in the car and walked back to the store. I suspected someone might have seen me but Marlene said to just be cool. She handed me another rack of stuff and when I got to the car and started to open it, these two security guards came from different directions and one said: 'Stop right there.' "

In the San Rafael police report of the incident Chuck was described as "being very cooperative" with the Emporium security guards, giving them "detailed information on the property recovered from suspect vehicle." He allowed them to search his car, where they found Marlene's purse containing dozens of price tags. He gave them permission to move the car closer to the store and helped them unload the stolen merchandise, which amounted to sixty-one separate items of clothing and jewelry worth $1,114, more than half of them taken from the Emporium that day.

The two girls were taken into custody along with Chuck, and when the San Rafael police arrived, all three were brought to police headquarters in handcuffs. Chuck was photographed (the picture shows him wearing a black leather vest, love beads, and a headband around his straggly hair, and it did him little good as a character reference when the prosecution introduced it during his trial), fingerprinted and sent to the Marin County jail charged with grand larceny. Marlene and Sue Evers were taken to the Marin County juvenile hall and booked under Section 602 of the California juvenile code. According to state law at the time, there were only two possible charges that could be lodged against a minor. Section 601, the "baby-sitter clause," accused the minor of being "beyond parental control" and was usually initiated by parents themselves. This is what Marlene would have been charged with as a runaway had Jim not convinced the arresting officer to release her in his custody. Section 602, Marlene's present offense, covered any adult criminal act without fine distinction—anything, that is, from the most minor misdemeanor to murder.

Seven

The Marin County Juvenile Hall consists of several long shed-like buildings surrounded by ten acres of grassy playing fields. It is fronted by the Lucas Valley road in Marinwood, just a half mile or so from Hibiscus Way, and backed by the spine of hills that runs from the freeway to the ocean, hills that were still a lush green from the heavy late-winter rains but would, by summer, become a parched fire hazard the color of old silver coins. Except for the cyclone fence that surrounded the compound, it looked more like a summer camp for children of affluence than a correction facility—which was exactly the charge that the increasingly vocal critics of juvenile justice in California lodged against the entire system. In fact, so in tune was the facility with the surrounding community that parents would often punish misbehaving youngsters by placing them in the hall for a day or two, and their children would return the favor by preferring the hall to home and showing up there again and again, eventually under police rather than parental escort, until by the time they reached their majority and faced adult court they were too often hardened criminals charged with major felonies.

A first-time offender at sixteen, Marlene was less typical of her fellow wards than her co-conspirator, twelve-year-old Sue Evers, who had already spent a considerable amount of time in the facility, as had her fourteen-year-old brother, who was there when the girls arrived. But if her age made her atypical, Marlene's serious family problems, which were immediately apparent to "intake officer" Clarence Underwood, fit precisely into the mold. "The Olive residence was contacted by this officer," Underwood wrote on the first page of what would become Marlene's extensive juvenile hall record. Naomi Olive "was quite irate, loud and angry, stating that, 'Why hadn't she been notified of her daughter being in detention?' " Under the heading "Impressions" in his report, Underwood wrote that Naomi was "a possible chronic alcoholic . . . which has a profound effect on her daughter. I suspect there are many other problems in the home and that it is not feasible to release Marlene to her parents at this point in time."

That judgment was confirmed the following day when Jim Olive came to see Nancy Boggs, a probation officer at the juvenile hall. Mrs. Boggs was a pleasant woman with swept-back silver-blond hair. She had been a juvenile officer in the Los Angeles ghetto of Watts for nine years before transferring to Marin County, and had found the affluent families she worked with now "much more seriously disturbed" than those she had left behind. "The kids here are angry at their parents, not at society. And the parents are more concerned with what the neighbors will think than with improving the situation at home."

When he came in to see her, Jim at first tended to place all the blame for Marlene's behavior on the influence of her friends, especially Chuck, whom he called a "bad egg." He explained that he had tried to prevent Marlene from associating with many of her other friends and would now forbid her to see Chuck. "You'll have trouble if you do," Mrs. Boggs replied. "That's like holding a red flag up to a bull."

Pressed by the probation officer, Jim reluctantly admitted that Marlene's problems were long-standing and involved a troubled home life. According to Mrs. Boggs's report, when family therapy was suggested Jim "stated that his wife is 'scared to death' of psychiatrists and refuses to participate in any form of counseling."

Marlene echoed many of Jim's remarks, although the probation officer was not prepared for the level of anger in her voice. "She states that the primary problem is her mother," Mrs. Boggs wrote, "who drinks to excess and talks to herself all the time, which 'drives me up the wall.' Marlene also stated that her father doesn't do anything about the problem, except to state that, 'We have to learn to cope with mother's problem.' " Despite her anger at Naomi, and to a lesser but growing extent at Jim, Marlene told Mrs. Boggs that "she wanted to go home and would try to go along with what her parents wanted."

Indeed, it did seem that Marlene's arrest and the five days she spent at the hall before her detention hearing made her reflect on her situation at home. At Nancy Boggs's suggestion Marlene drew up a long list of ways to improve her behavior that included such general prescriptions as "Go strictly by parents' rules" and "Once a week spend a day with my parents." She also made a list of specific activities calculated to please Jim and Naomi, some of which were: "Clean my room"; "Make dinner"; "Feed and groom cats"; "Help with fish tanks"; "Call Father Barnette about church activities"; "Talk to mother and keep her company"; "Teach her to crochet and have her teach me to knit" and "Go to bed early for school." Finally, Marlene bombarded Mrs. Boggs with juvenile hall "request forms" pleading to be sent home. "I had a good visit with my parents," one of them read. "I love them and I reassured both of them I love them. I feel that if we all work together we could prevent further trouble." Another note simply promised the probation officer "More of the *real* Marlene. She can be and is good deep inside."

Mrs. Boggs felt that Marlene would be better off in juvenile hall until her case could be heard in a few weeks. "Without therapy and some drastic changes at home you're going to be headed for serious trouble," she warned Jim. Initially he agreed to keep Marlene at the hall. As he told his bookkeeper, Winnie Stockstill, "We're just going to let her stew in her juices until she makes some sense of her actions."

It was the relentless barrage of entreaties from both his daughter and his wife that helped change his mind. Much to Marlene's astonishment, Naomi accompanied Jim to juvenile hall each of the five days she spent there. During the late-afternoon visiting hour Jim tried to draw up some guidelines for the future, as Mrs. Boggs had suggested, while the two women spent most of the time in tears, holding hands and reaching for the box of Kleenex that Marlene had brought with her from her room. After one visit Marlene wrote a poem called "Mirror, Mirror" that expressed a guarded optimism about her ability to improve her relationship with her mother:

> When you mouth your obscenities and your
> 　　eyes mirror your enjoyment
> Of the orgy of hatred you carry on verbally
> 　　with yourself
> With me as your audience,

Shall I share in the cacophony of
  self-hatred
Using you as my audience?
Shall we pick our roles and play a part?
If you can be an animal and reflect the
  beast in me,
Why can't I be a person and reveal the
  human in you?

The day before Marlene's detention hearing Jim came into
Nancy Boggs's office and told her, "I can't stand having my
little girl in jail. She and her mother keep begging me to take her
home and promise to get along better." The next day, after
formal charges were filed against Marlene, she was released in
her parents' custody. Legally it would have been difficult to
detain her without their permission despite Mrs. Boggs's strong
recommendation to that effect. "It is felt," she concluded her
report, "that although Marlene states she wants to go home and
will abide by her parents' requests, she will be unable to do so
because of the disturbed family situation." Nor was the investigating officer's recommendation for "a complete psychological
evaluation" of the Olive family accepted by the juvenile court.

After the hearing Peter Mitchell, the young San Rafael attorney
Jim had hired to represent Marlene, was witness to a scene
between mother and daughter that made him, too, fear that the
Olives' family situation was potentially explosive. Marlene was
being contrite and conciliatory with Naomi. "Mom, I hope I can
come home and start fresh," she said between sobs. "I want to
have a real family. I want us to get along." Mitchell, whose
round-faced, choirboy looks belied his years of experience as a
Marin County district attorney, was genuinely taken with Marlene's
sincerity. "If I were that girl's parents, I'd have been thrilled to
death," he remembers telling his wife that evening. "It was an
opening." If so, it was one that Naomi immediately blocked.
"How can I ever believe you?" she had responded. "Your
room's always a pigpen, you dress like a streetwalker, you stay
out all night. You hang around with all those delinquents who
keep getting you in trouble. And now all these people will be
poking around in our private affairs."

After the detention hearing Nancy Boggs made a special point
of asking her superior to reassign the Olive case to another
probation officer. "I felt that I was loaded up with crazy families

and couldn't do the situation justice,'' she recalls. ''There's going to be more trouble with this one,'' she told juvenile services director Dave Rogers. ''Marlene is angry at her parents—legitimately so. She has a disturbed mother, an ineffective father unable to make decisions, a boyfriend her parents disapprove of strongly. She's acting out. It's a classic blow-up situation.''

It did not seem so close to exploding when Marlene first arrived home. She remembers being ''so scared that I asked permission to open the refrigerator door.'' She began attending classes regularly and coming home after school to do homework. She signed up for an adult-education course entitled ''The Psychology of Crisis,'' thinking ''it could help me learn to deal with what was happening.'' In order to earn some spending money, she made inquiries about getting a part-time job as a bilingual telephone operator.

Marlene even tried to live up to the resolutions she had made to ''keep mother company'' and help out with domestic chores. For Mother's Day she bought Naomi a dozen white roses and a cute greeting card with a drawing of a cat that resembled Mishu, on which she wrote an endearing note. And on a couple of occasions Marlene and Naomi actually began to experience the kind of mother-daughter intimacy both clearly longed for.

One fondly remembered early-spring day Marlene cut school and went to the beach by bus, coming home to find Naomi resting in the master bedroom, drinking coffee and making out laundry inventories, a cat perched on her stomach. Until they triggered their almost reflexive hostility, the two talked more intimately than they had in years.

''What were you doing all morning?'' Naomi asked.

''Just walking around and thinking about stuff,'' Marlene said.

''You spend too much time writing those poems of yours. It puts you in a tizzy.''

''Can I ask you something?'' Marlene said, bringing up a subject that had been on her mind since she found herself physically drawn to a girl she had met at a recent concert. ''What do you think about bisexuality?''

''I think it's sick, that's what. You're a beautiful young lady. You'll have all you can handle dealing with men and their sneaky ways.''

''Was Daddy sneaky?''

''He wanted to sleep with me like the rest. But the way I was

raised, a proper young woman from a good home waited until
she was married. Nowadays—''

"How come you and Dad don't sleep together anymore?"

"He got me started drinking, though," Naomi said, ignoring
the question. "I never had a drop of liquor before I met your
father."

"I really wanna know," Marlene insisted. "Why don't you
and Dad ever sleep together?"

"Or cigarettes. Your dad smoked when he came home from the
war, so I started smoking too."

"Mom, I'm asking you a question!"

"Don't you give me your fresh mouth, Marlene Louise Olive!
How would you like me to tell your father?"

Unlike Marlene, as a first-time adult offender Chuck had been
"O.R.'d"—released on his own recognizance—after staying overnight in the Marin County jail. At the hearing to consider
releasing him Joanne Riley explained to the judge that "Marlene
Olive is my son's 'first love' and he is not using rational
judgment." A trial date was set for mid-July, two and a half
months away, and Chuck was intructed "not to have contact in
any form with Marlene Olive."

Since Oscar had recently visited the doctor for his high blood
pressure, Joanne didn't tell him about his son's arrest until Chuck
returned home, and the delay served to diffuse his normally
quick temper. He did remind Chuck of his old warning that he'd
"wind up in San Quentin someday," but by then Oscar was
feeling more concern than anger for his elder son.

In the interim Chuck had received a brief note from Marlene
hinting that she wanted to break up with him. "Don't bother with
my fantasies and trying to please me," the note cautioned Chuck.
"They are a sickness I have that is out of this world. They are
carried too far. Growing up for me is hard to do. Poetry, music,
acting and singing are only the far-fetched dreams of a neurotic
girl, nothing important, nothing to share." Over the telephone
Marlene confirmed Chuck's worst fears about breaking up, telling him that her parents intended to get a court order forbidding
them from seeing each other, and reporting her father's threat to
shoot him if he showed up at the house. Then she sat down and
wrote Chuck an apologetic farewell letter, sending it to him
along with the topaz "engagement" ring and some drug paraphernalia he had loaned her. "Dearest Chuck," it began:

I guess when goodbyes are near, I'm not too much for words. I wanna thank you for always being there when I needed you, and for not giving up when things looked away from you. I'll never forget you, that I'm sure of. It would be too long of a wait for us to see each other, so I'll let you on your way, and I'm sorry to have hurt you. I guess from now on school will be the first and only thing for me. It's for the best, I guess. My hopes and dreams are too far away. Maybe when I turn 18 I can have my happiness permanently, not temporarily. I feel only emptiness in me, and a prayer for you, my love. Please forgive me for everything. . . .

Chuck moped around the house for a few days in a despondent mood and then decided to go over to the Olives' house, hoping that by then Jim had "cooled down enough" so that he could both apologize and explain that he wasn't entirely to blame for getting Marlene into trouble. He never got the words out of his mouth. As soon as Jim heard the approaching sound of Chuck's unmuffled Buick he came outside to meet him. "Don't bother to come over here ever again," he yelled, his index finger gesturing accusedly and his face florid with rage. "And don't call Marlene. If I ever so much as hear of you being with Marlene, I'll make sure you regret it." Jim turned around and stomped inside. Chuck stared at the front door for a few minutes after it had been slammed shut, wondering if he should try again, and then left. He never saw Jim Olive again until the moment before he shot him to death.

The next day Chuck made his second half-hearted suicide attempt. He had tried to talk to Marlene at Pacific Crest and she had rebuffed him. Again he filled a medicine bottle with a variety of pills—Benadryls, Darvons, Valiums, and the Sinequan that Oscar used to control his bouts of depression. That evening he called the Olive house, telling Naomi, who answered the phone, that he was Tim Prather, a friend of Marlene's whose monotone drawl was easy to imitate. In the course of the conversation with Marlene, Chuck took out pill after pill, announcing what he was doing before swallowing each one. By the time he hung up he had swallowed several dozen pills and could barely stagger out to his car and drive to a far corner of the Civic Center parking lot. When he woke up it was still dark. It was not until

he saw a newspaper the next morning that he realized he had
missed a full day.

After a week of seeing her son "down in the dumps," Joanne
Riley decided to call the Olives up to ask if they would allow
Marlene and Chuck to see each other on a restricted, perhaps
even chaperoned, basis. "I remember when I was a kid," she
explained to Naomi, "if my parents didn't want me to see
someone, I'd want to all the more." Naomi was both obdurate
and nasty. In the course of a rambling, semicoherent monologue
she managed to say that she was accustomed to living a much
more luxurious life in South America, replete with several
domestics, that she preferred dictators to presidents for the stabil-
ity they provided, and that she and Jim were laying out a "pretty
penny" for Marlene to attend "private school" and didn't want
Chuck to spoil it for her. Joanne hung up when Naomi said, "I
understand you're a nurse's aide and live in a lower-income area.
I can't imagine why Marlene would want to see Chuck when she
knows so many boys from influential families."

Whatever the imbalance in Marlene's relationship with Chuck,
she had come to depend on his affection and emotional support,
especially during trying times at home. Her promise not to see
him—like the other resolutions that she had made in the juvenile
hall—faded as soon as she put the experience behind her and the
Olives' family life returned to normal. Unfortunately, "normal"
meant the quick collapse of any improvement in her relationship
with Naomi. As Marlene wrote in her poetry book around this
time:

> All of a sudden it's the same old thing:
> Yelling and screaming,
> Accusing everyone and everything.
> No, you haven't changed at all.

Then, two weeks after Marlene had returned home, she and her
mother had their worst argument ever.

Like all of Marlene and Naomi's fights, this one started with a
comically minor irritation and soon burst out of control, with
both participants expertly fanning the other's fury. It began in
the early evening when Marlene was helping her mother prepare
dinner. Naomi, who had been sipping Scotch all afternoon and
was now feeling the effects, became irritated at the way Marlene
was fixing the salad. "How many times do I have to tell you to

cut the celery on a bias?'' she snapped. ''You do that on purpose to annoy me.'' As usual Marlene was taken aback by her mother's sudden change of mood, and reacting with a familiar taunt, jumped to attention, gave her mother a Nazi salute and said ''Heil Hitler!'' From there the two women struck all the black notes of their long-standing discord.

''You look like a tramp,'' Naomi yelled. ''Can't you ever wear a brassiere?''

''Well, I guess if my mom was one, I'm one,'' Marlene answered back.

''Your so-called 'mom' gave you away, that's how much she cared about you. I'm your mother and don't you forget it.''

''The hell you are.''

''Sometimes I wish I wasn't. We were better off without you. All you ever do is tear this family apart.''

''All *you* ever do is drink and talk to your precious 'fitzes.' You're a real space case. How come you keep moving your eyebrows up and down, crazy lady?''

''You watch your tongue. Wait till your father hears about this.''

''You can't even make him a proper wife.''

''What kind of a daughter do you suppose you are?''

''Bitch! Crazy lady! One day they're gonna cart you off in a strait jacket!''

At this point Marlene began biting her right forearm in rage, something she had done so often over the years in arguments with Naomi that she had developed layers of scar tissue there. This time the deflection of her hatred onto her own person was not enough. She picked up the knife she had been using to cut vegetables and flung it at Naomi. It bounced off the kitchen cabinet behind her mother. ''If they don't take you away,'' she yelled, ''I'll kill you myself!''

By the time Jim came home he found Marlene behind the locked bathroom door and Naomi exhausted on her bed. When Naomi told him about the fight he was properly horrified—his ''fishermen's wives'' were becoming lethal. Instead of playing his usual mediator's role, he sided squarely with Naomi. After discussing the matter with his wife—a fact that angered his daughter more than the punishment itself—Jim decided to ''dock'' Marlene from seeing any of her friends for two weeks.

Inevitably, whenever Jim seemed protective of her mother, Marlene felt betrayed and lashed back at him bitterly. Throughout the spring Marlene's friends began to notice that she expressed almost as much hostility toward her father as toward her mother, and her often voiced intention to kill Naomi became plans to kill both her parents. The difference was that while Marlene never showed any ambivalence in her feelings about Naomi, she would jump between emotional extremes regarding Jim, condemning him one moment for being ineffective and praising him extravagantly the next. "There's only one man I ever loved . . ." she told Sharon Dillon, and just when Sharon thought that her friend had finally resolved her feelings for Chuck, Marlene finished the thought: ". . . my father." Shortly after Jim's latest attempt to "straighten out" his daughter, Marlene dedicated an eerily prescient poem to him called "Gentle Weeper," which began:

> I wish you could have stayed here
> Beside me father to keep
> Things straight.
> Who knows these days what might happen?
> I just might break.

It was in this state of intense family hostility that the Olives kept their mid-April appointment with Frieda Noll, the "investigating officer" at the juvenile hall. Mrs. Noll was a lively, good-humored woman who wore a bright-colored bandanna over her graying hair and almost as many rings on her fingers as Marlene herself. She had been working in the juvenile justice system for fifteen years but she was still taken aback by the response she got when she called Jim's business phone, as the note on Marlene's folder suggested, and Naomi answered anyway. After Mrs. Noll carefully explained that she needed to interview the Olives for a family evaluation that would be furnished to the juvenile court judge before Marlene's upcoming hearing, Naomi asked, "Why do you *really* need this information? Is this some kind of FBI investigation?"

When the Olives appeared in her office Frieda Noll, like Scott Nelson several months earlier, took note of the way the family arranged their seating. But this time Marlene deliberately positioned her chair between the interviewer's desk and Naomi, as if to block her mother out of the proceedings. Naomi still managed to monopolize the conversation, running on, according to the veteran juvenile justice official, "like a wind-up toy" until she was played out or Jim said gently, "Mrs. Noll isn't interested in that, dear." Listening to Naomi speak in a flat, even voice and with her head tilted sideways, Frieda Noll felt sure that the reports of her drinking were exaggerated, since she slurred her words even though she seemed perfectly sober, but not those of her deteriorating mental condition. "She was fearful of everything," Mrs. Noll recalls, "and probably should have been hospitalized, as Marlene had suggested to me earlier."

Naomi had started by talking about Marlene's friends, complaining that many of them came from broken homes, as if, according to Mrs. Noll, "they had red letters on their foreheads." Then she got on the subject of Chuck Riley, of whom she seemed genuinely frightened.

"He's a terrible person," Naomi said. "Every time he calls I jump through the roof, I'm so scared. The next time I'm going to call the police."

"See, Mrs. Noll," Marlene interjected. "See how she is. Chuck's harmless. He'd do anything for me."

"Mrs. Noll," Naomi continued, staring hard at the interviewer, "I'm going to be murdered in my bed."

What struck Frieda Noll about Naomi Olive as much as her "free-blown paranoia" was that, for all her disapproval of Marlene, she complained repeatedly about the fact that these days her daughter stayed away from the house as much as possible. And she was gratuitously smug about the fact that Marlene's attempt to find a foster home had not worked out well. "The mother's need for Marlene was very transparent, very 'clingy,' " Mrs. Noll recalled, "while Marlene was clearly struggling to break loose."

After the family conference Marlene asked Mrs. Noll if she could see her privately. "Now you know why I have to get out of that house," she sobbed. "When she closes the drapes during the day it's like a tomb in there." She also talked about her love for Chuck Riley. "Nobody can stop me from seeing him," she said.

"You're right," Mrs. Noll responded. "Nobody can stop you if you want to sneak around."

"I don't want to sneak around," Marlene answered. "I want them to know."

As Frieda Noll suspected, Naomi's mental problems were more evident than ever, the periods of relative normality shorter and shorter. She rarely went outside even to shop or make her midweek visit to the Northgate tropical-fish store, and she often spent the entire day in her room dressed in a housecoat. And all of her tenuous connections with the outside world—the television programs she watched, the calls she occasionally answered, the local newspaper she read—told her that she had better remain there. A poem her daughter wrote that spring describes Naomi locked inside her house, her room and herself:

> A lit cigarette
> the only light
> a radio turned down low
> a restless body
> a bed on which it lies
> only a ceiling to stare at
> a head filled with fear
> a face in the dark
> blank eyes concealing all.

Unfortunately, Naomi's further deterioration was occurring at a time when Jim was more preoccupied with work than ever. With two associates handling the day-to-day accounting details in his office, Jim had time to do what he did best—sell new clients on the GBS idea. He had also decided to buy the consulting firm's regional franchise for all of Northern California, which meant that he would spend most of his time finding and training other local area franchisers like himself in return for an override on their incomes. At a cost of $50,000, the purchase would take all of the Olives' savings and still require a hefty bank loan, a situation that fed Naomi's poor-girl fantasies and no doubt contributed to her worsening condition. Perhaps by way of compensation, Jim became excessively protective of Naomi, especially in her fights with Marlene.

To make matters worse, Jim's expanding business interests would soon require him to move his office from the spare bedroom at home to larger accommodations in San Rafael, so that he would be around less than ever to provide a much needed physical buffer between his feuding wife and daughter. Unable to confront Jim directly, Marlene, as usual, expressed her confused feelings of physical and emotional distance from him in a poem:

> Just like the tide that goes out to sea,
> you changed on me.

Just like a bird that takes off for flight,
you left me as silently as a thief in the night.

Tell me,
Where did you go that spring season?
And for what reason?

I am entitled to an explanation
of any variation.

Jim was finally showing the strain of work and family tension. He wrote a former Gulf colleague about his longing to return to the simpler life he had enjoyed in South America. ("I never get a chance to eat crab with my fingers, sit on the floor and listen to the *serranos* sing about the *tomate* that got sent to Caracas.") As his daughter was fully aware despite their growing differences, Jim "was holding everything together/While he slowly fell apart."

If the tension in the house was bad enough when Jim was away, these days it was sometimes even worse when he was there, more often than not adjudicating a family squabble in Naomi's favor. The shoplifting arrest and Jim's new protectiveness toward Naomi left Marlene feeling like an outcast in her own family, a theme that surfaced in her poetry around this time, most explicitly in "Outburst":

Am I alone?
Is my heart made of stone?
Would I be better off dead
And give everyone peace of mind?
That would suit them just fine.

Late one night Marlene was lying on her bed smoking marijuana and playing a favorite Elton John song, "Funeral for a Friend," over and over again, identifying with the world-weary lyrics. She began "dry-dropping" a powerful street downer the kids called Red Devils. She loved the "shush feeling" the pills gave her, the illusion of weightlessness and infinite possibility. Self-pityingly, she scribbled in her poetry book:

I'm gone, not making a sound.
Someone has buried me in the ground.
Please don't weep over my fate.

> You can eat what's left on my plate.
> I don't really care.
> You can even breathe my air.

Jim was finishing some paperwork in his office when Marlene came in, wobbly-legged and heavy-lidded, holding on to the wall for support and saying in a slurred voice, "Three's a crowd. Maybe you and Mom can make it better alone." Then she slid to the floor like an unhinged picture frame. When Jim found out what Marlene had been up to, he rushed her to the Marin General Hospital crisis unit, the same place where Mike Howard had taken Chuck months earlier. Marlene was not so comatose that she needed to have her stomach pumped, but she was stripped of her clothes and given a bucket and a vial of green liquid, a powerful emetic that forced her to vomit. Jim nervously paced the reception area for over an hour, and when Marlene rejoined him he reassured his daughter that he loved her and she should never doubt that again. "Just because your mother and I are married," he said, "doesn't mean that you're excluded."

The following day Marlene wrote:

> She stood in the doorway of death,
> Closed her eyes and held her breath.
> And although she was alive,
> She knew she couldn't survive.

That evening when Jim came home from work he gave his daughter a pair of stained-glass earrings he had bought at a client's store.

Although Marlene would later treasure the earrings, by then it was far too late for such a gesture. About that time the rift between father and daughter was widened further by a curious accusation leveled against Jim by Frank Geary, Sharon and Nancy's stepfather. Months earlier Geary, whose prison record and rumored employment as a police informer lent him a certain credibility in such matters among local teen-agers, had told Marlene and a group of her friends that her father, with his long residence in Latin America, was probably connected with the CIA, if not as a full-time agent, then at least as a part-time informer. It was a notion that Marlene was delighted to add to her tales about Jim's other, and equally fanciful, exploits.

But then Geary came up wth a story that had a good deal less allure for Marlene. He claimed to have seen the Olive car in the San Rafael police parking lot, and after asking around, to have learned that Jim was informing the authorities about teen-age drug pushers and their customers. Under pressure from her friends, Marlene confronted Jim with the allegation and seemed satisfied with his bemused denial. But the disturbing notion that he might be covering up remained in the back of her mind, and once or twice, when she herself spotted the family's green Vega in the police parking lot—actually a convenient municipal lot in downtown San Rafael, only part of which was reserved for police cars—the thought recurred to her.

Another fanciful notion that Marlene occasionally entertained resurfaced around this time—the idea, implanted by Naomi during arguments, that her natural mother had been a prostitute and that, judging by her own "sluttish" dress and "lewd behavior," she would become one, too. Insulted by the suggestion at first, Marlene soon took to fantasizing about the possibility in conversations with Chuck and in her poetry. ("Streetwalker cruising the freeway,/Sticking her thumb in the air./Her legs shone like a reflection,/Her love grows like an infection . . .") And then the usual line she maintained between fantasy and reality became dangerously thin. Jim Pickett, the black pimp Marlene had met through her friend Linda Fraser, had been trying to convince her for months to work for him. Marlene had always turned his suggestions down cold and, more recently, had tried to steer her friend away from Pickett's influence. One day Pickett and a couple of his associates ran into Marlene on one of the walkways connecting the streets around her house and an argument ensued. He slapped her face and pushed her to the sidewalk, leaving her with a black eye and a nasty bruise on her leg. The next day she came to school wearing a long skirt and sunglasses and told the story, adding several dramatic flourishes, to Joan James, who did not know whether to take her seriously or not.

She also told the story to Jim when he questioned her about the bruises. Once again Jim went to see Frieda Noll, whom he had come to trust, to reveal his concerns about his daughter and wife. But after giving her a brief history of the problem, beginning in South America, Jim suddenly stopped talking, as if the effort of personal revelation, so foreign to his nature, had become too much of a strain. "He was very aware of everything that was going on," Frieda Noll recalls, "but his way of dealing with problems was to keep them hidden. The poor man was overwhelmed and he had no one to talk to. He wanted help badly. He just didn't know how to get it.''

But even Jim could not have known how desperate the situation had already become. In her poetry and in letters to friends that she never mailed, Marlene was now regularly recording her fear of being overcome by fantasies of murdering her parents:

> There's a voice behind my step
> Calling me back to what I just left.
> I fear the tone in which it speaks,
> For it knows what I don't.
> In the coming weeks
> I wish it would vanish
> Or loosen its control.
> But I fear it's too late,
> For it has taken me over
> And is playing my fate.

In another poem, entitled "Space-Age Sacrifice," she wrote that no matter what she set her mind to "All that arises is/Murder./A sort of revenge." And then in May, two weeks after Marlene threw the kitchen knife at her mother in a rage, she calmly and deliberately tried to make her fantasy real.

The intervening period had been one of almost unrelieved hostility between mother and daughter, arguments whose specific origin vanished into the woodwork like layers of furniture polish. But the Saturday morning when Marlene tried for the first time to poison her mother had been relatively quiet. Jim was out on his rounds, Naomi was "resting" in bed and Marlene was in her own room across the hallway watching cartoons on television. In recent months she had wondered aloud to friends what it would take for Naomi to "space to death" on LSD or "nod out permanently" on downers, and that morning when her mother asked for lunch she decided to find out. She fixed coffee, cream of mushroom soup and a salad with bottled dressing, and then she emptied a dozen Darvon and Dalmane capsules into the food and drink, which easily camouflaged the white powder. She took the tray in to Naomi and went back to her room. A few minutes later Naomi called out, "There's something wrong with this salad, Marlene. It tastes bitter." And a few seconds after that: "The soup tastes funny, too. Maybe there's something wrong with my tastebuds." Even after Naomi drank the coffee, the effect of the drug was merely to prolong her habitual afternoon nap.

However far-fetched and inept, perhaps deliberately so, the poison attempt further erased the already razor-thin line between Marlene's fantasy life and reality dangerously close to the vanishing point. She wrote Chuck a long, rambling letter in which her free-floating fantasies—musical, sexual and parricidal—were punctured by her hostility toward Naomi like so many burst balloons. It ended:

> I hope this life will let me accomplish what is on my mind to the fullest. I have so many dreams but am afraid everything I wish will crumble like pie. To indulge in fantasies is Satan's command. (Did you know he lives partially through fantasies his followers must obey?) I'm counting on you to help me find my place.
>
> FUCK YOU. Strike this from the record, it was directed at my mom.
>
> Well, it's almost 5 p.m. and you haven't called. They better play those songs I requested on KTIM or I'll get mad. Asthma is gonna kill me.
>
> Talk to Gary's brother. Maybe he could find someone who would do it as a favor for two people's happiness. 'Nite, Marlene.

If, increasingly, Marlene had difficulty distinguishing her fantasies from reality, Chuck was even more confused. From now on he became hopelessly entrapped in the web of her imagination, lured there, in part, by her continued threats to break off the relationship if he failed to obey her. Chuck and Marlene managed to see each other frequently without the Olives finding out. Chuck still carried around rolls of dimes to "check in" with Marlene at all hours, as she insisted, using a friend's name if Jim or Naomi happened to beat Marlene to the phone.

Around this time Marlene began to talk about killing her parents almost daily, often in a disconcertingly casual manner. Marlene told Chuck she would pay the murderer $25,000, money that she assumed would eventually come to her once her parents had been declared "legally dead," either from the sale of the house (Jim had, in fact, mortgaged it to the hilt to pay for his new business venture) or from her father's $100,000 double-indemnity insurance policy. Marlene began urging Chuck to raise several thousand dollars from his drug dealing to pay a hired killer "front money" until the insurance came through.

"Did you ever talk to Gary's brother?" she asked him one day. Chuck was hoping that Marlene would forget about Fred Griffin, the name he had pulled out of thin air in desperation when she had first broached the matter of hiring a killer months earlier. At that time the supermarket clerk with supposed "Mafia connections" lived in the city and it was relatively easy for Chuck to tell Marlene that he hadn't been able to locate him, but she knew that Chuck had recently helped him move to nearby Fairfax. As Chuck recalled under hypnosis, Marlene repeatedly asked him to talk to Fred and finally threatened to stop seeing him if he did not drive up to Fairfax immediately with the proposition. "I drove to Fairfax and parked across the street and started to walk up to the door," his account continues. "But I didn't have the nerve. I turned around and sat in the car for a while smoking a joint. Finally I knocked on the door, but the lady who was living with Fred said he wasn't home. I phoned Marlene and said I had seen Fred and he would look into it, but he wasn't sure if he could find anybody because he had lost contact with the people who might be interested since he had left the city. Marlene said we'll just have to talk to him another time."

Again according to Chuck's hypnotic tapes, on "many occasions" Marlene asked him to bring his gun with him on dates. She would neither tell him why she wanted it nor even, after verifying that he had followed instructions, take it out of the glove compartment. What Chuck thought of as "Marlene's loyalty test" ended when he loaned the gun to Roger Kyle as security for a small loan.

Chuck, in turn, had received another gun from a friend whose sister had accidentally backed into his car, damaging a door. The gun he accepted in compensation was an old shotgun, and when the two friends attempted to fire it, the barrel split. Since he intended to file off the split portion anyway, Chuck decided to shorten the barrel as close to the legal limit for shotguns as possible, which someone told him was sixteen inches. Then he put the gun in the trunk of his car and forgot about it. In fact, the legal limit was eighteen inches; two weeks later, when Chuck and Marlene were arrested for the second time, the main charge was possession of a sawed-off shotgun.

Chuck's car, with its dartboard hood and its owner's high-speed habits, was a favorite target of the highway patrol. In addition to legitimate offenses, he had been harassed for allowing the air pressure in his left rear tire to fall too low and his front bumper to protrude over a crosswalk line. On this particular occasion Chuck and Marlene were on their way to rent a motel room when a highway patrolman noticed that the Buick's license plate registration tag had expired and pulled them over. As usual Chuck's car resembled a mobile head shop. According to arresting officer Arthur Lutzow's report:

> While subject #1 [Chuck] removed his license I observed an orange package of Zig Zag cigarette papers on the dash. I then observed a roach clip hanging on the left visor. This item caused my attention to focus on numerous small green seeds appearing to be marijuana seeds on the floor of the vehicle. . . . I observed a prescription bottle next to the seat. The bottle contained numerous small green seeds and debris appearing to be marijuana seeds. . . . A box was found under the right front seat containing numerous small green seeds appearing to be marijuana seeds. I also found a brass pipe in a side pocket which contained debris and smelled of burnt marijuana. I found another plastic bottle containing numerous small green seeds appearing to be marijuana seeds.

In addition to numerous small green seeds, the highway patrolman found seventeen bottles of prescription drugs in Marlene's purse, including several that held an assortment of pills, as well as "a black-handled knife with an approx. 5″ blade inside." He told her that the legal limit for concealed blades was three inches and was not overly impressed with her explanation that she had been using the kitchen knife to "sharpen colored pencils" at home and had inadvertently stuck it in her purse. When he asked Chuck if he could look in the trunk, "Subject #1 stated, 'Sure, go ahead, you won't find anything.'" He found the sawed-off shotgun.

Chuck was booked for possession of the shotgun, a felony that carried a possible prison term of seven years, and that same day bail was set at $2,500. Chuck spent three nights in jail before Oscar consented to put up the 10 percent the bail bondsman required—and even then he did so only when Chuck agreed to hand over the keys to his car and to abide by a strict ten o'clock curfew, conditions which Oscar had the bondsman write into the contract. Chuck came home looking like a "whupped puppy," according to Oscar, and that evening father and son stayed up late into the night talking. At first Oscar was insistent that Chuck find some other place to live, and he only relented the next morning when he found an apologetic note Chuck had left on the kitchen table that seemed to him "written from the heart—not apple polishing."

The police escorted Marlene to juvenile hall, but this time it was decided after several hours to release her to Jim. "Now you're a two-time loser," he told her during the drive home, more in disappointment than in anger. Marlene broke into tears, and that night Jim came home with another gift of costume jewelry from his client's store as a peace offering. For a while Jim enforced his standing restriction on incoming telephone calls (even reducing the time limit from ten to five minutes) and insisted again that Marlene return home immediately after school and only go out at night on weekends. But he believed her explanation for carrying the knife, and as with the shoplifting arrest, blamed Chuck more than Marlene for the entire incident. He did take his daughter to task for seeing Chuck and exacted another promise that it would not happen again. (Marlene told Chuck while he was in jail to write her in care of the Dillons "because if you send a letter to me here my dad will kill me and confiscate it.") Jim tried to think of new ways to get Marlene away from her circle of friends. He asked fellow Rotarian Clifford Campbell, the superintendent of San Rafael grade schools, if there was any way to enroll Marlene in a public school farther away from Terra Linda, and told him that he was even thinking of selling his business and moving the family elsewhere.

From Southern California, where she was staying with her daughter, Eunice called and offered to take Marlene to Maryland with her when she visited her son Peter, whose wife was about to have a baby, and then down to Panama for the summer. Jim rejected the first suggestion outright but said he would think about the other. ("My aunt would like me to visit her in Panama this summer," Marlene wrote Chuck in jail, "but I sure won't go without you. Don't worry, I won't give up on you. Never!") When Eunice came up to San Francisco to stay with friends in the city, Jim and Marlene picked her up at the airport and drove back to San Rafael for the day. Eunice immediately realized how much Marlene had changed in the year since she last saw her. At one point, when a San Rafael police car drove by, Marlene said, almost proudly, "They know me," and told her aunt about the weapon charge. Eunice was surprised that Marlene would discuss the matter so openly in front of Jim. "Well, that's nothing to be so smart-alecky about," she remembers telling her niece.

Despite her brave front Marlene felt more insecure than ever now that Chuck was not around to provide support. While he was in jail she sent him a steady stream of letters pledging her love and constancy. By now Chuck was aware that the only time Marlene grew affectionate toward him was when they were in trouble together or he became angry at her "games" and lashed back. The more explosive the situation, the more openly affectionate she became. Now she thought he might be taken away from her for years. "Oh, God, what am I gonna do?" one typically effusive note began. "I was hoping you'd be out today so I could see you and we could talk things over. Help me, Chuck. I can't live without you. I love you. Please believe me! Please!"

But interspersed with such romantic assurances were increasingly violent allusions to her situation at home, which she began referring to as a "disease," and to her mother, whom she took to calling "Mrs. Olive" in their arguments as well as in letters and poems. "We have to take care of a disease," Marlene wrote Chuck. "Talk to F.G. [Fred Griffin] some day soon. I could even get hurt a little if it was an accident. I told Mrs. Olive she wasn't considered my mother anymore, and that I smoked dope and took pills and was just as bad as you, just as savage. I'm going to be so good to you."

On June 3 Marlene and her parents appeared in juvenile court for the final disposition of her shoplifting charge. Peter Mitchell, the young lawyer Jim had retained, had already plea-bargained the charge down to petty theft, and on the recommendation of Frieda Noll's probation report (which was, she wrote in Marlene's file, "extremely bland because I was most concerned not to feed the mother's full-blown paranoia"), referee Noel Blaine let Marlene off with a verbal rebuke, placed her on a compulsory three-day week program with the county's parks and recreation department and directed that she and the family seek "psychiatric treatment" in the indefinite future. Blaine "ordered" the minor, who thereafter became a ward of the court in the custody of the Olives, to "lead a law-abiding life and follow the reasonable and proper directions of her parents, the school authorities and the probation officer." At Jim's insistence the referee also decreed that "the minor is forbidden to associate with Charles D. Riley under penalty of parole violation."

According to Frieda Noll's written remarks after the hearing, Marlene was very receptive to psychiatric treatment ("she wants this and is relieved it was 'ordered by the court' "). She was, however, quite distraught by the order forbidding her to see Chuck, and after asking if she could see Mrs. Noll alone, she cried bitterly about it, complaining that "Chuck is the only person I can rely on now."

Frieda Noll was just assigned to Marlene's case through the disposition hearing, and now she turned over her files to a supervising probation officer. She had recently asked to be reassigned to her old job investigating juvenile cases from her present counseling position, and the obduracy of the Olives' problem contributed to her decision. "In closing," she wrote on Marlene's record, "I can only say that this case is one reason I like investigation. Ready for transfer."

In the Olive household there were few immediate repercussions from the juvenile hearing. One reason for this brief truce was that two days after the hearing Naomi learned that Anna DeKay had died at the age of eighty-three. Although Naomi had not seen her foster mother for a decade, she had always thought and spoken fondly of her, and the sudden news of Anna DeKay's death left her disconsolate. Pleading the pressure of work, Jim refused to accompany Naomi back East for the funeral, and she decided not to make the trip on her own. Instead she retreated to her room and the Scotch in her sewing cabinet, refusing this time even to care for her tropical fish. In a poem ominously entitled "It's Nearly the End," Marlene wrote of Naomi:

> It's nearly the end of the world
> and you sit there idle in
> the cold, cold night
> wearing funny faces and reaching
> for a drink, all the while
> you read nursery rhymes.
> It's nearly time for you to fall
> asleep, so drunk from a hard
> day's labor over nothing.
> Shed no tears for we all must end.
> Sooner or later we all come to an end.

Concerned about her deteriorating mental and physical health following Mrs. DeKay's death, Jim was more than usually solicitous toward Naomi, even buying her the expensive living-room furniture—a couch and two easy chairs—she had been wanting for months. He also felt totally cut off from his daughter, unable to deal with either Marlene's erratic behavior or his own anger with it. One evening during a silent dinner Jim plaintively told his daughter, "I wish I knew what's going on in your head." "It's better you didn't," Marlene answered. "It might frighten you."

Marlene felt equally isolated from her father. In "Nightsong" she wrote about going into Jim's room when he was asleep and thinking: "What I would give to slip inside and take my/Place in the shadows and just for a /Little while pretend I play an important role."

In this supercharged atmosphere the events of the next two weeks moved swiftly, almost inevitably, toward their tragic conclusion. All of the key participants in the drama expressed the feeling that they were helpless, uncomprehending witnesses to an event that was happening to others. Marlene, especially, was whirling like a pinwheel and she knew it. "I wish I could change all this," she announced to Joan James one morning, "but I'm too caught up in it now." She described her emotional state in a poem called "Contradictions," which began: "My mind is being blown to pieces/My feelings are engulfing me./They are going their own way."

Marlene's poetry and other writings in these weeks reflect an intense internal debate about her own fantasy life, fear alternating with hope from one page to the next. "I'm trying to fight my way out of dreams I thought were reality," she warned herself, recognizing, as she put it in one poem, that she "may self-pretend/until the end." Finally the whole tortuous debate became so painful that she backed away from further reflection:

> Maybe, just maybe, I would be
> Better off not knowing
> Certain things about me.

Shortly before the end of school, Jim dropped by to offer Marlene a ride home and found that she had not been there for several days. Walking with him down the back stairs of the church building to the parking lot, Joan James said she didn't think Pacific Crest would be the best place for Marlene in the fall, since she had so thoroughly abused its loose structure. "Tell me, where *is* the best place?" Jim asked. "What can I do with her? I'm desperate." Miss James, who prided herself on "being able to feel optimistic about the most difficult kids," had no answer.

At the end of the first week in June, Mary Sigler, Marlene's new probation officer, was getting ready for a two-week vacation in Hawaii. She was a precise, attractive woman with closely cropped blond hair and the general case-hardened air of a "juvy" veteran. Besides writing to the parents of a half-dozen new charges, she sent the Olives an introductory letter explaining that if a problem arose while she was away, they could contact her superior, Mel Augustine. She also singled out Marlene as someone who might benefit from the special attention of a young "case aide," and instructed the volunteer to contact Marlene and try to get her to "open up." Her instincts told her that Marlene desperately needed someone to talk to she could trust, if it wasn't already too late. When Mary Sigler turned over the files of her new cases to Mel Augustine before leaving, she clipped a note on Marlene's that read: "This one could blow up while I'm gone."

And it was true that with the end of the school term a new urgency entered into Marlene's relationship with her parents. After speaking to Joan James about his daughter's truancy and failing grades, Jim decided that his only recourse was to send Marlene away to boarding school in the fall, and he wrote letters of inquiry to several institutions around the country that had been recommended to him. Since Marlene had no intention of starting over again in an unfamiliar environment, Jim's decision, together with his preoccupation with moving his office to San Rafael, further alienated her from her father. As for Marlene and her mother, they hardly ever talked these days; they either hurled abuse at each other, as likely as not accompanied by shoves and slaps, or passed each other by in stony silence.

Faced with so much hostility at home, Marlene drew closer than ever before to Chuck. In letters and notes she expressed her abiding love for him and, for the first time, her intention to marry him and raise a family. ("I love you. Freebird wants to be tied down to Chuck. I want your baby, too.") She talked about their future together "after I'm free of a certain disease." At times she would drew Chuck into the plot, implying that they could only get married while she was still a minor if her parents were killed. ("I hope you'll wait till I'm 17 to marry me or kill my parents.") Some of these letters, having never been mailed, were later found by the police in Marlene's bedroom; others were confiscated from the Riley house. Before her trial, when Marlene's lawyer asked her to read and comment on the evidence that the police held against her, she wrote on several of the letters, both mailed and unmailed, "Fantasy note." Chuck, of course, had no way of knowing.

When she was displeased with him Marlene would threaten to break off the relationship, often using the difficulty of escaping from her parents' constant vigilance as an excuse (although, in fact, they had no trouble arranging to meet on the sly). If Chuck balked at buying her something she wanted, or stealing it, she threatened to "turn tricks"—or simply turn to another, more compliant boyfriend. Under such inconstant conditions Chuck continued to rely on his "magic bracelet," empowered by Marlene's sorcery, to inform him in advance of her shifting moods and desires.

Occasionally Chuck would get back at Marlene with another "suicide attempt." Early in June, when she threatened to stop seeing him over some minor irritation, Chuck felt that she had "messed with my head enough" and reacted aggressively. At the time, the two were driving along the Lucas Valley Road. "No, you won't break up," Chuck said. "Take it back!" Suddenly he steered the speeding car toward the concrete abutment of a bridge. "Take it back, I said!" At the last moment Marlene reneged on her threat and Chuck swerved back onto the road. Afterward she edged closer to him and put her hand on his thigh.

From an occasional topic of conversation after arguments at home, the murder of her parents had become Marlene's constant obsession. Hardly a day went by now without her raising the subject with Chuck, generally to describe some new way she had dreamt up to commit the crime. One plan had the killer robbing the house or even beating up and "raping" Marlene in order to obscure the motive. Another, even more bizarre notion, which Marlene mentioned to several friends besides Chuck, called for placing a bomb in the trunk of the family car timed to explode when her parents were out on a shopping expedition. There was an even crazier idea of using another car to force the Vega to crash down the steep cliffs below the perilously twisting coastal highway. And, of course, there were the old standby plots to poison or shoot her parents or kill them in one or another well-timed "accident," such as a house fire or a hit-and-run driving incident.

It was impossible for Chuck to know just how seriously to take these schemes, for whenever he decided that Marlene was "just blowing off steam," she would convince him anew that she was, in fact, deadly serious. Just recently, after she found out that Chuck had given away his only remaining gun, she grew very upset and told him to get it back or buy a new one. Chuck asked around and learned that his friend Scott Seldin knew where he could buy a used, and no doubt stolen, 9mm Luger automatic pistol. Marlene wrote him a poem that, without mentioning specifics, was her most explicit demand for him to participate in her plans to kill her parents:

> Can I believe you'll help me in my future?
> Help me now to plan ahead.
> Can I believe you'll fulfill my fantasies
> With no arguing said?
> Can I believe you'll always be true
> And never leave me blue?
> Can I believe I still am Freebird
> No matter what it takes?
> Can I believe in you?

One afternoon two weeks before the murder, Gary Griffin came over to buy a lid of grass. As soon as he left, Marlene said, "Ask him about Fred." Chuck hesitated. "Chu-uck," Marlene said with that familiar threat in her voice. "Ask him or else . . ."

"Or else what?" Chuck balked.

"Or else I'm leaving you," Marlene said.

Chuck called to Gary through his bedroom window, and he and Marlene met him on the Rileys' side lawn. It was clear to Gary that his friend was suddenly very uncomfortable. After beating about the bush for a few minutes, Chuck finally said, "Do you know someone who can get rid of certain parties? Would you ask Fred?"

"I don't, Rocko," Gary said. "What do you have in mind?"

"No one in particular," Chuck demurred. "Just wondering."

But Gary had been around Chuck and Marlene enough to know exactly which parties they were talking about, particularly after Marlene said that "money would be no object." Gary later said he was so "weirded out" by the conversation that he didn't know how to react. At Chuck's trial he would testify: "Marlene was in visual contact with his eyes all the time. It was like it wasn't even him talking. It was like a trance he was in. His tone of voice was very soft, flat. He talked like a robot."

The next day Marlene spotted the Griffin brothers sitting on Fred's pickup truck outside their parents' house. After all Chuck's talk about Fred being a "hired gun" it was the first time that Marlene had actually seen him. Chuck was finally trapped in his lie. Again he took the initiative under Marlene's careful scrutiny. "Have you thought over what we talked about?" Chuck asked. Marlene added, "There's twenty-five thousand dollars in it for whoever's willing to help out." This time Gary said, with a finality that ended the brief conversation, "I don't know of anybody—and I wouldn't tell you if I did."

A few days later Chuck and Sharon were sitting under the big shade tree in the Riley's front yard sharing a joint, when he mentioned the automatic Luger that could be had for $50, although it was easily worth double the price. "I hope no one buys it before I can raise the cash," Chuck said.

"How come you want it so bad?" Sharon asked.

"I just like guns," Chuck said.

They smoked some more marijuana without talking. Then Sharon suddenly blurted out what was really on her mind. "Do you really intend to help Marlene find somebody to kill her parents?"

"The person we thought would do it can't," Chuck said.

"If it came down to it, would you do it yourself? Do you love her that much?"

"If it has to be done, I'd do it," Chuck said, mindful of the fact that Sharon might report the conversation to her best friend. "I'd die for Marlene."

For the first time since she heard Marlene and Chuck talk about killing the Olives, Sharon thought it could really happen. "There has to be another way, " she said.

On Monday, June 16, Marlene's Pacific Crest report card arrived in the mail, confirming Joan James's assessment of her scholastic performance. At this point Jim told Marlene about his decision to send her to boarding school in the fall. "No way, Father dear," she said. "I'd rather die."

"They're sending me away," Marlene announced to Chuck that evening when he picked her up at their usual meeting place

at the far end of the walkway between Hibiscus and Las Gallinas
Avenue. "You better do something fast or we're finished. If you
can't find someone else, you do it, Chuck. Do it yourself." She
nuzzled up to him in the car and spoke in the little-girl, singsong
voice she had always used so successfully with her father when
she wanted something. "Please, Chuck. Pretty please." Then
more coldly: "After we collect the insurance money we'll have
enough to get married and move away. We can go down to
South America. I still have some connections down there. We
can get the best coke for practically nothing. We'll be rich,
Chuck. And we'll be together. I just want to be with you. No
one else matters."

Until now Marlene had not involved Chuck as a direct participant in her plans to kill her parents, and he was, as he later said,
"shocked but not surprised" that she would. She had been
exhorting him almost every day to help her "do something about
the disease," saying that otherwise her parents would make it
increasingly difficult, if not impossible, for the two to see each
other. It was the one threat Chuck could not abide.

On Tuesday, June 17, four days before the murder, Tim
Prather, a friend of Marlene's who had been attending junior
college in Santa Barbara, ran into her in front of her house and
was invited inside. From her bed in the spare room Naomi asked
Tim about school and his plans for the summer, which were to
work as a lifeguard and "ice boy" at the Bohemian Grove
retreat on the Russian River. Marlene seemed impatient for Tim
to end his conversation with her mother, and when he did, she
told him that he should meet her new boyfriend, Chuck Riley.
"She seemed happy about him," Tim later recalled. "As I was
leaving she said, 'Maybe you can come over this weekend. My
parents will be in Lake Tahoe.' "

On Wednesday, Jim and Marlene signed court papers agreeing
to the conditions of her probation for the shoplifting conviction.
That night she told Chuck that her father had compiled a list of
all her friends who used drugs and was about to turn it in to the
San Rafael police. Chuck, of course, was prominently mentioned.

On Thursday, Marlene and Naomi got into one of their worst
rows ever. In the late morning two of Marlene's friends, Glenn
Erlinger and Ed Tucker, had stopped by to pick up some shirts
that she had promised to tie-dye for them. Marlene told Chuck
that the boys would drop her off at his house but instead accepted their invitation to "toke up" with them. The three drove

down the Lucas Valley Road until they came to a secluded creek bed, a favorite place for Terra Linda teen-agers to smoke marijuana and drink wine, which is exactly what they proceeded to do. On the way back they were all, according to Marlene, feeling "pretty wasted." Tucker dropped Erlinger off at home and drove on to Hibiscus, where Marlene invited him inside.

The Olives had recently turned part of the garage into a makeshift den, replete with their old living-room furniture, a radio and an extension of the house phone. Marlene showed Tucker into the garage and then went to her room to change into her "bikini jeans"—a pair of very short cutoffs that particularly infuriated Naomi—and a tank-top T-shirt. Marlene turned on the radio. She and Tucker began petting and disrobing each other. A telephone call from Chuck interrupted them. He wanted to know why Marlene hadn't come over to his house hours earlier, as she had intended, and even though she said she'd be there soon, the male voice he could hear giggling in the background indicated otherwise.

Marlene and Ed Tucker were making love on the couch when Naomi, drawn by the sudden silence, walked in and caught them in the act. She reeled back as if struck in the chest. "How dare you!" she screamed. "How dare you do that in my house! Wait till your father hears about this."

Tucker was hopping around the garage trying to put his pants on. "It's okay, lady," he said, trying to calm Naomi. "I'm leaving now. Excuse me. I'm sorry." Then he ran past her and out the front door.

Naomi screamed at Marlene for half an hour, calling her a "tramp" and a "whore" and indicating again that, in her words, "the apple doesn't fall far from the tree—the *rotten* apple." At one point she ran to get a dictionary from under the telephone and said, "You're promiscuous, Marlene. Do you know what that means? Look it up. P-R-O-M-I-S-C-U-O-U-S." Marlene did not, in fact, know the meaning of the word, and Naomi insisted that she read the dictionary definition aloud. At that point Marlene broke into tears and begged Naomi not to tell her father about the incident.

She was still sobbing when she called Chuck. "Something's happened," she said tersely. "I can't go out." Without being told, Chuck quickly guessed what had happened. It was hard to question Marlene further because she kept putting down the phone to argue with Naomi. Chuck heard her plead with her mother not to tell her father. When the two women finally calmed down and Marlene promised that nothing like that would ever happen again, Naomi agreed to keep the whole matter between them.

For the rest of the afternoon Naomi stayed in her room and Marlene sat on the living-room couch reading stacks of fashion magazines and hoping someone would call her. Jim came home around six. He had been in his new office all day arranging for the installation of telephones and carpeting. Naomi must have reached him there, for it was clear from his angry look that he knew what had happened in the garage. Marlene became furious at the thought of Naomi's betrayal and she stormed into her room yelling, "You bitch! You fucking bitch! You lied to me! I should kill you for this!"

Jim's reaction to the whole episode was, typically, anger followed by conciliation. At first he told Marlene that her mother was right, she was behaving shamefully. He forbade her from going out with boys "until further notice," and when Chuck called up a short time later to find out what was going on, Jim took the phone away from her and said, without knowing who it was, "Marlene is not available now. Please don't call back." But later on that same evening his attitude softened considerably.

After her parents were asleep Marlene called Chuck to tell him about the new restriction. She apologized for "messing everything up for us" and reaffirmed her love for him, at the same time telling Chuck not to reproach Tucker, because she had taken the initiative. She also said, "I've got to kill that bitch for betraying me." She seemed perfectly serious to Chuck. Later he would say, "I tried to talk her out of it but it was like talking to a fence post."

On Friday morning Jim picked Phil Royce up at his house shortly before seven and the two drove to the Airport Hotel in Sacramento for the regular monthly meeting of GBS area directors in the Northern California region. It was the first time Jim would chair the meeting since purchasing the regional directorship earlier in the spring, and during the ninety-mile drive he was full of plans for revitalizing the program, which the previous regional director had let slide. The slack attendance at the meeting did not prevent him from launching into what Royce later called "a typical gung-ho Jim Olive pep talk" to try to regenerate enthusiasm among the disgruntled ranks. After two years of grinding effort his business was about to lose what he jokingly referred to as its "nonprofit status."

Still, on the way home Jim seemed unusually pensive, and when Phil Royce asked him what was on his mind he explained that he was planning to hire Marlene to work in the office over the summer answering the phone and typing letters, and he worried that it wouldn't work out. "I have to tell you that she's constitutionally unable to tell the truth," he told his partner. "You've got to make sure that what she tells you isn't just something she's made up in her head."

Although Royce had heard Jim allude to Marlene's "difficulties" before, it was the first time he had spoken badly of his daughter. Once again Phil Royce reminded his partner that in the sixties he himself had raised five children in Terra Linda, including a daughter who was a "wild one." "It wasn't exactly smooth sailing during the whole hippie business out here," he said. "You let me know if I can help you out."

Friday afternoon Leslie Slote picked Marlene up while Chuck waited a block away, and the three of them drove to the Civic Center lake and then to Mike Howard's house. Marlene joked about the Tucker incident, which hurt Chuck, although he decided to "play along and not make a scene." But she also talked about running away to stay with friends in Oregon or Florida before her parents sent her off to boarding school. When she was alone with Chuck for a few minutes she became unusually affectionate. "I love you so much," she told him. "I'll never forget that no one's ever stuck by me like you have." Chuck felt there was something oddly final about her words, but at least she hadn't, for once, mentioned killing her parents.

When Marlene walked home to meet her ten o'clock curfew, Jim and Naomi were sitting in the living room waiting for her with faces even longer than usual. "Jody Swafford's father called" was all Jim had to say for Marlene to know that she was in for big trouble. Marlene hardly knew Jody, who lived near the Air Force base in Novato and attended a different high school, but she had spoken with her many times recently, usually attempting to disguise her voice.

What had happened was that a month or so earlier, Jody Swafford had heard through a mutual friend that Marlene could get her an ounce of Panama Red. Marlene had agreed, and Jody met her at Northgate Mall to give her $40 for the marijuana. Marlene told her she would return in a half-hour with the lid. It would not have been the first time that Chuck had sole her pot at cost and allowed her to keep the profit. Now, perhaps because she was not likely to run into Jody again, Marlene decided to simply hold on to the money.

Jody had called her many times over the next several weeks and either reached Naomi, who always sounded very angry, or Marlene's "younger sister," who promised to pass along the message as soon as Marlene returned home. Finally Jody decided to swallow her pride rather than lose the money, and she told her father about the incident. Air Force Colonel Martin Swafford promised to do something abut it. He called the Olive house and left word with Naomi to have Jim return his call as soon as he got back from Sacramento. When Jim did, the conversation was uncomfortable for both men.

"'Your daughter has extorted forty dollars from my daughter," Colonel Swafford began. "I don't condone Jody attempting to buy marijuana, but neither do I condone Marlene's taking money under false pretenses."

" 'Extortion' is a pretty strong word for what might just be a misunderstanding between the girls," Jim answered.

"Nevertheless, if Jody doesn't receive her money back, I'm going to contact the Narcotics Agency about Marlene's drug dealing."

"Now, that kind of talk doesn't get us anywhere. I could just as easily report your daughter for soliciting."

After the two men calmed down, Jim said he would talk to Marlene as soon as she came home, and if what Jody claimed was true, he would personally reimburse her the next day. Marlene would call the Swaffords in the morning to arrange a meeting.

By the time Marlene returned home Jim and Naomi had been waiting anxiously to talk to her for three hours. Backed into a corner, Marlene admitted keeping the money, but whatever hope Jim might have taken from her candor was offset by her explanation. "I didn't even know the broad," she said. "Besides, it was only pot. It could've been heroin."

For once Jim's own temper kept Naomi quiet. "I'm at the end of my rope with you, Marlene," he said in carefully measured tones. "Like it or not, next fall you're going away to boarding school. This summer I don't want you to associate with any of your friends. In fact, you won't go out of the house for any reason unless you have my express permission. I've a mind to let you stew in juvenile hall for the summer—you and the rest of your no-good friends.''

As Marlene had arranged earlier, Chuck called her from the telephone booth late that night. Sobbing, she told him what had happened. "I'm completely grounded—no telephone, no seeing friends, no going out, no nothing. He says he's going to turn us all in. That's it for us, Chuck."

A final poem alluding to her murder plans, possibly written that evening, reads:

> No more time to stand alooking.
> No more time for child's play.
> Now we're down to the nitty-gritty.
> There's no back door that way. . . .

Emotionally spent from the events of the day, everyone in the Olive household was soundly asleep long before midnight.

Chuck arose early Saturday morning with his usual "wake-up snort" of cocaine. Because Marlene was restricted to her house and he had nothing to do but "kick back" all day, he also swallowed a half tab of windowpane acid. It was a bright, clear morning, unseasonably warm for the first day of summer. Skipping breakfast to allow the drug to take effect, Chuck called Mike Howard to find out if he and Nancy Dillon wanted to head for the beach later on. Mike was somewhat surprised to hear his friend's voice, since the two had not seen much of each other in recent weeks, an estrangement that Mike attributed to Chuck's "total absorption" with Marlene. But he agreed to come for Chuck, whose own car was out of commission, as soon as he could "get it together."

At that point Chuck called Marlene, more to allay his apprehension over their last conversation than to make any plans to see her. He could not have chosen a worse moment. Marlene and Naomi had both awakened early, and the temporary lull of the night before was shattered even before Jim left the house to run some errands. Naomi had begun drinking early. Marlene was watching the Saturday morning cartoons on television that preceded her favorite *Creature Features* show. She was dressed in jeans and a skimpy T-shirt and had gone to a utility drawer in the kitchen for a hammer—a red-handled, claw-necked tool meant for heavy work—to fix a leather strap that had come loose on her

six-inch-high wooden platforms, the very scrape of which on her
linoleum floors was enough to spark Naomi's fury. With all the
commotion of the night before, the sink still held the dirty dinner
dishes that Marlene was supposed to have washed. Afterward
Marlene was never certain exactly what prompted their latest—
and last—argument. Perhaps it was just the concurrence of the
dirty dishes and the platform shoes—the symbol of Marlene's
"whorish ways" to her mother. Perhaps it was Naomi's gnawing
awareness that Colonel Swafford's call meant that Marlene was
still "broadcasting family problems." Certainly their argument
was fueled by Naomi's drinking and Marlene's disgust with it.

Marlene remembers that her mother insisted that she do the
dishes when she came into the kitchen for some orange juice.

"I'm watching television," Marlene said. "I'll do them later."
She walked back to her own room."

"It'll only take a few minutes," Naomi, trailing her, insisted.
"You can watch television after."

"You don't do anything around the house yourself but drink
and stumble around and mumble to yourself," Marlene shot
back. "So why should I?"

"At least I'm not a dope pusher like some people I know!"
Naomi yelled.

According to Marlene, the two of them kept "hassling each
other." After hearing her mother allude again to her promiscuity,
Marlene started shaking her rear end the way she had seen
Naomi do in imitation of Eunice. Whatever her mother said,
Marlene would answer "Shut up" to try to block it out.

"You stop parading around like a—"

"Shut up."

"—of trash."

"You're nothing but—"

"Shut up."

"—Latin swine—"

"Shut up."

"—gutter tramp."

"Shut up."

"Your mother was—"

"Don't talk about my mom. She's a million times better than
you."

At that point Marlene put her hands over her ears and half
chanted: "Shutupshutupshutupshutup . . ." She stared at Naomi,
who continued to berate her soundlessly, her eyebrows and

wrinkled forehead moving in perfect synchronization with her overlipsticked mouth. Marlene could only hear odd snatches of her mother's monologue, but she knew it was about the "Norfolk whore" who had gotten "knocked up" and "gave you away."

Naomi's last remark, according to Marlene, "blew it completely." At that point Marlene kicked Naomi and she pushed her daughter against the wall.

"I hate you!" Marlene shouted.

"I hate you too!" Naomi screamed back.

"Bitch!"

"Shut you damn foul mouth!"

Chuck's call scarcely interrupted the argument, since Marlene repeatedly threw the receiver down to hurl insults back at her mother. It was when Naomi left the dining area that Marlene, as she would later admit, "opened my big mouth one time too many. Everything exploded. Everything that was building up inside me for years."

"Get your gun," she told Chuck. "We've got to kill that bitch today. They're gonna put me in the hall all summer."

"Roger's got my gun," Chuck reminded her. "It's not mine anymore."

"What about the one Scott told you about?"

"Scott's probably at work. Anyway, I can't use my car."

"If you don't do it, Chuck, I'll never speak to you again."

By now it was after nine. Chuck called his friend Scott Seldin at home and found out that he was indeed at work. He walked and hitchhiked through the center of San Rafael to the Shell station in Fairfax, at the other end of the Miracle Mile, thinking, as he later recalled, that he'd "play Marlene's little game and that would be the end of it."

Scott Seldin was busy servicing customers when Chuck arrived at the gas station, so Chuck called Marlene from a nearby pay phone just to "check in" with her, as she had instructed him to do. By then Marlene had conceived the idea to trying to poison her mother again.

"What kind of things are poison?" she asked Chuck.

"If it's poison, it says so on the label," Chuck answered. "That's the law."

"Maybe I should try putting pills in her soup again to get her to sleep. Then we could hit her with something heavy. How would I do it? What with?"

By then the acid Chuck had taken an hour earlier had made

him "fairly well spaced." For the first time he became frightened that Marlene might be serious; he might not be able to "brush her off my back" so easily. The hypnotic tapes, which would be played in court, reveal his thoughs at the moment: *"Spinning around and around. I'm just spinning around. I'm in Fairfax. She is talking about putting some kind of pills in the food, in some soup. I'm trying to . . . I'm trying to . . . I don't want to do it. I want to get around it somehow. But I have to do it because she says so. I can't avoid it. She told me I had to do it. . . . That's all we talk about. She asked me on the phone there in Fairfax, 'Where do I hit my mom to kill her? How hard do I hit her?' I don't know. I don't know. I tell her I never hurt nobody before. I don't know how to. [She says] 'Just tell me where. That's all. Where to hit her.' "*

Scott was surprised to see Chuck in Fairfax early on a Saturday morning, especially since Chuck owed him some money for a bag of marijuana. When Chuck asked about the gun, Scott told him he couldn't get it until Monday at the earliest. Chuck said he needed it sooner and left when more customers arrived. Relieved, he called Marlene from the same phone booth to report the news. *"She wants me to get my other gun. She wants me to go to Roger's and get my other gun. She says why did I ever give that gun to him. She gave me the story to get the gun back. She said to insist on getting it back. So we talked. [Then she said] 'What if we use a hammer?' No, not a hammer. A rolling pin. Something heavy. 'How hard do I have to hit?' She kept asking that question all day, all day. I didn't say nothing then. Later, I did."*

The "story" that Marlene had given Chuck involved telling Roger Kyle that he had found a buyer for the gun and would thus be able to repay the loan in cash. Chuck hitchhiked back to San Rafael, getting a ride almost immediately with a fellow who was returning from a successful fishing trip and had a bucket of trout beside him to prove it. Chuck was now "good and high" from the acid and could hardly keep from laughing at the "old-timer" in his flannel shirt and porkpie hat with fishhooks in the brim. They traded fish stories. "Once I lassoed a fish," Chuck said. "Honest to God. Brought him in with the line tied around him instead of on the hook."

The man left Chuck off at the unemployment office in downtown San Rafael and from there he walked the few blocks to Roger Kyle's apartment. It was eleven o'clock by the time he got there. Kyle, his wife and a neighbor, Alice Kearns, were home. Chuck accepted a cup of coffee.

"I need the gun back," he announced.

"You gonna shoot someone, Rocko?" Roger joked.

Chuck "looked away," according to Alice Kearns, who felt "strange vibes coming from him."

"I think I've got a buyer for it. I can let you have the cash in a few days."

Kyle, who had come to enjoy having the gun around, offered to cancel the debt to keep it, but when Chuck said he could get "extra bucks" in the sale, he relented, reaching under the couch to retrieve the shiny black pistol in its tan leather holster. At Chuck's request, he put it in a brown shopping bag. After a few minutes Chuck made a hasty call to Marlene to let her know he was on his way and excused himself by saying that someone was waiting for him downstairs. When Kyle asked him why he was so "jumpy," Chuck said it was the effect of his "allergy pills."

Chuck started walking toward San Rafael's main business district, hoping to catch a ride back to Terra Linda with his friend Gary Griffin, who drove a delivery van for Burn's Florist. But none of the vans were there, so he continued walking. By now he was "really climbing" from the acid and was beginning to feel "paranoid" about being on drugs and carrying the gun through town. At the corner of Fifth and Lincoln he saw a San Rafael police car stopped at the light and felt sure that the cop knew something was wrong.

"I called Marlene again—there was a phone right there—and asked her for some help. 'Send somebody down to get me.' [I was] scared. Something's wrong. Something is wrong. I have to bring my gun to her house. I have to give it to her. She is going to do it. No. No."

Since the lock on the living-room phone prevented her from making outgoing calls, Marlene told Chuck to hold on while she went to Jim's office to telephone Mike Howard and ask him to pick his friend up in San Rafael. When she got back to Chuck, he mentioned that he had no bullets for the gun. Marlene told him to ask Mike if he'd like to go shooting later in the day, then to stop off at the Sears store in Northgate Mall to buy a box of ammunition, making sure to give his friend the money to purchase it and—as was required by California law—sign the registration book. Marlene asked him again how many tranquilizers she would have to put in Naomi's soup to poison her, as well as how hard she had to hit her mother with the hammer to kill her.

The conversation ended when Mike Howard arrived in Nancy Dillon's car. The two friends proceeded to Sears, where Mike bought the bullets "without really thinking about it" and then picked up some groceries and headed home. Marlene had already called there once, asking for Chuck. According to Nancy Dillon's statement to the police ten days later, she and Marlene had a "casual conversation, nothing important. She said she'd had just about enough of her parents and was getting tired of them and that she was going to bump them off. She said she was gonna put sleeping pills in her mom's soup. . . . I didn't believe her."

By that time, shortly before noon, the argument between Marlene and her mother had quieted to a barely suppressed rage. Jim, who had been transporting equipment and files to his new office all morning, left to take some clothes to the dry cleaner, telling Marlene to call Jody Swafford and confirm their two o'clock appointment at the shopping center. Marlene tried to cancel the appointment by asking Jody if she wouldn't be satisfied with the ounce of marijuana, after all, but Jody said that now that her father was involved, she needed the money back. Marlene also mentioned that Jim was going to turn her in to the "narcotics squad" as soon as he paid off the debt, a statement she later admitted to be false. (In fact, aside from restricting his daughter to the house for the time being, Jim had merely insisted that she repay the $40 to him out of her weekly allowance.) After the conversation Marlene made a second half-hearted attempt to "poison" Naomi by emptying the contents of a dozen or so 30mg Darvon capsules into the soup, salad and tea she had promised her father she would prepare for Naomi, who was resting in her bedroom when Marlene brought it to her on a tray. But as she had done a month earlier, Naomi rejected the food for its "funny" taste, although once again the few spoonfuls of soup she swallowed may have made her habitual afternoon nap sounder than usual.

When Jim returned home a little past noon he, too, decided to take a short nap before going to meet Jody Swafford. The house was suddenly still. Marlene later admitted that she took the claw hammer and walked "very slowly" down the hallway to the master bedroom, where her father was sleeping. "I stood over him. I started to bring [the hammer] down and pulled back. And tried it again and pulled back." She went out to the garage to work on her shoes. "All that anger came out. I didn't want to see Jody Swafford. I didn't want to face her. I kept on hitting my finger with the hammer while I was fixing the shoes." After that "everything happened so fast."

In the next half-hour there were several calls between Marlene and Chuck at the Howards' house. Mike, Nancy and Chuck were sitting around the kitchen table drinking beer, listening to records and talking, mostly about the upcoming Yes concert in San Francisco that they all had tickets for the following Wednesday. There was no further mention of going target shooting at China Camp, although at one point Chuck took the gun out of the paper bag and loaded it. Instead, plans were made to drive to the beach later in the afternoon. Chuck rolled and passed around a number of joints from a quarter-pound stash of marijuana he had brought with him in a freezer bag. At one point he removed a mirror from the wall and they all did some lines of coke.

Since Chuck normally spent so much time on the phone with Marlene, neither Mike nor Nancy was surprised at how often he got up to call or receive calls from her. Nancy answered one call from Marlene and remembers her saying, "We've had it up to here with my parents. We're gonna blow 'em away," before she handed the phone to Chuck. To Nancy the remark seemed "typical Marlene"; later she would testify to being more struck by a remark she overheard while cooking breakfast near the kitchen phone. "I heard Chuck say, 'I guess hit her as hard as you can. Harder than you've ever hit anybody.' "

Around one-thirty in the afternoon Chuck left Mike's house, explaining that he was going to meet Marlene in the walkway that connected Las Gallinas Avenue with Hibiscus. He said he'd be back soon, possibly with Marlene, and then they would all head for the beach. (Mike and Nancy waited for an hour before they decided that Chuck was "playing his typical games" and left by themselves.) Instead Chuck walked directly to the Olives' house, hesitating only when he approached it and saw the green Vega still in the driveway and Marlene at the kitchen window waving him away. Realizing that Jim Olive was still at home, Chuck drew back beyond the fence between the Olives' house and their neighbor's. He heard Marlene shout to her father, "I'm just going to get the paper," before she came to the edge of the driveway and whispered to him, "We'll be gone in a few minutes. Then go in."

Eventually Chuck hid behind some azalea bushes on the lawn

of a house around the corner. He waited "five to fifteen minutes," lost in acid-inspired wonder at the intricacies of the undergrowth. Just after the Olives' car passed by, with Marlene searching for him out the passenger window, a postal truck and jeep stopped directly in front of his hiding place, and the drivers engaged in what seemed to Chuck countless minutes of "mailman talk." (He was being "extra careful," he would tell the court, "because I had been told by Marlene that people in the neighborhood were alerted to watch for me . . . by Mr. Olive.") When their conversation ended, Chuck went over to Marlene's house, already well behind their agreed-upon schedule.

Jim and Marlene arrived at the Safeway parking lot in the Northgate shopping center, only a few blocks from Hibiscus, "sometime between a quarter to two and two," according to Jody Swafford's later reckoning in court. Jody herself was early for the two o'clock appointment, and the transaction was quickly completed. "Her father said, 'You must be Jody,' and I said, 'Yes,' " she would testify. "I gave him my driver's license to prove it and he looked at it and asked if a check was good and wrote one out. And that was it." Marlene "didn't look too happy" seated beside her father in the Vega, Jody reported. "She looked quite angered."

In the meantime Chuck entered the house by the front door, which Marlene had left unlocked for him. According to Chuck's subsequent confessions, he found the red-handled hammer leaning against the wall inside the front door, where Marlene had carefully placed it before joining her father in the car. Picking it up, he was suddenly startled by his own image reflected in the full-length foyer mirror. Chuck's hypnotic account of the next several minutes—begun in a barely audible, slow, monotone voice—grows increasingly animated at this point:

"I see myself. I am terrified to walk in the house. It has been so long since I have been there. And I was really unsure about being there. Mr. Olive was going to kill me if he saw me enter that house again. Yes. He told me so. I was afraid of Mr. Olive. He was making me do without Marlene a lot. He was driving me hard. Looking around. Looking around. I was looking at all the different furniture. The table was the same. New couch and chair. And I stood there for a couple of minutes. It was so quiet. Just remembering all the time I spent in the house months before, hours and days. I look around the house. Walk up the hallway to be sure the house is empty. It was all eerie . . . I

thought everything was cool. I had made enough noise going up the hallway to attract anyone's attention. Mr. Olive's office looked half empty. The desk wasn't there. And I walked into the master bedroom just a little ways. I walked into the big bedroom at the end of the hallway, just to make sure. I am listening for any noise, anybody moving about. When I started to walk down from the bedroom the cat, Rascal, ran by me really fast. Ran out into the living room. Empty house so far. And I walk back down by the bathroom, and there is a door. And it was closed. It was Marlene's bedroom.''

Chuck opened the door and entered the room, which had been Marlene's bedroom the last time he was in the house but was now her mother's. Lying on her back with her face tilted toward him, Naomi, still wearing her reading glasses, was in a drugged sleep. A plate on the nightstand beside the bed held a kitchen knife and some apple parings. Chuck was vaguely conscious of soft music from the stereo in the living room, tuned to Marlene's favorite rock station, KTIM. Although he would eventually change his account of the murder, two hours after his arrest Chuck told Marin County jail nurse Dick McGovern that he struck Naomi "many times." (Asked for the same information in a more hysterical state, he would tell arresting officer Bart Stinson: "I don't know. I just hit her. I don't even remember. My mind went blank and I don't remember anything after that.") The blows crushed Naomi Olive's forehead above the left eye. The first one shattered her metal-frame glasses, sending them flying off her face. Its force was so hard, Chuck would later tell Roger Kyle from the county jail, that the gun wedged in his belt fell to the floor, discharging a bullet that narrowly missed his foot. (The police eventually found the intact shell embedded in the floorboards.) After another blow the hammer became stuck in Naomi's skull, and Chuck, placing his left hand on Naomi's head for leverage, only dislodged it with great effort. A "gush" of blood followed its release, and thereafter Chuck made sure to tilt the hammer head sideways before bringing it down, closing his eyes against the sight of his victim.

At this point in Chuck's hypnotic account he is sobbing convulsively: *"I had to touch her to take the hammer out. It was really hard. It wouldn't come loose. I just about broke the hammer. Blood. Blood. No. No. It is burning my hand up. My left hand. Blood. There was blood everywhere. It shot out when I pulled the hammer. It spurts out as soon as the hammer came out, all over my hand. Fire. I have to do something to get the blood off. I'm flinging it off my hand like you do with a paint-brush when you're cleaning it. I can't stand it, I can't stand it. It's burning my hand. Then I saw the hem of a dress and I picked it up and wiped my hands on it.''*

Horribly battered, Naomi refused to die. She was choking on the blood now pouring out of her mouth, and her gasps for air produced a "raw, gurgling" sound that Chuck found "almost deafening." Her jaw was trembling. *"She wouldn't die. She wouldn't die at all. Please, God, let her die. I just couldn't see her living like that. It hurt so much to see that. So much."* According to Chuck's account of the murder to Nurse McGovern, he ran into the kitchen, grabbed a steak knife and stabbed Naomi in the chest. She was still gasping for breath, so he pulled the blood-soaked pillow from under her head and attempted to smother her. At that instant he heard the Olives' car pull into the driveway.

Marlene and Jim had returned unexpectedly early from the shopping center, just a few minutes after two. At the front door Marlene pretended to adjust the strap on her shoes so that Jim would enter the house first. (Later she would tell a court-appointed psychiatrist that she warned her father, "Don't go in there. You're going to die," and that Jim "just giggled and walked in.") Chuck's hypnotized "revivification" of what followed is spoken with all the emotion that attended the original event:

"The car's back. They're home. Mr. Olive's home. What do I do? I don't know what to do. I run up the hallway, look around. There's nowhere to go, nowhere to go. I'm trapped. I'm trapped in the house. There's only one way out—through them. I stop in the hallway and hide behind the bureau, a big dresser or something. I am terrified. I don't know what to do. I'm trapped. I see Mr. Olive. He is walking towards me. He looks in the room and he sees Mrs. Olive. He screams. He runs over towards her. 'Oh, my God, Naomi. Oh, my God.' I can hear that screaming echoing in my head, just echoing. And then—no, no—he sees me. He sees me. 'I am going to kill you, you bastard! I am going to kill you!' There's a knife right there on the night stand by the bed. 'Don't pick it up.' No, no. He is picking up the knife. He comes stepping towards me, lunging. I shoot him. I shot him. I shot him. I just pulled the trigger, never even took the gun out of the bag. He didn't even know I had it. I shot him. He spun around, facing me again, and I shot him three

more times before he hit the floor. I couldn't stop pulling the trigger.''

Immediately afterward Chuck was overcome by a wave of contrition. *''Oh, no, I can't do that. Can't kill him. Why'd I do it? I didn't want to die. Now I do, now I do. I started to shoot myself . . . I almost couldn't stop. I just had to fire the gun.''*

Standing at the entrance of the room, he fired the remaining bullet into the floor beside Jim and lowered his arm. Then, blood-splattered and blank-eyed, he walked slowly into the living room and slumped onto the couch. *''I sat staring into the fireplace. Just staring, staring.''* It was then that Marlene came over from the hallway and tried to comfort him. ''Everything's all right, Chuck,'' she said. ''Everything's all right. Don't worry. Everything's all right.'' In the sudden quiet Naomi could still be heard taking her last savage breaths.

Eight

In the hours that immediately followed the murders, both Chuck and Marlene began to repress the full horror of the event even while meticulously carrying out their plan to incinerate the corpses. When Marlene called home from Mike Howard's house that afternoon and pretended to talk to her father, it was an act of deception directed at herself as much as others. Throughout the week she would experience the unsettling sensation that her parents were not dead at all, that she could turn a corner or open a door and find them alive and well, the whole episode a dimly remembered nightmare. Chuck, in turn, could put the murders out of his mind so long as he basked in the glow of Marlene's renewed affection for him, but he would be brought jarringly back to reality when, as happened several times that week, she seemed to be trying to give away their shared secret—and future together.

Marlene's carelessness in this regard was first apparent after Chuck had returned home before his parents awoke on Sunday morning. Instead of waiting a half-hour before joining him there, as they had agreed, she appeared on the Rileys' doorstep only moments later. But Oscar and Joanne did not seem to suspect that they had spent the night together. Marlene helped Joanne prepare Sunday breakfast, while Chuck told his father about the drive-in movie he had found so disappointing the night before, *Death Race 2000*.

After breakfast Marlene wanted to go out to China Camp to check the cistern. Chuck drove behind Long's drugstore to load more pine flats into the Vega in case another fire had to be started, but he knew that wouldn't be possible as soon as he turned into China Camp and saw all the Sunday dirt bikers riding the trails. At the cistern Chuck became frightened that they had been discovered. (Fireman Turrini had recently left, having shoveled the ashes over the low wall and wet down the entire area.) He and Marlene piled the wood from the back of the Vega into the cistern but drove off without lighting it. On his way out, Chuck stopped to ask a biker what had happened at the cistern and was relieved to hear him say, "Somebody almost burned the place down last night roasting himself a deer."

In the afternoon they decided to return to China Camp once more to light the wood they had left there, after first stopping off at the Olives' to collect the box spring that still remained on Naomi's bed, although the mattress it had supported had been burned the night before. While they were carrying it to the car the cats got into the bedroom and seemed to be driven half crazed by the smell of blood. Marlene had great difficulty getting them out of the room, and when she finally succeeded, they stood sentry in front of the closed door. For the rest of the week, she would tell the police, "I didn't want to look at that room, but it's kitty-corner to my bedroom. The cats lay next to the door and I kept looking at it and being able to see through it."

The bikers had abandoned China Camp by the time Chuck and Marlene arrived. Chuck had a hard time lighting a fire until he dragged an oily-leafed eucalyptus branch on top of the pile of wood. Then the flames leaped high enough to singe the lower limbs of surrounding trees, and Chuck, fearful that "the whole place would go up," sped out of the forest.

Chuck thought his parents might be suspicious if he didn't sleep at home that night, since his friend Doug Nolan planned to stop by early Monday morning and drive him to Waterbeds West in Sausalito for their first day of work at a new job. Marlene had no intention of spending the night at her house alone, where the smell of death was a lumpy presence beneath the thinning blanket of Lysol, and the cats, their fur upended and their tails raised high, skitted along the hallway in front of the closed door like cartoon animals. She called Leslie Slote and asked her if she could sleep over, adding, "Tell your mom my parents are away and I don't like being alone."

Since Leslie's parents were out that night, the two girls had the house to themselves. They sat on Leslie's waterbed gossiping about boys and the Yes concert coming up on Wednesday. To .

her friend, Marlene looked "emotionally wigged-out," but the reason did not become apparent until Leslie mentioned her own mother in a casual way. At that point Marlene broke into tears and sobbed, "I don't have a mom."

"I go, 'What do you mean?' " Leslie recalls.

With no further prodding Marlene told Leslie everything that had happened the day before. "My dad was going to take me to the hall that afternoon and turn in all of us for smoking dope," Marlene finished. "He said he had a list. We couldn't let that happen."

After all Marlene's empty talk about killing her parents Leslie didn't know for sure whether to believe her now, but the emotions she displayed certainly seemed genuine. "She gave me the impression it was just a split-second thing," Leslie recalls. "Also that Chuck did all the dirty work." Leslie became frightened, the more so when Marlene warned her not to tell anyone. "Chuck told me that he'd kill me if I said anything," Marlene explained. "He'll kill you, too." With Marlene exhausted and Leslie "too freaked out to ask any questions," the two girls smoked some dope that Chuck had provided and went to sleep before the Slotes returned.

When Leslie left for work early Monday morning, Marlene took a bus home. Entering the house alone for the first time since the murders, she felt "spooked." She walked from room to room to make sure she was indeed alone, avoiding only Naomi's bedroom. Coming into the living room, she thought for an instant that she saw her father sitting by the dining-room table playing with the cats. In his office she turned Jim's datebook from Saturday, where he had jotted down the name of a man he had hired to help him move to his new office, to Sunday, where Jim had written "Hispanic festival" to remind him of an event at the Marin County Civic Center he and Marlene had planned to attend together, to Monday's notation of a Rotary Club dinner and Tuesday's of an afternoon dental appointment. These ordinary reminders of her father's activities suddenly filled Marlene with anxiety, not so much a fear of being caught, she would later recall, as of "facing the future without him there." She reached into her "goody bag," with its pharmacopoeia of prescription pills, and popped several Darvons in her mouth.

She couldn't stand being alone in the house another minute and called Mike Howard to see if he would drive her to San Rafael to pick up Sharon. Mike wondered why Marlene had

permission to use the family car but didn't question her then.
Sharon thought it was odder still that Marlene had asked her to
stay over. Ever since Jim had found Marlene living at the
Dillons' house in January, the Olives had made no secret of the
fact that they considered Sharon, after Chuck, the principal "evil
influence" on their daughter and had forbidden her from entering
the house.

After the girls dropped Mike off at his house, Sharon took the
wheel of the car. Alone with Marlene, who seemed unusually
withdrawn, Sharon felt, as she told the police a week later,
"weird vibes." At the corner stop sign she turned to Marlene
and asked, "Did you croak your parents?" When Marlene said
yes, Sharon's reaction was "instant goose bumps." Once inside
the house, Marlene told Sharon the whole story. The hammer
that Marlene said Chuck had used to kill her mother was lying on
an easy chair in the living room. But Sharon didn't believe her
friend until Marlene led her into Naomi's bedroom and showed
her the pinkish stains that still remained visible on the carpet
despite the effort to wash them out the day before—a large
bloodstain beside Naomi's now dismantled bed, one almost as
big near the door, where Jim had fallen, and several smaller
ones by the entrance to the bathroom. In addition, there were
countless other specks and streaks of blood on the walls, furniture and bric-à-brac of the small room that had escaped the first
hasty cleanup.

Marlene asked Sharon to help her clean the room more thoroughly and brought out some equipment—a plastic bucket filled
with water, a sponge mop and an armful of towels from Naomi's
vast collection, towels that had found a use in her death they had
never found in her life. Repeatedly the two girls poured liquid
detergent onto the larger bloodstains, scrubbed them with a
handbrush and used a vacuum cleaner set at the lowest position
to suck up the soapy residue. They wiped any possible finger-
prints from the doorknobs, reached the high places on the walls
with the sponge mop and cleaned the furniture and the china
figurines on the bookshelves. According to Sharon, Marlene
"freaked out" when she once again noticed the streaks of blood
on her portrait behind the bed. All the time they were cleaning
the room Marlene felt the odd sensation, which she had also
experienced at the firepit, that someone was looming behind her,
and she kept looking nervously over her shoulder. When they
were finished, Marlene and Sharon moved the couch and end

table from the garage into Naomi's room to replace the bed (whose only remaining part, a metal frame, they stored in a rafter in the garage), giving the impression that it was a spare den or sewing room. They placed an ironing board directly over the largest bloodstain.

Sharon took a laundry bag full of dirty clothes she had brought with her out to the washing machine in the garage, but both the washer and the dryer were stuffed with the bloody towels and bedding that Marlene had already run through the machines several times, as she would again and again throughout the week without entirely being able to remove the stains. While Sharon was in the garage she heard Marlene let out an ear-piercing shriek. She ran back into the living room thinking that the Olives must have just walked through the front door, which she, too, half expected would happen all week long. In fact, Marlene had turned on the TV and immediately "jumped two feet off the ground" at a commercial for a horror movie, one of several films that summer trying to outdo *The Exorcist* in ghoulish goings-on.

After that, Marlene was anxious to leave the house. Using the checkbook she had found in the master bedroom, she cashed two checks totaling $65 at Scotty's Market down the block, getting away with signing her mother's name to them by writing a note that said: "Hello, this is Mrs. Olive. My husband isn't here now and I'm sending my daughter Marlene over with the checkbook. Would you cash?" Scotty did not notice—as both Marlene and Sharon did—the specks of blood on the vinyl checkbook cover.

After a quick stopover at Sharon's boyfriend's apartment to smoke some dope, the two girls went shopping at Wanda's Gemini, a fashionable boutique on San Rafael's Miracle Mile. Marlene picked out a pair of silver-colored six-inch-high platform shoes for herself—the kind Naomi especially hated—but since all of her mother's identification was either out of date or from South America, she could not use Naomi's BankAmericard and left the shoes on layaway. The problem was easily solved by a quick trip to a local printing shop, where for $3 she bought an impressive-looking plasticized ID card with her picture but with her mother's name on it.

Toward evening the girls returned to the Olive house. Neither Marlene nor Chuck had given much thought to what they would do now that the Olives were dead; they certainly had no immediate plans for escape. According to Sharon's grand jury testimony, they were going to wait until the Olives were declared legally dead—"in about a year"—and collect the insurance and other money that would be coming to Marlene before moving away, perhaps to Ecuador. It was all set in the vague future. More immediately, Marlene asked Sharon to provide her with an alibi by telling the police, should the occasion ever arise, that the two of them had gone on a camping trip to Lake Tahoe on Sunday (Sharon often visited the area) and had not returned until the following Wednesday. On a scrap of paper that she left by the telephone in Jim's office for the police to find, she wrote out and memorized her alibi: "Sun.—Wed. Tahoe. Wed. concert, out night. Thurs. home. Fri. S.F., movie, dinner." But that evening when she turned to the fire calls column in the back of the *Independent-Journal*, she was reassured that there would never be a need for an alibi. For there, among several other notices of fire calls in the county on the previous day, was the following unassuming item: "9:49 A.M. Santa Venetia—small grass fire in Flattrack Area on North San Pedro Road; cause undetermined."

Like Marlene, Chuck spent much of the week frantically trying to push what he had done from his conscious mind, and it was in tune with his character that he was much more successful than Marlene at doing so for long stretches of time. His new job at Waterbeds West helped. From the moment he changed into the paint-stained coveralls and work shoes he had brought with him on Monday morning, he loved the work, which involved assembling and finishing various models of bedframes and occasionally delivering them to the company's other outlets in the Bay Area or directly to customers' homes, where Chuck would also install the waterbed. Although it wasn't really his job, Chuck even sold a few of the beds to customers during busy periods in the showroom, on one occasion pursuing a skeptical middle-aged woman to her car in a successful attempt to close a deal.

After work on Monday, Chuck went home so full of enthusiasm that, according to Oscar, who was delighted that his son had finally found a way to channel his energy, "he couldn't stop talking about waterbeds." He called Marlene to say that he'd be over soon and was reminded of the Olives for the first time that day.

Chuck was a little surprised to see Sharon at Marlene's. When it became clear to him that Sharon knew all about the murder,

Chuck grew inwardly angry, sure that Marlene had "blown it."
He also noticed that she had rearranged the living-room furniture,
just as she had changed the murder room into a makeshift den,
but this time less to disguise the crime than to eliminate the last
vestiges of her mother's presence in the house. They all smoked
the dope Chuck had brought over, did some lines of coke and
listened to tapes on the stereo. To Chuck's further discomfort,
Marlene began telling the whole grisly story again, adding new
details such as the fact that she had tossed her father's favorite
Panama hat into the funeral pyre on Sunday morning. Occasionally Chuck nodded agreement, but he said little. When Marlene
went to the bathroom, Sharon confronted Chuck with "the question that was boiling up inside me until I had to get it out":
"How can you go around knockin' off people and not worrying
about it?"

"Let's not talk about it," Chuck said. And then: "We had no
choice. They wouldn't let me see her." To Sharon the words
sounded frighteningly unremorseful, particularly coming from
someone she had always found so warm and good-natured. Her
retelling of the incident at Chuck's trial would become damaging
testimony against him.

Later Marlene suggested that they all go to bed together in the
master bedroom. As the three had done once before after the
body massages, Chuck first made love to Marlene and then, at
her insistence, to Sharon. Sometime before dawn Marlene awakened
with a start from a nightmare in which her father was standing
over his dying wife, crying out, "Nomi, Nomi, my God, Nomi!"
Awakened by Marlene's screams, Chuck dressed and drove
home so that he would be in his own bed when Oscar got up for
work.

During the day, while shopping with Sharon, Marlene called
home several times from pay phones in the mall, as she would
on other occasions throughout the week. It was an odd thought
pattern, but perhaps less schizophrenic than it might appear.
Marlene knew perfectly well that her parents were dead, but in
some hidden recess of her mind she harbored the hope that one of
them would pick up the phone and the nightmare she was living
would end. In a recurrent dream that would plague her for
months Jim did just that, but as soon as Marlene started to speak
the line would be disconnected.

It was early evening by the time the girls got back home. The
shopping bags and unopened boxes were already beginning to

clutter up the living room to the point where it was hard to find a place to sit down. In other respects the house was equally untidy—beer cans everywhere, a pile of unwashed dishes and food-encrusted pans in and around the sink, an unwrapped package of bologna spoiling on the kitchen counter. Marlene was, however, careful to feed the cats every day; more surprisingly, she regularly took time to sprinkle food in Naomi's fish tanks throughout the house. But she would certainly not do the two tasks her mother was always getting after her to do—wash the dishes and straighten up her room. Not anymore.

That evening Nancy Dillon came by to drive her sister and Marlene to the Lion's Share in San Rafael, a popular club that featured rock bands and dancing. By the time the girl's arrived many of their friends were already seated at adjoining tables in one corner of the bar. The Tuesday gatherings at the club were a weekly ritual, since that was local talent night, when Marin groups auditioned for future jobs and admission was free.

Because Chuck worked later than usual it was eight o'clock before Mike Howard reached him at home and offered him a ride to the Lion's Share. On the way Chuck wanted to stop off at Roger Kyle's apartment, insisting that Mike stay in the car. During the brief visit, Chuck returned the murder weapon, telling Kyle that the intended buyer had "crumped out on the deal." Kyle was happy to have the Ruger back and agreed to cancel Chuck's debt in exchange for it. He noticed that the gun was cleaner than when it had left his apartment three days earlier, and also that there was a small chip in the butt that hadn't been there before.

Chuck's happy demeanor that evening would become an effective argument for the prosecution at his trial despite his explanation that he went to the Lion's Share because he "needed to be around people." He drank a lot of beer and bought several pitchers for the others; he danced with Sharon, Marlene having turned him down. After the first set he went backstage, more to show off his easy access to the musicians than to try to make a drug sale that night.

The following day Chuck arranged with his employer to take the afternoon off in order to run some errands and then drive to the Cow Palace for the Yes concert. He went to pick up Marlene and became annoyed when he found out that she had been answering both the office and the home phones. Since Jim had not shown up for his appointment on Tuesday, the receptionist at the dentist's office had called to reschedule it—and, more ominously, Phil Royce had talked to Marlene.

Since Monday, when Jim had failed to appear for his first day in the San Rafael office, Royce had been calling the house frequently without getting an answer. He was puzzled by his partner's continued absence. As he later explained, "Jim was a man of such precision that if he said he'd be somewhere at 6:15 he'd be there at 6:15, not 6:12 or 6:17." A number of urgent messages had accumulated for Jim at the office. So Phil Royce was very relieved, by late afternoon on Wednesday, to reach Marlene, who, sounding quite normal, promised to have her father call the office as soon as he returned home. She also took down the various phone messages for Jim on a piece of paper that she left beside the office telephone, where the police eventually spotted it.

Without her mother around to shock, Marlene found herself dressing for the concert in jeans and a sweater, far less provocatively than usual. At the Cow Palace some kids were working the ticket line, offering a variety of psychedelic delights—the new candy counter. Chuck bought some powerful opiated hash and Thai sticks to add to the grass and cocaine he carried on him. He and Marlene also took some of the windowpane acid that had been left over from the Yes concert a year earlier, when Chuck and a friend had brought three hundred tabs and sold most of them on the ticket line at $1 each. Yes was not a pile-driving, get-it-on rock group, but one that packaged a soft-focus, post-flower-child fantasy world of love and cosmic consciousness, Kahlil Gibran filtered through a Moog synthesizer. To listen to Yes without being stoned out of your mind, the kids felt, would be equivalent to taking a warm bath in a raincoat.

Rock impresario Bill Graham's minions gave everyone entering the enormous pillbox of an auditorium a quick frisk for booze, a symbolic laying on of hands considering that one could get high on three deep breaths of the fragrant air inside. Chuck and Marlene's friends had come hours earlier to get front and center seats, and when they found the group,' there was only room to sit beside them on concrete steps already sticky with spilled Coca-Cola. Chuck passed around his wares as the auditorium darkened until only the phosphorescent coils the kids bought as necklaces were visible, and the preliminary group, Ace, came on stage.

High on acid, Marlene was having trouble controlling the

almost subliminal flashbacks to the murder scene that seemed to pulsate through her mind to the beat of the music. There was a fellow sitting nearby wearing a painted-on silver face with a large red tear on one cheek; later, that was what she remembered feeling like, a "sad clown." She couldn't understand the general hilarity among her friends. Didn't they *know?* Leslie Slote certainly knew. Sharon knew. What about the others? Didn't they at least suspect what had happened, seeing her and Chuck driving around town so free and easy in the Vega? When Ace began their hit song, "Rock & Roll Runaway," Marlene felt that it was beamed right at her and thought of her father picking her up at the Dillons' house back in January, how gentle he was with her at the time. A few minutes later, when Yes opened its set with "Out on the Edge," she sensed the same intensely personal connection with the music. She was feeling more and more paranoid in the cavernous hall, lit now only by a beam of light glinting off the mirrored, spinning globe near the ceiling. Could the band even know? As a kind of dare or test of fate, or maybe just seeking confessional relief from her anxiety, she began chanting, first under her breath and then louder and louder: "I killed my parents! I *killed* my *parents*! *I killed my parents!*" . . . But no one heard her in the general cacophony.

Marlene was glad when the concert was finally over, and she asked Chuck to drive straight home. For the first time since the murders he was feeling some of her old indifference toward him, and he turned off the freeway on the Marin side of the Golden Gate Bridge, hoping that the lights looping across the water and those outlining the San Francisco hills—one of his favorite views—would serve as a romantic backdrop to a mood-changing walk. But both Chuck and Marlene became uncomfortably aware that they were walking along a stretch of the same road Chuck had driven to calm himself after leaving China Camp early Sunday morning. The cold damp air of the place—and Marlene's chilled response to the question that had plagued him for days—turned them back.

"When are we going to get married?" Chuck asked.

"As soon as everything gets cleared up," Marlene said distractedly.

On Thursday, Marlene was still in a sullen mood, and once more she avoided thinking about her father by going on another whirlwind shopping binge with Sharon. When Marlene returned home she again felt Jim's presence in the house and went from room to room looking for him, knowing all the while how bizarre her behavior was. In the closet of the master bedroom she came across his prized Ecuadorian machete in its leather sheath, took it out to feel its heft and balance, as he used to do, and left it leaning against the bureau for the police to puzzle over.

As soon as Chuck came over from work she transferred her hostility to him, and they had their first argument since the murders. She had little remorse about Naomi's death but her father was a different story, and no matter how skillfully she had engineered the deed, she began to blame Chuck for carrying it out. For his part Chuck was angry to have sensed at the concert that Marlene had told Leslie Slote about the murders as well as Sharon, and he demanded to know who else she had informed. The argument went back and forth for a time and then it ended abruptly. "Why don't you just kill me!" Marlene yelled. "Kill me like you killed my parents." In a blind rage at the injustice of the remark, Chuck wound up and struck Marlene a closed-fisted blow on her arm that would leave a large black-and-blue mark. Once again he was astonished to see how soon after his physical outburst Marlene calmed down and became coyly affectionate toward him.

Afterward Marlene suggested going to some of the topless bars in North Beach. They drove into San Francisco, parked in a lot off Broadway and were pulled into the first place they passed by a barker in a tassled fez. It turned out to feature belly dancers rather than strippers, but neither Chuck nor Marlene was disappointed with the show. They drank several tequila sunrises each, and when one of the performers danced near their table, Chuck, following the lead of other customers, put a $5 bill in her waistband. Next they went to a place called the Garden of Ecstasy, where the principal attraction, according to the marquee, was the "Naked Dance of Love" prominently featured in a recent issue of *Penthouse* magazine. That was enough to lure Marlene. Chuck could sense that she was really turned on by the act's smoothly choreographed, if simulated, copulation. On the ride home she made Chuck pull over on Van Ness Avenue so she could perform fellatio on him. And then in the middle of the Golden Gate Bridge she astonished him by sitting astride the gear lever and getting off on the vibrations, until the car almost stalled out on the long upgrade into Marin and Chuck had to force her to move off the knob in order to down-shift.

Friday morning Marlene went over to La Familia to try out the alibi she had thought up after the crime. She hadn't spent much time at the Spanish cultural center since her first year in Terra Linda and was pleased to find her old friend Raul Fernandez there. Marlene helped him mimeograph and staple together a monthly newsletter the center put out, mentioning in the course of the conversation that she had gone to Tahoe with a friend for a few days and returned Wednesday afternoon to find that her parents had left without a word of explanation. At lunch in a downtown cafeteria Marlene kept trying out new details of her alibi, saying that her mother was a very tidy person, so it was odd that she had left a pile of clothes in the dryer and the milk out and the breakfast dishes unwashed.

Chuck and Marlene again spent the evening in San Francisco, revisiting some of the same bars they had gone to the night before and adding a few others. At one of the new ones Marlene was captivated by a striptease done by a female impersonator. The bright lights and glitter of Broadway, the hints of sex for sale and profitable perversion, connected with her fantasy life, her secret plans for her own future. Back home late that night she wrote a poem about a young girl who becomes a prostitute in New York.

Chuck and Marlene spent most of Saturday doing still more shopping, despite the fact that by now the week's purchases, mostly unopened, were piled high on every surface in the living room. Slowly they made their way from boutique to boutique, through Mill Valley and Sausalito and into San Francisco. By the end of the day Marlene had spent several hundred dollars on clothing—including four pairs of women's shoes—that filled the back of the Vega.

By late Saturday afternoon Phil Royce had become so worried about his partner's week-long absence that he contacted the San Rafael police. According to a diary he kept at the time, after talking to Marlene on Wednesday he had called the Olives six times on Thursday and eight times on Friday. The home phone was always busy (Marlene, in fact, had taken it off the hook at Chuck's insistence) and no one answered the business phone. He had, of course, also spoken to others with whom Jim might have been in touch, especially the two bookkeepers who worked closely with him. All that week Winnie Stockstill had been surprised that Jim hadn't contacted her, since it was nearing the end of a payroll quarter and there were customers' accounts that needed attention. And Elfie Kuehn had been dreading Jim's call, having failed to complete some work for him on time because of the visit of relatives from Germany. "I just thought, how typical of his consideration. He knows that I have company and he's not bothering me."

Friday afternoon and Saturday morning Royce had stopped by the house on Hibiscus Way and knocked on the door. He peered through the kitchen window and saw that the place was "an ungodly mess." Harriet, his wife, who kept a meticulously neat house while studying full-time for an advanced degree, felt that something was very wrong as soon as she heard about the disrepair the house was in, but for all Royce knew about Naomi, such a state of affairs might have been perfectly normal. Around four o'clock he decided to stop by the house again and perhaps talk to neighbors this time. "You're not going alone," Harriet said firmly. "Call the police." Although Royce was not a man who enjoyed bringing outsiders into a friend's private affairs, his wife was so insistent that he called the San Rafael police station and explained his concern. The duty officer agreed that under the circumstances a "welfare check" on the occupants was in order and asked Royce to meet the patrol car at the house.

After peering through the kitchen window at what he would describe to the court as "an extreme amount of mess," Officer Paul Bell felt that a forced entry was justified (a point that would be hotly disputed by Chuck's lawyer) and he kicked in the back door leading to the garage. Bell immediately noticed that while there was no car in the garage, a full set of luggage remained in an overhead rack. In the dining area he saw a bankbook and several credit cards on the table as well as a man's wallet with a driver's license sticking out—all belonging to James F. Olive. Walking through the house, he judged that nothing was missing that might indicate a robbery—the TV and stereo were in place and Naomi's jewelry box seemed untouched on her dresser— although in other ways the house had the appearance of having been ransacked. Sheets and blankets were stripped from the bed in the master bedroom, and on the nightstand there were several empty beer cans, a half-filled bottle of tequila, a shoebox lid filled with marijuana seeds, and a bottle of Making Love body lotion. As for Marlene's room, Bell would testify that it was "difficult to get a footing without stepping on all the articles on the floor." Along with clothing and shoes there were knee-high stacks of *Playboy*, *Penthouse* and *Oui* magazines.

When Marlene arrived home a short time later she sensed, without detecting any obvious signs of intrusion, that someone had been there. Then she saw the note—marked "Urgent!"—that Phil Royce had left by the telephone. Marlene called the number on the note, and sounding very upset, sobbed, "Colonel Royce, where are my folks? What's happened? Their clothes and luggage are here but I haven't seen them since I got back from Tahoe on Wednesday." Royce told Marlene not to worry and invited her to stay at his house until her parents returned, an invitation she politely refused. Afterward he reported the conversation to the San Rafael police department, which promised to contact Marlene at home.

In the meantime Marlene offered to treat Chuck to a roast beef dinner at a swank Terra Linda restaurant, the Velvet Turtle. They both dressed for the occasion, Marlene in the green satin dress with tassled belt she had bought that day and Chuck in one of Jim's best shirts, which Marlene picked out for him, saying, "You can be my dad tonight." After a leisurely dinner they drove back to the Olives' house, but moved on past it when they saw a patrol car in the driveway and two cops with flashlights circling the house. By then Chuck had so totally blocked the murder from his mind that his first thought, as he later recalled, was, "My God, I'm not even supposed to be with Marlene and here I am driving around with her in her dad's car."

Earlier in the evening Marlene's old boyfriend Larry Pederson had called to ask if she could sell him some dope, and she had told him to call back later. Now Marlene directed Chuck to drive to Pederson's house, and while he waited in the car she ran inside and explained that she and Chuck could not be seen together. Could Pederson give Chuck a ride home and then come back to her house to collect his marijuana? Like Marlene, Pederson didn't have a driver's license, so he asked his friend Tim Prather, who lived nearby, to do the driving. The two boys dropped Chuck off at his house and then returned with Marlene to Hibiscus Way, by which time the police had left.

Marlene explained that she had no idea where her parents were and, according to Prather, "acted real concerned." The three of them smoked some hash and started listening to records on the stereo. After a short time Marlene saw a flash of headlights through the kitchen window and quickly ran into the garage, where she taped the remaining hash to the inside of the washing machine. A moment later three policemen entered through the unlocked door. One of them, Sergeant Bill Hool, asked Marlene if she would mind coming down to police headquarters to answer a few questions concerning her parents' whereabouts.

For the next fourteen hours Marlene was questioned almost continuously by three different policemen and a psychiatric intern at Marin General Hospital. She gave them a half-dozen different accounts of her parents' disappearance, some more fanciful than others, all of them containing glaring contradictions and obvious holes that the police probed, forcing Marlene to improvise even more fanciful versions of events. Included among these stories was one that her interrogators let pass as the wildest and lest credible of all—the truth.

Bill Hool, a fair-haired, soft-spoken juvenile officer, began questioning Marlene under the assumption that her parents had simply gone away for a few days and she could either tell him where they were or give him the names of people who might know. Marlene started with her well-rehearsed Tahoe alibi. Lending credibility to the story in Hool's eyes was the fact that Marlene seemed so upset, breaking into tears as she was talking and afterward saying, as she had to Phil Royce, "Sergeant Hool, can you help me find my father?" On the other hand, Hool thought, why hadn't Marlene called the police for help in the four days since she returned home? Her explanation—that she "kept expecting my parents to walk in any moment"—didn't make much sense to him, particularly after having just seen how messy the house was, not exactly the way a kid anticipating her parents' imminent return would keep it. And then there was the matter of the missing credit cards and the packages in the living room, clearly recent purchases. Even though it was after midnight by now, Hool thought he had better telephone his colleague Bart Stinson, the San Rafael police detective whose two specialties, missing persons and murders, fit the extreme possibilities such a case presented like parenthetical brackets.

Stinson was watching a late movie on television when Hool called, but after listening to the details of the case he readily agreed to drive the twenty miles from his home in Petaluma to San Rafael. Physically unprepossessing—an average-sized, middle-aged man growing soft around the middle and bald on top—Stinson, at forty-nine, had spent thirteen years on the San Rafael police force, the past five wearing a detective's shield. But he still loved police work the way he had as a rookie cop, any kind of police work but particularly cases that had a mystery at their core—as was generally true of those involving persons missing or murdered. (The spilling over of city tensions into suburbia had strained even Stinson's enthusiasm for murder cases in the past year, when there had been eight of them, more than he had encountered in the previous decade.)

Outside the juvenile bureau at police headquarters, where Marlene was being held, Hool told Stinson that he was convinced Marlene was lying or at least withholding information. Stinson taught a course in police interrogation at the College of Marin and he knew all the tricks of the trade. Anyone could figure out a plausible general alibi, but it took a criminal with a novelist's bent to fill in the specifics. He aimed a barrage of questions at Marlene designed to probe holes and discrepancies in her story. How many rides did it take her to hitchhike to Tahoe? Where did she stay that night? What did she do the next day? The one after that? Whom did she meet? Always skillful at ad-libbing extravagant lies, Marlene came up with quick answers to all the questions, if not always the same one when the question was repeated. But Stinson only knew for certain that Marlene was lying when he asked her about the weather in Tahoe. "It was pretty good but it got a little cold at night," Marlene shot back. As it happened, Stinson's married daughter lived in Tahoe and was visiting him at the moment. They had discussed the bizarre weather the Tahoe area had experienced the previous weekend—a freak summer storm that mixed snow, hail and rain. Not exactly camping weather.

Stinson didn't call Marlene's bluff yet. Instead he decided to try to locate the missing bankbook and driver's license, for Jim Olive was not likely to have left without the latter, at least. According to Stinson's trial testimony, by the time he handed Marlene over to a policewoman at the front desk she was "crying uncontrollably and appeared to be very despondent."

The stereo was going full blast when Stinson and Hool let themselves into the Olive house to discover that Prather and Pederson had found the events of the evening too compelling to leave. Stinson pat-searched the boys to make sure they weren't carrying off anything and sent them on their way. He began opening the boxes in the living room, in the process pushing aside a hefty red-handled hammer lying on an easy chair. The first two receipts he came upon were dated June 25 and 28, a time when the Olives, according to Marlene, were already gone.

Now Stinson was fairly certain that he knew what had happened. While the Olives were on vacation their daughter had gone on a shopping spree, using their credit cards and possibly forging checks as well, and although she surely knew where her parents were, she had good reason not to welcome their return. The Tahoe story was her way of covering her tracks. So Stinson was not too surprised that he couldn't find the bankbook or checkbook where Marlene said they would be.

He decided to search the car for any clues to the Olives' whereabouts. In the glove compartment he found a note that seemed to be a version of Marlene's Tahoe alibi. On the reverse side, in a different handwriting, were several names and telephone numbers, including TWA's. A separate note in the glove compartment, signed by Naomi, read: "This is my daughter. It's OK for her to use my bank account." After securing the house, Stinson and Hool drove back to headquarters hoping that the mention of an airline meant that the Olives had flown back to New York for Anna DeKay's funeral, as Marlene had suggested might be the case.

It was two-thirty in the morning. Stinson felt that Marlene had calmed down enough to continue the interrogation, although, as he wrote in his police report, she would "intermittently cry and occasionally say that she wanted her daddy." Because criminal charges of forgery were now a possibility, Stinson read Marlene her rights "per *Miranda*," got her to sign a waiver agreeing to talk to him and began to tape-record the proceedings.

Presented with the sales receipts, Marlene finally admitted cashing her parents' checks and using their credit cards, but insisted that she had made up the Tahoe story because she had spent several days with Raul Fernandez and didn't want Chuck to find out. At that point Stinson called Eunice Richard, who was visiting friends near Boston. She told him that something "very fishy" must have happened, since it was unthinkable that Jim and Naomi would leave Marlene alone and go off on a trip by themselves. After the call Marlene suddenly said, "I know something terrible's happened to my parents. They're both dead. Sometimes I get these strong feelings about things and they're almost always true."

When the questioning resumed, Marlene began spinning out her new alibi about being with Raul Fernandez before Stinson interrupted her. "You know, I find it very hard to believe anything you've said," he told her firmly. "Even your second story is not plausible to me."

"What I should really do," Marlene said, "is just sit down and think."

Clearly, Marlene wasn't getting anywhere with Stinson. Several times during the interrogation he had felt Marlene trying to stare him down and thought it important for him to stare back until she looked away.

"Some people may forget my name," she told him at one point, "but they'll never forget my eyes."

"I can believe that," Hool said. "You do have pretty eyes."

"I can believe it too," Stinson joked. "We've got a fellow in the department whose eyes I'll never forget—one's blue and the other's black."

So it wasn't too surprising when Marlene told Stinson, "Your eyes are bothering me," and asked if she could talk to Bill Hool alone. Stinson was happy to oblige if it would break the stalemate. While he waited in the hallway Marlene broke into tears again. "Every time I close my eyes," she said between sobs, "I can still see my father standing over my mother in a pool of blood. He's yelling, 'Nomi, Nomi, Nomi.' I know something terrible has happened to my parents. I know they're dead. I've been seeing this vision ever since I came home Monday with Sharon and found so much blood on the carpet in the sewing room and on the wall behind the couch where my picture is."

A few minutes later Marlene walked out of the office leaning against Hool, who was trying to guide her to the bathroom. "Here's another story, Bart," Hool said after a policewoman took over. He related Marlene's latest account. For the first time Stinson sensed that "the Olives may have been the victims of foul play." When Marlene came out of the bathroom he pressed her for details about the size and exact location of the bloodstain as well as her method of cleaning it up. Since Marlene was so distraught, Stinson instructed someone to take her to the Marin General Hospital's crisis unit for a psychiatric evaluation and then called the department's other juvenile officers, Sergeant Louis Foster and Scott Nelson, at home, telling them to meet him at the Olive house. It was just about daybreak.

The first thing that Stinson noticed about the "sewing room" was that it was the only clean part of the house. Indeed, a vacuum cleaner was still plugged into a wall socket. Removing an ironing board, he could immediately see a large discolored area on the shag carpet. He knelt down and worked his fingers through the pile. There was what looked like dried blood at the base. The odor of the stain proved to be identical to the detergent that Hool, following Marlene's directions, located under the kitchen sink. Stinson also noticed the "streaking effect" on the wall behind the couch, as if someone had recently washed it. Looking around the rest of the house, he found a note by the telephone similar to the Tahoe alibi in the Vega's glove compartment, as well as some brownish stains of undetermined origin on the car's spare-tire cover. At this point in the investigation Stinson was considering several conflicting explanations to fit the evidence, foremost among them being the possibility that Jim Olive had killed his wife and fled, while his daughter, whose loyalty clearly belonged to her father, was stalling the police with conflicting stories to give him more time to get away.

While Stinson was searching the house, Lou Foster checked with the Olives' neighbors to see if anyone could help the investigation. As might be expected, given both the neighborhood and the family, they all reported having very little contact with the Olives. (According to Foster's subsequent police report, the neighbors directly behind 353 Hibiscus said that "the only way they know the Olives are there is sometimes somebody waters in the backyard and a little water runs under the fence.") But one woman did tell Foster that she had heard arguments from time to time between the mother and daughter, including one recent fight about Marlene staying out either too late or all night. About a week ago, the woman added, she heard several sounds that seemed like firecrackers going off in quick succession and took them to be early harbingers of the coming July Fourth festivities.

Scott Nelson was not exactly overjoyed at having been awakened at six o'clock on a Sunday morning to transport an "acting-out" teen-ager to the crisis unit, a job he felt any rookie cop on duty could have performed just as easily. Only after he arrived at the Olive house and Stinson explained the circumstances of the case did it make sense that he should have been called in, since he was the only one in the department who had had extensive contact with the family. Nelson drove over to Marin General with instructions to place Marlene in juvenile hall on a seventy-two hour BPC (Beyond Parent Control) hold. A psychiatric intern had interviewed Marlene briefly and determined that although she was emotionally distraught and had some "neurotic fantasies," her condition was not bad enough to justify keeping her in the ward. Wary of charges of impropriety from a seductive girl, Nelson called in his mileage and destination before leaving the hospital for the juvenile hall.

En route Marlene asked Nelson if she could stop off at her house to pick up some personal effects. "Only if you promise to come clean with me," Nelson said. Marlene agreed. Once at 353 Hibiscus they walked through the house to a section of the back porch covered by a trellis barren of vines. It was eleven-thirty on Sunday morning. Nelson read Marlene her rights again and turned on his tape recorder.

For the next several hours, first at the house and later at the juvenile hall, Marlene poured forth a series of fantasies woven from threads of truth to an increasingly skeptical and irritable Nelson. Her mother had killed her father and fled. Her father had killed her mother and fled. Both of her parents had been killed by a house burglar . . . a hired gunman . . . an irate Hell's Angel client of Jim's. The only constant in Marlene's tale was her tearful refrain, "I want my daddy." Finally, as Marlene edged nearer the truth, Nelson's attitude changed from skepticism to outright incredulity, and he cautioned her that he was through listening to any more of her "sand bagging." At that point the police transcript continues:

Q. I thought we weren't going to bullshit, Marlene. I want to find out what the hell's going on. Where are your parents at?
A. They're dead. That's no bullshit.
Q. How do you know they're dead?
A. Because I know they are.
Q. Did you just pull it out of the air?
A. No, because I saw their bodies.
Q. Where?
A. In a room.
Q. Where are they at now?
A. China Camp.
Q. Where in China Camp?
A. Firepits.
Q. How do you know?
A. Because I took 'em there.
Q. How did you get two heavy people like that into a

car, get them all the way out there with nobody seeing you, get them into the firepits, nobody seeing it, no blood inside the car, no blood inside the house other than that little splotch that's in that room that you say is blood. Don't you think it's about time you really came across straight?

A. I tell you they're dead and you don't believe me. It's true.

Q. There's no blood in there.

A. It's blood. Why don't you wait and get the damn report and you'll find out.

Q. OK, where does that leave me if we do find blood? All you got is a little puddle of blood in there.

A. Little!

Q. You can leave that blood with a cut finger, because there's a Band-Aid in the bathtub.

A. All that blood from a cut finger?

Q. Sure.

Scott Nelson's refusal to believe that she was involved in her parents' death reassured Marlene. She began to relax and smile for the first time since the interrogation began. Also for the first time she looked at him right in the eye instead of staring at the floor or off into space, an indication, Nelson felt from his previous experience with Marlene, that she would stop lying to him. (A few days later, after the crime broke, some pranksters in the police department made an enlargement of Marlene's eyes from a mug-shot negative and stuck it under Nelson's glass desk top, where he kept it permanently as a kind of penance.) But instead she began her sixth and most fanciful story of all, the only one with scarcely a shred of truth in it. And, of course, it was the story that Nelson bought, as he put it later, "hook, line and sinker." It was now two in the afternoon. By then the two were sitting in the juvenile hall reception area, where Nelson bought Marlene a candy bar from a vending machine as a reward.

According to Marlene's last account, her parents had been bickering ever since Naomi's foster mother died. They took a long drive through China Camp on Saturday to talk the matter over and must have decided to leave for a short vacation on Sunday, because by the time Marlene came home from Leslie Slote's house on Monday morning, they were nowhere to be found. Two suitcases were missing, as were several of her mother's dresses, some of her father's sport shirts and jackets, his tennis shoes, and his favorite Panama hat, without which he would never leave for more than a day or two at a time.

At that moment Nelson remembers "feeling an enormous sense of relief. That was the stuff I wanted to hear. I didn't want a homicide. I wanted to hear that her parents were dumb for taking off and leaving her to run wild, not that they were butchered and burned. I'm a trained police officer. Somebody gets shot in a bank robbery, I can handle that. But in my contact with Marlene I couldn't imagine that sort of pent-up violence was in her personality."

Q. Before we go further, there's no blood at all, is that right?
A. Uh, there was blood but that was because somebody got hurt there.
Q. How do you mean?
A. Well, we had a glass table in that room, a real nice thing we were going to put out on the patio and put a small fish tank on it. I kind of slipped when we were carrying it over and we both fell down and she [Naomi] cut herself on the foot. So that was where the blood came from. . . .
Q. It's nice to talk to you now that you're coming to me straight.

It didn't make a great deal of sense that Marlene would confess to murder in order to get off the hook for using her parents' credit cards and cashing their checks, but by now Nelson was hearing only what he wanted to hear. "There's a good possibility your mom and dad will probably be home tonight or tomorrow, right?" he suggested. "Because your dad has appointments coming up this week. They're probably out hoofing it somewhere, along the beach or in a hotel or motel."

Nelson told Marlene that she would have to stay at the juvenile hall until her parents returned home and contacted the police, then he went back to the Olives' house and left a note on the door to that effect. A reassuring check of the storage rafter in the garage turned up a woodframe coffee stand without its glass top (which had, in fact, broken when Sharon and Marlene were changing the furniture in the sewing room). Then Nelson went

back to police headquarters, telephoned Phil Royce to let him
know that the Olives would be back that night or the next day at
the latest, and wrote up his report on the case, which consisted
of a summary of Marlene's last story, "when," as he put it,
"she finally broke down and told me the truth."

A short time later Bart Stinson awakened to learn from his
wife that the Olives had not, after all, been victims of foul play
and were expected home soon. Like Nelson, he was enormously
relieved, but he was also miffed at the man-hours needlessly
wasted on the case. A year earlier he had gotten an ulcer
investigating a case involving the supposed rape of a San Rafael
police officer's wife. Her husband had come home late one night
to discover his furniture cut to shreds, his wife on the bed
bleeding from knife wounds and a note scrawled in lipstick on
the bathroom mirror that read: "This is how we deal with pigs'
wives." But after working on the case for several weeks Stinson
got the woman to admit that she had faked all the evidence in a
pathetic attempt to convince her husband to find less dangerous
and time-consuming employment than police work. So Stinson
was not very sympathetic to people making false confessions,
and this time he resolved to talk to police chief Larry Kelly first
thing Monday morning about making the Olives reimburse the
department for the cost of their impulsive vacation to taxpayers.

But the next morning, after Stinson had read the full transcript
of Nelson's interrogation, his anger at the Olives quickly subsided.
He found Marlene's final account no more believable than any of
the others. Less so, in fact. He was especially struck by one
brief exchange. "OK," Nelson had said, "where does that leave
me if we do find blood? All you got is a little puddle of blood in
there." "Little!" Marlene had quickly exclaimed.

As soon as Stinson found the exchange on the tape he was
convinced that one or the other parent would never come back
from vacation—or wherever they were. Marlene's response to
Nelson's understatement was simply too reflexive and surprised
to be part of some story she had concocted. Stinson called
Nelson at home and asked him to report in, saying, "I've still got
a bad feeling about this one." Then he directed Lou Foster to
find Sharon Dillon and see if she could corroborate Marlene's
story—any of Marlene's stories—and left to keep an early-
afternoon dental appointment.

Sharon heard from her stepmother that the police were looking for her and called Foster, agreeing to meet him near her boyfriend's house. Along with a girl friend, she had spent the weekend in the Tahoe area looking for a summer "mother's helper" job. She had tried to come to terms with Marlene's revelation all week long, but every time she thought about what went on in the sewing room she got "a bad case of the willies." She knew full well how much Marlene hated her mother but couldn't understand how it had ended in murder rather than the couple running away, or why Chuck had gotten involved at all. At a campsite on Saturday night she had told her friend what she knew, but her nervousness persisted.

By the time Foster, sitting in the front seat of an unmarked police car, asked her if it was true that she had spent several days at the Olive house the previous week, Sharon appeared, according to the officer's report, "quite upset and confused." She lied half-heartedly for a few minutes before admitting that she did have something to say but wanted to talk to a lawyer first. Foster took her to the Marin County public defender's office in the Civic Center and an hour later (during which time the district attorney agreed not to prosecute Sharon for being an "accessory after the fact" in return for her cooperation) drove her back to police headquarters, where a taped interview was conducted. While still minimizing her own role in the cleanup, Sharon told Foster everything else she knew, and in the late afternoon she agreed to show him the place where Marlene and Chuck had, as she put it, "crispy fried" the Olives.

The two of them proceeded to the flattracks area in one police car, followed by two other policemen in another. They were met there by Stinson, who had called in from his dentist to learn that his worst suspicions about the Olive case had been confirmed: it was a probable double homicide. The small caravan turned off North San Pedro Road onto a dirt track, skirted a burned-out mattress several hundred yards farther ahead and continued, at Sharon's direction, through a sloping laurel grove to a concrete cistern at the bottom of a shallow basin.

Nothing appeared out of the ordinary during a preliminary walk-through of the area. There were wet ashes outside the cistern next to a charred tree stump, and more of the same inside, along with a partially burned box spring, tin cans, a variety of picnic debris and empty shells from all manner of weapons—just about what one might expect in an area frequented by hunters taking target practice and roasting their game.

At the base of a double-trunked tree twenty feet east of the cistern there was a foot-high mound of wet ashes shaped like a pyramid with a flat top. Detective Fred Castillo dug two or three feet through the chalky soil of the cistern until he came to its gravel base. There were no signs of the Olives' remains in sight, and Stinson, tired of false leads and improbable stories from overly imaginative teen-agers, was about to call it a night when fireman Turrini, who had been routinely contacted at home by the police, arrived at the scene. After surveying the area, he was certain that the mound of wet ashes under the tree, clearly part of the debris he had shoveled into the cistern, had not been there at that time, nor had the burned box spring.

On closer inspection one of the policemen found bone fragments in the ashes outside the cistern. Two others, sifting through the ashes inside by hand, came up with many more small pieces of bone, all charred to a semiporous, lavalike consistency. When Stinson placed the fragments in an evidence bag, he noticed that while their outer surface was blackened, the ends were not, indicating that someone had mechanically broken the bones *after* they were burned. None of the fragments were large enough to be recognizable parts of a skeleton until one of the cops came up with a tooth and another found the largest bone yet, a two-inch vertebra. After Foster brought a sifting screen from police headquarters, the mound of ashes by the tree was examined closely and still more bone chips were recovered. By then it was nightfall. Stinson left a guard at the site overnight and drove back to his office.

He immediately called the Marin County coroner's office and requested assistance in verifying the evidence. Deputy coroner Ervin Jindrich told Stinson he'd be right over. From among the many bone fragments that Stinson had laid out on his desk, Jindrich picked up the tooth and held it up to the light between his thumb and forefinger. "Human," he pronounced. Then he examined the vertebra. "Definitely human."

On Tuesday morning a team of policemen went back to the firepit accompanied by Dr. Rodger Hagler, a professor of physical anthropology at San Francisco State University and an expert at identifying skeletal remains. Hagler used string to lay down a grid divided into twenty one-foot-square sections. Each square was painstakingly sifted for bone fragments down to the hard-packed dirt, and the findings placed in separate, numbered plastic bags so that the area could be reconstructed on an evidence table back at the coroner's office. Within the cistern the fragments were placed in a single bag, although Hagler separated out those that he felt were sufficiently large or well-defined to be identifiable—or "diagnostic." There were remarkably few. Whatever doubt lingered about the animal or human nature of the remains vanished when several gold fillings were found, one of which fit smoothly into a recovered tooth. To Hagler's expert eye it was likely, from the different thicknesses of cranial and limb bones, that two people had been burned, most likely a man and a woman. And calcium deposits on joints told him that the victims were middle-aged, probably between forty-five and fifty-five years old. By the end of the search the team had collected only a few pounds of skeletal fragments, none bigger than the vertebra that Foster had already recovered. Even assuming, as Hagler did, that some of the larger, least destructible bones such as the pelvis had been removed, it was, to use his words at the trial, "quite a thermal incident."

By early afternoon Stinson felt he had enough evidence to obtain a warrant to search the Riley house and arrest Chuck at the waterbed factory simultaneously. Lou Foster led the four-man search team to 210 Corrillo Drive. When the two patrol cars pulled up, Joanne Riley was mowing the front lawn while Oscar, who had finished work early that day, was rewiring a floodlight on the side of the house. Since he was dressed in street clothes, Foster identified himself and asked the Rileys if they could all go inside the house to discuss an important matter relating to Chuck. At the kitchen table Oscar read the search warrant, which reviewed the course of the investigation to date. He found it hard to take in all the information but said, "We've always been law-abiding citizens. Of course we'll cooperate," adding that he was sure his son, who wasn't "the violent sort," was innocent of the charges. While Oscar told the police what he knew about Chuck's activities during the week, Joanne prepared a fresh pot of coffee for the group.

Then the Rileys conducted the police through the house. From the boys' room Foster took a pair of dirt-encrusted cowboy boots, a hunting knife in a leather sheath, a black binder containing letters from Marlene, and the shoebox full of Villa Rafael room keys. In a storage area between the side of the house and a fence, the police seized three red gas cans of varying sizes. While these items were being placed in the patrol car Joanne came out with an unopened letter that had arrived earlier in the day for Chuck. As the return address and postmark indicated, it had been sent by Marlene from the juvenile hall the day before. "You might as well take this, too," Joanne told Foster.

It proved to be a disjointed, emphatically underlined six-page note that Marlene had scrawled in pencil at a time when she had not slept in two days, but it became the most damaging piece of evidence against her, since it seemed to show a lack of any mitigating remorse following the killings. Clearly meant for Chuck to pick up personally (Marlene had written "Do not mail out. Please exchange" on the envelope), it was sent by mistake. The letter read, in part:

> I said my parents went on a trip as far as I knew. I said we had an accident in room with glass table. That's why blood. Even when I did say something true they didn't believe it happened or I'd do it or anyone would do anything. I settled down and looked Nelson in eyes and started to talk with no lying eyes and he believed me. They couldn't believe me when I said they were probably hurt or something or any other story I gave, but the last worked. I smiled and relaxed! I said they took a suitcase and beer and were in process of or already bought a second-hand Chevy Malibu for $500. . . . They think my parents will be home tonite or tomorrow. I hope you get to Sharon before they do. I have no guilt feelings at all about my folks. NONE. NEITHER SHOULD YOU! Relax. We should have gotten married! Then you could probably bail me out. . . . Please help me!! What are we going to do now? What should I expect? Who will have custody? When will we marry? I want now.

While Foster and his colleagues were searching the Riley house, Stinson and others went to arrest Chuck, having first ascertained that he was at work by calling Waterbeds West. The factory, a low concrete shed with a glass storefront, was located near one of the Mill Valley off-ramps. As uniformed police surrounded the building, guns in hand, Stinson and Nelson, in civilian clothes, approached the front door. Chuck was staining a bedframe when he saw them enter and he dropped the brush he was holding. According to Nelson's report, "the suspect's eyes got extremely wide and his face immediately flushed." But

Nelson misinterpreted Chuck's surprise. His first thought, Chuck later recalled under hypnosis, was that he was being busted for dealing cocaine, not for murder.

By that time Chuck had nearly succeeded in pushing the crime from his mind. His greatest fear, one that had gripped him for months, was that he would be sent to prison for selling drugs and thus lose Marlene. He had spent all day Sunday hanging around his house hoping to hear from her, and in the afternoon he had gone over to the juvenile hall to leave her a note expressing his "undying love" and promising to try to get her out soon. If he felt any anxiety about his own safety, he hid it in work. Oscar had been amazed to see Chuck pour himself into one activity after another—repairing the back patio, mowing the front lawn, even beginning a long-promised brake job on his father's car.

Now Nelson motioned him forward and said, "Chuck, could we see you outside, please."

"Let's walk down to the end of the building," Stinson said calmly, leading Chuck past the glass storefront. Stinson then told Chuck to place his hands on the concrete wall, step back and spread his legs so he could search him.

"What am I under arrest for?" Chuck said.

"Suspected homicide," Stinson said calmly. Then he hand-cuffed Chuck's arms behind his back and turned him around. "Don't be scared of me," he said. "I'm not mad at you. We're going to police headquarters. You'd better not make any statements right now."

"He said 'homicide,' " Chuck later told the hypnotist when asked to recall his thoughts at the time. *"I couldn't even figure out what it meant right then. I got in the back seat and asked for a cigarette. Nelson put one in my mouth and lit it for me. I was telling them how much I liked the new job. They were asking me about prices and I was saying how much the different types of beds cost and the accessories you could add like heating pads, thermostats and pillows. Then we pulled into the station and they read me my rights. They told me I was being arrested for the murder of Mr. and Mrs. Olive. That's when it hit me. And I said, 'You got to be kidding. What do you know about that?' "*

Stinson was surprised, as he would testify at the trial, at how "calm and friendly" Chuck was. He left Chuck in a small interrogation room and instructed another officer to sit in an adjacent room behind a two-way mirror and take notes, since he found that tape recorders used too early in interrogations tended

to impede what he liked to call "the free flow of information."
Much better to get an admission of guilt and then tape a full
confession. He read Chuck his rights from a standard form and
was not at all surprised that Chuck agreed—indeed, seemed even
anxious—to talk to him, checking the appropriate box on the
waiver and even writing "Yes, OK" beside it. One thing Stinson
always told rookie cops in his interrogation course was that
guilty parties usually waive their right to remain silent, since
they're so impatient to learn how much the police already know.

"Now, Chuck," Stinson began in his most avuncular manner,
"we know Mr. and Mrs. Olive are dead and we think that you
killed them. Are you curious as to what we know?" Chuck
nodded and Stinson briefly described how the murders occurred.
"Are you curious as to how I know this?" Stinson then asked.
"Sharon Dillon told us that you and Marlene killed the Olives.
We have a tape-recorded statement from her. We've been out at
the firepit, Chuck, and her story checks out. We have bone
fragments and teeth that I'm convinced we can identify as the
remains of Mr. and Mrs. Olive. We even have tire marks that
match the Olives' car."

Chuck remained composed. Stinson was content to let him
absorb the information in silence.

"Can I hear the tape?" Chuck asked after a time.

Stinson pushed the Forward button on the tape recorder, and
he and Chuck sat listening as Sharon said:

> Okay, I'll start with Monday. Marlene called me
> Monday morning around ten, maybe earlier, and asked
> me if I could come over and stay with her for a few
> days because her parents were gone. And she called my
> sister's boyfriend, Mike, and asked him to drive her to
> San Rafael to pick me up. And after we dropped Mike
> off we drove over to Marlene's house and I asked
> Marlene if she, ah, croaked off her parents because I
> just had weird vibes about it. And she said, yes, that
> she had, and she asked me to help her clean house. I
> helped her clean the shelf that was in the sewing room
> where, ah, Chuck and Marlene killed her parents by
> hitting Marlene's mom over the head with a hammer
> when she was asleep and shooting Mr. Olive. There
> was blood, big bloodstains on the—

At that point Stinson turned off the machine and asked Chuck, "Do we need any more of this?" Chuck said no, and Stinson saw his chin begin to quiver. He buried his face in his hands, rocked forward toward his knees and cried out, "I did it! I did it! I didn't want to do it. Marlene made me do it. She kept asking me and asking me, begging me and begging me for months. Telling me to do it or she wouldn't love me anymore. And I finally did it. I loved her so much I didn't think I would get by. Please help me."

Stinson calmed him down somewhat and after a while asked him if he wanted to make a tape-recorded confession. Chuck nodded agreement. The interrogator then led his subject step by step through the events of June 21: the early-morning phone calls, the battering of Naomi Olive, the shooting of Jim Olive when he came upon the scene, the disposal of the bodies. Although Chuck was highly distraught throughout the half-hour confession, it was only toward the end, when Stinson addressed the motive for the crime, that he broke down completely. At that point the police transcript reads:

STINSON: Tell me why did you do this?

CHUCK: Because Marlene told me to.

STINSON: And why did she want you to do this?

CHUCK: Because she wanted me to. I don't know. She said they were going to take her away from me. I don't know. She told me her dad's going to take her away from me forever. She said I had to do it. I had to. (Suspect crying in between words.)

STINSON: You did it because Marlene said they were going to take her away from you?

CHUCK: Yeah. They'd already done it. So many different things. All the time they were messing me up. They were always hurting my head, always hurting my head. She just told me to do it, so I did it, that's all. I don't know what I did. I really don't. (Suspect still crying.)

STINSON: It's all right. Is there anything I can do for you?

CHUCK: Help me.

STINSON: I'll help you every way I can.

CHUCK: Please help me. I have to see her and talk to her. I have to. Please.

STINSON: All right. I'll try everything I can.

CHUCK: I have to. I don't want to be by myself.

STINSON: OK. Anything else you can tell me about this thing? That you'd like to tell me at this time?

CHUCK: I didn't want to do it. I didn't. She told me to.

STINSON: OK, I believe you.

CHUCK: I really didn't want to do it. She told me to.

STINSON: How long have you been thinking about this?

CHUCK: She kept telling me a long time, a couple of months. She kept telling me to do it. Find someone to do it. And I said no, I don't want to. I'm afraid. She just kept telling me to do it and finally she said that I had to do it or she wouldn't love me anymore.

STINSON: OK, son.

Nine

"Two Teenagers Held in Couple Slaying," ran the banner headline in the following day's *Independent-Journal*. "Remote Sewage System Yields Cremated Remains." The sensational aspects of the story made it front-page news in the San Francisco papers, too, where the crime was quickly dubbed the "Barbecue Murders." Local TV news teams swarmed over the China Camp area and the house on Hibiscus Way in search of "visuals" to go with their interviews of neighbors and friends, and the case made the *CBS Evening News* that first night. But it was within the community of Terra Linda that the murder of Jim and Naomi Olive struck the loudest chord.

For many of their neighbors the crimes came to symbolize the ultimate suburban nightmare, just as the school system, the library and the shrub-bordered lawns had once symbolized the dream. Parents could not help but wonder about the aftermath of *their* next family quarrel. And despite the fact that they had often heard Marlene threaten to kill her mother and father in the preceding months, her friends were as shocked as their parents when it finally happened.

For those who knew either the victims or their killers, the initial reaction of astonishment often gave way to a feeling of inevitability. "Hearing what happened was like peeking ahead to the end of a book I was in the middle of," Chuck's friend Bob Miller said. "I was stunned but I could almost say, 'Oh well, that figured.' " It was a sentiment echoed by an older generation. "Afterward," said Phil Royce, "given what I knew about the Olives—where they came from, who they were, how they related to each other—I could look back and see the track of doom leading right up to the final explosion.''

In the days that followed Chuck's confession the police continued their investigation of the murders, but it was clearly a mop-up operation. After their search of the premises they went to 353 Hibiscus on two other occasions, both times to accompany defending lawyers in their own search. Marlene's lawyer, Peter Mitchell, found two undeveloped rolls of film in her room that the police had missed. They turned out to be the nude pictures of Marlene that she had intended to send to *Penthouse* magazine. Some were traditional pornographic poses in dubious taste (there was a whole series of Chuck performing cunnilingus on Marlene while she was seated on the plywood hood of his car), but others were more artfully conceived. When Mitchell turned the photographs over to the authorities (after exacting a promise that they would not be used against his client), Stinson set aside the ''muff-diving shots'' but was captivated by a picture of Marlene standing at Nicassio Lake, nude except for a diaphanous green scarf blowing in the breeze.

Stinson also accompanied Chuck's lawyer, William Weissich, when he went through the house, and found himself equally intrigued by an item seized on that occasion. As evidence of Marlene's control of his client, Weissich removed her library of books on drugs and the occult, along with several packs of tarot cards. Back in his office Stinson began playing around with the cards, aided by one of the paperbacks that explained how to read them. Earlier, in the binder of correspondence the police had confiscated from Chuck's bedroom, he had come across the typically melodramatic letter that Marlene had written to Chuck after her father had found her at the Dillon house in January, in which she said ''goodbye'' to him and apologized for having treated him badly. At the end of the five-page letter she had laid out Chuck's tarot, drawing the positions of the cards for him and instructing him to ''go to Brentano's and read the divinatory meaning in a complete guide. . . . Your question was, 'Will I be yours in the end?' '' Stinson could now understand why Chuck, who did as he had been instructed, was so heartened by what he had learned. To represent him, Marlene had chosen the Page of Swords, which the guidebook said was an appropriate card ''for an energetic boy or girl with brown hair and brown eyes.'' She had placed it at the center of the tarot pattern she preferred to use, a Celtic cross. The card that had fallen to its immediate

right, signifying the near future, had turned out to be the Two of
Cups, which indicated "harmony of the masculine and the
feminine" or "the beginning of a friendship or love affair." The
card that had shown up in the "final outcome" position was the
Empress, who is the goddess of love and fecundity, and indicates,
according to the book, "marriage and fertility."

On the Sunday after the story of the crime broke, Rev. David
Barnette conducted a requiem mass for Jim and Naomi. "This
week," he began his sermon, "discombobulated, mind-boggled,
struggling in utter disbelief, faced with the incomprehensible,
now the time has come for letting go." The church aisles were
lined with vases of red gladiolas given by a couple celebrating
their twenty-fifth wedding anniversay, and in his sermon Rev.
Barnette referred to the flowers as "a symbol of rebirth—whether
the new life after marriage or our hope for a new life after
death." He concluded by saying: "Lord, into Thy hands I
commend Jim and Naomi, and also into Thy hands those who
must live with the memory of this crime for the rest of their
lives."

The following day Eunice Richard, who had interrupted her
vacation on the East Coast as soon as the police called with word
that the remains had been discovered, visited her niece in juvenile hall. All week long Marlene had alternated between periods
of apparent lucidity and bouts of hysterical sobbing, during
which she would cry out, "I want my daddy!" By the time
Eunice arrived, Marlene had heard of Chuck's arrest, but since
she was kept isolated from other wards and forbidden to read
newspapers or watch television, she couldn't be sure exactly
what the police knew. Eunice was instructed to keep the conversation away from the crime. When she entered the visiting room,
Marlene, dressed in the hall's regulation green smock and looking apprehensive, embraced her tearfully.

"Auntie Eunice," she said when she recovered her composure
and they were seated at a table, "you don't think I did the
horrible things they say I did, do you?"

"I don't know what to say about that, Marlene. The evidence
is pretty clear that someone did it. I don't think we should talk
about it now."

"But how could I kill my daddy? I love my daddy. He's one
of the two people I love most in the world."

"Who's the other?" Eunice asked before she could catch herself.

"Chuck," Marlene said.

They were both silent for a time. Marlene began biting her nails. Then she turned the conversation to less sensitive concerns, asking Eunice if she would make sure the cats were fed. "If Mishu's gotten outside, you have to take the box of Friskies to the door and shake it to get him back in," Marlene explained. She also asked Eunice to locate her poetry books and some clothes, and then, sensing the older woman's discomfort, she said, "You don't really want to be with me, do you?"

As the week went on, Marlene's observation, true enough then, was even more apt. Learning the details of the crime from the police made it much more difficult for Eunice to visit Marlene. She did what she felt obliged to do for her only brother's daughter, buying Marlene candy and fruit and, in San Francisco, some books in Spanish, but their conversation became increasingly strained. Along with others at the hall, she noticed that Marlene generally referred to Jim in the present tense and only Naomi in the past tense, and she asked herself if it was possible that her niece had blocked the crime from her consciousness. She was also plagued by the thought that "all this might not have happened if only I had insisted that Jim send Marlene down to Panama for the summer."

Eunice and Phil Royce did look after the cats. Mishu had escaped during one of the police searches and could not be rounded up, but Rascal, Marlene's favorite, was just as sleekly self-satisfied as ever, having managed to knock down the box of cat food from the kitchen shelf and overturn one of the dozens of milk bottles on the floor that Naomi kept full of water at room temperature for her fish tanks. Phil Royce tried to find a home for the cat, but as soon as he mentioned the Olives' name one excuse or another would be offered, a local reporter having mentioned the black cat in connection with Marlene's "occult activities."

Royce immediately undertook to be the executor of his friend's estate, and his first "official act" was to give away Naomi's fish tanks, two of their choice to the Edemadfars next door and the rest to a local private school. (With unintended appropriateness, Royce also sent Naomi's huge larder of canned foods to a nearby rehabilitation home for alcoholics.) The coming months, as he later reflected, would prove to be "the worst period in my life, not excepting plebe year.'' It had begun with premonitions of his friend's fate even before the police called him with the bad news. On the Monday after Marlene's arrest, Royce had been searching through the desk that Jim had just moved into the new GBS office for some clue to his partner's whereabouts, when he noticed, on top of the ''in'' box, Jim's will. Afterward he wondered if it was entirely accidental that the murders were committed on the day his partner moved his office out of his home, thereby isolating himself further from his daughter.

Marlene had several other visitors that first week in the hall, among them Rev. Barnette, who saw her ''out of a sense of priestly obligation'' nearly every day. On the first visit he gave Marlene a Bible and a ''little sermonette'' he had prepared: ''You don't have to tell me the truth, Marlene, because that's not important. What is important is that you're honest with yourself and with God.'' But despite his sentiments, on these early visits the reverend found himself, much against his better judgment, ''pushing to find out what actually went on in that room.'' Marlene couldn't bring herself to talk about the crime, but she did mention repeatedly how much she missed her father and, once, softened her account of Naomi's cruelties by saying of her, ''She didn't know how to express love.'' Marlene asked Rev. Barnette if he would visit Chuck and personally deliver some poems addressed to her ''Diamond Boy,'' including one called ''Chant at Sunrise'':

> Breath of incense
> legs of stone
> eyes of topaz
> every bone
> of him is mine.
> I take my time.

Peter Mitchell, who had been contacted by the juvenile hall when Marlene was merely charged with a parole violation for associating with Chuck, also visited her regularly. As her lawyer, Mitchell had less interest in learning ''the truth about what actually went on in that room'' than in defending her alibi and hoping he could make it square with the police reports. The truth could only complicate his life. Gingerly, he asked Marlene if she had told anyone or written down anything that might contradict her final account to Scott Nelson, and she mentioned the letters she had written to Chuck from the hall. After Mitchell left Marlene he rushed over to Riley's house to retrieve the letters, but Joanne had already given the most incriminating one to the police.

On July 10 the charges against Marlene were changed from a minor parole violation to multiple murder. At the same time the court authorized money for a psychological evaluation of the defendant, and Mitchell hired Dr. Stanley Upshaw, a prominent Marin County psychiatrist, to do the job. Dr. Upshaw interviewed Marlene twice and determined, as he would later testify at her hearing, that she "suffered from an elongated diminished capacity that culminated in killing," but was by no legal definition the word insane.

In his evaluation he was guided by a battery of standardized tests that a local clinical psychologist, Dr. Lawrence Katz, administered to Marlene. On the Incomplete Sentences Blank test, Marlene often burst the bounds of a single sentence with what the psychologist, in the report he turned in to the court, called "highly affect-laden descriptions" of her inner feelings and relationships with Chuck and her parents:

> *The happiest time* . . . of my life is when my father cried and said I love you and Chuck, but I don't want to lose my child.
> *Boys* . . . are boys. I only have really loved two—my father and Chuck. I still do.
> *A mother* . . . should love her daughter.
> *I feel* . . . very hurt, lonely, scared and I want to see a familiar face.
> *My greatest fear* . . . is that I will lose my life (convicted) and Chuck his.
> *I can't* . . . live without the emptiness replaced.

On both the Rorschach and the Thematic Apperception Test (TAT) cards Marlene "showed a very striking tendency to be oversymbolic" and to give images "more concrete reality than most people do," reactions that Katz found "suggestive of a very highly schizoid view of the world." Marlene interpreted one TAT card as "showing a woman dead, with her husband finding the body, and she turned the card face down, stating, with some apparent anger, 'You're showing me this on purpose.'

She then began to weep and continue to do so for some minutes."
Given a Rorschach ink blot often seen, according to Katz, as the
"mother card," Marlene's comment was: "Desolation, sorrow
and emptiness."

In his summary of the test results Katz was careful not to label
Marlene with facile psychological tags. "This is a very interesting young woman and one who is obviously very troubled," he
wrote. "Miss Olive is functioning intellectually in the High
Average range. She does not give evidence of an overt thinking
disturbance. On the other hand, she seems to be someone whose
judgment could be poor in those areas where love is involved,
even though in many respects her capacity to perceive reality
clearly seems to be intact. She shows an unusual mixture of
maturity in some areas and considerable immaturity in others,
with a tendency to be quite hysterical and histrionic and very
easily given to poetic flights of fancy and oversymbolic, vague
and amorphous styles of relating to the world."

Marlene told the psychologist and anyone else who would
listen how much she loved Chuck, and in letter after letter she
told Chuck himself. "Oh, please, love, remember *I love you*
and we'll always be together," went one typically effusive
outpouring. "I love you more than the world. I don't care how
long I have to wait for you, because I want you. I don't want to
live if I can't be with you in the end. Just as the night turns into
dawn, you're my man for the future or they'll be none."

Shortly after her arrest Marlene, having missed her period,
became concerned that she might be pregnant. Eventually a visit
to Dr. Tapley would dispel her fear, but in the meantime she hinted
delicately at the situation as a way of tying Chuck even closer to
her. "I want you to know that I need you as soon as I can," she
wrote him. "Because what I've got to tell you is the business of
no other man. Here is a hint to the thing I need to say: 'You are
there and two are here.' "

Marlene's motives for trying to reach Chuck included a large
measure of self-interest. On the advice of Peter Mitchell she tried
desperately to warn Chuck not to let any of the self-incriminating
letters she had written him in the first days of her incarceration
fall into the hands of the police. There were three such letters,
including a rambling account, written over a two-day period, of
life at the hall and her fears for the future. "Now what are we
gonna do about our plans?" she asked at one point. "In six and
a half months I'll be 17 and be able to marry you. What are they

gonna do now, Chuck? I'm afraid. I need to be beat up, just for general purposes. Just for the pleasure rushes it sends through my body.'' Then, after instructing Chuck, who was still at large, to ''feel some vibes for me'' at an upcoming Robin Trower concert she would ''probably miss,'' and to ''rip me off some mascara (black) and eye shadow (to match green clothes),'' Marlene came up with her most bizarre plan yet, this time to conceal the deaths of her parents. ''I said they probably bought a Chevy Malibu,'' she wrote Chuck. ''We need to get ahold of one—any color. Need plastic explosives or something to blow it up so it'll burn. And someone to report it after time for a normal body to burn away completely. And a man's shoe and part of a woman's old pocketbook, if possible. Doesn't matter if car doesn't work. Tow it yourself and dump it. Just make sure they can't tell it didn't work. Something has to be done by weekend.''

All three letters eventually came into the possession of the police, and after several days in the hall Marlene concentrated on convincing Chuck not to ruin their chances in court by confessing to ''those ridiculous charges against us.'' ''You are innocent and so am I,'' she wrote him two weeks after her arrest. ''And I believe *we* will survive. *We* is an important word, remember. It seems to me that they've got you on so much medicine you can't think straight. I think you know better than I that it will always be *us* together. I just have the feeling that it will be alright. Right now, as things stand, they don't particularly have enough evidence to convict.'' But even in the midst of these outpourings of love and concern for Chuck there were early hints of Marlene's eventual disaffection: ''Please don't put your address on back of letters. Put Mr. and Mrs. Wood. The girls make fun here and want to read them.''

Because he was considered a suicide threat, Chuck was placed in the jail's infirmary after his arrest, where he could be monitored around the clock by a mounted closed-circuit TV camera. A note he scribbled the following day—addressed ''Dear World''—gives some indication of his confused state of mind: ''Write this to keep my mind together. It's falling apart. There is a camera on me. It's driving me up the wall. I don't know what I've done or am doing now. It's hard to say. God should help me but I won't even see him now. It's the Devil I must see now. He's been my master for the past ten months, ever since I met her. I love Marlene. She's got control of my heart, mind, soul, all of me. I do all she says. Love is strange. Please don't take her from me. I need her now more than ever.''

After his initial (and according to prison chief Larry Nabor, quite typical) ''cleansing'' period, when he confessed to several on-duty officers as well as to Nurse McGovern, Chuck withdrew from his surroundings into a trancelike stupor, but he continued to plead for the return of his magic bracelet. Withdrew, that is, except for a torrent of correspondence he addressed to Marlene that far exceeded the jail's limit of two three-page letters per day for each prisoner. He refused to eat and slept most of the day. (''It's about 12 p.m. and I haven't got out of bed,'' he wrote Marlene. ''Nor have I eaten. I find no reason to eat. I feel nothing but anguish, sorrow, heavy heart. What's going on, Marlene?'') Failing to hear from Marlene or to obtain his bracelet, he painstakingly tattooed her name on the back of his left hand, using an improvised ink made from mixing the ashes of burned candy wrappers with water, which he injected under his skin with a straight pin.

After a week in the infirmary Chuck was transferred to a single-occupancy maximum-security cell and then, as soon as he seemed to be coming out of his period of withdrawal, to a cell he shared with a man who had broken his foot when a safe he was attempting to rob fell off a shelf and, as Chuck put it to Marlene, ''chased him down a staircase.'' Everyone in the jail had a nickname, and after viewing a TV movie about the Lizzie Borden trial, inmates started calling Chuck ''Lizzie Riley.'' But the nickname that stuck was ''Barbecue,'' prompted by the media's references to the ''Barbecue Murder Case.'' Chuck accepted the teasing in good grace, the way he had when his classmates called him Large Charles in grade scool. He also tried to curry his fellow prisoners' favor with gifts of cigarettes and candy from his commissary fund. Dick McGovern, a male nurse who had struggled hard to win the inmates' respect, tried to warn Chuck not to be such a ''jellyfish.'' Under McGovern's guidance Chuck began to get himself into the best physical shape of his life by dieting and doing hundreds of push-ups and sit-ups in his cell every day. Soon he could write Marlene that he was ''reducing so fast my skin feels loose. I'm exercising three times a day. I'm down to 180 lbs. or less with a 32–34 waist and will soon wear a 30–32. I hope I'll see you when the time comes. I do want to be the man for you.''

As he became integrated into prison life Chuck's withdrawn

and remorseful moods alternated with periods of bravado. In the topsy-turvy prison value system someone accused of a multiple murder—one of the few crimes that called for an automatic death penalty in California—had a kind of status that he was not above exploiting. He taped newspaper articles about the crime to his cell wall and often, in conversations with other inmates, exaggerated Jim Olive's wealth and importance. A few days after the crime he used one of the two calls he was allowed to make each week to telephone Roger Kyle, mainly to assure his friend that he would repay the money he still owed him, now that the police had confiscated the murder weapon he had used as collateral on the debt. With the exception of the tape-recorded confession, Kyle's testimony about that call became the most damaging evidence the prosecution used against Chuck at his trial.

"I hit a real big guy," Chuck began the conversation. "A CIA man."

"How'd it happen?" Kyle asked.

"I got to take the Fifth on that."

"C'mon, you can tell me. I won't tell nobody."

"Marlene's a witch. She's got me under some kinda spell. She set the whole thing up and I carried it out."

"Were you high?"

"Is the sky? The whole thing was a bad acid trip. Blood spurtin' out all over me when I finally could pull the hammer out of her head. The damn gun even fell to the floor and almost blasted my damn foot off."

"I guess that finishes you and Marlene."

"I still love her, if that's what you mean. She says when all this blows over we'll move away from here, maybe settle in South America. Her dad left her a bundle."

"You think you'll get off that easy?"

"I'm insa-a-a-ne," Chuck said, his voice trembling in mock hysteria. "A couple of years on a green lawn and I'll be back out."

In general Chuck was a model prisoner and felt proud when his father reported that Lieutenant Nabor "wished he had a jailful of Chucks." Passive by nature, he adjusted to the boredom of prison life without complaint. He spent much of his time reading the Bible and Carlos Castaneda's Don Juan trilogy, recommending the latter to Marlene as a work which "is changing my outlook on life." He listened to the radio and called KTIM whenever he could to request songs he associated with

Marlene, such as "Lady Stardust" and "Free Bird," even though, he wrote her, listening to them "makes me so sad I sometimes cry." Because he found it so difficult to remember the events of his first days in jail, he began to keep a diary of his activities. The first entry, dated July 17, reads: "I got out in the yard today for about an hour. All I did was run 'til I almost fell. The sun was nice. Got to see my bro and a lot of friends. Thank you Lord for one beautiful day."

Hoping to please Marlene, Chuck wrote a great deal of poetry to her, mostly romantic doggerel except for a few fragments that expressed his gratitude to her for, as he put it in one of them, "making me whole." One such poem began:

> I think of you
> at sunrise
> which is God's beginning.
> For you were there
> at the beginning of me,
> when I came alive
> and discovered my place,
> my worth.

But mostly Chuck spent his time writing Marlene impassioned letters, often dozens of pages each and written at such white heat that they were barely legible. Many of them ended "I'll love you forever and a day" and were signed "your slave and lover." Nearly all expressed an intensity of devotion that one court-appointed psychiatrist would characterize as "akin to magical enthrallment." Occasionally Chuck's letters to Marlene were textbook expressions of what another psychiatrist, borrowing a popular term from biology, would call their "symbiotic relationship." "When I see you again I will be reborn to a life somehow taken from me," Chuck wrote her after two weeks in prison. "Without you I am nothing, a part without a counterpart. If I don't have some kind of contact soon I will die, as my dreams have shown. I live not so much for as because of you, and if I can't feel your presence I haven't any. Love and life are yours to give and take away."

Chuck never failed to express his joy at receiving any response at all from Marlene. ("To me a letter from you is like hearing from God, like being free to run, like deep, deep happiness that can't be explained to anyone.") But as weeks went by with scarcely a word, he began to voice his displeasure, until by the end of the summer he was writing her: "You told me you do love me, you care, you can't live without me. Well, haven't you? Or was that just talk without meaning to you? If all I am is a pawn in a game of chess, tell me so. Do it and be done with it."

In the fall Chuck stopped calling KTIM to request songs that reminded him of Marlene—and then he stopped listening to the radio altogether. For weeks the number one rock song in the country, which the station played with nerve-pinching regularity, was called "Bad Blood." Chuck could not help but identify with the Neil Sedaka lyrics:

> Bad blood, the woman was born to lie
> Make promises she can't keep
> With the wink of an eye
>
> Bad blood, brother you've been deceived
> It's bound to change your mind
> About all you believe . . .
>
> Bad blood, the bitch is in her smile
> The lie is on her lips
> Such an evil child
> Bad blood is takin' you for a ride . . .

Chuck was certainly correct in perceiving that Marlene's feelings for him had cooled as time passed. In her first month at the hall he remained the only tie to the past she had not severed, and she needed him desperately. Her letters continued to be supportive and loving, often expressing a degree of passion that embarrassed the rather stiff-spined lawyers who perused them. ("Would you still like to stir the gravy and check that the meat is tender, hot and succulent. I hope so. I got plenty of new recipes saved up.") But soon her replies became so grudging and sporadic that Peter Mitchell took to sending them to Chuck's lawyer with notes that read, simply: "At long last!"

Initially the juvenile authorities put Marlene in a single-occupancy room and placed her on strict "in-building" standing, which meant that she was never allowed out of the girls' unit. Meals were brought to her, and a private tutor gave her lessons in the morning and came back in the evening to check over her homework. Because her general despondency and occasional hysterical outbursts made her a high suicide risk, a hall monitor looked in on her every half-hour around the clock. Worst of all, the enormity of her crime isolated her from the other girls, the great majority of whom had been placed in the hall by their parents for breaches of behavior rather than of law (what the authorities called "status," or noncriminal, offenses). For legal reasons the juvenile hall staff was instructed not to talk to Marlene about her crime and to change the subject if she initiated such a conversation.

In the beginning considerable effort was expended to make sure that the other girls not learn the charges against Marlene, but this quickly proved futile. During a regular Wednesday night "coed" a few days after she had been arrested, a group of boys and girls watched a movie on television. Afterward a local news special about the crime came on, and before a monitor could turn the set off, everyone sat transfixed with horror, while Marlene quietly returned to her room. After a month in the hall Marlene would write Chuck about her sense of isolation: "Girls here seem to care a lot, but they're nosy, too. So you really are alone, if you think about it. New chicks who come in find it hard to confront me after they know who I am. Some worried parents have called because I'm in the same hall with their kids." And a few days later, in a more despondent mood: "I find it hard to stay alive. Not that I don't love life, but I am alone basically. I have no family and no real friends because I have been damned by them. I don't have your family, either. And your words are becoming distant . . ."

Marlene's juvenile hall supervisors noticed that she was especially depressed before bedtime and that she talked in her sleep and often awakened with a start from nightmares. She wrote Chuck that "there are a couple of nights when I feel like I've been struck by lightning and everything falls apart." The dream she was plagued with was always the same. "I kept seeing myself standing before the closed bedroom door," she would later recall. "I'd try to keep myself from going in but I'd always find myself turning the handle and looking inside. The bodies wouldn't be there but there'd be holes where they were in the same shapes, like a jigsaw cutout."

Despite some minor infractions of juvenile hall regulations, Marlene's behavior was considered generally satisfactory and her spirits lifted as the months went by. She formed a close and enduring relationship with a young volunteer worker named Carolynn Shaalman. Mature well beyond her twenty-three years, Carolynn had always enjoyed working with problem kids, from her high school tutoring days, to the time she spent manning the Haight-Ashbury switchboard during the flower-child summer of '68, to Vista volunteer work during college at Lewis & Clark in Oregon. Perhaps because she brought to her volunteer work at the hall fresh memories of her own troubled adolescence, when continual conflict with her father prompted her, for a time, to live with foster parents, Carolynn was able to gain Marlene's trust in a way that the regular staff could not ("She fills up a hole in me that my mother never could," Marlene wrote to her aunt), and the two quickly became inseparable companions. Several months after they met, Carolynn would actually realize Marlene's long-standing fantasy about a surrogate mother by becoming her legal guardian.

With the help of such sympathetic adults Marlene seemed to live less in the world of her fantasies. By late August she was writing Chuck: "Please don't let this Satan bit get to you. I swear, it'll tear up your brain." On another occasion she told him: "And, no, I'm no longer 'Freebird.' That is a fantasy world which I can escape to sometimes, but not reality. I love the song and it still moves me, and I may be a representative of it once in a while, but not always." A poem called "Death" that she wrote in the hall, concludes: "You built a world of fantasy/And now it's become reality." And once, when she signed a letter to Leslie Slote "Stardust, Inc.," she quickly added in a postscript: "No, it's not a fantasy trip. Just a nickname."

Nor did it hurt Marlene's morale to have a number of male admirers at the hall, especially after she put herself on a crash diet and shed the twenty pounds she had put on earlier in the summer. These flirtations seemed harmless enough until one of the boys was released from the hall and mailed Marlene some marijuana. "A letter was intercepted by staff," her hall counselor, Mary Sigler, wrote in Marlene's record. "It contained marijuana. There was nothing in letter to indicate that she solicited it, however. But tone of letter is disturbing in that it indicated promised sexual favors and in that he refers to her as 'my goddess.' "

A few weeks later Marlene asked another boyfriend who had been released from the hall to send her "some acid taped to your letter—they don't check my mail anymore." She was mistaken.

But, once again, given what Mary Sigler called "Marlene's history of sexual manipulation," the staff was less concerned with the requested contraband than with the way Marlene tried to arouse her boyfriend's jealousy, so reminiscent of her relationship with Chuck. Even more ominous to the hall staff were the references to herself in the correspondence as "Lady Stardust" and to her new boyfriend as "Diamond Boy." It appeared that Marlene had not so much relinquished her fantasies as redirected them.

Marlene's neglect of Chuck masked the anger she was beginning to feel toward him. She could take some responsibility for her mother's death but had convinced herself that Chuck was solely to blame for killing her father. "I hate to say it," she wrote to her new boyfriend in the middle of September, "but I hope that the man who killed my parents pays. He broke my heart, killed part of me, took what I loved most in life—my father—and now smiles. I can't forgive him. I am sorry."

There was no doubt about Marlene's contrition over her father's death. She tacked a newspaper picture of Jim that the *I-J* had printed to the bulletin board in her room and placed a much older photo of him wearing his service uniform, which she had begged Peter Mitchell to retrieve from the house, on her night table. A poem she wrote that summer, called "In a Quiet Mood," begins: "Here I am/Alone in my room,/Not wanting out,/Not wanting in./Not wanting anything/But forgiveness for my sin."

Marlene couldn't talk to Mitchell about the crime for nearly a month and then only by fits and starts, in great emotional distress. She told him that when she and Jim came back to the house from paying off the drug debt, she tried to warn him not to go inside. When she heard the shots she was in the kitchen, and she covered her ears with her hands and banged her head against the stove. Later, in the murder room, she spoke of apologizing to her father's corpse. "He died like a soldier," she said on a number of occasions. There were many times during the following weeks when she thought the murder was "part of a bad movie," or "a nightmare I would wake up from," and it was on those occasions that she would call home half expecting her parents to answer the phone.

Again and again Marlene would sob, "Why did my daddy die?" The lawyer was convinced that Marlene genuinely did not know the answer. Clearly, it was not, as the prosecutor would imply, for financial gain: Marlene did not even know the meaning of the word "estate" when Mitchell broached the subject. "I came to believe," he said later, "that Chuck was put in motion by Marlene—or rather by her fantasies. She told him so many times that she wanted her parents dead that one day he took her up on it. Then she came home and said, 'Jesus, what did I do now?'" The only poem Marlene ever wrote that mentions the scene of the crime seems to support Mitchell's conjecture. "Sheets and pillowcases torn all to pieces./Bloodstains on the wall./Lord, I wasn't aiming when I left."

But even if Marlene did not kill her parents with her own hands, she clearly had initiated the crime and thus was equally responsible in the eyes of the law. Mitchell's main job was to make certain that her case was tried—"heard," actually—in juvenile rather than adult court, where at least she could not be equally punished.

The problem was that the law considered the ages between sixteen and eighteen a gray area and allowed judges some discretion in remanding a case to juvenile or adult court. Fortunately for Marlene, who was four months shy of her seventeenth birthday at the time of her "fitness" hearing in September, the seriousness of the crime was not alone sufficient to allow a judge to rule for adult court, as it would have been only a few months later. At that time the state's Welfare and Institutions Code was changed in this regard as part of a continuing, nationwide tightening of juvenile procedures—the result, itself, of ever rising rates of serious crime for minors. In California, typically, more than half of all major felonies were being committed by minors—and no one expected the permissive juvenile justice system to stem the tide.

After several days of testimony from a parade of police officers, forensic experts and family friends, juvenile court referee Noel Blaine ruled that Marlene was, as the law specified, "amenable to the care, treatment and training programs" of the Youth Authority and remanded her case to juvenile court. Soon afterward Peter Mitchell agreed that his client would plead *nolo contendere* to a vastly reduced version of the original two counts of murder. The new petition, deliberately vague in its wording, charged that "said minor did . . . aid in the unlawful killing of human beings, to wit, James Olive and Naomi Olive." The petition skirted the usual categories of murder and manslaughter, said nothing about intention, and might even allow Marlene to inherit her father's small estate. "The way it reads now," assistant district attorney Josh Thomas complained to his neighbor Peter Mitchell, "the charge could just as well be a hunting and fishing violation."

But by the time of her court hearing several months later, Marlene had decided not to accept the limited admission of guilt that Peter Mitchell had worked out on her behalf with the juvenile authorities, and she had hired a new lawyer, Terrence Hallinan, the son of famed radical lawyer Vincent Hallinan, to mount a go-for-broke defense for her. She herself was the principal defense witness in the closed-door juvenile hearing before Judge Charles Best of the Marin County Superior Court. Dressed in a turquoise jumper and green blouse, and without any make-up on, she "gave every appearance," the judge told reporters during a recess, "of being a normal, clean-cut, average American kid." In an articulate and composed manner she denied participating in the murder of her parents. Marlene contended that she had argued bitterly with her mother early on June 21 and that Chuck, who had called several times that morning, heard the row. In the early afternoon she and her father drove to the shopping center to pay off her marijuana debt, and when they returned, Marlene went to the kitchen for a glass of orange juice while Jim Olive looked in on his wife. Marlene heard her father cry out, "Oh my God, Naomi. What's happened to you?" and then she heard sounds "that seemed to be blasts from a weapon." She was "frozen in place" and fearful for her welfare. A few minutes later Chuck Riley came into the living room carrying a pistol in one hand and the blood-splattered childhood portrait that had hung above her mother's bed. "He was just a madman," Marlene testified. "His eyes were bulging, his face was red, he had blood on his shirt and his hands looked gigantic."

"Are you going to kill me, too?" Marlene claimed to have asked him, whereupon Chuck began beating her. Marlene became even more "fearful for my welfare." After dinner with two of Chuck's friends at a Chinese restaurant, the couple returned to the Olive house and Riley entered the murder room again. He asked Marlene to help him drag what she "assumed" to be the bodies of her parents, wrapped in sheets and blankets, to the car, and they drove to China Camp. Marlene said she stayed in the car the whole time and did not see or participate in the actual cremation, but she did admit to cleaning up the sewing room with Sharon. For the next week Marlene claimed to have been held a virtual prisoner, watched constantly by Chuck and several of his drug-dealing friends, who had begun to suspect that Jim Olive knew of their illegal activities and was preparing to turn them in. Once, when Marlene told Chuck that she would call the police, he beat her again. All this kept Marlene in a "state of shock," and the heavy dosages of prescription drugs she took further numbed her resolve to communicate her plight to friends and the authorities.

The story made little impression on the handful of people who attended the hearing. "After listening to the witnesses and the evidence presented," supervising probation officer Mel Augustine began his written "assessment" of the proceedings, "there was no question that Marlene instigated and was a leader in this crime. Her boyfriend, although a willing participant, must have acted in the belief that he was acting for their future." Neither could Judge Best "buy the whole nine yards," as he put it in one of his favorite phrases. He ruled that "Marlene Olive did encourage, instigate, aide, abet and act as accomplice in the homicides of her parents."

Best would have liked to sentence the defendant to a term in prison more appropriate to her crime—murder in the first degree—but he felt that his "hands were tied." The Youth Authority could keep Marlene, who had recently turned seventeen, until she was twenty-one, but it was more likely to release her earlier. Technically, as a juvenile she was only guilty of violating Section 602 of the state's Welfare and Institutions Code—which could have been any crime committed by a minor.

Despite his strong feelings about the inequity of justice in the case, Best gave Marlene some fatherly advice after pronouncing sentence. "You are an intelligent young lady and I hope you will take advantage of the opportunity to finish high school and start college in prison," he said as she stood before him. "You have no family or real friends in Marin County now. When you're released from custody my advice is to change your name, move to another part of the country where people do not know about your crime and start all over again. Someday, however, you will meet a man you will want to marry, and then you should sit down with him and admit the truth, even though there is some risk involved. Otherwise, you will forever live under the cloud of a disclosure that could ruin your future.''

A week later Marlene was transferred to the Ventura School, north of Los Angeles, California's only coeducational institution for youth offenders.

Ten

Chuck Riley was facing a compulsory death penalty. According to California law at the time, any adult charged with first-degree murder was tried in two stages: the first to determine guilt or innocence, and the second to ascertain if any of eleven "special circumstances" applied, such as a murder in the commission of a crime, the murder of a police or corrections officer, or the charge Chuck faced—the murder of two or more people. Upon conviction for one of the special circumstances, the death penalty was automatically imposed by the judge. The law had been adopted, after much public discussion, when the Supreme Court overturned the state's old death penalty for allowing juries too much discretion in its imposition.

Because there could be no mitigating circumstances in Chuck's case, either of age or the lack of prior convictions, the choice of a lawyer became all the more crucial. By common agreement the best criminal lawyer in Marin County was William O. Weissich, a short, slight, bespectacled man who, in the utter plainness of his dress and manner, resembled a small-town pharmacist but enjoyed a reputation as a brilliant courtroom tactician. In fact, the Marin County Civic Center, where the trial would be held, was built on its commanding hilltop site because of one of Weissich's most ingenious arguments. The property was not within the boundaries of San Rafael, the county seat, as the law said it must be, but Weissich uncovered a century-old letter from the Archbishop of San Francisco to a group of Dominican nuns asking them to take charge of "St. Vincent's orphanage at San Rafael." Since the orphanage was sixteen miles north of the town's present boundary line, Weissich, representing the local government, argued that the law merely specified that the Civic Center must be built within the city limits but not necessarily the *current* city limits. Besides listening to Wagnerian opera, winning seemingly hopeless cases was the fifty-four-year-old Weissich's great passion in life.

It did not hurt Weissich's reputation as a crackerjack criminal lawyer that he had never lost a death-penalty case for either the prosecution or the defense. Throughout most of the fifties he had been Marin County's district attorney, much respected by the police as a tough-minded, vigorous prosecutor. Such views were perhaps best typified by Weissich's outspoken advocacy of capital punishment. For many years, whenever a bill to abolish the death penalty was introduced at each session of the state legislature, Weissich would travel to Sacramento to lobby for his hard-line viewpoint. While he recognized the "logical possibility that an innocent person might be put to death," he also firmly believed that capital punishment served as a "deterrent to some murders" and was convinced that the benefits to society outweighed the risks.

The trouble was that if Weissich was clearly the best criminal lawyer in the country, he was also the most expensive. When Oscar Riley first approached him about taking on the case soon after Chuck's arrest, the lawyer told him that it would cost a minimum of $25,000 in legal and expert-witness fees to mount a proper defense. "I'll raise the money if it takes my last penny," Oscar had said, but when he started talking about cashing in his life insurance policy and refinancing his home (his only assets), Weissich realized that it would take just that, Oscar's last penny, and he eventually agreed to accept a court appointment to be Chuck's lawyer at a fraction of his normal retainer.

Weissich first met his client three days after he had been arrested. Despite the constant sedation he was receiving, Chuck still appeared extremely agitated, rubbing his wrist and, the lawyer later said, "sort of clawing the wire" separating him from Weissich in the jail's closet-sized attorney-client room. The version of the crime that Chuck related to Weissich was essentially the same as the one he had told to Stinson and several others since his arrest. "Frankly, I've heard my share of gory confessions," Weissich would recall, "but listening to that story made me sick to my stomach."

The source of Chuck's nervousness as well as his principal

concern was not the crime but the need to recover his "magic" bracelet so that he could communicate with Marlene. At first Weissich misunderstood his client's meaning.

"They took my bracelet away," Chuck said, continuing to rub the wrist where he normally wore it. "Please help me get it back. I need to talk to Marlene so bad."

, "You can't see Marlene now," Weissich cautioned. "They won't let you."

"If I had my bracelet I could talk to her."

"How can you talk to her through the bracelet?"

"She sends me signals through it. She's a witch, you know."

"What do you mean by a witch?"

"Whatever it means, Marlene's one. She can control people's minds."

"You really believe Marlene can do that?"

"Yes."

On this and subsequent visits with Weissich, Chuck could remember details of the crime and its immediate aftermath well enough, but the time from then until the present, including the crucial period of his arrest and confession, was very hazy to him. By then Weissich had listened to the tape of Chuck's confession to Stinson while reading the transcript at the same time, and its emotional context, more than its actual contents, convinced him that his client was telling the truth. Legally, Weissich's options were very limited: he could plead Chuck insane if he could get supporting psychiatric evidence or he could bargain for his client's life with a diminished-capacity defense. The lawyer, under the assumption that his client was guilty as charged, proceeded along both avenues.

Chuch had already told Weissich about the drugs he had ingested on the morning of the murder—marijuana, cocaine, LSD and alcohol. Unfortunately he had also indicated, and the prosecutor would have little trouble proving, that such usage was by no means unusual for him. But what about witchcraft as a cause of diminished capacity? Weissich wondered. He desperately needed something to counteract the emotional wallop Chuck's tape-recorded confession was certain to have on any jury, and besides, the idea appealed to his sense of courtroom theatrics. Through a priest he got the name of a local expert on exorcism rituals, Rev. Kent Fillpot, who ran a combination bookstore and religious counseling service from a storefront in San Anselmo. Fillpot had moved to Marin County in the late sixties to counter what he called the "Satan boom" among local teen-agers, including a group that had held cat sacrifices on the Terra Linda High School football field during lunch period. But he had encountered only "isolated cases" of demonic possession in recent years and had turned his attention to combating the widespread influence of astrology, which he considered the devil's "door opener."

Eventually, after talking to Fillpot and other priests, Weissich decided that he would be "laughed out of court" if he argued the possibility that Marlene was in fact a witch. But since it was clear to the lawyer that, whatever the reality, Chuck believed she was demonic, he would talk about the psychology of witchcraft as a motivating factor in the murders. Such a defense—as well as a possible insanity plea—required expert testimony of a more conventional sort, and to explore both approaches Weissich hired Dr. Charles Cress of San Francisco to interview Chuck.

The thin, sharp-featured psychiatrist spent a total of seventeen hours with him and also talked to his parents and brother and sister. Since he was not a court-appointed psychiatrist, Dr. Cress submitted no written report of his findings, but he hired a clinical psychologist and fellow professor at the University of California Medical School, Dr. John Steinhelber, to probe Chuck's background and administer a battery of psychological tests. The latter's written report to the court reads, in part:

> [Chuck] readily admitted killing Marlene's parents, describing the event as something that Marlene directed him to do and that he couldn't help doing. He couldn't explain what he meant by his conviction that he couldn't help it, and he was uncertain whether Marlene's powers as a witch were or were not involved. He said that he felt sorry during the process of killing them and during times when he thought about what he had done, but that at other times he seemed able to dismiss the incident from his mind. . . . He feels that he has had a number of "visitations from Satan." During these experiences he "felt firey red hot, but cool and comfortable." He could see and hear Satan as clearly as he would experience another person.

In his "psychological assessment" of Chuck's mental state Dr. Steinhelber wrote that "Charles Riley has average intelligence, a chronic psychotic thought disorder, and current extreme emotional distress." Among the factors influencing his "participation" in the crime was an "extreme subjective need for Marlene as a real and symbolic fulfillment of his inadequately met social and sexual needs" as well as "his perception of her parents as symbolic sources of his frustrations."

Unlike Dr. Steinhelber's comprehensive report, Dr. Cress's notes from his many interviews consisted of barely decipherable scribbles on scraps of paper, a circumstance that would considerably reduce his courtroom effectiveness. On his first visit to the jail a week after Chuck's arrest, Dr. Cress found that his account of the crime had a "melodramatic, soap-operaish quality." A few of the notes he took on that occasion, all brief phrases from Chuck's version of events, were: "I didn't want it to happen"; "I couldn't stop it"; "there was blood in the air"; "I'll do anything for her, including drop dead." Describing Naomi's charred corpse when he returned to the firepit the second time, Chuck said that "the skull was laughing, as in a dream." At that point he "apologized to Mr. and Mrs. Olive." He referred to Marlene as "a high priestess" and an "official witch" who could "talk with the devil." He said that "Marlene and I make one" and that "sometimes I don't know where she ends and I begin."

From the start Dr. Cress was "skeptical" of Chuck's account. At one point during that initial interview Chuck said, "Everything's so confused in my mind, I wonder what really happened"—a remark that he would repeat in different words a half-dozen times over the next several months. On other occasions he would use the phrase "legal suicide," sometimes adding, "If I can't have her I might as well let them kill me." But it was Chuck's manner during his first meeting with Dr. Cress more than anything he said that triggered the psychiatrist's suspicions. The account of the crime seemed to him almost "recited by rote." Chuck would sometimes caution Dr. Cress against interrupting, saying, "You'll confuse me." As Dr. Cress later recalled, "It wasn't the way you review traumatic events. After the first few minutes Chuck shifted into a trancelike state, as if he were actually reliving the murder. He was like an actor who wanted his audience—me—to feel the full horror of the event. 'Then after I'd done it,' he'd say, 'blood dripping down my arm . . .' " In fact, the very repetition of the word "blood" in Chuck's account struck Dr. Cress as significant, as if the murder itself was "some sort of blood connection to bind Marlene to him."

After several interviews Dr. Cress began to see Chuck as a "borderline personality," someone who appeared perfectly normal most of the time but would occasionally slip into psychotic behavior. Not legally insane, but plagued by such a weak sense of self-identity that his personality could literally be taken over by a strong individual he came to feel was necessary for his very existence. There was even a psychological term for this little-understood phenomenon, "symbiosis," a word borrowed from biology to describe, as Dr. Cress would explain to the jury, "an attachment between two people in which at least one of them . . . feels that he or she cannot survive without the other." In a curious way, Chuck was right about Marlene being a witch—at least she had quite literally cast a spell over him. "He met Marlene Olive and something happened," Dr. Cress would explain to the jury. "I think the usual expression is 'he fell in love.' Now, the something that happened I don't think is an ordinary falling in love at all. 'Enthralled' sounds somewhat poetic but I think it fairly accurately describes the state of mind that this man has towards Marlene Olive. He felt in her power. . . . She was able to direct his activity, whether she was in the room or not. In a fairy tale he would be said to be 'under her magic spell.' "

Both Chuck's lawyer and the psychiatrist were operating under the assumption that he had committed the crime he had confessed to. Only Oscar Riley believed his son could never have murdered anyone, and proving Chuck's innocence, despite the weight of evidence against it, became an obsession with him. At the moment, with Chuck still proclaiming his guilt, there was little that Oscar could do, besides interrupting his rounds delivering Dolly Madison baked goods every time he was near Weissich's office in order to try to convince the lawyer and his staff that Chuck was "covering up for Marlene" and offer to pay for lie-detector and sodium-amytol tests to prove it. That and watch helplessly as his own already high blood pressure rose steadily despite his usual medication until, by early August, his doctor put him in the hospital for a few days of enforced rest.

The Rileys saw Chuck during the jail's visiting hours on Thursday nights and weekend afternoons. Often they would bring along some of Chuck's friends, nearly all of whom remained loyal to him, blaming Marlene for the crime no matter who did the actual killing. During those occasions when Chuck and his parents were alone together in the tiny visiting room, there were long, awkward silences once the Rileys had delivered the latest news about relatives along with the most recent proof that Rascal, the family dog, missed his master, for no one felt free to speak his mind about the crime itself. Occasionally such forbearance was beyond Oscar and he would plead with Chuck to stop "covering up" for Marlene, but Chuck's evident discomfort and his wife's sharp elbow would make him desist. As often as not he would go home, and late at night, while Joanne was working the night shift at the hospital, pour his heart out in long, emotional letters to his eldest son. One such letter, typical of many others, read:

Hi Son,

I just wanted you to know your mom and I and all your family from all over the country are behind you 100%. You in your normal state of mind would never do harm to anyone. Your mom and I and everyone knows you better than that. You are either covering knowingly or unknowingly for someone else, either temporary insanity or under hypnosis by another party that made it known to anyone would would listen to her that she hated her parents.

I cannot help but believe you were programmed just as a computer is programmed to fulfill the wishes of the person you loved so much. I'm not going to in no way knock that love you have for her, but, son, your attorneys and us, your family, are fighting to save your life, a life we hold so dear.

Keep in mind you are being tried in adult court with the D.A. seeking the death penalty. On the other hand her attorney is pointing his finger at you as the culprit, only she is being tried in juvenile court and if found guilty of involvement will get a minimum sentence and then inheritance time.

This is the last I will talk on this all-important matter. Please try to reach back into your mind and think if you can see where a definite transition came over you in the last few months you were being programmed and help us help you. The rest is up to you and the God above.

Love you,
Dad

Besides such parental coaching on Oscar's part, the Rileys were doing whatever else they could to help prepare their son's defense at his upcoming trial, which was now scheduled to begin in Marin County Superior Court in late October and to last for six weeks. Over the summer Sharon Dillon had gotten kicked out of her mother's house after one of their frequent disputes, and since she had nowhere else to stay, the Rileys took her in. It was an act of kindness more than calculation, but neither did it escape Oscar and Joanne that Sharon would be the state's principal witness at Chuck's trial.

Then, after Marlene was remanded to juvenile court in mid-September, Joanne Riley sent her the following plea:

Marlene—
Can you really sit there and let Chuck get sentenced to death for 2 counts of first degree and see you getting sent to CYA when, if you copped to one of them you'd only get 3–4 years and possibly getting him a 7 yr. sentence for manslaughter. Is four years of your life too much to ask in trade for a hundred of his. Is there anything you can do?
Your "Family"

Marlene never answered the note, but the Rileys did get the one break that they had been hoping for most. In late September, Chuck recanted his original confession and dramatically changed his version of the crime. There had been indications all along that he wasn't really sure what had happened on the day of the murders, and as the event receded into the past his doubts only increased. Early in September he had written in his diary that he wished "to clear my name with friends and family and to let the Law and Lord know I didn't do it. All other statements are false, for the protection of the one I love."

At that point a new and unexpected element entered the story—the very real possibility that Marlene, and not Chuck, had killed Naomi Olive.

By then Chuck had not heard from Marlene in several weeks. He spent his nights rereading her earlier letters to him. "It seemed to me that my whole life was reduced to the time I knew her," he recalled later. One night he cried out for duty officer Richard Todd and begged again to be allowed to see Marlene's bracelet. This time Todd relented and led Chuck to the lockup room where it was stored, leaving him alone there for twenty minutes. Chuck clipped the turquoise-and-silver bracelet on, noticing a crack in it that he thought must have happened when the police handcuffed him at the waterbed factory. A feeling of "enormous calm" engulfed him. Chuck returned to his cell and slept peacefully for the first time in many weeks.

Since his arrest Chuck had been plagued by a recurring nightmare in which he replayed the events leading up to the murder of the Olives. He would always wake up with a start at the point when he entered the Olives' front door—having waited in the bushes beside the driveway for Marlene and her father to leave—and saw himself in the full-length mirror on the opposite wall. The night he wore the bracelet Chuck dreamed the dream all the way through. He walked into the house carrying the gun in a paper bag and prepared to wait for Marlene to return, as she had instructed him to do. He went from room to room making sure no one was home. He opened the door to Naomi's bedroom, thinking it was still Marlene's. Naomi was lying in bed in a pool of blood with a hammer embedded in her forehead. Her eyes were closed but she was still alive, emitting a harsh gurgling noise. Chuck was transfixed with horror and could not leave the room without first trying to remove the hammer from Naomi's head. Just as he was struggling to dislodge it he heard the Olives' car pull into the driveway. At that point Chuck woke up in a cold sweat, screaming.

Chuck did not tell anyone about his dream immediately, although it further convinced him that he did not kill Naomi Olive. He changed his story publicly only when he received outside confirmation that his original confession might be false—confirmation that seemed to come, through an intermediary named Danny Lyon, from Marlene herself.

Danny was a slight, wiry sixteen-year-old who had been in and out of juvenile institutions a dozen times in the previous two years, most recently for armed robbery. Sometime in August, he claimed, Marlene had approached him on the lawn of the juvenile hall and during a brief conversation admitted that she had killed both her parents, striking her mother on the head with what she termed a "mallet." She added that if "things got too hot for Chuck," who was only involved in disposing of the bodies, she would come forward with the truth. Danny, who had known Chuck and Marlene only casually at Terra Linda High School, kept the information to himself when he was released from the hall two weeks later, in part because he immediately ran away from home and was afraid of being apprehended if he spoke out, and in part because, as he would later testify, he "figured it was [Marlene's] beef, not mine." He only came forward with the information when he told the story to two friends of Chuck's and they mentioned it to the Rileys, who immediately called Bill Weissich. Weissich met with Lyon and prevailed on him to tape-record his recollection of his conversation with Marlene. That same day the lawyer played the ten-minute tape to Chuck Riley. Afterward he looked fixedly at his client and spoke with unaccustomed sternness. "Goddamn it, Chuck," he said, "will you level with me before it's too late. What really happened?"

At that point Chuck's new story, in the lawyer's words, "came pouring out." It was essentially a more detailed version of his dream, with Chuck walking in on Marlene's mother while she was dying and shooting her father in self-defense—a crime of involuntary manslaughter instead of multiple murder. The problem was that while Chuck told his new account with as much conviction as he had his original confessions, it came nearly three months later, prompted by a dream and patently self-serving. Moreover, Chuck's revised account did not even correspond to Danny Lyon's story, since Chuck admitted shooting Jim Olive. Weissich was sure that no jury he had ever impaneled would "touch it with a ten-foot pole" without corroborating evidence, which was in hopelessly short supply.

"Frankly, I didn't know what to believe," the lawyer recalled, and his first thought was to get some sort of confirmation through a polygraph examination. Chuck readily agreed, and an appointment was arranged with a San Francisco polygraph expert named George Harman. In a "pre-test interview" with Harman, Chuck was ambiguous about which version of the murders was the truth, saying "I still believe both of them. I'm not sure which is true." During the examination itself, he was asked a dozen questions, some of which were easily verifiable control questions designed to establish a base line on the polygraph chart. The results of Chuck's answers to the key questions about the crime were mixed, supporting his revised version of events but indicating that he was still protecting Marlene. According to Harman's report:

There were no significant emotional disturbances indicative of deception reflected in Riley's polygraph charts on the following test questions:

"Do you have a reality memory of killing Naomi Olive?" Answer: "No."

"Do you have a reality memory of shooting Jim Olive?" Answer: "Yes."

It is the opinion of the examiner, based on Riley's polygraph chart, that he probably is telling the truth on the above-listed questions.

There were significant emotional disturbances indicative of deception reflected in Riley's polygraph charts on the following test questions:

"Do you know for sure who killed Naomi Olive?" Answer: "No."

"Did Marlene ever talk to you about killing her mother?" Answer: "No."

"Are you now deliberately lying to Mr. Weissich in any way?" Answer: "No."

It is the opinion of the examiner, based on Riley's polygraph charts, that he probably is not telling the truth on the above-listed questions.

But the good news of the lie-detector test was mitigated by the fact that polygraph results were not considered reliable enough to be admitted as evidence in a trial. Weissich, it seemed, was forced back to a purely psychological defense, although even there the experts did not entirely agree. Dr. Cress would have been willing to plead Chuck insane at the time of the murder, but the psychiatrist Weissich had hired to provide a second opinion, Dr. John Hess of the Langley-Porter Institute, who had interviewed Chuck on three separate occasions, did not concur. Like most states, California still used the nineteenth-century M'Naghten rule of determining insanity, which specifies that the defendant must be incapable of telling right from wrong when committing the act. Hess did not want to go that far, although he would testify that Chuck "did not have the freedom to choose to kill or not to kill," nor the "capacity to form an intent to kill any particular person," the intention to kill being the difference between first- and second-degree murder, or, in Chuck's case, between life and death.

Both Drs. Hess and Cress would agree that Chuck's mental

state was "seriously impaired" by his relationship with Marlene and that it was as plausible for him to have killed the Olives under her influence as it was for him, under that same influence, to have confessed to a crime he did not commit—and impossible to ascertain the truth. (Privately, Dr. Cress leaned toward Chuck's second version, since it was elicited with less "external pressure" than the original confession at the police station, but the opinion was not one he was willing to defend in court.) With the trial fast approaching, Weissich was left with his original diminished-capacity defense and, seemingly, no independent corroboration of his client's eleventh-hour protestations of innocence. In separate conversations with the lawyer, the two psychiatrists had unwittingly suggested a way out of the dilemma, describing Chuck as "extremely suggestible" and his behavior as "trancelike," but neither they nor Weissich drew the logical inference until a local family therapist named Loyal Davis suggested that he could test the truth of Chuck's statements through hypnosis.

As a Marin County resident, Loyal Davis had read about the crime in the newspapers, but he knew the more recent, unpublicized developments because he was treating Chuck's friend Mike Howard for a speech impediment. When Davis telephoned Weissich to offer his services, the lawyer was "willing but skeptical." As a criminal lawyer and former D.A. he knew that hypnosis was being used more and more in police work as a way to jog the memory of witnesses and uncover leads for further investigation. Indeed, California police departments, and particularly Los Angeles' (where several dozen officers in the Behavioral Sciences Division were trained in the use of hypnosis), had pioneered the field, solving scores of crimes ranging from hit-and-run driving to murder and rape cases by means of information elicited from hypnotized witnesses. But Weissich also knew that even as a device to uncover leads that could be independently verified, hypnosis was under increasing attack from scientists and civil libertarians, who could cite mounting evidence that witnesses were perfectly capable of distorting the truth in a deep trance (or, to use the more technical terms, "confabulating" to fill in "memory gaps"), especially if they sensed the biases of the investigator, and that their memory would be tainted forever afterward. That was why no court in the land had yet admitted hypnotically induced testimony except under restrictions that severely limited its usefulness.

Controversy, as Weissich's research would quickly show him,

had always surrounded hypnosis as it passed through cycles of acceptance and rejection in the two centuries since Franz Mesmer's experiments with "animal magnetism" were condemned by a French royal commission headed by Benjamin Franklin, which attributed the reported benefits of the treatment to his patients' "imagination." Fifty years later, well-documented use of hypnotism as an effective pain-control technique was superseded by the discovery of chemical anesthesia. Then, in the late nineteenth century, the subconscious having by then come into its own, hypnosis was widely used to treat nervous disorders such as hysteria, until the growing psychoanalytical movement stole its thunder. For decades the little-understood phenomenon receded to the demimonde of faith healing and stage hypnotism, where psychopathological disorders were miraculously cured and sedate middle-aged women made to perform belly dances. Not until World War II, when hypnosis was found to be a quick and effective treatment for battle fatigue and other war neuroses, did the technique gain some sort of scientific footing. After the war, studies of "hypnotic susceptibility" and its correlation with personality types confirmed this new respectability by answering long-puzzling questions about why some people could be sent into a deep trance at the snap of a practitioner's fingers and others could never be hypnotized.

In the late fifties the American Psychiatric Association issued a policy statement that recognized hypnosis as a useful technique, and hypnotherapy soon became a flourishing practice within the profession. But an aura of quackery still clung to it in the public mind, as illustrated by something that happened to one of its leading medical practitioners, a Columbia University professor named Dr. Herbert Spiegel, around the time that Bill Weissich called him for advice. Dr. Spiegel had recently treated a woman who complained of a persistent urge to coo at an imaginary bird she held in front of her, an hysterical symptom the psychiatrist had never encountered in his thirty years of practice. When he questioned the woman he realized that a stage hypnotist had told her that she would carry a canary around on her finger after she came out of the trance, and had forgotten to remove, as Dr. Spiegel hastened to do, the posthypnotic suggestion.

After listening to Dr. Spiegel's experiences as an expert witness in other murder cases, Weissich was encouraged to prepare a defense based on hypnotic interviews, although he fully realized that the professional qualifications of Loyal Davis, the hypnotist and (according to his business card) "psychonutritionist" who first broached the subject, were far from unimpeachable. A large, florid-faced man given to wearing his graying hair fashionably long and his bold-patterned shirts outside an ample beltline, the forty-year-old Davis was a building contractor turned, in therapy-happy Marin, hypnotist. The career transition was made largely on the strength of a five-day course in the technique that he took in 1965. But when Davis opened up his one-man Hypnotherapy Institute of Marin in Mill Valley he did not lack clients— women who wanted to give up fattening foods or cigarettes; men who wished to improve their sexual potency or golf scores; kids whose parents hoped they could be persuaded, by a simple posthypnotic suggestion, to like dope less and history more. He was even frequently employed by the Marin County probation department to hypnotize newly released prisoners and give them, as he would shortly put it in court, "suggestions that they should be more content with their lives and no longer want to do acts that are unlawful." Two months before he contacted Weissich, Davis had received a master's degree in psychology from Sonoma State College and began practicing "family therapy" along with his original specialty. But it would not escape the prosecution's attention—and hence the jury's during the trial—that Davis had been advertising himself as an M.A. in the Yellow Pages before he had the parchment in hand.

Even though Davis was clearly the least qualified of the three experts who would hypnotize Chuck, the other two being psychiatrists, the two-and-a-half-hour interview he conducted at the county jail in late October, a week before the start of the trial, was by far the most revealing. This was no doubt partly because a hypnotizable subject tends to be most emotive the first time he is put in a trance. But it was also due to the time and care that Davis took to put Chuck at his ease about the process and to hypnotize him in slow, if somewhat unorthodox, stages.

When Davis, before putting Chuck in a trance, ran a few preliminary tests out of an old hypnosis primer, he was amazed at how suggestible his subject seemed. He gave Chuck a "special stone"—actually a piece of Pyrex attached to a foot-long chain— and asked him to hold it over a drawing of a circle intersected by arrows pointing clockwise, suggesting that "no matter how tight you hold your finger the stone still goes around and around and around, the circle getting larger and larger and larger." In no time the stone was indeed making a wide loop in a clockwise direction, and when Davis changed the card to one that showed three horizontal lines with arrows at each end, the stone Chuck was holding began, as the hypnotist suggested it might, "to move from side to side, side to side." Similarly, when Loyal Davis asked Chuck to close his eyes, extend his hands out with the thumbs up and "visualize a great big balloon tied to your right hand going upward and backward and a big heavy book on top of your left hand," it did not take more than a minute of further coaxing for Chuck's arms to be two feet apart. "This is from a test to see how well you can be hypnotized," Davis announced. "With you—no problem."

After reassuring Chuck that entering a trance would be similar to "floating off on a good LSD trip," Davis asked him to close his eyes and count backward from a hundred, suggesting to himself that he was becoming more and more tired after reciting each number. Chuck began the process: "One hundred. Sleep. Ninety-nine. Deep sleep. Ninety-eight. Sleep. Ninety-seven. Deep sleep . . ." All the while Davis kept up a steady patter that seemed laughably close to the stereotyped hypnotist's monologue: "Your eyes are closing. Now very shortly they will be so heavy you can hardly keep them open. Closing. Very, very sleepy. The muscles around your eyes are more relaxed. Very, very relaxed. Closing. Very, very heavy. Very, very heavy. Closed . . ."

He continued this for some minutes, telling Chuck to ignore the jailhouse noises that often intruded into the visitor's cubicle and to "just let go" of the tiny wrinkles in his forehead, the muscles under his eyes and around his cheeks and jaw. Slowly, as Chuck sank into the pillow of his consciousness, his face seemed to attain the peacefulness of a sleeping child. Even hypnotizable people differ widely in the degree to which they can be hypnotized, and Chuck, from all evidence, was in the deepest possible trance. One such indication is that many of his answers to Davis' questions were in the present tense, a "revivification" of experience with all the emotions appropriate to someone who cannot distance himself from the scenes he is describing—emotions that were often lacking when Chuck talked about the crime in a normal state.

In his most lulling voice Loyal Davis first took Chuck on an imaginary walk along "a nice, wide, safe trail" above a beach, which was designed to deepen his trance and sharpen his sense impressions under hypnosis and finally, with the introduction of his reflection in a tidepool, to bring him back to his current predicament. Chuck's involvement in the walk was written on his face. When Davis told him to "pick up a stem or grass and start to chew on it," his mouth grimaced from the bitter taste, just as his nose twitched as he followed the instruction to "smell the sweet smell of wild honeysuckle." When the imaginary walk was over, with Chuck in the deepest part of his trance, Davis set up a series of conditioned reflexes in his subject that would react instantaneously to signals from the hypnotist, by-passing any rational control so as to make them impossible to fake. Then the hypnotic interview, as it was tape-recorded and later played back to the jury, began. Slowly, painstakingly, Davis led Chuck to the front door of the Olive house:

DAVIS: You are very, very relaxed now. You are walking in the house. You are walking in the house now. What do you see, Chuck?

CHUCK: I see myself [in a hall mirror].

DAVIS: Yes, you see yourself. You see yourself walking in the house. What is happening, Chuck?

CHUCK: I am terrified to walk in the house. It has been so long since I have been there.

DAVIS: You were scared to walk in the house?

CHUCK: Mr. Olive was going to kill me if he saw me enter that house again.

DAVIS: Were you really afraid of Mr. Olive?

CHUCK: Yes, I was afraid of Mr. Olive. He was making me do without Marlene a lot. He was driving me hard.

DAVIS: You see yourself walking in the house. Then what happened? It becomes very clear now.

CHUCK: Looking around. Looking around. Just remembering all the time I spent in the house months before, hours and days.

DAVIS: You look around the house?

CHUCK: Walk up the hallway to be sure the house is empty. And I walked into the master bedroom just a little ways.

DAVIS: I can hardly hear you.

CHUCK: I walk into the big bedroom at the end of the hallway, just to make sure. I am listening for any noise, anybody moving about, and I walk back down by the bathroom, and there is a door and it was closed. It was Marlene's bedroom. I opened it and there was Mrs.

Olive on the bed and she was dead. There's a hammer in her head.

DAVIS: There's a hammer in her head?

CHUCK (very agitated now; sobbing hysterically): Yeah, coming out of her forehead. I didn't know what to do. The more I stood there, the more I had to get the hammer out. Do you know what it is like to see a hammer in somebody? I didn't know——I think she was dead. I couldn't tell. I was hoping she was because I just couldn't see her living like that. I couldn't see it. It hurt so much to see that.

DAVIS: It hurt you?

CHUCK: Yes, so much, oh. I had to touch her to take the hammer out. It was really hard. Blood. Blood. No. No.

DAVIS: Blood on you?

CHUCK (in a high-pitched, gasping voice): Yeah, it got on me from the hammer when I took it out. No.

DAVIS: It is going to be all right, it is going to be all right, you are going to make it. It is going to be all right. You can get through it. You will feel much, much better afterwards. You had to take the hammer out. Something you had to do. What's happening now, Chuck?

CHUCK: I have to get something to get the blood off. I'm flinging it off my hand. I can't stand it, I can't stand it. It's burning my hand.

DAVIS: It is burning your hand?

CHUCK: The car's back. They're home.

DAVIS: Who is home?

CHUCK (with rising emotion): Mr. Olive's home. What do I do? I don't know what to do. I run up the hallway, look around. There's nowhere to go, nowhere to go. I'm trapped.

DAVIS: You are trapped?

CHUCK: I'm trapped in the house. There's only one way out. Through them. Marlene and Mr. Olive. I know she's with him. I stop in the hallway and hide behind the bureau, a big dresser or something, I can't tell. It is in the hallway, though. I am terrified.

DAVIS: You are terrified?

CHUCK: Yes. I don't know what to do. I'm trapped. I see Mr. Olive. He is walking towards me. He looks in the room and he sees Mrs. Olive. He screams, he runs over towards her.

DAVIS: He screams and runs over towards her. What is he screaming? You can hear him screaming.

CHUCK (great emotion): "Oh, my God, Naomi, oh, my God." He is there. I can hear that screaming echoing in my head, just echoing. And then he says . . . No. No. He sees me. He sees me. "I am going to kill you, you bastard. I am going to kill you."

DAVIS: "You bastard, I will kill you"?

CHUCK: There's a knife right there. No. Please.

DAVIS: Where is the knife?

CHUCK: It's on the night stand by the bed, on a plate by a cup of coffee, a lamp. "Don't pick it up." No. No. I shoot him.

DAVIS: I can't hear you.

CHUCK: I shot him, I shot him. I had to. I was trapped. Where could I go? Where could I go? I just shot him. I didn't even think about it. I just pulled the trigger and shot him. Never even took the gun out of the bag. He didn't even know I had it.

DAVIS: How many times did you shoot?

CHUCK: I shot him four times. I couldn't stop pulling the trigger. He spun around, facing me again, and I shot him three more times before he hit the floor, just shot him.

DAVIS: You shot him?

CHUCK: Oh, no, I can't do that.

DAVIS: You can't do what?

CHUCK: I can't do that. Can't kill him. Why did I do it? Why, why'd I do it? I want to die.

DAVIS: You know why you did it. Why did you do it, Chuck?

CHUCK: Because he was going to kill me. I didn't want to die. Now I do, now I do. I want to die.

DAVIS: What you want is truth. You are going to find the truth. What happened then?

CHUCK: I started to shoot myself. Marlene stopped me. I almost couldn't do it. I almost couldn't stop. I just had to fire that gun. I just had to fire it two more times, empty it, and I emptied it in the floor. I just shot it in the floor. Just shot it. Then I brought my arm down.

DAVIS: You brought your arm down and shot the gun in the floor? What happened then?

CHUCK: I walked out of the room, just walked down the hall to the living room, just walked down there and sat staring into the fireplace. There's nothing going on, just staring, staring. Marlene comes over to me. "Everything's all right, Chuck. Everything's all right. Don't worry. Everything's all right. Everything's all right."

Chuck had been sitting erect and motionless on a straight-backed chair for nearly two hours, and after he came out of the trance he felt emotionally and physically "emptied out" and very puzzled by the passage of time. At the crucial moment in the interview, when Chuck exhibited his fright and horror upon entering the murder room, Loyal Davis whispered to Bill Weissich, "Every fucking word of this is true." The lawyer was convinced that the hypnotist was right. In a long career spent listening to people confess to or deny every conceivable variety of crime, he had trained himself to detect telltale signs of fabrication with a polygraph needle's precision, and he had "never seen such an impressive performance before." Throughout the interview Loyal Davis had repeatedly touched Chuck's left wrist, and every time his index finger automatically jumped in response, as it had been conditioned to do. After he was taken out of the trance Chuck examined the soles and insides of his shoes for specks of sand that would confirm the mysterious walk along the beach he recalled so vividly.

As he left the jail Weissich realized that in terms of its impact on the jury the tape recording of the hypnotic session was the only evidence he had that might match the persuasiveness of his client's original confessions—if, that is, he could convince the trial judge to admit it into evidence. He also knew that to do so he would need to have Chuck rehypnotized by someone with more impressive professional credentials than Loyal Davis and hope that the results were just as favorable for the defense.

The man Weissich chose to rehypnotize Chuck two weeks later was Dr. Gerald Hill, a Marin County psychiatrist who had successfully used the technique to treat patients suffering from a variety of phobias and traumatic memory loss, including several hit-and-run victims who had glimpsed and then quickly repressed the license plates of the cars that had struck them. Hill had learned the uses of hypnosis five years earlier in a course that

Dr. Herbert Spiegel taught at Columbia University's College of Physicians and Surgeons, and he employed Dr. Spiegel's Hypnotic Induction Profile (HIP), a quick, relatively foolproof way to gauge the hypnotizability of a subject, in his own practice. The HIP included a number of components, but the one part of the test that could not be faked, because it seemed to be an inherited trait that did not change with age or practice, was a simple eye roll. Dr. Spiegel had discovered that his most hypnotizable patients had very mobile eyes, a fact that had eluded earlier investigators in part because, viewing hypnosis as analogous to sleep (it is in fact a form of intense concentration, the opposite of sleep), they put subjects into a trance with their eyes closed. Before attempting to hypnotize them, Dr. Spiegel began asking patients to look upward while keeping their head level, and he noticed that a few of them, the most hypnotizable, could roll back their eyeballs until only the whites were visible and that others who could not be put into a trance at all had a fixed gaze; most of his patients could roll their eyes upward to one degree or another and were correspondingly hypnotizable.

Eventually Dr. Spiegel formulated a scale of measurement for the eye roll and associated tests that ran from 0 to 5 and wrote a celebrated paper called "The Grade 5 Syndrome: The Highly Hypnotizable Person," in which he attempted to provide a thumbnail personality sketch for these subjects. After discussing such common Grade 5 characteristics as a "posture of trust," the "suspension of critical judgment" and a "telescoped time sense" that is rooted entirely in the present, Dr. Spiegel remarked: "Because they so urgently need direction, certainty and faith, grade 5s are likely to be receptive to all kinds of forces, even those antithetical to their best interests. They are uncritical and thus have difficulty in distinguishing between what is and what is not good for them. . . . They tend as well to look at a simple proposal as a demand, and to concretize a proposal without appreciating the full metaphorical meaning of it; so much so that they may at times use a metaphor as a concrete command to perform."

Dr. Hill gave Chuck the Spiegel test before interviewing him and found that "he was one of the most hypnotizable people I have ever tested," as the psychiatrist would soon testify in court. "Every observation I made," he continued, "was as strongly positive as it could possibly be," including Chuck's high eye roll, his quick arm levitation in a trance (it took Chuck only seconds to raise his forearm to a vertical level, a position he maintained throughout the forty-minute interview), his ability to regress to past ages and revivify experiences, and finally, the fact that he had no recall of the hypnotic state after leaving it. Chuck Riley was clearly a Grade 5 subject, placing him in the top 10 percent of the population in terms of hypnotizability, and making the information elicited from him in a trance, according to most experts, highly reliable. "I would say that if a person is in the upper third of the population in terms of hypnotizability," Dr. Hill would tell the court, "there is an extremely high probability, possibly 90–95 percent, that the information is truthful."

Dr. Hill's hypnotic interview with Chuck was much shorter than Loyal Davis', since he was covering the same material and could ask more pointed questions. Because the initial questions answered in a trance often meet with the least resistance, Dr. Hill began by asking Chuck what Naomi Olive's last remarks to him were, thinking that if there had been an argument between them on the day she died it would come out. Instead, Chuck reached back to a remark that Naomi had made several months earlier, which was, in fact, the last time he had actually spoken to her. " 'I just can't understand kids today,' " he recalled her saying. " 'They never learn responsibility.' " The interview continued in the same vein:

HILL: Now, I want you to tell me next the best remarks she ever made to you, the kindest words she ever said to you.

CHUCK: "You're really looking good. You lost a lot of weight."

HILL: Now, I want you to tell me the worst words she ever said to you.

CHUCK: "You're not any help for Marlene at all."

HILL: What else?

CHUCK: "Get out of my house!"

HILL: Why was she saying, "Get out of my house"?

CHUCK: We had been picked up by the police.

HILL: Now, I want you to think very hard about the day that Mrs. Olive was killed. And while you're thinking this, you'll not be afraid about anything that Marlene could tell you about how her mother died.

CHUCK (quoting Marlene): "I sneaked back into the house

while my dad was waiting for me in the car, and I went and killed my mother, hit her with the hammer and went back outside.''

HILL: All right. Now, I want you to change to another scene, the scene in which you last saw Mr. Olive, and I want you to describe exactly what happened.

CHUCK: I was hiding. He comes in the house. Closes the door. There he is. ''Oh, my God, Naomi!'' ''Don't do it!'' ''I'm going to kill you, you bastard!'' I shot him. I reached into the bag and shot him.

HILL: Now, I want you to think of the way in which you felt about Marlene when you told the original story and believed it.

CHUCK: I loved her so much, and I was looking for the answers from her. I would do anything to save her, even give my life for her. I know she loves me.

HILL: It is all right, now, to let yourself feel angry at Marlene. Let yourself feel angry at Marlene, then say all that you feel about her right now out loud. It is all right.

CHUCK (loudly; his face tightening): God damn it, straighten up! Can't I do enough for you? Can't I, damn it? I do love you. Can't I prove it?

HILL: Now, I want you to tell me the secret that you have been keeping.

CHUCK (very agitated): Marlene killed her mother. She did it. She did it. I never did believe it. She did it.

The People of the State of California vs. *Charles David Riley* got under way October 30, 1975, in Courtroom Five of the Marin County Civic Center, the futuristic Frank Lloyd Wright–designed pink-stucco palace that leaped from hillside to hillside above arched driveways. As a news event the final resolution of the murder of James and Naomi Olive suffered greatly from competition with a peculiar string of violent confrontations that had kept the Bay Area in the nation's headlines for weeks, from the capture of Patricia Hearst the previous month to ''Squeaky'' Fromme's and Sara Jane Moore's attempts to assassinate Gerald Ford. In the Marin County courthouse itself the trial of the San Quentin Six, a group of prisoners accused of killing two guards during an escape attempt, had turned the suburban landmark into an armed camp, which all visitors entered through a series of finely calibrated metal detectors and body searches of increasing intimacy.

Judge Warren McGuire, who presided over the walnut-paneled high-domed courtroom (*everything* in the Civic Center, from the judges' chambers and courtrooms down to the drinking fountains and bathroom sinks, was relentlessly circular), was a silver-haired, mild-mannered jurist who never allowed the proceedings to get out of hand. But his sense of fair play would at times be sorely tried by the contentiousness of the opposing lawyers, especially the assistant district attorney, Josh Thomas, who was hardly unaware of the public passion aroused by the murder of the Olives—a parricide in a family-oriented community torn by generational conflict. (The long line of spectators waiting to get into the courtroom each day—and the frequent surprise encounters of parents with their hooky-playing teen-age children—provided a daily reminder.) Thomas, a self-made man and proud father who had successfully raised five daughters in what he considered an overly permissive time and place, was convinced that the crime was motivated by nothing more complicated than thwarted lust and the financial greed of coddled children. Outraged that Marlene had gotten away with a "slap on the wrist," he was determined to see that Chuck at least was punished to the fullest extent the law allowed.

As theater for a packed gallery, the first week of the trial was short on drama, taken up as it was with the selection of an unbiased jury from a panel of over a hundred media-saturated citizens. A dozen of them at a time filled the jury box, each to be replaced by another upon being eliminated for cause by the court or on one of the many "pre-emptory challenges" allowed both the prosecution and the defense. The routine was repeated over and over again. Judge McGuire asked each prospective juror to "tell us something about yourself," then gently probed the person's attitude toward the case itself, the legal system in general, capital punishment, various fields of expert testimony and "the proposition that people sometimes confess to crimes they don't commit."

In the end every wrinkle and blemish had been removed from the face of justice, leaving it looking perfectly acceptable but somewhat boring, like a department-store mannikin. Three of the five men selected were engineers, five of the seven women were full-time homemakers, and all but one, a twenty-eight-year-old secretary, had children, up to six of them, many the same ages as Chuck and Marlene. As Josh Thomas made certain, each juror had either voted two years earlier for the reinstitution of the death penalty in California or was in sympathy with the result.

That afternoon Thomas' opening statement to the jury—aggressive, doggedly thorough and somewhat graceless—characterized the man and the prosecution he would mount. Tall and funereal in a dark suit and a dark tie with flecks of color, like a sprig on a casket, he spoke in measured tones, his arms crossed under his ribs, promising to "prove beyond any reasonable doubt, to a moral certainty, that the defendant, Charles D. Riley . . . personally murdered two human beings." Moving from his lectern to the jury box as the narrative reached its climax, Thomas talked about Marlene's difficult adjustment to Marin County ("it being an unstructured society, she being a conservative individual in dress and attitudes"); her falling in with a crowd her "somewhat old-fashioned" parents objected to; the fact that Chuck was "deeply infatuated" with Marlene, in part because of "the sexual favors that she bestowed upon him."

Thomas' highly dramatized account of the murder itself—drawn largely from Chuck's initial confessions—had its intended effect. While he was talking, his voice gravely hushed, several of the women jurors blanched and were visibly shaken, one of them signaling to the bailiff for a glass of water. When he finished, the courtroom seemed to let out a single collective breath. People looked in embarrassment at Oscar and Joanne Riley, who remained motionless in their front-row seats, a small man and a large woman dressed in their church-going best, their faces displaying a mixture of incomprehension and anger. They would be there every day of the trial, Oscar having received a leave of absence from the Dolly Madison Company and Joanne, who continued her job as a night-shift nurse's aide, simply doing with less sleep. She always held a large paperback Bible on her lap—whether for the jury's or the Lord's sake was never clear—but certainly the look she fixed on Josh Thomas for long moments did not speak of Christian love.

Only Chuck seemed impervious to the drama of the moment, his distracted demeanor more appropriate to traffic court than his own murder trial. He sported newly grown mutton-chop sideburns and a mustache, and wore a print shirt with a space motif and neatly pressed pants. If, as Dr. Hill testified, a Grade 5 subject was "completely absorbed in the present, with no thought of future consequences," Chuck Riley would daily prove the accuracy of the diagnosis. Throughout the proceedings he would pay more attention to the packed visitors' gallery than to the trial itself. For the past two hours he had been listening to the prosecutor with that fraction of his attention not occupied by a long letter he was writing—a letter, as it turned out, to Marlene. "These past four months have shown me a great deal of the world and myself," he began, "a lot of which I don't completely understand yet. My beliefs have changed, all for the better. Someday we will make it. I am always here and ready." Then a short time later: "The D.A. just went through his opening statement. You couldn't believe how badly he made me out to sound. What a bunch of head trips." And still later in the afternoon: "I've got some really nice clothes to wear to court. I think you'd like them a lot. Since I've been losing weight here I am down to a 32 size pants. I feel that I look rather nice." Back in his cell after court, Chuck concluded the letter with a poem for Marlene:

> She figured out
> the jigsaw of his heart
> and placed the pieces
> with such precision
> nothing came apart.

For the next ten days Josh Thomas called a well-rehearsed parade of witnesses to substantiate the prosecution's case, beginning with Phil Royce testifying on the Olive family's background. Then came the San Rafael policemen involved in the investigation, the younger ones looking well-scrubbed and eager, the best knot-makers in their Boy Scout troops, the veterans, professional witnesses who had been there many times before, speaking with a matter-of-factness that undercut the emotional impact of their testimony. In this sea of words, occasionally an object washed ashore that would startle the jurors to attention: the red-handled claw hammer, a lethal weapon whose heft each juror measured before quickly passing it to his neighbor; the palm-sized Ruger pistol, no bigger nor more dangerous-looking than the holstered capgun that hung nearly to the ground in Joanne Riley's favorite childhood photograph of Chuck.

Rodger Hagler, the physical anthropologist (or "well-qualified bone identifier," as Weissich kept referring to him in his *voir dire*) who had been called in by the Marin County coroner's office to sift through the remains at the firepit, testified to what he had found, using anatomical words that sounded like the final rounds of a spelling bee: scapula, coracoid, ulna, condyle and—the last identified bone fragment—a "basel minus its mandible." As the numbered manila envelopes full of "grid contents," the plastic Baggies containing major bone fragments, along with a cigar box of "odds and ends," piled up on the evidence table, a delayed reaction registered on the jurors' faces—the sudden realization that beneath the scientific wrapping, they were looking at all that was left of two human beings.

The state suffered a setback when its principal witness, Sharon Dillon, took the stand. At the grand jury hearing five months earlier she had testified that on the evening of June 23, two days after the murder, Chuck had told her in the living room of the Olives' house that "he hit [Naomi Olive] in the head with a hammer." Both before and after those proceedings she had given somewhat different accounts of that crucial conversation. Now she indicated that Marlene had done all the talking about the murder, with Chuck simply nodding in agreement.

"What did she say?" Thomas asked her in court.

"She just told me that when she hit her mom on the head with a hammer, that the blood and stuff went all over the place."

"Did you say that 'she' hit her mother over the head with a hammer, or 'he'?"

"I don't recall."

But Sharon's memory loss was only a temporary setback for the state. Thomas had wisely saved his most impressive witness—Chuck Riley himself, in his tape-recorded confession—for the conclusion of the prosecution's case. When it was finished and the court recessed, the jury filed out more grim-faced than usual. That day even the one woman who had habitually tried to give Oscar and Joanne a sympathetic glance at the conclusion of the court sessions failed to look their way.

The remainder of the trial became a battle of expert witnesses, with the defense psychiatrists, for the most part, defeating themselves. Dr. Cress testified at great length about the "symbiotic relationship" between Marlene and Chuck, along with his conviction that there was "no way to establish which confession is true," but his notes from his interviews with Chuck were so disorganized that it was easy for Thomas, using a standard prosecutorial technique, to trip him up on dates. Dr. John Hess's basic diagnosis was virtually identical to Dr. Cress's and it was couched in the same terminology. Asked by Weissich to describe Chuck and Marlene's relationship in scientific terms, Dr. Hess answered, "What took place was a kind of psychological merging in which he, in exchange for the continued fulfillment of his needs and his fantasies, would trade in, as it were, his own capacity to think objectively, to act independently. He became essentially enslaved." The testimony continued:

> Q. Now what is the difference between Mr. Riley's relationship with Marlene and any other young man who has a first love for a girl?
> A. His relationship with Marlene was a kind of grotesque caricature of love, filled with fantasies of dying for her, filled with fantasies of stealing for her, filled with fantasies of sacrificing anything in accord with her wishes. . . . Finally, his relationship with Marlene was so intense and her role in his life, psychologically speaking, became so great as to actually destroy—not totally, but to a large degree—his very sense of himself as an independent, separate individual.
> Q. Now, can you describe to the jury the degree of control that Marlene exercised over Chuck in your opinion?
> A. Yes. I think that the control was essentially total.
> Q. Essentially total?
> A. Yes. I have a very firm opinion that had Marlene proposed in an appropriate way that, for example, Mr. Riley jump off the Golden Gate Bridge, that he would have done so.
> Q. Doctor, does the term "psychological robot" aptly describe Charles Riley's condition on June 21?
> A. Yes. I think it would.

Midway through the trial Weissich became convinced that Chuck's only chance for an acquittal or, at least, a reduced sentence lay in the hypnotic tapes that confirmed his second confession. In such a controversial area he felt he needed an authority in the field more pre-eminent than the two hypnotists who had already interviewed Chuck, and he called Dr. Herbert Spiegel in New York to ask him if he would come to California. Dr. Spiegel had other pressing commitments but he suggested that Weissich contact his son and collaborator, David, a Harvard-trained psychiatrist who was then teaching hypnosis at the Stanford Medical School.

David Spiegel visited Chuck in the Marin County jail on a Saturday afternoon in the middle of the trial, and the resulting hypnotic interview was in many ways the most interesting of the three. This was true not so much because of the account of the murder Chuck related in a trance, which supported the others in nearly every detail, as because of an age-regression test that the doctor performed during the initial Hypnotic Induction Profile. It is the ability of a person in a trance to regress in time, answering questions about past events in the present tense and defining words from a standard IQ test, that provides the final confirmation of a Grade 5 hypnotic subject. Not only were Chuck's answers to Spiegel's questions "age appropriate," but even his tone of voice became progressively younger until, at the age of one, it was reduced to an infant's babble.

SPIEGEL: Today, now, is November 29th, 1975, and what we're going to do is go back to a younger time. Let's go back five years, to your fifteenth birthday. All right, today is your fifteenth birthday. Hello, Chuck, can you tell me what you're doing now?

CHUCK: School.

SPIEGEL: You're in school, and what are you doing at school?

CHUCK: What I'm doing? Just going to school.

SPIEGEL: And what class are you in?

CHUCK: English.

SPIEGEL: You're in English class. Who is your teacher?

CHUCK: Mrs. Sullivan. I don't like her.

SPIEGEL: You don't like her?

CHUCK: No. She gives a lot of work.

SPIEGEL: She gives you a lot of work, uh-huh. And you don't feel like working, huh?

CHUCK: Not today.

SPIEGEL: How come?

CHUCK: I want to celebrate.

SPIEGEL: You want to celebrate. What are you celebrating?

CHUCK: It's my birthday.

SPIEGEL: Oh, it's your birthday today. How old are you?

CHUCK: Fifteen.

SPIEGEL: What are you going to do?

CHUCK: Just fool around with a lot of friends. Go to the show or something, get high.

SPIEGEL: Uh-huh. Okay. And let me ask you a few words, Chuck. Like in the English class, can you explain what a lecture means?

CHUCK: It is when the teacher explains something.

SPIEGEL: Okay. How about an envelope? What is an envelope?

CHUCK: An envelope is what you send a letter in.

SPIEGEL: Okay. And an eyelash?

CHUCK: It's a hair.

SPIEGEL: Now, we're going to go back farther, Chuck. The years will go, and you're now going to be younger. You're now just approaching your eighth birthday. Today, you're eight years old. Hello.

CHUCK: Hi.

SPIEGEL: Who are you?

CHUCK: Chuck.

SPIEGEL: You're Chuck, huh?

CHUCK: Yes.

SPIEGEL: How old are you, Chuck?

CHUCK: Eight.

SPIEGEL: What are you doing?

CHUCK: Just playing down at the creek.

SPIEGEL: Uh-huh. And what are you doing down there?

CHUCK: Just digging some tunnels and throwing rocks in the water.

SPIEGEL: Oh, I see. Is this a day off from school today?

CHUCK: It's a weekend.

SPIEGEL: Anything special about today?

CHUCK: We're getting ready to move.

SPIEGEL: Oh, I see.

CHUCK: Back to Arkansas.

SPIEGEL: Let me ask you some other questions, Chuck. What is a lecture?

CHUCK: Something my folks go to.

SPIEGEL: Something your folks go to, okay. How about an envelope?

CHUCK: It is what you get letters in.

SPIEGEL: Okay, an eyelash?

CHUCK: Something in your eye.

SPIEGEL: Okay. How about an orange?

CHUCK: A fruit.

SPIEGEL: Just close your eyes. All right. More years are going off now: seven, six, five. Today is your fourth birthday. Today you are four years old. Hello.

CHUCK: Hi! Who are you?

SPIEGEL: Who am I? I am a friend of your parents. You have never seen me before?

CHUCK: No.

SPIEGEL: No. They asked me to talk with you today. How old are you?

CHUCK: Four.

SPIEGEL: You have got a smile on your face.

CHUCK: Yeah.

SPIEGEL: Why?

CHUCK: Because . . .

SPIEGEL: Because why?

CHUCK: I am getting big.

SPIEGEL: How come you are getting big?

CHUCK: I am four.

SPIEGEL: You are four, now, you mean just today?

CHUCK: Yeah.

SPIEGEL: Today's your birthday. Well, happy birthday.

CHUCK: Thank you.

SPIEGEL: Did you get any good presents?

CHUCK: I ain't got them yet.

SPIEGEL: What are you hoping for?

CHUCK: I am hoping for a space station set.

SPIEGEL: A space station set. What are you doing today?

CHUCK: Oh, just playing in the backyard with my trucks.

SPIEGEL: Where is home now?

CHUCK: Shaver Street.

SPIEGEL: What number on Shaver Street?

CHUCK: I don't know. It's just a big house.

SPIEGEL: It is a big house, huh. You like it?

CHUCK: Yeah. it's nice.

SPIEGEL: You got some good friends around here?

CHUCK: Yeah, I've got a couple of good friends.

SPIEGEL: You seem like a bright fellow. Can you tell me who the President of the United States is?

CHUCK: No, I don't know who the President is.

SPIEGEL: Okay. Are you in school now?

CHUCK: Not yet. Next year.

SPIEGEL: Next year, huh?

CHUCK: Yeah.

SPIEGEL: You want to go to school?

CHUCK: Yeah.

SPIEGEL: Good. Let me ask you some other questions. Can you tell me what a lecture is?

CHUCK: What is a lecture?

SPIEGEL: You don't know what it is?

CHUCK: No. What is a lecture?

SPIEGEL: Okay. How about an envelope? Do you know what an envelope is?

CHUCK: Grandmothers and grandfathers send things in them.

SPIEGEL: How about an eyelash? What is an eyelash?

CHUCK: Eyelash?

SPIEGEL: Yeah.

CHUCK: I don't know.

SPIEGEL: Okay. An orange, what is that?

CHUCK: It is good.

SPIEGEL: It is good?

CHUCK: Yeah.

SPIEGEL: What is it?

CHUCK: Fruit.

SPIEGEL: It is a fruit?

CHUCK: Yeah, it is a fruit. Don't you know that?

SPIEGEL: Yeah. I just wanted to know how much you knew. Okay, we are going to go back even earlier now: three, two, one year old. Today you are one year old. Hello, hello. Hello. Hi.

CHUCK: (Giggles.)

SPIEGEL: Who are you?

CHUCK: (Giggles.)

SPIEGEL: You are giggling. Hi.

CHUCK: (Giggles.)

After the age-regression test the psychiatrist led Chuck through another emotional reliving of the crime. When Chuck came out of the hour-long trance he felt exhausted, as he always did after these hypnotic interviews, and was curious to know why his right arm was raised in the air and his eyes were wet with tears. With the tape recorder still running, the psychiatrist assured him that the interview had been "pretty consistent with what you said the previous times."

"I would just as soon let them kill me," Chuck said.

"I wish I had something comforting to offer," Dr. Spiegel remarked. "It's hard to live with that."

"I just wish I could undo things somehow."

"Well, I think you are doing the best you can now. Where do things stand with you and Marlene?"

"You can't turn off how you feel about somebody," Chuck said, "but I was used. Not just this time—a lot."

"What was the reason you did it?"

"I needed her. I would do anything to keep the relationship together."

By the time Dr. Spiegel walked out of the jail to hand the tapes of the interview to Weissich, he was convinced he had heard the truth—and not merely because Chuck was so easily and deeply hypnotized or so emotive in reliving his experiences. "I gave him a chance to save his neck by suggesting that Marlene may have held the gun and killed her father," Dr. Spiegel explained to the lawyer, "but he didn't take it. He stuck by his story. That impressed me."

There was still another reason why Dr. Spiegel became convinced that Marlene killed her mother—one that had nothing to do with Chuck Riley. From what he had learned about the broader aspects of the case, the Olive household provided a casebook illustration of a concept that family therapists called the "parentification of the child." "There's always a little seduction between father and daughter," Dr. Spiegel explained later. "But it becomes more serious when the mother has abdicated her role by telling the child, in effect, 'I don't want to be a mature provider in this family. I want to be a kid. You run the show and in return you can enjoy all the sexual excitement that's going on.' Often the mother has taken on adult responsibility before she was ready to handle it, as may have been the case with Naomi Olive after her mother died, and she decides to cash it in early. Usually the daughter's real rage is toward the mother and not the father. In effect she asks, 'Why don't you make this your house and put me in my place? If you had any self-respect you'd be the wife.' " Even the fact that Marlene encouraged Chuck and Sharon to make love fit in with Dr. Spiegel's theory. "Symbolically, using her friend in place of Naomi, she's saying,

'For Christ's sake, Mother, *you* score. Take Daddy back and let me get on with my own life.' "

Of course, Dr. Spiegel was not allowed to speculate so freely before the jury when he testified in court two days after the hypnotic interview. In fact, he was not even permitted to go into Chuck Riley's account of the murder under hypnosis. Nor was it even clear that the judge would decide to allow the tapes of the interviews to be played in court, so tentative and confusing was the current state of the law on the subject of hypnosis. For while the police frequently used hypnotically induced evidence to further their investigation of a crime, such evidence, uncorroborated by other facts and witnesses, had never been allowed in an American courtroom for what was called the "truth of its contents." In California there was some precedent for introducing hypnotic tapes into evidence for the limited purpose of providing the jury with the background information that helped a psychiatrist judge the defendant's "mental condition" at the time of the crime or—in this case—his subsequent confession. But if the judge felt that the evidence's "probative value" would be outweighed by its "prejudice"—in other words, if he did not trust the jury to keep such a fine distinction in mind—he could still prohibit the playing of the actual tapes.

Dr. Spiegel was allowed to tell the jury that he thought it was "highly improbable" that Chuck Riley could lie in a trance, given what an "extremely highly hypnotizable" subject he proved to be, but under cross-examination by Thomas he also admitted that such a possibility was "conceivable." Moreover, it was Dr. Spiegel's opinion that Chuck had slipped into a "spontaneous trance state" during Bart Stinson's interrogation, and that his false confession was induced both by the "desire to comply with the police"—to be a "good arrestee"—and by "the suggestion that was given to him by the evidence that he read."

After Dr. Spiegel left the stand the state continued for "foundational evidence" on hypnosis by calling its own expert witness, Dr. William Andrews, a specialist in psychosomatic medicine. He testified that while a hypnotic subject may indeed "confabulate" in a trance, the information obtained is generally "accurate as far as the patient is concerned. This is what he believes. . . . A person may see a light in the sky and believe that it is a flying saucer. Well, that doesn't mean that it's a fact. It is his interpretation of the situation."*

Now it was Weissich's turn to further confuse the matter. "Assuming a highly hypnotizable person," he asked Dr. Andrews on redirect examination, "and assuming a competent hypnotist, one who does not suggest to the patient what he wants to hear from him, and assuming a state of deep hypnosis and a vivid recounting in the present tense accompanied by appropriate emotional responses, would you think that the story you get is more likely to be the truth than not?"

"More likely to be the truth, yes," the state's witness admitted.

Faced with such contradictory testimony about hypnosis, Judge McGuire decided against extending the case law on the subject, ruling that the hypnotic tapes could be introduced into evidence but only with the standard restrictions. As he instructed the jury in a carefully worded written statement: "These tapes are being played for you for the very limited purpose of allowing you to know all the data that an expert relied on in making any opinion expressed to you during this trial. These tapes are not being admitted and may not be considered by you for the truthfulness of their contents and they are not independent proof of any facts stated in those tapes."

For the next several days the jury listened to the nearly five hours of hypnotic interviews that had been introduced into evidence, along with a great deal of testimony on trance-induction techniques from the interviewers themselves. Although the judge repeated his cautionary instructions before each interview was played, Weissich was clearly betting that no jury could hear such a detailed and emotional re-enactment of the murder three times over without incurring some reasonable doubt about Chuck's original confession. But he knew that he was betting against heavy odds, given the poor quality of the tapes themselves (large sections of which were spoken in a barely audible whisper that

---

*Even such a firm believer in forensic hypnosis as Dr. Herbert Spiegel had termed just this phenomenon "the honest liar syndrome" in a scientific paper he published entitled "Hypnosis and Evidence. Help or Hindrance?" Writing about the "Janus-like quality" of trance-induced information, he concluded: "All data obtained under hypnosis are vulnerable to the counterclaim of memory contamination or coercion (innocent or designed), even though incredibly accurate information can at times emerge. . . . The most one can legitimately expect from hypnotic interrogation is further data, which may serve as *leads* for more conventional evidence gathering."

was rendered unintelligible by jailhouse noises) and the skepticism about hypnosis of a group of literal-minded engineers and housewives.

The effect of the hypnotic tapes was further mitigated by a surprise prosecution move on the last day of testimony—Josh Thomas' insistence that the jury be allowed to inspect the Olive house. The judge, the defendant, court aides, lawyers and jury members piled into an old school bus for the ten-minute drive up the freeway to Hibiscus Way. The house had hardly been touched since police seals had been placed on the doors nearly six months earlier. The dirty dishes that Marlene had left piled in the sink when the police arrested her still awaited washing, and a gray-green mold had spread to the adjacent counters. Thomas led the jurors along the path Chuck claimed to have taken on the morning of the murder. They peered into Marlene's bedroom, where the unmade bed was still piled high with discarded clothing and papers; squeezed by the bureau that Chuck hid behind when he heard the Olives' car; and congregated in the master bedroom, with its sliding glass door leading onto an outside patio. Then the entourage came back down the hallway to Naomi's bedroom, which Marlene had remade into a sewing room and which was, as a consequence, the only clean, bright-looking room in the house. "It's so small," one woman juror was overheard to tell another, which was precisely the impression Thomas hoped the jury would form. The cluttered tract house did indeed seem smaller than the blown-up floor plan in the courtroom indicated. Certainly, it was smaller than the house the jurors must have formed in their minds after six weeks of testimony about the events that had taken place within it.

Back in the courtroom, Thomas hammered home his point about the physical layout of the Olive house. "There was a sliding glass window in the master bedroom and there was one in the living room . . ." Thomas addressed the jury. "And what was stopping Mr. Riley from running out the front door, just a few paces away? Instead of that, he stays there after Mr. Olive supposedly looks up, and he transfers the gun in a bag from his left hand to his right and is able to pull off four shots, boom, boom, boom, boom." Here Thomas took the .22-caliber semiautomatic pistol from the evidence table and tried to demonstrate the awkwardness of such a maneuver, since the trigger had to be cocked by hand before firing each shot.

As to the killing of Naomi Olive, the prosecutor had his own theory about Chuck's hypnotic testimony. "I think what happened is that Mr. Riley has amnesia for that particular point, his actual striking of Mrs. Olive repeatedly and sinking the hammer into her head. And what he is doing when he describes the hammer sticking out of her head, reaching down and pulling it out and having a lot of difficulty—that's what occurred. But he omitted how the hammer got there, ladies and gentlemen."

Brusquely dismissing Weissich's "attempt to depict Marlene as a kind of green-eyed monster" who controlled her boyfriend through a "walkie-talkie bracelet," and psychiatry in general as "more an art or a philosophy than a science," Thomas got to the heart of the defense's case—Chuck Riley's supposedly false confession after his arrest. "If his desire at the time he talked to Sergeant Stinson was to protect Marlene," he argued, "that's what he should have done. 'I did it because they weren't going to let me see her.' Not, 'I did it because she made me do it.'"

"Can there really be any doubt in your minds," Thomas concluded, "based on the physical evidence that's been presented in this case; the cold, calculating way in which this was carried out; the fact that it was thought about for a period of at least two weeks before it was done; the manner of its execution and the disposition of the remains, indicating a high degree of comprehension and awareness? . . . What other logical conclusion can you draw from that kind of evidence? Are you just going to disregard it and say, 'Well, maybe they were just kidding around.' They weren't kidding around, ladies and gentlemen, because it was done. It was done."

In the defense's closing statement Weissich attempted to rebut some of the prosecution's specific points, including Thomas' "Oscar-winning" performance fanning the pistol, reminiscent of "John Wayne playing the role of Rooster Cogburn" (Weissich in turn demonstrated that the gun could indeed be fired in quick succession from within a paper bag). But his main arguments were more general. Allowing that the jury had sat through "one of the most gruesome, sordid, bizarre cases that it's possible to conceive of," one which would not exactly dispose it to "look upon this defendant as a fair-haired boy," Weissich argued that "the evidence before you is such as to make any reasonable person incapable of achieving that state of mind the law requires—namely, moral certainty." He insisted that the hard facts of the case "at most prove that Mr. and Mrs. Olive are dead, and that they met their deaths as the result of somebody's criminal act. They do not in any way identify the killer or killers." To do that the jury would have to face "the God-awful problem of deciding which version of Mr. Riley's story is the true one."

The lawyer further suggested "there's something that doesn't ring true" about Chuck's original confession. "We have here a young man who loves guns, who has shot that revolver something like 5,000 times, who has bought hundreds and hundreds of rounds of ammunition, as the records of Sears will show, and he walked into a house to kill Mrs. Olive with a hammer." But it was not Weissich's purpose to plead for one version of the confession over another, but only to insist that "there's no one in this courtroom, including Chuck Riley, who really knows for sure what happened on June 21. It is not the law of this land that a person accused of two first-degree murders with special circumstances alleged can be sent to the gas chamber based on guesswork," he concluded his argument. "You are going to have to live with this decision for the rest of your lives."

The jury deliberated for four days after it received Judge McGuire's instructions on the law. The prosecution had asked for a guilty verdict on two counts of first-degree murder—an automatic death penalty. But if the jury had bought that Weissich called his "second line of defense"—"diminished capacity"—resulting from Chuck's use of drugs and his belief that Marlene was a witch—it would likely return a verdict of voluntary manslaughter. Finally, if, influenced by the hypnotic tapes, the jury discounted Chuck's initial confession for his current one, the killing of Jim Olive was justifiable homicide and Chuck would be acquitted.

Lawyers generally feel that lengthy deliberations favor the defendant, since as time passes it becomes more and more unlikely that a jury will be able to reach a unanimous judgment. But Weissich and Thomas both found this jury particularly difficult to read. Each day except the last it reassembled in the courtroom with a different request for Judge McGuire. During the second day of their deliberations the jurors wanted to hear Sharon Dillon's testimony reread, which the opposing lawyers took turns doing for the sake of even-handedness. The next day they requested a scaled ruler to measure the floor plan of the house as part of lengthy discussions about whether Chuck felt trapped behind the bureau when Jim Olive walked in. The following day Judge McGuire received a note from the foreman of the jury requesting that he reread his instructions on murder, manslaughter and justifiable homicide, and asking a question that lifted the spirits of the defense: "Where does irresistible impulse fit in?"

By midday of the following Monday, at the beginning of the seventh week of the trial, the jury had reached a verdict and court reconvened. The bailiff handed it to the judge, who gave it to the court clerk to read aloud: "We the jury in the above-entitled cause find the defendant, Charles David Riley, guilty of a felony, to wit: Murder."

Chuck's shoulders had slumped slightly when the verdict was passed to the judge, since he was familiar with the form of the document and could see that the top box, for first-degree murder, had been checked. Standing beside his lawyer as the verdict was read, he showed no outward sign of emotion other than the whitened fingertips he pressed against the defense table.

Since the penalty phase of the trial was now a foregone conclusion, it took the jury less than fifteen minutes to affirm the "special circumstances" alleged in the indictment—that Chuck had "personally committed" both first-degree murders. By then the Rileys had arrived in court and they sat in the front row holding hands while the clerk read the new verdict, which would automatically condemn their son to death. At that point Joanne broke down, and her crying only intensified when Chuck smiled wanly and gave her a thumbs-up sign before being led away.

After listening to the judge praise them for their "remarkable attention and concentration" throughout "one of the most unusual cases that most of us have had an opportunity to be exposed to," the jurors were dismissed. The Rileys visited Chuck briefly and then asked Bill Weissich and co-counsel Suzanne Graber over to their house to give them Christmas presents. Weissich received a silver-plated cigarette lighter. From the number of times Joanne Riley had asked about her birth date, Suzanne Graber guessed that her gift was a necklace with her astrological sign on it, but she could not be certain because, under the circumstances, she never had the heart to open the small package.

Most of the jurors went for a drink together at a local watering hole, the Velvet Turtle, the same restaurant Marlene had taken Chuck to just before she was arrested. One juror who did not go was Joan Lucas, the trim blond housewife from Tiburon who had seemed so sympathetic to the Rileys during the trial. From the start of their deliberations none of the jurors had believed Chuck's story about killing Jim Olive in self-defense, but until the final ballot Joan Lucas had not been convinced that he had killed Naomi, and even though she finally acceded to the majority view, she was emotionally shaken by the verdict and would be for months to come.

To a lesser extent the other jurors had all been affected by the long ordeal, and the barroom banter—about Weissich's single pin-stripe suit, Suzanne Graber's puffy sleeves and knee socks, Josh Thomas' self-described "artillery ear"—reflected their relief. From their conversation it was clear that they had not been much impressed with the defense's diminished-capacity arguments. After hearing the evidence about Marlene dabbling in the tarot, one woman juror had brought in her own deck and laid out the fortunes of several others. And at a crucial point in the discussion about Chuck's drug use, the youngest member of the panel, twenty-eight-year-old Cheri Martin, had announced, "I smoke pot and it doesn't make you crazy." Then she invited the others over to her house to prove the point for themselves. As for the expert testimony, a male member of the jury commented that the defense's psychiatrists "sounded like they'd been paid off" and another pronounced the cumulative effect of the hypnotic tapes "boring." Clearly, in their minds Weissich had never been able to make much of a dent in the original confession. "You just don't wake up one fine morning three months later," a by now well-lubricated juror commented to general accord, "and say, 'Hark, I didn't do it.' "

Few observers of the long trial argued with the verdict. Murders are rarely as clear-cut in life as in fiction. It is certainly possible that Marlene attempted to kill Naomi and was interrupted by Jim's return home or temporarily thwarted when the hammer became embedded in her mother's skull. It is even possible, as Chuck, under hypnosis, quoted Marlene as saying, that she went out to the car to meet her father, excused herself momentarily, returned to batter her mother and then rejoined her father for the trip to the shopping center. These scenarios are possible, but they are not plausible. The job was simply too messy.

At the end the jurors had to believe either Chuck's original confession to Sergeant Stinson or his hypnotic recollections, and even if they had been allowed to give both stories equal weight, they would still have chosen the first, which was told under enormous emotional stress and contained the kind of detail that would be difficult for a more imaginative person than Chuck Riley to dream up in a calmer moment. They did not necessarily think that Chuck was lying under hypnosis, but rather that the process of repressing the full horror of the crime that had begun in the immediate hours and days afterward continued in the succeeding weeks, and that Chuck, pressured in subtle and not so subtle ways by his parents, friends and lawyer, became convinced that he did not kill Naomi Olive but entered the room to find her in the throes of death. By the time Bill Weissich sought to confirm his client's new story through hypnosis, Chuck believed it so firmly that his trance-induced recollections were as convincing as his initial confession.

A month after the verdict was reached, Chuck Riley, together with his parents and lawyers, returned to the courtroom to hear Judge McGuire declare: "It is the judgment of this court that you shall suffer the death penalty at San Quentin State Prison in the manner and time prescribed by law."

Epilogue

Less than twenty-four hours after his sentencing, Chuck Riley
was transported from the Marin County jail to San Quentin's
death row in time for lunch. He left behind a note pinned to the
bulletin board thanking his jailors for "making this time as
pleasant as possible." The ride to San Quentin covered a distance of only five miles, but the prison's barricaded, gun-turreted
entranceway marked the border to another country, a place where
it is definitely not appropriate to thank one's keepers. The sprawling yellow-stucco facility juts into San Francisco Bay, a gangre-
nous limb attached to the otherwise well-toned body of Marin
County. Like so many prisons, which require the same zealously
guarded isolation as vacation retreats, San Quentin is a choice
piece of real estate, a condemned Club Med surrounded by
verdant mountains, boat-filled waters and, of course, a twelve-
foot-high concrete wall topped by coils of electrified barbed
wire.

In the adjustment center Chuck was stripped naked, skin-
searched, issued a set of prison blues (jeans and a workshirt),
assigned a number, photographed, handcuffed to belly chains
and marched across the concrete Big Yard at gunpoint. As
someone with nothing left to lose, he was assumed to be among
the most dangerous and desperate characters in a violence-prone
population and was automatically assigned the institution's highest security rating—"Condemned HVP" (for High Violence
Potential). Thus, every few yards on his walk the two guards
who flanked him fore and aft yelled out, "Dead man coming!"
and the other prisoners gave him a wide berth, a ritual that would

continue for the next six months every time Chuck was off "the row." Although Chuck had been briefed about life in San Quentin by some of the older cons in the county jail, the sudden attention shocked and embarrassed him, and he was relieved to arrive at the ground-floor elevator of the north cell block.

The block itself was an enormous open space, a human warehouse consisting of five tiers of cells facing an equal number of well-patrolled catwalks, replete with all the lingering odors and echoing noises of nearly six hundred caged men, a quarter of the prison population. Death row—actually two rows of thirty-four cells each—was a separate "penthouse," a segregated world within a segregated world. Charles D. Riley, prisoner number B-70738, was at present its thirty-seventh occupant.

In a predominantly young group (two-thirds were under thirty) Chuck, at twenty, was the second youngest (an eighteen-year-old had killed a woman after stealing $2 from her, thus barely qualifying, by age and crime—murder in the commission of a robbery—for the death penalty). On its own perverse terms the row was a rapidly expanding but still exclusive club. Some four hundred men had been executed in San Quentin since the facility opened in 1893, about half by hanging and the rest, after 1938, by gas. The last man executed had made the trip to the glass-enclosed, octagonally shaped gas chamber—conveniently located opposite the elevator on the ground floor—in 1967, at which time the country began a particularly turbulent decade in its love-hate relationship with capital punishment.

In 1972, when the Supreme Court struck down all thirty-five state capital punishment statutes, the 104 people then awaiting execution on San Quentin's death row, among them Charles Manson and Sirhan Sirhan, had their sentences commuted to life imprisonment, and the facility was closed down. Two years later the California legislature passed a new statute that imposed a mandatory death sentence for certain categories of crimes, and the row slowly began filling up again. But no one had yet been executed, or even received an execution date, because the law had not been tested by a Supreme Court appeal. Since that situation was expected to be remedied during the Court's current session, the tension on the row was particularly high at the time Chuck moved in, a state of affairs that would by itself reduce the inmate population by three over the next several months, during which time two men hanged themselves and another was murdered.

Chuck was marched to cell 20 on the back bar of the north

side (each side of death row being divided into a front and back bar separated by a gate). His first impression was of endless lines of steel rivets marching in formation, like the helmets of toy soldiers. (Later he would think of the zoo in Golden Gate Park that his parents took him to as a young boy, for here was a high-rise zoo housing equally torpid animals.) Although it was early afternoon, most of the inmates he passed were sprawled across their beds, asleep or resting. Since the concrete walls of their cells protruded a foot or so beyond the bars, which were painted a fulsome apple green, there was little communication between the prisoners. Chuck was startled by the tiny size of the cells, four-and-a-half feet wide and ten feet long, barely room enough for their meager provisions: a narrow concrete-based bunk attached to the side wall; a three-legged stool; a stainless-steel, seatless toilet and a basin on the back wall; and on the ceiling a bare light bulb encased in a metal cage. Each prisoner decorated his "house" with individual touches: some improvised clotheslines out of prison-issue string too weak for hanging oneself, others fashioned makeshift cabinets out of cardboard boxes, nearly all covered the mustard-yellow walls with *Playboy* or *Penthouse* centerfolds whose corners were curled by the all-pervading moisture that emanated from an open pink-tiled shower area. The weak light filtering through a few small, dirty, chicken-wire-covered windows high above the cells was in perfect consonance with the row's emotional gloom. Only the encaged fluorescent ceiling lights in the corridors never dimmed.

Even so, death row was, in many ways, a privileged unit within San Quentin. It was a kind of intensive care ward ending in death. Only the condemned in San Quentin were issued 10-inch black-and-white television sets along with portable radios, or allowed to purchase tape decks. The food, while no longer better than the general population's, was nevertheless adequate, and it was served (from a hotcart on trays pushed through a slot in the bars) at precise, if somewhat untraditional, hours: break-fast at seven-thirty, lunch at eleven and dinner at four. As a result of a two-week-long hunger strike in which Chuck partici-pated shortly after he arrived on the row, condemned inmates were given a hot lunch, one of fifteen "demands" that also included the right to use the prison law library and the extermina-tion of the huge white cockroaches that fed on the prison's crumbling limestone walls.

Daily showers were provided along with a two-hour exercise

period, during which groups of prisoners were allowed out either on the tier in front of their cells or on the rooftop yard, a long, narrow, fenced-in cage with a basketball goal at the far end, a board for handball along one side, and a punching bag. From the floor of the exercise yard the prisoners could not see beyond the prison walls, but if they climbed atop the punching bag and then shimmied up an adjacent waterpipe, as someone was always doing, they could on a clear day get a magnificent view of the Bay Area: Mount Tamalpais on one side and, across the water, the white hills of San Francisco sparkling in the sun. Such a view was available to the "mainline" population only vicariously: along the prison's Number Eight wall a public-spirited group of local artists had recently completed a giant forty-five-foot-long mural depicting in exact detail the panorama of green-and-yellow hills that would have been visible from the Big Yard if the wall were not there.

For Chuck Riley the row had still another clear advantage over the mainline. As a young baby-faced inmate with a reputation for being "pussy-whipped" by his girl friend, neither especially wise in the ways of prison life nor trained to defend himself physically, he would have been a classic victim of homosexual attack—a "punk," in prison parlance. On death row, where there were no hiding places and inmates were kept locked in individual cells twenty-two hours a day, this was not possible.

Visitors from the "free world" provided Chuck's principal relief from the numbing boredom of the row, and he could gauge his mood on any particular day by whether he expected a relative or friend from his "approved" list to go through the time-consuming process of filling out the required forms, enduring two separate searches, having one's hands stamped with invisible phosphorescent ink (a procedure inevitably accompanied by the guard's feeble joke that "If you don't glow, you don't go") and then waiting until an "escort" was free to lead Chuck to the visiting room. At first he could have ten visits a month, then fifteen and, finally, daily visits. Since he never gave the guards any trouble ("He's just trying to do his time quietly," the row's chief security officer told an *I-J* reporter, paying Chuck his highest compliment), his classification was changed to "Condemned—non-HVP" ahead of schedule, which meant that he did not have to walk to the visiting room with his hands bound in clanking bodychains. (Around the same time the prison changed the warning for mainline inmates to clear the way from "Dead man coming!" to the less intimidating "Escort!")

Death row and other maximum-security prisoners were only allowed "no contact" visits that took place behind a Plexiglas shield with holes punched in it at mouth level. Chuck, who had the advantage of family and friends living nearby, received more visitors than any other inmate on the row, generally three or four a week. He was there on such a regular basis that he formed a friendship with the visiting-room guard, a kindly, florid-faced sergeant named T. E. Prout, who affectionately called him "Chuckie" and, on occasion, unlocked the door to the maximum-security reception area to allow him briefly to hug his mother or the girls who visited him ("Hurry up, Chuckie. I guess what I don't see won't hurt me"). Prout was convinced by one detail of the crime that Chuck had not killed Naomi Olive. "If you have a gun in your hand," he felt, "you don't use a hammer. It don't make no sense. Besides, you don't beat someone over the head you don't know *very* well and work up a full head of steam about."

Soon after he arrived at San Quentin I began meeting with Chuck once and sometimes twice a week. After watching him in court for so long I was surprised by how clear-eyed and coherent he appeared, until he explained that contraband was much more difficult to obtain on the row than in the county jail. For the first time in many years—including, he later admitted, the day he testified in his own defense—he was drug-free. We spent the early visits getting comfortable with each other, not an easy task given the visiting-room din and the plastic shield that separated us. But the discomfort was more mine than Chuck's (I never entered San Quentin without half suspecting that I would not be allowed out; he knew he wouldn't), and when we finally began talking about his life he did so with the kind of candor and concentration that characterizes the best hypnotic subjects.

I generally visited Chuck on Saturdays. Prodded by Oscar's telephoned reminders, Chuck's friends came in small groups during the week, and once they realized how hungry he was to learn about their daily activities despite his circumstances, they relaxed and enjoyed themselves. Oscar and Joanne came on Sundays, sometimes bringing a family friend or relative. If Chuck's new environment could be said to have resulted in a single benefit, it was his vastly improved relationship with his mother and father. Few young men spend as much time simply talking to their parents as Chuck Riley did or are in a position to daily appreciate their love and devotion. They never wavered in their insistence that he was innocent and would be judged so on appeal.

All along Joanne had taken Chuck's imprisonment better than Oscar, although every time she read about a murder or maiming at San Quentin, which was quite frequently, she would suffer from the same nightmare, one in which Chuck was stabbed to death by another inmate in the dozing presence of a prison guard. After months of hypertension and heavy drinking that resulted in two brief stays in the hospital, Oscar, too, had adjusted to his son's situation and was generally careful to keep his visits "on a light note." It was only late at night, after Joanne left for work and alcohol had weakened his resolve, that he tried to relieve his despondency with long, maudlin letters that reviewed his son's entire life in great detail, sometimes beginning before Chuck was even born. "Dear Chuck," one such letter started, "I remember as if yesterday when I learned your mom was 'expecting'—and was very elated. I remember bragging to co-workers long before your birth that I was going to be the father of a boy. My bragging turned out to be factual. I remember the first time I was allowed to get a peek at you through that glass. My heart turned somersaults with joy at such a beautiful baby, my son." Only then did Oscar go on to talk about Chuck gradually "maturing into a young man before my happy eyes." Sometimes Oscar would even mention Chuck's feelings for Marlene and his first brushes with the law, but at that point he would always break off his chronology, which was rapidly approaching events he did not want to think about or recall to his son.

Of course, Chuck thought about them constantly—particularly as the first anniversary of the crime approached. He had not heard from Marlene since his arrival at San Quentin and thereafter was not allowed to write her. In January, a week before she was sentenced, he had sent her a note on her seventeenth birthday that read: "I'm writing you now to wish you a Happy Birthday and also to say I still think of you very much. Marlene, I'm sorry what happened did. I wish I could erase history to start fresh but this is so very impossible. I hope some day we'll meet once again, if only for a few words. I've written many times but could not bring myself to send them to you because the things I said of hate for you were but words on paper. You were my first love, a love I wanted so very badly. I was heartbroken so badly that I thought I would die. Now I probably will.''

Understandably, Chuck had been depressed the week of his birthday, after having spent three months on the row. (''This is a hell of a place to turn twenty-one,'' he told me during one visit.) Then, for a few days before June 21, he had constant ''flashbacks'' to the morning of the murder, events that seemed ''ten years instead of a year away,'' and had already receded into an impenetrable fog. He could remember the confusion of telephone conversations with Marlene, going to San Rafael after a gun, his acid-induced fear of being stopped by the police in town, the time at Mike Howard's house before he walked over to the Olives'. He could even remember shooting Jim Olive. But he had completely blocked Naomi Olive's death from his consciousness, although he was more than ever convinced, from listening to the hypnotic tapes in court if for no other reason, that he had not killed her.

It was partly in an effort to recapture these repressed events that Chuck suggested one day that I have him rehypnotized. I agreed, provided he was willing to be questioned in a trance about events far afield from the crime in order to recover details that he had not so much repressed as merely forgotten. We discussed the matter with the Rileys and also with Bill Weissich. There was some concern that Chuck's memory could be permanently ''contaminated'' by any false statements made under hypnosis, even, as seemed more likely with such a highly hypnotizable subject, if they were not deliberate lies. But it also seemed that the risk had already been run. After three nearly identical hypnotic accounts of the murder, no one raised the objection that new information might contradict the evidence presented in court.

Loyal Davis, who by then believed firmly in Chuck's innocence, consented to rehypnotize Chuck, asking questions that I would hand him during the interview. San Quentin gave us permission to use one of the quieter attorney-client booths off the main visiting room. Here, too, a sheet of Plexiglass isolated the prisoner across a narrow bench, but toward the ceiling the solid divider was replaced by chicken wire, allowing us to drop a microphone close enough to Chuck to hear his nearly inaudible responses. We held six hypnotic sessions over as many weeks during the spring of 1977. By now Chuck was such a practiced subject that Davis could place him in a deep trance in seconds, which was always followed by a "finger check." (Chuck was told that the index finger of his right hand would jump whenever he was lying or Davis gave him a prearranged verbal signal, generally the number three.) The process of bringing Chuck out of such a deep trance was more elaborate and involved recalling a pleasant boyhood experience, usually one of his many newspaper-sponsored trips to Disneyland.

Twice during these hypnotic sessions Chuck relived the day of the murder with what seemed to be all of the emotions that attended the original event. They were grueling ordeals that left him exhausted for days, although buoyed by the knowledge that both times his account was identical in every significant detail to the hypnotic tapes that had been played in court. During another session, when he relived the original confession to Sergeant Stinson that led to his conviction, his emotions were equally convincing: tears overflowed his closed eyelids and he sobbed so heavily that Davis thought it best to bring him out of the trance. On the other occasions Chuck sat for as long as three hours at a stretch with his arms resting on a bench, his eyes lightly closed, his mouth slightly parted, not a muscle in his body visibly stirring except when he spoke. In a low, deliberate and uninflected voice he recounted in great but seemingly untroubling detail the events that had led him to his current circumstances.

As the Supreme Court's 1977 spring session approached its end, the tension on the row could be measured in the number of tranquilizers handed out in the morning or food trays returned half-eaten in the evening. There were now sixty-seven men in the facility (a third tier had been opened) waiting to learn their fate. A kind of gallows humor developed around the "green room" five floors below, with its two leather-strapped, barbershop-type chairs marked "A" and "B." Inmates joked about their predecessors' last requests or told stories about the race between the big wall clock outside the gas chamber, always set a few minutes slow, and the black wall telephone connected to the governor's office. One night a local television station showed the movie *I want to Live!*, starring Susan Hayward, part of which was actually filmed in San Quentin's gas chamber, using dry ice to give the effect of cyanide pellets. For days afterward prisoners joked nervously about the film, greeting one another with the last exchange between the tough-talking prostitute who was framed for murder and her sympathetic guard. "Take a good whiff. It won't hurt," one prisoner would say, to which the second would reply, imitating Susan Hayward's contemptuous snarl, "How the hell do you know?"

On the final day of its session, the Supreme Court upheld the constitutionality of capital punishment but seemed to outlaw mandatory death penalties such as California's. (That evening Chuck was interviewed on the local news expressing the prevailing sentiment on death row: "We're about to enter the twenty-first century, sending people to the moon and curing rare diseases, but in some ways we're still in the Dark Ages.") It took until the following December for the state's highest court to rule that the decision did indeed overturn the California law, at which time inmates on the row began having their sentences commuted to life imprisonment and being transferred to San Quentin's mainline or other state facilities. At that point, as well, pressure began to build for the state to fashion another death penalty that met the court's new guidelines. Not long afterward the Rileys, as registered Republicans, received a fund-raising circular in the mail from the "Law and Order Campaign Committee" that said: "Dear Friend, I'm sure by now you've heard the shocking news about the death penalty. Right now vicious and ruthless murderers on death row are celebrating their great victory. If you and I don't get a new death penalty law passed, murderers could be back on our streets to kill again and again."

Chuck was one of the last prisoners to be transferred off the row before the facility was shut down in June of 1978 (only to be reopened the following year, when the state passed a new capital punishment law). He and his parents were of two minds about his impending reassignment from what he called a "ghost town," weighing the convenience of San Quentin's mainline for visits of friends and family against the possibility that he could be transferred to a much less dangerous, although more distant, institution. In the end, after nineteen months on death row, Chuck was reassigned to the California Men's Colony, largely on the recommendation of his prison guards, who praised him, in their final report, for being "a good conforming individual who programs well."

The California Men's Colony is a medium-security prison located off the state's main costal highway just north of the town of San Luis Obispo. Like San Quentin, it is situated in a spectacular scenic setting—lush rolling hills that fall to the ocean a few miles away—but unlike that implacable institution, CMC is known as a relatively easy place to do time, a chink in the state prison system's armor. From the outside it looks like a friendlier place, with a wide, manicured lawn leading to a freshly painted green-and-yellow administration building, flanked by two flower-bordered trailers for family and conjugal visits. Its eight triple-tiered cell-blocks form the exterior walls of four quads, each with its own baseball diamond and exercise area.

Inside, too, there were marked differences from San Quentin, notably the absence of armed guards and catwalks as well as the more commodious cells and greater emphasis on rehabilitation (the institution virtually hummed with industrial and trade facilities, including a shoe factory, a knitting mill, a printing plant, an upholstery and handicraft shop, and a bakery.) But CMC's reputation as a "gofer" institution was in no small measure due to the fact that it contained an unusually high percentage of the two categories of inmates that other prisoners held in the greatest contempt—snitches (or "rats") and sex offenders ("tree jumpers"). The presence of so many of the former kept guards' "suggestion boxes" full and meant that those suspected of providing such helpful hints were not, as they would certainly have been at San Quentin, automatically killed by fellow inmates, since the task would have been too ambitious. Similarly, heterosexual prisoners—even young, good-looking ones such as Chuck Riley—were not prey to homosexual attack, if only because the presence of so many sex offenders, many of them homosexual, provided a surfeit of consenting adults.

Still, there were more than enough indications that CMC was very much a prison, most immediately the five fortresslike gun turrets manned by guards bearing M-14 rifles and the double row of ten-foot-high chain-link fence topped by coils of razor wire. Many of the facility's 2,400 prisoners (by design more or less equally divided into whites, blacks and Chicanos) had committed very serious, even heinous, crimes (Tex Watson, the former Manson gang cohort and, subsequently, reborn Christian, was there), but they were all judged to have a low "violence profile." This did not mean that they were by any means model inmates. Most varieties of prison crime were regularly practiced at CMC, including frequent escape attempts—generally "walkaways" by prisoners whose security clearance allowed them to work outside the fenced-in compound.

Shortly after he left San Quentin, Chuck's automatic appeal to the California Supreme Court was rejected, none of the minor irregularities his new lawyer cited in his brief being deemed sufficient to overturn the original verdict. Since Judge McGuire had presided over Chuck's trial with what was universally considered an even hand (and one eye cocked on just such an appellate process), and since no new information had come to light in the interim, it was considered fruitless to appeal to an even higher court.

Faced with life imprisonment, Chuck's basic strategy for survival, as he recently expressed it in a letter, is "to take only one day at a time, keep my hopes down and try to get the maximum freedom I can from the system." Such a strategy involves getting along both with "the man" and with fellow inmates but keeping a certain distance from both, a position of independence that Chuck feels he would not have been capable of before entering prison but, strengthened by its rigors, is now. Like most prisoners Chuck divides his life into his years in the free world and his years of incarceration, and as with most, the division is marked by a prison nickname, "Q," a shortening of his nickname in the county jail, "Barbecue."

Chuck's routine at CMC is considerably less confining, if even more invariable, than his routine on death row. In the morning he works out for two hours in his quad, jogging and lifting weights. He can press three hundred pounds, and after losing the flab that resulted from the forced inactivity of death row, considers himself in the best physical condition of his life—a taut 180 pounds. Physical strength and the ability to defend oneself is important even in a relatively nonhostile prison environment such as CMC's, but Chuck is also keenly aware that he could on short notice be transferred back to San Quentin or one of the state's other maximum-security facilities, where it would be crucial. Chuck, who has thought about the psychology of obesity more than most people, also recognizes that there is a subtler motivational component to the enormous emphasis on physical fitness in prison. "Society punishes us with wasted years," he wrote me recently. "One way to get even is to come out looking younger—or at least in better shape—than when you went in."

Every inmate must volunteer for a job or face assignment to the kitchen or clean-up crews. On the strength of his typing proficiency, Chuck has worked his way up to head ducat clerk and is responsible for providing prisoners with the special passes they need to attend activities outside of their normal "program"—meetings of religious and rehabilitation groups, vocational classes, medical appointments, etc. He enjoys the work and the camaraderie with the "educated types" in his office (who include Bill Harris, the Patty Hearst kidnapping figure).

The job has a number of perks for Chuck. Because of its long hours and the unpredictability of the workload, he is allowed to attend any session (of which there are two on Saturdays and two on Sundays) of the weekly movie (generally, major motion pictures a year or two after their release or minor ones sooner). He can also "outcount" in his office during the two daily lockup checks at four in the afternoon and again at ten, when other prisoners must return to their cells. But Chuck's most prized job-associated privilege allows him to stock up at the prison commissary at any one time during the month, rather than having to wait for an assigned turn, as other inmates must.

Chuck usually leaves his job around 9 P.M. and may spend the next two hours in the common television room on his tier (where the inmates' overwhelming favorites are cop shows, exceeded only by the rare prison film or documentary), but by eleven he must be back in his cell for lockdown. There he listens to music (using earphones) for a few hours before turning in. He also makes it a rule to write at least two letters a day.

The routine rarely varies, and the sheer boredom of it leaves Chuck depressed and spiritless for long stretches. "The only way I break up my routine is by telling people about my routine," he said recently. Sometime ago he came across a book by Malcolm Braly called *False Starts: A Memoir of San Quentin and Other Prisons,* and in a letter to me he quoted one paragraph from it that captured the way he felt:

> The hardest part of serving time is the predictability. Each day moves like every other. You *know* nothing different can happen. You focus on tiny events, a movie scheduled weeks ahead, your reclass., your parole hearing, things far in the future, and slowly, smooth day by day, draw them to you. There will be no glad surprise, no spontaneous holiday, and a month from now, six months, a year, you will be just where you are, doing just what you're doing, expect you'll be older. . . . Most of the outrages that provide such lurid passages in the folklore

of our prisons are inspired by boredom. Some grow
so weary of this grinding sameness they will drink
wood alcohol even though they are aware this potent
toxin may blind or kill them. Others fight with knives
to the death and the survivor will remark, "It was just
something to do."

Chuck has far fewer welcome interruptions from his routine at
CMC, five hours by car from home, than he did in neighboring
San Quentin. A few friends such as Mike Howard and the Dillon
sisters made the trip soon after his transfer, but as time passed
they were less willing to expend the effort until now, four years
later, it is all Chuck can do to get them to answer his letters
occasionally. He is allowed to place a weekly collect call, but
the ten-minute time limit is barely enough for a superficial
exchange of pleasantries. I moved back to New York in 1979,
and although we correspond regularly, I can only visit him on
the infrequent occasions when I find myself in California on
magazine assignments. The Rileys see Chuck as often as they
can, generally on holidays when they can coordinate their
different work schedules.

Partly because of the strain placed on their marriage by Chuck's
arrest and imprisonment, the Rileys separated for six months
after Chuck left San Quentin, although they are now reconciled.
Oscar is still subject to high blood pressure and bouts of depression,
conditions that were not helped by the ordeal. In addition, some
of the old tension in his relationship with his son has returned
because of Oscar's disappointment that Chuck seems to have
resigned himself to his fate. For his part, Oscar is still struggling
to come up with enough new information about the crime to
merit a retrial; lately, his efforts have led him to visit psychics.
This began when Oscar and Joanne, on an anniversary trip to
Reno, Nevada, attended a performance of a stage telepathist
known as The Amazing Kreskin, who singled them out of the
audience as parents whose son had been falsely convicted of a
crime. More recently, Oscar has seen a Bay Area psychic, a Dr.
Georgiana Segee, who told him that there had been another
person at the scene of the crime, a woman who is now a
schoolteacher living in the nearby town of Ignatio, and that the
District Attorney's office was aware of her presence in the
house. Since his efforts to locate the woman have been
unsuccessful, and Josh Thomas vigorously denies the claim,

even Chuck and his mother find Oscar's hope of reopening the trial—on grounds that the state suppressed evidence during the discovery procedure—far-fetched.

More than obtaining a reprieve, Chuck's dream is to have a steady girl friend who visits him and perhaps will even eventually marry him. (At CMC he could have conjugal visits in the family trailers every sixty days.) Toward that end he spends much of his free time writing letters to lists of women he gets from the lonely hearts clubs that advertise in the back of men's magazines, or to women who answer his appeal for pen pals in *Rolling Stone*'s "Prisoners Dialog" column. Several such women have become regular correspondents, exchanging photos and promising to visit, but so far the only one who has made the trip is a neighbor of the Rileys', a single woman in her late thirties. With all these women Chuck finds himself in a peculiar dilemma. He desperately wants a steady companion, but after years of masturbating to airbrushed fantasies in *Playboy* and *Penthouse*, those available, big-hearted but blemished, leave him unmoved.

Chuck's worse period at CMC was the six months he was forbidden to have "contact" visits as a result of disciplinary action. He had already been reported for two "115s"—violations, often petty ones, of the California Department of Corrections code. The first was for agreeing to use his weekly call to telephone an inmate friend's wife and allowing him to speak to her momentarily. The second was for permitting another inmate to step inside his cell to relieve himself. The third, more serious charge, for which his visiting privileges were revoked, was that he tried to flush marijuana down his toilet after a guard discovered him smoking it. Chuck denies the specific allegation but not his use of marijuana, which is his surest "escape" from the deadening prison routine. In that sense he is back to his old dope-dealing days in Terra Linda, although the setting and what he jokingly refers to as the "difficulty factor" have changed.

But only in that sense, really. In other ways he has grown in the years I have known him from an insecure, unreflective kid to a much more independent and confident young man with opinions of his own. In a hate-filled place he has very little bitterness in him, whether toward Marlene and his past or his life in prison and a future he knows will be bleak. Some of the changes are no doubt due to the passage of time and the trial by fire that prisoners emerge from either better or worse but never the same. Chuck, however, attributes his growth to prison psychology classes that he began attending two years ago because the credit would look good on his record and soon found absorbing his attention. He now spends much of his free time reading books in the field and was recently appointed a group leader in the prisoners' own "peer counseling" sessions.

In May of 1981, a week after his twenty-sixth birthday and nearly six years from his arrest, Chuck went before the parole board, under California's recent determinate-sentencing law, possibly to learn his release date. He approached the event with considerable trepidation. "I'd really rather not have a date, to tell you the truth," he wrote. "Five years away can be much heavier than an indefinite time. Without a date no one can set you back. You can live from day to day without any disappointments."

There was another factor in his thinking. The board was certain to ask him if he was now willing to admit to both murders and to expect an affirmative and properly penitent response. But Chuck is convinced more firmly than ever that he did not kill Naomi Olive. It is not a subject that he discusses readily, however, and he fully expects to serve out his prison term. The reason for his resignation is that he realizes that he will never be able to prove his innocence. Over the years he has consistently maintained that a day or two after the crime Marlene started to explain to him how she struck her mother with a hammer when her father was out running errands but that, having decided to take the blame, he cut her off with an angry: "I don't want to hear about it." Marlene denies any such conversation.

Even if Chuck could have lied under hypnosis, he was surely not lying now. The most ardent proponents of hypnosis in the courts admit that the technique can permanently erase from consciousness any version of an event at odds with trance-induced statements. Thus, as regards the murder of Naomi Olive, the unenviable dilemma Chuck faced as the date of his resentencing hearing approached was whether to admit to a crime he does not believe he committed or tell the parole board the truth as he understands it, and thereby add years to his prison term.

Chuck decided to insist on his innocence, and the parole board refused to act on his case. As a "lifer" without an expiration date he could theoretically spend only the minimum seven years behind bars, but this is so unlikely that he doesn't even think about it. Realistically, he expects to remain in prison at least twenty more years, with a few years off for good behavior, and he knows he could be there even longer. That would make him about forty-five upon his release around the turn of the century, someone who will have spent nearly all his adult life in prison—a world he will know far better than the one he will then be forced to face.

At the time Chuck was struggling with this dilemma, in the winter of 1980–81, Marlene had been out of prison a full year. As California juvenile law requires, all record of her participation in the crime had been destroyed upon her release a few days before her twenty-first birthday. She had served a total of three years of "restrictive placement" at the Ventura School in Camarillo, California, an hour north of Los Angeles, which was six months more than the average sentence for California youth offenders convicted of murder. If she had entered the system a troubled teen-ager with fantasies of living a life of petty crime, she emerged from it a young woman fully prepared to realize them.

The Ventura School, a complex of single-story brick buildings within a flat, fenced-in compound, is the largest of ten such facilities run by the California Youth Authority and the only one that admits girls. It's 500 "wards," a third of whom were female, were assigned to residential "cottages" according to their age and the seriousness of their offense. Both categories had been escalating precipitously since the mid-sixties to the point where a correctional system designed to handle younger juveniles convicted of minor offenses had become overwhelmed by older youths (the average was 18.6 years), nearly half of whom had committed violent crimes. By the time Marlene entered the Ventura School in the spring of 1976, there were 227 other wards convicted of murder in Youth Authority institutions.

Even so, the public attention Marlene's case had received set her apart from the others and contributed to her "institutional adjustment" problems at Ventura. She had to face what she described in a poem as the "hissing words" of other inmates. In a "behavior report" she received shortly after arriving, one of her teachers wrote: "Marlene and I were talking at the desk when [three girls] started asking her what she knew about some girl burning her parents in a fireplace. Marlene paled, said, 'I'll see you,' and walked out the door. Comment: I counseled Marlene regarding the proper way to excuse herself in class." Along with other petty rule infractions, Marlene was accused and convicted of having violated "bubblegum restriction" and of keeping a "cluttered room." In a poem about losing her identity in prison she wrote:

> I chased you down endless halls,
> I lost you to those concrete walls.
> To censored mail and jingling keys,
> To silent tears that no one sees.
> To paint-chipped bars made of steel,
> To phony people trying to be real.
> To uniformed police in green and white,
> To freaky nightmares I have at night.

Marlene attended required group-therapy sessions in her cottage and a voluntary drug-therapy program for "brownie points." She saw the institution's one psychiatrist weekly until she "couldn't stand him shaking his head and going 'uh-huh, uh-huh' no matter what I said." The nightmares that startled her from sleep all concerned her parents. ("Heard my mother crying,/She was calling out my name;/Whispering in the darkness,/Saying who's to blame.") The nights "seemed to fluctuate with pain," "swarm with entities of gloom." Nevertheless, Marlene refused to talk about her parents with the psychiatrist and walked out of the group sessions the few times the subject was raised.

During her early days at Ventura I visited Marlene frequently, often accompanied on the long drive south from San Francisco by her guardian, Carolynn Shaalman. Marlene would talk about the past more easily with us, but it took many months before she could touch upon the murder, and then only briefly, glancingly. Afterward she would burst into tears or retreat into herself. It was clear that she was feeling great remorse about her father's death but she could only articulate it in her poetry, where she could admit to herself that "The slow stain of your judgment/rusts the moment."

Her depression lifted somewhat when she fell in love with a girl in her cottage, the only relationship she had ever entered that rivaled the intensity of her feelings for her father. Homosexuality was too common a practice at Ventura to jolt the authorities, but they were concerned, as a counselor put it in a behavior report, that the girls might "reenforce each other's negative qualities." Toby Franklin, the daughter of a Beverly Hills doctor, was smart, tough and violence-prone (she was at Ventura for attempting to burn down the previous institution in which she had been incarcerated). Marlene's relationship with her was the mirror image of her relationship with Chuck Riley, for now she played the submissive, beseeching partner. All attempts by the authorities to break off the affair—including transferring the girls to separate cottages—only rekindled its passion, which Marlene expressed in dozens of explicitly erotic poems, such as the opening lines from "Some Unsaid Things": "Nor will I say whose body/opened, sucked and whispered/like an ocean, unbalancing/what had seemed a safe position."

During our weekend-long visits Marlene would read me her poems and long excerpts from a diary she kept. Mostly the diary catalogued her everyday activities at Ventura, but there were occasional references to her parents tagged on almost as afterthoughts: "I'm fat. How awful. I miss daddy"; "Uneventul day. Missed parents"; "Dreamed that dad and me were skating and checked out"; "I cried Sat. nite because I miss my mom and dad." A short poem from those days reads:

> I've longed for you near me, father.
> I know there's no way you'll come back,
> But think how long it's been
> Since I really smiled.

On special occasions Marlene wrote longer "letters" to her parents that she signed "your loving daughter," in which she poured out her often sentimentalized recollections but also her genuine regrets. Her first Easter at Ventura she wrote: "I remember spending Easter Sunday in the hall last year. How I'd cry every time you'd both come. Why didn't I die instead of you?" The following Christmas she regretted that "there will be no rushing out to buy things, no wine brought in, no snapshots to add to our sorrows. Daddy and his Old Spice, Mama and her Fabergé. I could kill myself for not showing more appreciation for the two of you. Now this season arrives and you are gone." On her seventeenth birthday a few weeks later: "I'm hoping the two of you have kept a watch on me and can see that I have you in my mind and heart. Not a day has slipped by that I haven't thought of you both. If only I could reach out and hold you." And, more despairingly, she wrote them on the first anniversary of their deaths: "I wonder if I ever made you happy. Oh, please, if you love me, give me a sign I ever made you happy. I've searched for so long, hoped and prayed—yet nothing.''

Although she continued to write her parents every June 21, she soon curtailed her letter writing on other occasions. The reason was that a few days after the first anniversary of the Olives' death, when she mentioned the letters in her group-therapy session, her counselors insisted that such a one-way correspondence had no place in the ''reality therapy'' that was practiced at Ventura.

But if Marlene became less preoccupied with Jim and Naomi, she fantasized all the more about her ''real'' mother. (A long, maudlin poem she wrote about a dying woman forced to give away her infant daughter ends with the mother saying to the child, ''But before I go I have one cry:/Darling, I love you, take care, goodbye.'') She had lost the baby beads she had puzzled over for so long, but could not forget the individual letters that had never quite fit together to spell a name. She was now nineteen, only two years short of the age when her father had promised to tell her the little he knew about the woman, and she felt more than ever determined to learn what she could by herself.

It took surprisingly little effort. A call to the hospital in Virginia where she knew she was born from her amended birth certificate elicited only the information that in those days the baby bracelet would have spelled out the mother's first initial and last name. But another call to the law office of her father's old friend Russell Sommer, who, Marlene knew, had drawn up the adoption papers, proved more informative. Believing that Marlene needed the information to obtain a passport, a secretary found the old adoption file and simply read aloud the consent decree, including the name of the woman who had signed it: Jeanette Ellen Etheridge. Russ Sommer himself revealed the further information that Miss Etheridge had been a nineteen-year-old girl at the time, the daughter of an old-line Norfolk family who had become pregnant by a sailor on shore leave (a Scandinavian, the lawyer vaguely recalled) in those pre-pill days. Sommer felt sure that the woman had married long ago and didn't know—or refused to reveal—her married name or current whereabouts. When Marlene learned the news she had wondered about for so many years she did not know whether to laugh or cry. Jeanette Ellen Etheridge. J-E-T-H-E-R-I-D-G-E. The baby beads never made sense because three of them were missing and the first initial was included.

Several times over the next few weeks Marlene called Norfolk, Virginia, information to ask for a Jeanette Etheridge, but each time the operator told her that there were two columns of Etheridges in the local directory, none of them with the first name Jeanette although several started with the initial "J." For the moment Marlene felt relieved to have reached an impasse. She would have liked to obtain a photograph of her mother to go with the name, but now that she knew the woman probably had a family of her own, she had decidedly mixed feelings about pursuing the search.

As time passed at Ventura, Marlene seemed to grow more stable emotionally, her thoughts directed toward the future as much as the past. She completed a two-year junior college program with high grades, majoring in political science. By the fall of 1978, after she had spent two and a half years in the institution, the Youth Authority parole board recommended that she be transferred to the minimum-security SPACE (Social, Personal and Community Experience) center in Los Angeles, in preparation for her final release three months later. Although it considered Marlene's relationship with Toby Franklin a "negative factor" in her rehabilitation, the board noted that she benefited from a close and mutually supportive friendship with Carolynn Shaalman and seemed to have developed a growing sense of self-worth. Indeed, Marlene had been accepted into UCLA to complete her final two years of college, and then planned to attend law school, an interest sparked by her ability to successfully represent friends during disciplinary hearings at Ventura. Clearly, Marlene was apprehensive about re-entering society (after she was allowed to leave the institution for the first time to shop for clothes in the company of a Ventura security officer, she wrote me that "people looked at me like I had a sign around my neck"), but such a reaction did not seem inappropriate after three and a half years as a ward of the state.

A week after she had been transferred to the pre-parole facility in Los Angeles, Marlene escaped. Late at night she crawled out a window in the institution's laundry room, climbed over an eight-foot fence and fled in a car that had been provided by Toby Franklin, who had been released a few weeks earlier, and was driven by a thirty-year-old black man, Earl Brooks, who had been serving as Toby's pimp. The escape seems to have been

motivated by Marlene's fear of the straight world combined with
Toby's misguided sense of adventure. The three took a bus to
San Francisco so that Marlene could meet with Carolynn
Shaalman, who tried unsuccessfully to convince her to turn
herself in. By then sensationalized reports of the escape (both
San Francisco dailies ran front-page articles, one of them accompanied by a menacing-looking photograph captioned ''Marlene
Olive: She Lives for Today''), together with the Youth Authority's
description of her as ''potentially dangerous,'' had fanned a
certain amount of hysteria among some Terra Linda residents,
who feared that she was heading north bent on revenge.

No one heard from Marlene for the next nine months, during
which time I moved back to New York but kept in touch with
Carolynn Shaalman and others she might contact. Then, in July
1979, I got a call from a member of the New York City police
department's runaway unit, saying that ''Nina Reed,'' a young
woman he had just picked up on suspicion-of-prostitution charges,
had requested to see me. Marlene had often written about her
long-standing fantasy of becoming, as she once put it, ''an
educated call girl/in a New York City whirl,'' and besides, the
name Nina Reed had the ring of an alias. I took a cab to the
Women's House of Detention in lower Manhattan and met Marlene in a visiting room.

She seemed very different, years rather than months older than
the last time I saw her. She had lost all of her adolescent
chubbiness and was wearing a tight-fitting, low-necked evening
dress of an iridescent green. The outfit, which was comple-
mented by gold jewelry, lots of make-up and a high-styled
hairdo, seemed almost surrealistically incongruous on that steamy
July weekday morning in such a drab institutional setting. But it
was not her best ''going out'' clothes that suggested the change
so much as her manner, so street-wise and brassy compared to
her old diffidence. I was used to coaxing information she considered embarrassing from her over days of conversation. Now she
told me about her life on the run in a self-assured, seamless
monologue.

After she left Carolynn Shaalman in San Francisco the previous September, Marlene knew that she had to avoid airports,
since an all-points FBI bulletin had been issued for her. Instead, she
and her two accomplices traveled by Greyhound, first to Las
Vegas and then Chicago and, finally, New York. For Marlene
the next nine months were a cram course in a scabrous urban

nightworld. Within a few days she had a falling out with Toby, but Earl introduced her to a woman named Nikki, who became her mentor. Nikki ran a small but exclusive brothel out of a two-bedroom apartment on Manhattan's Upper East Side, and she quickly taught Marlene the tricks of her trade: how to put a client at ease with small talk at the living-room wet bar, how to make sure he did not "lolligag" in the bedroom (after a half-hour the girls were into overtime), how to dress and make herself up to take advantage of her youthful good looks. She provided Marlene with a list of doctors (the madam required a weekly medical check-up), hairdressers and clothing boosters who were often willing to trade services. Under the name Nina Reed (the last name borrowed from Jim's old Quito friends, Alicia and Francis Reed) Marlene soon had her share of bookings, often as many as a dozen a day. Some of them became "regulars," including a prominent New York attorney who enjoyed dressing in girl's clothes and being spanked. Nikki would negotiate the fee with each client (anywhere from a minimum of $50 to $200 for one wealthy Arab businessman) and give Marlene half of it plus whatever tips she earned. There were also "outcalls" to hotels, in which case Marlene kept 60 percent of the fee and received cab fare. It added up to good money, some weeks as much as $2,500, but it all went to Earl, with whom Marlene lived in a hotel on West Forty-fifth Street.

If business was slow at Nikki's, Marlene would try to get bookings at other houses around town, and if that wasn't possible, she'd work the city's better hotels. The advantage of the hotels was that she kept all the money—never less than $100 a "date"—and could sometimes "sting" a careless john for more by stealing his wallet or jewelry. The disadvantages were the need to lay out "fronts" for drinks and bribes to doormen and bartenders, as well as the lack of security. Once at the Waldorf a trick bruised her badly. But another night she earned $900 just for going to discos with a Japanese businessman who kept handing out $100 bills to Marlene and two other girls from a wad of money two inches thick.

When business was slow at the hotels, Marlene and a girl friend named Fern would prowl the "bump track" along lower Park Avenue, where the object was as much to lift tourists' wallets as to lure customers into seedy sidestreet hotels. Although she avoided the Times Square area as too "lowlife," occasionally Marlene was reduced to walking the streets off Park in the late afternoon, satisfying commuters in their cars before they entered the Midtown Tunnel headed home to the suburbs. One time she was arrested by the vice squad and spent the night at the Women's House of Detention before Earl could bail her out in the morning.

Twice Marlene took her trade out of town. In January she accepted the offer of a client at Nikki's to fly to Chicago and work for a large cosmetics company during a sales convention at the Merchandise Mart. She stayed for three days in a suite at the Hyatt Regency and earned $1,000 a day even though a blizzard that weekend kept customers away. Business was a lot less lucrative during a mid-winter car trip to Florida she took with Earl (who had bought a Cadillac Fleetwood from her earnings). Miami hookers either walked the streets or worked out of telephone escort services where every third client seemed to be an undercover cop (Marlene learned to check their luggage for shaving gear or, whenever possible, verify home addresses with information). She soon found herself meeting tour boats returning from the Caribbean or hanging around shopping malls. Driving through Norfolk, Virginia, on the way back to New York, Marlene considered trying to locate her natural mother, but her old fear that the woman would have her own family, which now seemed confirmed by the lawyer, deterred her.

Although she found her life in New York exciting, Marlene was oddly relieved when she was finally busted and sent back to California. That night she had been warned by the cabbie who drove her downtown that the vice squad was "riding hard," but she never expected to be picked up by a runaway unit for looking underaged. A routine police check revealed that Marlene was wanted by the California Youth Authority as an escapee. She spent a week on Rikers Island waiting for a CYA guard to arrive and escort her back to Los Angeles. By then she was nearly twenty-one, and although Marin County petitioned the Youth Authority to have her held longer on grounds that she was "a danger to herself and society," by law the parole board could only add a few more months at Ventura to her sentence before finally releasing her early in 1980, a few days short of her birthday.

Since Marlene did not even have to report to a parole officer, she was left without any support at a difficult juncture in her life. Earl had vanished with the Cadillac and the little money they had saved. Her relationship with Carolynn Shaalman had deteriorated since the escape. Eunice Richard, her aunt, couldn't bring herself to answer Marlene's pleas for communication. ("I can't find words to make things better, and I can't change the past. But I haven't lost all feeling. I'm so alone in myself.") To earn money Marlene worked part-time with the lawyer who had defended her against the escape charge. She found an inexpensive apartment in Hollywood and reapplied to UCLA.

But within a few months the lure of the streets overcame her better instincts. She stopped showing up for work at the lawyer's office and began hooking again and passing bad checks to support a growing drug habit, this time speed and heroin instead of the downers she had been addicted to in Terra Linda. She became part of a Hollywood drug subculture comprised of kids who raced from pharmacy to pharmacy using phony prescriptions to get diet pills or, in larger quantities, dealt methamphetamine crystals obtained from underground chemists. At first she was content to swallow increasing numbers of pills, but she soon began to inject speed. Every few weeks, with the build-up of tiny "regressions" on the surface of her arms from blood that had backed up and hardened, she was forced to tighten the belt around her upper arm another notch in order to make ever smaller veins available to the needle. Soon she became a full-fledged speed freak, living only for her next fix, for the moment when her heart would seem to burst its bounds to shoot warm rushes throughout her body, and as she put it in a poem entitled "What's Been Goin' On," she "heard razors slice the air." It was as if she had gathered enough momentum to crash through to the other side of frenzy, where the world was still and clear and protected, like those snowy farm scenes built inside of paperweights or, it often occurred to her, Naomi's aquariums.

I heard from Marlene infrequently in those days, and the news was never good. She had been beaten up by a boyfriend she was living with and had to find a new apartment. She had overdosed on speed and almost killed herself. She had been caught passing a bad check and narrowly escaped being sent back to prison. More often than not she was so spaced out on uppers or downers—either skitting along in a heedless monologue or spitting out words like loose teeth—that it was difficult to understand her. Occasionally she needed small amounts of money to cover some "emergency." She exaggerated, of course, everything was always an emergency, but I usually sent the money. It was conscience money. I was no longer there for her and didn't really want to be, and by then, she would remind me, she had no one else to turn to. One night I got back to my apartment after a late dinner to hear her voice on my answering machine saying, "I'm so unhappy. I'm going to kill myself." But when I called her back her mood had changed—or her connection had arrived— and she sounded fine.

During one conversation she surprised me by mentioning that she had been thinking about visiting Chuck and wondered if I would accompany her during an upcoming trip to Los Angeles. By then, in the winter of 1980–81, Marlene hadn't seen Chuck in more than five years and had spoken of him mostly in anger, but in her increasingly unstrung life he was at least a tie to a past that she badly missed, especially during the holiday season. Her last letter to him, written several years earlier, had swung so wildly from regret to reproach to a posturing rage that Carolynn Shaalman, who was charged with sending it, had decided on her own against doing so. ("I am also sorry for our fate and all that has happened," the letter began. "All the hatred, bitterness, revenge, sorrow. Sometimes I think about that valley of lies with its easy real estate and its easy preaching and I'm glad I'm away from it. 'He that doeth the will of God abideth forever.' Abideth forever also my father with the small airhole there in the center of his forehead. His ashes are scattered over a place I cannot visit, where my name is always harshly whispered . . .'")

Marlene still held Chuck responsible for her father's death, but more than ever recognized her own complicity in the crime (as she had recently written: "Once it's done / you can't turn around / and say, Why did I do that? / You loved him / deep in your heart / but took his life instead"). For his part Chuck, who had rarely expressed anger toward Marlene over the years, wrote me that he thought he could finally see her again without raising any "old ghosts." In his new psychologically oriented jargon he mentioned that he was hoping for "a kind of completion to what I recognize was a sick relationship," but it was clear that he wanted her to visit him, in some part, because so few others did.

One weekday afternoon shortly before Christmas, Marlene and I drove the two hundred miles from Los Angeles to San Luis Obispo and rented motel rooms near the prison for the night. She was worried that Chuck, jealous of her freedom, would act vindictively toward her. Early the next morning she shot a larger than normal dose of speed into her arm to help allay her fears, and we left for CMC. While our visiting applications were being processed, we waited in the prison reception area, surrounded by glass cabinets full of trade school products—everything from cutaways of shoes to urethaned baked goods. It was an anxious hour, for there was always the possibility that the guards would discover that Marlene had a criminal record—not for murder but for escaping from the halfway house when she was no longer a juvenile—and disqualify her from visiting.

But suddenly Chuck was at the reception-room door. His hair was shoulder-length and receding somewhat, and he had grown brawnier over the years in prison, but Marlene had no trouble recognizing him. They greeted each other warily. Chuck led us into the visiting room, cheerlessly decorated with silver-foil bells hanging from crepe-paper streamers. There were alternating rows of salmon-colored and yellow vinyl chairs, a bank of vending machines, and signs printed in red lettering that warned: "Greetings and Farewells are limited to 'momentary' *contact* in the immediate foyer area *only*. Prolonged embracing and kissing is prohibited in the visiting room and other areas designated for visiting." Despite the warnings—or perhaps because of them—the sexual longing in the room was as thick as the icing on the urethaned display cakes. Women proudly wore T-shirts emblazoned with their man's prison name ("My lover is D-70524"); "momentary" was variously interpreted.

"You haven't changed," Chuck said after directing us to chairs.

"Your hair's longer," Marlene said. "Otherwise you look the same." There was a long awkward pause.

"Well, how've you been?" Marlene asked.

"I'm surviving," Chuck said. Searching for small talk, he gave Marlene news of the old group in Terra Linda. "Mike Howard's working as a chimney sweep and renting a house in Santa Rosa with Sharon Dillon, who's working for a car-parts dealer. Nancy Dillon and Leslie Slote are still at the same insurance company. Nancy's sharing a house with Steve Donnelly, who's a big success—going to college and working on the school paper. Steve visits every once in a while when he's down here for military training but my dad can't lasso the others into it. He doesn't understand, but I do. Our lives are too far apart."

All the time he was talking Chuck avoided Marlene's glance except when he was sure she was looking elsewhere, and then he turned his eyes on her with a searing intensity that resembled a miner's lamp in a dark tunnel. "I'm apprehensive," he announced suddenly. "In fact, I'm nervous as hell. I just thought I'd say it." The admission helped break the tension, but Chuck still found himself doing nearly all the talking. He spoke about the psychology classes he had been taking recently, at first to please "the people who run my life" and then because he became intrigued with what he was learning about himself.

"I was very passive," he said. "I'm trying to become more assertive, to express emotion instead of allowing it to bottle up inside me and explode. The psychologist in group pointed out that I depend on my job now the way I had on you—obsessively. There was a time when I really felt I couldn't live without you. I was played on, but I allowed it to happen." He held out his hand to show a small crescent-shaped scar above the thumb where Marlene had once bitten him, and said, "Remember this?" The recollection seemed to jar Marlene back into the conversation, which now flowed easily.

"It happened right after we met," she answered.

"We were sitting in my car in your driveway," Chuck said.

"Remember the Robin Trower concert when the lights changed every time they struck a new chord?"

"I got jealous because you hit on some chick," Chuck added. "I was really possessive. Now I'd realize it didn't necessarily concern me."

"Remember the little girl we picked up the day we got busted for shoplifting?" Marlene asked.

"Your long-lost sister."

"That whole thing got so crazy. Taking out racks of stuff."

"It developed into a game we got wrapped up into," Chuck said. "We fed each other's weaknesses."

"Two plus two back then was making five."

"Our lives were so haywire. Nothing was ever thought out. We weren't acting, we were reacting to everything."

"A day or two after it happened I couldn't realize it was happening. Lots of times I thought my dad was still alive. I couldn't get in touch with half my feelings."

"We were so far out of touch. I was hanging on to what I thought we had."

"What a trip." Marlene fell silent for a moment.

"What are you thinking about?" Chuck asked her.

"I was just thinking what had gone down. We just lost our marbles."

By early afternoon the visiting room had become crowded.

Chuck led us outside to a small concrete courtyard whose only solid wall was covered with a garish autumn landscape. His friend Bill Harris, carrying an accordion folder full of legal papers, came over to say hello, as did a man named Geronimo Pratt, a former Black Panther leader whose murder conviction had received considerable publicity a few months earlier when two sympathizers scaled the Statue of Liberty to protest it. An inmate and his girl friend were frantically taking advantage of the fact that the attention of the visiting-room guard was otherwise occupied. The guests at a wedding that was scheduled to take place in the prison chapel that afternoon were posing for Polaroid pictures. "I was the best man at a wedding here," Chuck said. "I even caught the garter belt. Too bad there was no one to match it up with."

When the photographer was finished, Chuck called him over. He moved closer to Marlene on the bench but restrained himself from putting his arm around her. "I don't have a picture of you, and my folks would be freaked out if I asked them to send one," he said when the awkward moment had passed.

"I would have sent you one, but I didn't know where your head was at. I always felt bad that I got off so easy."

"I used to feel really cheated, but it wasn't your fault."

"You were over eighteen."

"It wasn't the sentence as much as the character assassination," Chuck explained. "People don't know I'm not the same person who was involved in an atrocity."

"You're much more intelligent. You've come a long way."

"Not as far as I'd like. But in terms of being self-destructive, I know I've pushed ahead."

"I'm still self-destructive. If anything, I've slipped."

"Maybe we can help each other out."

"I could send you drugs," Marlene said, misunderstanding Chuck. "I was thinking Desoxyn, Preludin and a half-gram of crystal mixed up in a syringe and ready for takeoff."

"No, I meant as friends. I don't love you in the same crazy way, but I still care for you. You just can't erase some things."

By midafternoon Chuck and Marlene had moved to the only patch of sunlight left in the courtyard. The wind had picked up, sending empty coffee cups scurrying along the concrete. Sparrows pecked at leftovers from the food machines.

"Maybe it's time for me to head back," Marlene said. "I'll write soon and visit again." Chuck walked her to the reception desk and they hugged briefly before the guard pressed a button that unbolted the door with a loud snap.

I stayed a few minutes longer to say goodbye. "It seems like such a long time ago," Chuck said. "I really was a different person." He paused to watch Marlene disappear out the prison's front gate and then added, "I'll never hear from her again."

Although the visit lasted five hours and went more smoothly than she had expected, Marlene was disturbed by it. Chuck's progress seemed to underscore her own deterioration. "The past is past," she shrugged when I caught up with her in the parking lot. "I don't need to stare at it." She would never visit Chuck again nor answer his letters.

As we drove to Los Angeles, Marlene put on dark sunglasses and seemed lost in her own thoughts. The freeway cut into pleated hills tumbling to the ocean, their mane of grass now lion-colored in the winter. Marlene took a sheet of notepaper from her pocketbook and carefully tore it into ten small pieces. She printed one letter of her lost baby bracelet on each and played with them on the dashboard for some time, rearranging the paper squares into different combinations the way she used to do late at night on her bed in Terra Linda. Finally she spelled out J. Etheridge. "I wonder what my mom's doing for Christmas," she said softly. Then she stared out the window for a long time. It was dusk. High in the hills, grazing horses flashed their darkness against the lilac-lit, sage-scented air.

About the Author

RICHARD M. LEVINE has written for *Harper's*, *New York*, *Rolling Stone*, *TV Guide*, *Playboy* and other magazines. He is a past winner of an Alicia Patterson Foundation Fellowship, and currently lives in New York City.

Titles of Related Interest from SIGNET